*Love, Money
and Friendships*

Love, Money and Friendships

David T. K. Wong

BLACKSMITH BOOKS

Love, Money and Friendships
ISBN 978-988-75547-4-5

Copyright © 2021 David T. K. Wong
www.davidtkwong.com

Published by Blacksmith Books
Unit 26, 19/F, Block B, Wah Lok Industrial Centre,
37-41 Shan Mei Street, Fo Tan, Hong Kong
Tel: (+852) 2877 7899
www.blacksmithbooks.com

Also by David T. K. Wong:

Memoirs
Hong Kong Confidential: Life as a Subversive (2018)
Hong Kong Fiascos: A Struggle For Survival (2015)
Adrift: My Childhood in Colonial Singapore (2015)

Novels
The Embrace of Harlots (2011)
The Evergreen Tea House (2003)

Short story collections
Collected Hong Kong Stories (2016)
Chinese Stories in Times of Change (2009)
Connections: Stories of East Asia (2001)
Hong Kong Stories (1996)
Lost River and Other Stories (1990)

All rights reserved. No part of this publication may be reproduced, stored in a retrieval system, or transmitted in any form or by any means, electronic, mechanical, photocopying, recording or otherwise, without the prior written permission of the publisher.

CONTENTS

1	Introduction	7
2	Terms of Engagement	44
3	Transition	74
4	Exits a Bureaucrat	108
5	Enters a Trader	130
6	Fireworks	153
7	China, My China	172
8	Karma at the Great Wall	197
9	Suze the Matchmaker	226
10	The Runes of History	256
11	Making Millions	281
12	Unforeseen Consequences	296
13	Getting Married	311
14	Awkward Passages	331
15	Mistress of Mao	355
16	Taking Up the Pen	386
17	Old Friends Reunited	401
18	Gathering Storms	425
19	Breaking Up	451
20	Odds and Half-Ends	479

CHAPTER I

Introduction

WHEN I WAS A CHILD and not literate in any language, I felt very pleased with myself when I thought I had found a cunning short-cut to knowledge. That happened shortly after my parents had divorced and I was sent from Canton to stay with my paternal grandparents in Singapore.

My grandfather had been employed by the British colonial service as a "Registering Medical Officer". He had graduated from the Hong Kong College of Medicine in 1900 and was immediately afterwards and assigned to work in Singapore, which was then an integral part of the Straits Settlements.

By the time I arrived at his home in Blair Road in the early part of 1935, however, my grandfather had not only retired from the British Colonial Service but he had also ended a considerable spell as a ship's surgeon on vessels plying between the coastal ports of China and Southeast Asia.

He had many glass cabinets and cupboards filled with books in English and Chinese at his home. The stately leather-bound volumes of the *Encyclopaedia Britannica* stood out majestically among those collections. So too did the six volumes of Gibbon's *Decline and Fall of the Roman Empire*.

It soon occurred to me, in that reckless and childish way of ignorance, that books had to contain knowledge. And the thicker the book, I reasoned, the more likely its store of knowledge would be greater.

Since I could not read, I began riffling through the tomes, searching for those with pictures or illustrations. Both the *Encyclopaedia Britannica* and

Gibbon's *Decline and Fall of the Roman Empire* did not contain enough illustrations to retain my attention. So I turned to another thick volume which I later learnt had been used as a textbook by my grandfather during his medical studies. It was called *Gray's Anatomy*.

It was filled with fascinating pictures of bones, muscles and internal organs. With the help of some of my maiden aunts then living at my grandfather's home, I began to learn the names of some of those funny-shaped organs. I was told I had all of them, neatly tucked away out of sight inside my own body. That was a revelation.

After *Gray's Anatomy* I delved into some amazing books on anthropology. They were filled with pictures of naked dark-skinned peoples from different parts of the world. Some of the women had elongated necks while others had saucer-like lower lips. The men often had marks on their bodies and on their faces; some had spikes driven through their noses. They carried spears and blowpipes.

The pictures shocked and surprised me. Did such people really exist? If so, where could they be found? How come I never saw any of them on the streets of Canton or Singapore?

Subsequently, I did see a procession of ash-splattered Indians with metal spikes and hooks through their cheeks, chests and backs. I was told they were devotees of the Hindu god Lord Murugan, celebrating the Thaipusam festival and performing a form of religious penance.

Seeing the pictures and witnessing the procession gave me a sense of wonder over the diversity of peoples and cultures in the world. Their existence became a demonstrable reality, which was far easier to accept than the stories told at Sunday School about Jesus and his miracles. I could not visualise how anyone could turn water into wine at a dinner at Cana or how a person could walk on water across the Sea of Galilee.

As soon as I began to grasp elements of written languages, however, I realised how vast stores of knowledge could be opened up for those with the ability to read. My efforts thus far had barely scratched the surface. So I began supplementing what I was being taught at school by dipping regularly into the books at home.

It was an altogether hit or miss affair, however. Sometimes I would stumble on a Sherlock Holmes mystery and would devour it in double quick time, fascinated over how the Baker Street sleuth had put simple clues together to make deductions to solve mysteries. That wonderful skill had me scouring for more accounts of how he had tackled other crimes.

His cocaine habit, on the other hand, got me wondering about its roots and whether it was related to my grandfather's and his friends' fondness for the opium pipe. After my grandfather started taking me with him to their homes to smoke, I rapidly developed a fondness for the sweet aroma of the burning drug myself. Would that cause me to become addicted later? That possibility worried me vaguely.

Sometimes, when rummaging among the dusty tomes, I would come across volumes way beyond my level of comprehension. It would then be like hitting my head against an intellectual brick wall. That had been the case, for example, when I tried to make sense of Schopenhauer's *The World as Will and Idea*. It transpired that the book had been one of those my father had studied at the University of Hong Kong at around the time I was born.

My introduction to memoirs happened also in that same haphazard way. I found among the books the memoirs of Julius Caesar, detailing his military campaigns in Gaul. I had no precise idea of where Gaul was; many of the other names he mentioned foxed me as well. But I did gain the impression that Julius Caesar had done something highly commendable by his fellow citizens at that time.

Then I found the *Confessions* of Saint Augustine, that celebrated fourth century Algerian theologian, sometimes referred to as "the Christian Aristotle."

His memoir resonated with me, especially when he recounted how he had stolen fruit from a neighbour's garden for no good reason. I too had stolen things for no good reason, sometimes just for the thrill of getting away with it undetected. The saint's revelation niggled my conscience a little and left me wondering whether my clerical maternal grandfather had been correct in asserting that all human beings had been born loaded with sin.

On the basis of those casual encounters I concluded that memoirs should be serious works, left to those who had actually done great deeds or those who wanted to recount experiences from their own lives in order to illustrate some moral purpose. People interested in such matters could then read them if they wished or else leave them as historical testaments. My own interest in memoirs thus faded away for a time.

* * *

The years seemed to fly by as swiftly as clouds driven by celestial winds. Before anyone knew it, World War II was upon us. When the Japanese invaded Singapore, I was forced to flee to Australia as a refugee. When the war ended, I found my way back to Canton in the spring of 1947, at the age of 18, to see my mother, with whom I had had virtually no direct contact for some 13 years.

I had undertaken the journey with an ulterior, not only to reunify with her but hoping that she would finance me in university studies in America. I figured that she owed me something, at least for those long years of separation and neglect. But I was soon to discover that rampant inflation in China had destroyed most of her wealth and savings. Financing a university education was out of the question. Furthermore, she did not seem to have a high regard for my academic potential. She thought I should just learn shorthand and typing, to secure some steady secretarial position in a Western commercial firm, as she had done herself. Her assessment dealt a crushing blow to both my pride and my ambition.

With the loss of hope for further education, I saw no point in remaining in a Canton, a city roiled by runaway inflation and the threat of civil unrest. Besides, my mother had remarried a Filipino doctor and had recently given birth to a baby girl. By remaining in Canton I would become one more distraction she could well do without.

So I headed for Hong Kong to see how I might salvage my dream of a foreign education. Although Hong Kong was the place of my birth, I was not familiar with it and I was fast running out of money. I was apprehensive over how I might survive. On the advice of my mother, I wrote to my Fifth Maternal Aunt and asked if I might impose on her hospitality for a while, until I could find suitable employment. On a positive response from her, I headed for the British colony.

There appeared to be jobs aplenty there but most of them were of a menial nature, openings as a *foki* or a menial live-in employee in a traditional Chinese enterprise or a clerical assistant in some foreign corporation. They were too lowly and without prospect to attract me, for I had already spent four years during my boyhood washing greasy bowls and dishes in a Chinese restaurant in Australia just so that I get enough to eat. But on the other hand, I was conscious that my lack of qualifications counted against me.

After failing to find suitable employment for a few weeks, I was forced to seek the help of the Right Reverend Victor Halward, the Assistant Anglican Bishop of Hong Kong. Bishop Halward had been a former close associate of my departed maternal grandfather, Mok Shau-Tsang, the first Anglican Bishop of Canton. Bishop Halward kindly offered me the hospitality of Bishop's House while he sounded out employment prospects for me.

* * *

It so happened that while my search for work was proceeding, I received news that my father had also arrived in Hong Kong from Singapore. He had apparently been offered a post as headmaster of a traditional Chinese middle school and was staying at the home of my Eighth Granduncle and Grandaunt at Leighton Hill Road in Happy Valley.

Although I knew that my Eighth Granduncle and Grandaunt were close and important relatives, I had initially been reluctant to seek out my father at their home because I saw myself as a junior who had failed to call on them earlier, as courtesy and custom demanded. I had shied away from my duty partly because I was ashamed of my impecunious and jobless state and partly because I had no memory of what those elders were like. I did not want to give them the impression I was just another poor relative turning up for a hand-out.

My lack of memory about my Eighth Granduncle and Grandaunt was understandable because my mother had taken me to Canton when I was about three and a half and I have had no contact with those elders since. It seemed unbecoming for a scarecrow of a young man to insinuate himself upon them out of the blue after 15 years.

Moreover my relationship with my father had been rather anomalous over the years. I feared that he might regard my precipitous journey to Canton and my inability to find a job and stand on my own feet afterwards a reflection on my own inadequacies and lack of judgement. Neither of us really got to understand one another till much later in life.

When I was a child living with my grandparents in Singapore, for example, he had seemed remote and not very approachable. My siblings and I seldom saw him. He was then working as a sub-editor for an English newspaper called the *Malaya Tribune*. When my siblings and I got up for school in the morning, he would still be fast asleep. By the time we got back from school and had our lunch, he would be getting ready to leave for work. He never returned till long after our bedtime.

Such brief and infrequent engagements left me with the impression he preferred children to be seen but not heard. He rarely uttered more than a word or two to any of us, though we could all note that he could be much more charming, witty and loquacious among adults. When in company he always appeared debonair and well turned out. His habit of smoking cigarettes with an ebony holder endowed him with an air of sophistication, like that of a matinée idol.

For a number of years during my childhood, even though I was completely ignorant of why my parents had split up, I secretly yearned that I might grow up to be like him. But sadly I never did.

For a start, I remained, even in adulthood, a few inches shorter than he. Secondly, I had failed to put on weight till I was in my twenties, no matter how much I ate. I therefore looked pretty much like an unappealing scarecrow and was shy, excitable and lacking in self-confidence. There was no way I could have acquired my father's type of *sang-froid*. I nursed a suspicion that my father must have regarded me at the age of 18 as a poor specimen for an eldest son.

World War II had further separated us. While my siblings and I — under the care of our grandmother and their mother, Anna — headed for the relative safety of Australia, our father had to remain in a Singapore under Japanese occupation, to look after the rest of the family.

The differences in experience during those traumatic years and our mutual reluctance to speak about what each had actually gone through made for further misunderstandings once we had been reunited.

During my adolescence, I had tried to construct for myself a framework of values and ideas through books and through what I had learnt at school. I thus arrived at rather idealised and overly simplified notions of right and wrong, curled around with a mishmash of ideals — patriotism, human courage, justice, truth and the rest.

I had been made aware, after my return to a post-war Singapore, of the massacres, rapes and random beatings that had taken place during the Japanese occupation. My grandfather and his friends had much earlier recounted tales of Japan's crimes in China. Those subsequent happenings merely deepened my antipathies towards the Japanese, though I had never lived under their rule.

When I also learned that my father had opened a restaurant called the Blue Willow during the occupation which catered exclusively to Japanese military officers, I was thunderstruck. Why did he do such a reprehensible thing? My father did not explain his decision or tried to justify it. My grandfather and aunts also offered no explanation. In my eyes, their silences seemed tantamount to admitting that my father had acted dishonourably, like a traitor. Or at least he must have been a pliant collaborator. All of those possibilities bothered me.

I felt immensely ashamed of him. Ashamed of myself too for having such a father. I could not understand how he could have bowed and scraped before Japanese officers for so many years, especially after a trio of Japanese soldiers had broken into our home at Blair Road and had raped a number of my aunts at gunpoint. What had happened to the man I had once wanted to emulate? Had his human weakness been revealed or was he simply a coward? What had happened to his courage, his pride and the Chinese patriotism he should have inherited from my grandfather? My heart became filled with reservations and resentments I could not articulate.

A frostiness began to creep into my attitude towards my father. Fortunately, no permanent damage was done because other members of the family who had shared the hardships of the Japanese occupation spoke up for him and stemmed my rush to a flawed judgement. It was pointed out to me that I had no idea of how harsh life had been under the Japanese. Apart from the random brutalities and war crimes, food had been rendered extremely hard to come by. Almost everything in Blair Road which could be sold to buy food had been sold. Many unfortunates had to survive by foraging or by digging up tapioca roots to assuage their hunger.

My father's decision to open a restaurant catering for Japanese officers had been in fact a stroke of genius, they explained. He had foreseen the shortages to come and had calculated that an eatery catering to the wellbeing of Japanese officers would be among the last to suffer from curtailed supplies. He had been proved right and throughout those lean years he had been able to sneak home remnants of food and leftovers to prevent the ten members of the family depending on him from starving.

"Sometimes when your father brought home even a crust of bread, it tasted like manna from heaven," my young Uncle Yan-Wing told me one day.

That remark struck me forcefully. I had impetuously wronged my father. The risk in passing hasty judgements on inadequate information dawned upon me. I realised that beneath his dandyish exterior, my father actually had a reservoir of courage, strength and responsibility I had never previously given him credit for.

* * *

My failure to land a job and the exhaustion of my slender financial resources eventually forced me to seek out my father at Leighton Hill Road. I wanted to report that my expectation of my mother financing me for university in America had come to nought. I also needed his advice on whether I should remain in Hong Kong to keep seeking employment or head back to Singapore.

When I told my father that my mother would not be in a position to finance my studies in America, he nodded understandingly, as if he had expected no other outcome. After a few moments of reflection, he suggested an alternative.

He said our family was not as well off as before but he could still scrape together enough to fulfil my desire to study overseas. However, there had to be a condition. If I were to be financed, he said, then I would have to undertake to support all my younger siblings through their university education after my graduation.

I instinctively declined his offer. I was conscious that my youngest brother, Tzi-Seng, was ten and a half years younger than myself. And there was no telling whether my father, then aged only 47, might not produce more children. After all, my grandfather had a son with one of his subsidiary wives at the age of 59!

To accept his offer could mean I might be paying for the education of my siblings till well into middle age. I thanked him and said I would find my own way of getting to a university.

As to whether I should return to Singapore, my father asked me what my financial situation was. When I told him I was almost down to my last dollar, he took out his wallet and gave me its contents. The amount came to exactly HK$600.

That sum was the only money I had ever received from him during my entire life. But he gave no indication as to whether I should use the money to pay for a passage back to Singapore or to use it to continue looking for a job in Hong Kong. Was he leaving me the choice of deciding or did he want me to discover for myself the validity or otherwise of Nietzsche's dictum that whatever did not kill a person would make him stronger?

I left Leighton Hill Road that evening with more money in my pocket than I had imagined possible. But the question of how I should use it continued to nag me.

* * *

The real achievement of that evening, however, was that I finally got acquainted with my granduncle and grandaunt in the flesh rather than merely through the abstraction of kinship.

When my father presented me to my grandaunt, a plump, elegant lady of around 50, she said: "Oh, my goodness; how you've grown since I last saw you years ago!"

Her remark took me by surprise, for I had not the slightest memory of ever having met her before. I offered my salutations and added: "I'm sorry, Grandaunt, but was it in Canton that we originally met? I can't quite remember, I'm afraid. I've only been in Hong Kong a couple of weeks."

My grandaunt gave me a kind and indulgent half-smile, "Of course you won't remember," she replied consolingly. "You were just a baby then." Her voice was soft and filled with understanding.

She then went on to explain that she used to visit my grandmother when she was looking after me at her home in Hill Road. I also used to to taken to Happy Valley occasionally to play with her children, until my mother took me to Canton.

"I see," I said, nodding with gratitude for that fragment of family history. That had hitherto been one of the long-missing pieces in the jigsaw of my early life. It occurred to me at once that my grandaunt might be able to help me find other missing snippets of information concerning how and why my parents' marriage had fallen apart. Most other elders had been reluctant to discuss that subject in my presence. The warmness and grace and the apparent willingness of my grandaunt to speak about such matters quickly drew me to her.

Her name was Kwok Yee-Hing. She was the mother of seven children, the eldest three of whom were all older than myself. She had a clear brow and gentle eyes and her smiles were very affecting. There was something subtle and mysterious in the way she conducted herself. It was as if she were a custodian of certain secrets which, on a good day, she might be persuaded to share. She seemed right up my street.

My granduncle too was a jolly and agreeable man. His name was Chau Wai-Cheung. He was a medical doctor with a flourishing practice on the ground floor of No. 33 Leighton Hill Road. He was portly and double-chinned and was a couple of years older than my grandaunt.

My Eighth Grandaunt and Granduncle

My grandaunt must have noted my lean and hungry look during the course of the evening, for she said earnestly upon my departure: "Don't stand on ceremony. We're all family. Come around for a meal whenever you feel like it. It will be just a simple matter of setting out an extra pair of chopsticks."

* * *

Within two or three days of my visit to Leighton Hill Road, Bishop Halward managed to arrange a job interview for me with Mr. Henry Ching, the Editor-in-Chief of the *South China Morning Post*. The upshot was that I was offered employment as a cub reporter for a probationary period of three months.

I jumped at the opportunity. I was placed under the wing of a senior Indian reporter who initially taught me how to cover the four courts at the Central

Magistracy and to report their proceedings. Gradually I was also sent out to cover traffic accidents, fires, natural disasters, funerals, social events and some sporting activities.

Such assignments were absorbing and exhilarating for they exposed me to life in the raw, to aspects of human existence I had never encountered before. For example, I had watched with bewilderment an endless tide of humanity brought before the courts day after day, charged with hawking without a licence, causing an obstruction, mendicancy, soliciting, pimping, larceny, smoking opium and so forth. Lines of incomprehension or resignation had appeared etched upon their faces as they listened dully to interpreters reading out the various charges.

Some assignments also took me into squatter encampments, where people lived without electricity, running water or latrines and had to endure the vagaries of the elements. Something in society seemed to be seriously awry. I wanted to stay with journalism, to expand my vision of society, so that I might gain insight into why things should be that way.

But there was one serious snag hampering me. My probationary salary was only HK$150 per month or five dollars per day, a sum barely sufficient for two modest meals. It was not a living wage. I soon discovered that other local journalists were just as badly paid and many had to take on additional work in order to make ends meet.

Well before I had received my first monthly pay, I already knew I was in serious trouble. Although I was living rent free at Bishop's House, I had already gone through a major part of my father's six hundred dollars for food, transportation and other daily expenses. There had been a promise of an adjustment in salary after my probationary period but what could that amount to? Certainly not to a living wage. And I could not possibly abuse indefinitely the hospitality of Bishop Halward.

I needed to secure a job paying well enough to support an independent life. But what better job could I get when all I had by way of qualification was a Cambridge School Leaving Certificate? Stark reality stared me in the face. I had no means of getting into university and no qualification for landing a job with a higher wage. I felt totally trapped.

After mulling over my predicament for two or three days, I decided the only viable option was to ask my father to send me back to Singapore. There I would at least be assured of free board and lodgings at my grandfather's house even if I got a poorly paid job.

So thinking, I made my way to Leighton Hill Road to appraise my father of my insoluble situation. I got there late in the afternoon and found my father engaged in a leisurely conversation with my grandaunt. My granduncle had gone off on his hospital rounds at the Yeung Wo Hospital. I knew that as soon as he got back the family would be gathering for the evening meal and I did not want to explain my problem in front of too many people. So I immediately set out my predicament with my grandaunt present.

When I had finished my narrative, my Eighth Grandaunt was the first to speak. She addressed my father and said he should allow me to move into her home, where my father was already a guest. There was no point for a young man to give up a likeable job simply because of inadequate pay. That was when families should help out, she concluded.

My grandaunt's spontaneous invitation took me completely by surprise. When my father indicated it appropriate for me to accept, I thanked my grandaunt profusely and moved in.

The next two and a half years spent at the Leighton Hill Road address turned out to be among the happiest and most formative periods in my entire life. Beyond offering hospitality, both my grandaunt and granduncle shaped me and helped me in many other ways. I shall never be able to repay in full all the generosity, mentoring, affection and kindness they bestowed on me.

* * *

Memoirs are often exercises in vanity. Ex-politicians, celebrities and other public personalities frequently feel compelled to try their hand at it, if they could somehow string together enough sentences without too many grammatical mistakes. If they could not, there were always ghost writers willing to do so for a fee.

Human nature being what it is, a person who has a bad reputation is likely to do better financially with a memoir, for he would attract the readership of the millions of scandalmongers and subscribers to racy newspapers like the now defunct *News of the World*. Fidelity to truth remains only an optional requirement in the genre.

The market for such efforts is as fickle as that for any other commodity. Books nowadays are being churned out more or less like tins of baked beans. The average shelf life of a book at a bookshop is probably just a few months. Few over time have stood up as well as Casanova's *Histoire de ma Vie*. Fresh editions of it are apparently still being printed in different languages.

During the Victorian era, memoirs filled with pedestrian accounts of everyday activities did enjoy a certain vogue. That was at a time when many British city gentlemen took to retiring to country estates. They seemed to take to writing memoirs as readily as they might take to the bottle and probably for the same reason — the utter boredom and ennui of retiring in the countryside. After all, there was only so much riding to hounds that ageing bones could put up with. And the seasons for blood sports like shooting grouse or partridge and stalking stag or water deer were unsatisfactorily restricted.

Once in a while, however, an amusing parody of such memoirs would emerge to tickle the public fancy, like *The Diary of a Nobody* by the Grossmith brothers, George and Weedon.

* * *

In 2011, after the publication of my second novel, *The Embrace of Harlots*, I began toying with the idea of a family memoir. Both my grandfathers had led interesting and significant lives but neither had been inclined to pen a memoir. My maternal grandfather, however, did have two or three biographies written about him by other people, because he had been the first Anglican Bishop of Canton and had been responsible for carrying out a variety of charitable works. But that still left many holes in our family history. The thought that I might be able to plug a few of those gaps teased me.

I had no thought of writing anything about myself. I was just another Joe Everyman who had stumbled through a medley of mundane callings — journalism, teaching, civil service, commerce and fiction writing — and had failed to achieve distinction in any of them. No startling scoops or exposés, no elevation to high office, no spectacular commercial coups, no literary renown. Neither had I any particular attainment in sports, the arts or other spheres of human activity. With some stretching of the truth, I might just manage claiming to be an expert in the game of *mah-jong*. But that would be all.

The 50 or so short stories and the two novels I had published had been pretty ephemeral stuff, set in locations which seemed almost to be changing right before one's eyes. So too their long-established verities.

I first tried my hand at writing fiction when I was studying at Stanford. I had regarded that activity as essentially a private pleasure. Although as a young man I had once in a while entertained those secret and exaggerated dreams of one day attaining literary immortality, I never took those dreams very seriously. I considered how others might react to what I had written to be none of my business; I had already had my fun in writing the stuff and that seemed a sensible attitude to adhere to.

Some time back, when the internet was sweeping the world, I had set up a website so that my fiction could be freely downloaded by all who might be interested in it. Notwithstanding that my website had received more than a million and a half hits within the last couple of years, I have maintained my original attitude. I have seen too many popular writers vanish from the scene without trace within a couple of decades, like tiny pebbles tossed into a boundless and indifferent ocean, causing hardly a ripple.

My peripatetic life had also left me with two broken marriages, a protracted period of trying single parenthood, frequent shortages of cash, plus the usual quota of missteps, misjudgements and missed opportunities. I imagined my life experiences must have been commonplace for millions of other ordinary Joes.

But one other thought did occur to me when I was reflecting on my past. It seemed that at every crucial juncture, whenever I had found myself in a tight spot with no discernible way out, a family member, a caring teacher, a bosom friend or a helpful colleague had appeared to offer kindness, support, illumination or some form of escape. I must have been truly blessed to have had so many instances of that happening so frequently!

As my memory reached back over the decades, I could visualise a teeming succession of exceptional teachers — Miss Nice, Miss Fox, Tutor Tam, Mr. Harold Lewis and Mr. Maurice Zines. Likewise other mentors — among them the twice-decorated war hero Jackie Wong Sue, who taught me how to live off the land and to catch poisonous snakes and butterflies, Mr. Henry Ching and Chan Hon-Kit, who drilled into me the ethics in the craft of journalism, and Sir John Cowperthwaite, the greatest Financial Secretary Hong Kong ever had, who adroitly separated out for me some of the humbug infesting common sense economics.

Sadly, all those decent, honourable and dearly beloved associates have gone the way of all flesh. Another few more years and I would be left willy-nilly as the sole custodian of the memory of their goodness. With my own demise, who would be left to remember their deeds, their kindness and their generosity?

That thought pierced me. They had all been sterling characters who should be remembered, for they had lived their lives with simple dignity, humility and purpose. They had truly been the proverbial salt of the earth. It came to me that, apart from my two sets of grandparents, I ought to try to extend their lives a little also, by writing a few paragraphs about them and introducing them to a wider audience.

Excited by that possibility, I began planning a family memoir. It became obvious that I could not introduce any of my benefactors as mere caricatures. To do them justice I had to present them in the round and within their relevant settings, full-blooded and in chiaroscuro, with their strengths and foibles and even their prejudices and eccentricities accounted for. By metaphorically extending their lives, I could also acknowledge publicly the immense debts of affection and gratitude I owed to each of them.

But I immediately faced a problem. In order to introduce them properly, I would have to provide chapter and verse on how our paths had crossed and the circumstances under which we had interacted with one another. I hesitated over revealing all such details.

I had always been a very private person, possibly due to some unexpressed and unfulfilled yearnings buried deep inside my psyche during childhood. Perhaps, if I were to submit myself to the tender mercies of a headshrinker, I might even discover that I had been subconsciously repressing many of my urges and feelings. Could even a saint who had taken the three public vows of chastity, poverty and obedience to become a member of the consecrated life afford to lay bare his innermost thoughts and his darkest fantasies and desires before a headshrinker? And I certainly had been no saint.

In the end, however, faced with the simple choice of telling the stories of the kindnesses and human-heartedness of people who had so fundamentally affected my life or of remaining silent just to preserve my own privacy, I felt compelled to choose the former.

*   *   *

Let me begin by giving an example of how complicated my relationships with my Eighth Granduncle, Chau Wai-Cheung, and my Eight Grandaunt, Kwok Yee-Hing, had been. And how they had evolved over the years.

Who was Chau Wai-Cheung and how did we originally become connected? He was one of the eight younger siblings of my grandmother, Chau Shui-Lin. My grandmother was the eldest child in a family of nine children, with a recorded history dating back 26 generations. Her earliest known ancestor was a Hunan scholar and calligraphist of the Sung Dynasty, by the name of Chau Len-Ti.

After a couple of generations, an accident occurred in the Chau family home in Hunan when it was under renovation. A fatality resulted. Because of the family's belief in certain aspects of geomancy, it was decided that the entire family should move from Hunan Province to Kwangtung Province.

Thereafter, different branches of the family spread out all over Kwangtung, pursuing different callings. The head of my grandmother's branch of the family ended up in Tung Koon, where he practised herbal medicine.

During his practice, he befriended a Christian missionary. In those days, it was neither politic nor advisable for anyone to openly preach a foreign religion. Nonetheless, the missionary managed not only to do so but also to convert the son of the herbalist to the faith. That converted son was my grandmother's grandfather. From that point onwards, that particular branch of the Chau family became Christians.

One of the grandsons of the herbalist even became a Methodist priest and he was subsequently sent by his church to Hong Kong as a missionary. One of his sons, named Chau Chung-Park, later married a local girl and together they opened at Caine Road one of the first missionary schools in Hong Kong.

They gave birth to nine children, with my grandmother, born in 1875, being the eldest. My Eighth Granduncle was their eighth child.

It has remained something of a mystery as to why Chau Chung-Park should have allowed his eldest daughter to marry my grandfather, because my grandfather was at that time still a medical student and the youngest son of an impecunious school teacher, without any substantial inheritance coming his way.

No oral history by any Chau elder has been found giving a reason for approving the marriage. It could be that the Chaus had spotted in my grandfather a common trait among the young of his generation — a burning idealism to restore the honour of the nation by ending the interferences of foreign powers in the affairs of China.

The willingness of my grandmother to marry an unqualified young man without clear prospects could be more easily explained. Back in those days, daughters were generally considered to be wasting assets, to be married off as soon as possible. My grandfather was, after all, a handsome devil and by all accounts had a charming way with women. His subsequent reputed acquisition of nine wives attested to that. Perhaps good looks and charm were about all that a young woman could reasonably expect back in those benighted times.

* * *

As to my Eighth Granduncle, he was born in 1894 and, like my grandfather, had studied medicine. He graduated from the University of Hong Kong in 1916 and soon established a flourishing practice. His waiting room was usually crowded with patients.

Unique among medical practitioners of his time, he did not fall in with the easy option of dispensing the "one-pill-suits-all" touted by the big pharmaceutical corporations. Instead, he employed a pharmacist to prepare medication with mixtures of ingredients he considered best suited to the malady of each patient, in much the same way his herbalist ancestor had done.

He married my Eighth Grandaunt, Kwok Yee-Hing, in 1921. Her father had come to the colony from Chung Shan when he was in his early twenties to work as an interpreter. Unfortunately, he died of a tropical disease well before he could see out his twenties, leaving behind three young daughters, one of whom was my grandaunt.

When World War II came, my granduncle sent his family to the relative safety of the fabled city of Kweilin to escape the Japanese occupation. The city, located with its uniquely-shaped hills in the interior of China, was said to have inspired Picasso into his Cubist phase.

But my granduncle himself remained behind to look after his father, Chau Chung-Park, who was too frail to travel. However, as the war took a turn for the worse for the Japanese, the authorities threatened to draft him into the Japanese Army to attend to its mounting war casualties. He too had to escape into China.

* * *

My grandmother had been my only memory of any connection with the Chau family, at least until I called on my Eighth Granduncle and Grandaunt in the middle of 1947. The unexpected invitation to become a guest in their home was the real start of our relationships.

Over the next two and a half years, I noticed a number of eccentricities about my granduncle which I could not fully comprehend at the time. For example, although he was quite prosperous, he was dead set against purchasing any property for either professional or domestic use. He preferred renting.

Such a decision had seemed rather quixotic and impractical in my then jejune eyes. Property prices after the war were already on an upward trend and since he had ample means I could not understand why he insisted on renting instead of buying. Later, I was given to understand it had been a matter of principle with him; he did not want to own property in a place already ceded to foreigners in perpetuity.

On the other hand, he did purchase a holiday bungalow called "The Abode of Butterflies" located on an outcrop on the island of Tsing Yee. The island was then little inhabited; all that was there were a couple of small villages engaged in fishing and small scale farming. The usual way of getting to the island was to travel by road to Tsuen Wan and then to engage a fisherwoman to row one across by sampan.

It was a delightfully rural place, with an abundance of bees, ladybirds, butterflies, dragonflies, grasshoppers, crickets and other insects. It also had no roads and hence was free of motorised traffic. Going there on weekends with my grandaunt and her children became one of my favourite treats.

Indeed, I was probably a more frequent visitor to the bungalow than any member of the Chau family because whenever it was not in use I would take a group of my financially straiten journalistic friends there for a picnic, a hike, a swim or dancing to some big band music played on a gramophone. It proved a thoroughly enjoyable and economic way of enjoying a day in the countryside.

My granduncle, however, always seemed too preoccupied with his patients and hospital rounds to indulge in the amenities of the bungalow. I imagined his rationale for purchasing the bungalow had something to do with his patriotism. The island was part of the New Territories, a slice of the motherland which had not been ceded, but only leased, to the British for 99 years.

Another puzzling aspect about my granduncle was his apparent appetite for acquiring antiquated Chinese books and ink rubbings from ancient Chinese monuments.

Above and overleaf: A day at the "Abode of Butterflies" in 1958 with journalistic associates. Among those pictured are Beatrice Greaves, Olga Tarvares and Chan Hon-Kit.

There had long been rumours of an underground cabal of dealers trading in questionable antiques, books and other Chinese imperial treasures stolen or looted from China over the decades. They often went to private collectors and museums in foreign countries, as well as to astute speculators. The trade began after the sacking of the Old Summer Palace in Peking in 1860, during the Second Opium War.

My granduncle never had any connection with that nefarious trade. After

World War II, however, large numbers of mainland refugees began fleeing to the colony to escape the rampant inflation and civil strife in China. They came with whatever they held dear. The parents of my first wife, for example, fled with a pair of antique vases. Others, if they had a scholarly inclination, brought out objects they might have treasured but they did not necessarily coincided with items that were most marketable. They might have consisted of out-of-print Chinese classical texts, personal seals or stone rubbings.

Somehow, one of those refugees found his way to my granduncle's medical practice and offered to sell what he had. I never discovered whether my granduncle was instinctively against ancient Chinese books of uncertain provenance falling into foreign hands or whether he just wanted to help out a person in obvious financial need. In any case, once he had bought the initial offering, word got around and others with similar offerings soon came calling.

In very little time, he had acquired so many antiquated books that the domestic quarters ran out of space for storing them. He then had cupboards put on the landings of the stairs to accommodate them.

* * *

It might be appropriate at this juncture if I were to sketch in some background about this questionable trade in looted Chinese treasures. It all began during the Second Opium War, when an Anglo-French expeditionary force of approximately 4,000 men was sent in 1860 to attack the Old Summer Palace or Yuan Ming Yuan, in an attempt to cower the Chinese authorities into submission.

The Yuan Ming Yuan was in fact a vast complex of palaces, pavilions, temples, halls, galleries and gardens covering some 860 acres, or approximately eight times the size of Vatican City.

Its construction began in 1707. After it had been brought into service, a succession of Ching emperors used the facilities as both royal residences and their place for conducting affairs of state. The buildings therefore became filled with all manner of exquisite objects of art, copies of ancient classical works and other rare literary compilations scoured from all over the country.

When an Anglo-French delegation went under a flag of truce to demand the surrender of the Chinese, the delegation somehow got intercepted by Chinese forces and its members got some rough and rather undiplomatic treatment. Orders were then issued by the Western powers for their troops to loot and raze Yuan Ming Yuan to the ground. Palace maids and eunuchs who took shelter in some of the buildings were burnt alive. The place was so vast and extensive and its structures so scattered that it took the troops three days to complete the job.

The items seized by the soldiers were then sold off in auctions and the proceeds divided among them. That was how the first wave of Chinese imperial treasures fell into the hands of outsiders. It should be remembered that at the time looting was considered a normal part of the income of soldiers.

What was also evident by then was that the myth of white superiority had been firmly planted so that even its minions accepted it as a truism in the British imperial adventure. Racism extended even to the sphere of looting! The British troops sent to China during the Opium Wars included contingents of Indian soldiers. But after looting, the items they pillaged had to be sold in auctions and the proceeds distributed according to a scale based on the ranks of individual looters. In the case of Indians, however, they would receive payments not on their actual ranks like comparable European soldiers but one rank lower. A sergeant, for example, would be paid as if he were a corporal.

Victor Hugo, in commenting on the plunder of the Yuan Ming Yuan, had characterised it as akin to two bandits named France and Britain robbing a museum. He then expressed the hope that one day France would feel guilty enough to return the plunder.

Introduction

In 1899, all the Western powers involved in China signed the Hague Convention outlawing looting. Nonetheless, when the Boxer Rebellion erupted in 1900 and foreign legations came under siege by mobs of Boxers in June, troops sent in by foreign powers to relieve them carried out widespread looting of private homes and public institutions in both Peking and Tientsin.

Among the latter was the Harlin Academy, the oldest and richest library in the world. It was a complex of courtyards and buildings housing the quintessence of Chinese scholarship. Unfortunately, it was located adjacent to the legation quarter.

When some Boxers attempted to start a fire near the dividing wall to smoke out some of the people seeking refuge in the legation quarter, a sudden shift in the wind caused the fire to ignite some of the Harlin buildings instead.

According to informed sources, some 23,000 plundered artefacts are supposed to be in the British Museum while UNESCO estimates that some 1.6 million stolen relics from that period can still be found in more than 200 museums around the world. Naturally, many additional antique items are also in the hands of private collectors.

*　*　*

My granduncle did not strike me as a serious collector of such material. I had never seen him studying any of his acquisitions or attempting to catalogue them. He was usually too busy with his practice to do much else, except that once in a while he would gather with a small coterie of friends for a meal and engage in composing Chinese poetry and exchanging couplets.

After I had moved out of his home to study at Stanford, I did not keep track of what eventually happened to those cupboards full of ancient books.

*　*　*

My relationships with my grandaunt had been infused with a certain mother-and-son flavour from the very start. Perhaps that had partly been due to wishful thinking on my part, because she had been so good-natured, welcoming and compassionately understanding of my ambitions and my predicament. She seemed to epitomise many of the qualities I had expected to find in my own mother but which I never found.

Long years of separation had estranged me from my mother. Although she had offered a perfectly logical explanation on why she had chosen to give me up when I was five while retaining custody of my younger brother, Tzi-Choy, I could not help being assailed by doubts as to whether she cared for me at all.

When I moved into the Chau residence at Leighton Hill Road, my Eighth Grandaunt's eldest daughter, Miu-Yee, had already gone to Peking to study at Yen Ching University while her second son, Yiu-Suen, was in America studying medicine. I was assigned a bed in a large dormitory-like room accommodating her four youngest children. The youngest one was Miu-Yan, who was eight years younger than myself.

My grandaunt's third daughter, Miu-Kwan, who was six months older than myself, was a jolly, self-assured and outgoing young lady. The war had interrupted her studies so that at that time she was still trying to complete her secondary education. She occupied a small cubicle outside the large dormitory-like room to which I had been assigned.

My relationship with my various cousins got off to a slightly rocky but not altogether unfriendly start. This arose because I addressed Miu-Kwan by her name. She quirkily got onto her high horse and declared that she, being an elder to me by family reckoning, ought to be addressed by her title as aunt and not by name.

"There are more than a hundred extended family titles," I replied. "Who has time to remember them all when extended families are in fact shrinking fast? In the West we would be considered merely as cousins and that seems a much more practical approach."

"But we're not in the West," Miu-Kwan retorted. "Hence we should follow customary Chinese practices."

"Yes, and we're all your uncles," some of her younger brothers chimed in.

"But Hong Kong is a British colony. So whether anybody likes it or not, Western systems of law and practices prevail," I said.

"You have spent too much time overseas; you've become a semi-barbarian," Miu-Kwan declared with finality.

My grandaunt looked upon our exchange with a sort of bemused nonchalance, probably regarding it as only a passing sibling argument which would soon be resolved without any outside intervention

* * *

Moving into the Chau household at once exposed the poverty of my wardrobe. I had left Singapore for Canton with only a small rattan suitcase holding a couple of shirts, two pairs of shorts, one extra pair of slacks, one change of undergarments and just the clothes I was travelling in. I had no jacket to wear for work in the magistracies and certainly no pyjamas suitable for sleeping in a room with several children. I was racking my brains over how I could squeeze enough out of my meagre salary to meet the most urgent needs.

But I needed not to have bothered. My grandaunt had identified my shortages and had fulfilled them without my having to breathe a single word. Later, when the Hong Kong weather started turning too cold for my tropical garments, she likewise supplied me with woollen vests and sweaters and a padded jacket of blue Chinese silk.

* * *

Miu-Kwan's put-down of my being a semi-barbarian hit me on a tender spot, however. I had been deeply conscious that both my spoken and written

Chinese had deteriorated during my years in Australia. Following the death of my grandmother, I had no one to speak Chinese to except Mr. Wong Sue, the restaurant owner who employed me as a dishwasher. And our conversations seldom extended beyond work schedules and food. Even my siblings, trying to navigate the Australian educational system, began automatically to speak in English.

After Japan surrendered in August of 1945, international shipping remained largely in military hands. By the time my family was allocated passages to return to Singapore, it was well into 1946. We did not reach home till the middle of that year, when the local academic year was already well advanced, What happened then was a frantic effort to get all my siblings into appropriate schools at the appropriate levels.

As for myself, I was anxious to complete my Cambridge School Leaving Certificate as soon as possible, rather than to wait for the start of the next school year. I therefore persuaded St. Andrew's to insert me into its first post-war School Certificate class, promising to make up on my own for all the missed lessons. I also got permission to take the examination for French, although no classes in that language was being conducted at the school. Those commitments prevented me from finding time to get my Chinese up to snuff.

* * *

Immediately after World War II had ended, the Chinese government issued an appeal to Chinese all over the world to return to China to assist in the reconstruction of the country. My grandfather mentioned that appeal to me when I was preparing for my School Certificate examinations. But he was scrupulous in not offering advice or urgings as to how I ought to respond.

By the time I got to Hong Kong, I had got myself in an emotional tangle of paradoxes and contradictions concerning my identity. Who was I and where did I really belong? Although the colony had been the place of my birth, I had felt no real attachment to it. It seemed just an alienated fragment of a much larger and more significant whole. Yet I did not feel I had a place in that larger whole either.

Up to that point in my life, I had been a constantly rolling stone, driven here and there by the winds of Fate and by circumstances beyond my control. I had spent a couple of years of my infancy in Canton with my maternal grandparents, before being taken abruptly and without explanation to Singapore, to live with my paternal grandparents. Then came the war and throughout its duration I was in exile in Australia.

That peregrinating history had left me unsettled and adrift, with no sense of belonging to any particular place. Some of the conversations I had overheard between my paternal grandfather and his friends had steered me towards a vague but unstable belief that I was a Chinese, and, as such, should really belong somewhere in China.

But I had practically no real experience with that country. What connections did I have with it? A few remembered poems from my kindergarten days under Miss Nice; a few references by Tutor Tam to its fabled cities, majestic hills and mighty rivers when teaching me the Three Character Classic; and then the stunning reality of an untidy Canton plagued by runaway inflation and rumours of unrest during the visit to my mother.

Could I, on such a flimsy basis, commit my destiny to a virtually unknown country, as my grandfather had done during the Revolution of 1911? He at least knew a fair bit of Chinese history and culture and had seen many parts of the country before coming to a decision. I myself was helmed in by vast swamplands of ignorance.

For instance, I was not on top of its language, Often, when my granduncle and my father were talking about the Chinese secondary school they were both involved in, they would employ Chinese epigrams or archaic allusions I was not familiar with. That underlined the pathetic state of my command of the language. I would then be forced to turn to my grandaunt for elucidation. Although I could tell that it pleased my grandaunt when I made such efforts to improve my command of the language, I could not help wondering whether I had really turned myself unwittingly into a semi-barbarian.

Before my very eyes, contradictory behaviours among the Chinese were taking place. Significant numbers were trying to escape from the factionalism and poverty in the country while at the same time others from Hong Kong and from overseas territories were returning to take up the call for reconstructing the country. Why was there not a unified heart or a common purpose? Had the nation remained as lacking in cohesion as the plate of sand as Dr, Sun Yat-Sen had referred to half a century ago? If so, then why was I struggling so hard to become a part of that disunity?

My upbringing had been quite mixed. I had developed no particular attachment to any of the places I had grown up in. Why not accept reality? I belonged nowhere. I was just a second class British subject living under colonial rule. I was bound to be discriminated against and considered inferior to any European. That was the future before me so long as I remained in Hong Kong. No possible change was in sight. Why not just accept it?

I imagined that accepting a subjugated identity would be far simpler than trying to make sense of five thousand years of recorded Chinese history. After all I had been taught many of the ways of the colonisers. I could intone English poems like a ritual or a prayer: "Oh, to be in England now that April's there." Though I had never had sight of England in April or at any other time, it was an easy abstraction to pay lip service to, an agreeable mirage conjured up by the words of others. But something in the blood stubbornly resisted my taking that route.

In my confusion and uncertainty, I sought the advice of Chan Hon-Kit, my friend and journalistic mentor. He was a university graduate and had much more working experience.

"Hong Kong seems pretty much a dead end for me," I said. "Should I go to China to help in its reconstruction?"

Hon-Kit shook his head. "You should stick to your original plan to study in America," he said. "Acquiring knowledge is the best contribution you can make to China."

"But that is such a long way away. Finding the money is no joke. I feel I'm being left behind by everybody. You know, when my grandaunt was a refugee in Kweilin, she got a job making parachutes for the airmen in General Claire Chennault's Flying Tigers who were attacking Japanese forces to protect China. I also had a good friend in Australia who volunteered to be dropped behind enemy lines in New Guinea to ambush Japanese troops. He became a decorated hero twice. But all I had ever done during the war was to go on a few night patrols as an Air Raid Warden."

"Your turn to make a difference will arise sooner or later."

"Well, what would you suggest that I read in the meantime, to improve my understanding of China?"

"Proudhon."

And that was how I began exploring Proudhon's concepts of property being theft and why the great only appeared great because we were on our knees.

* * *

At the end of my probationary period, my pay at the *Morning Post* was doubled to the magnificent sum of HK$300 per month. When I had completed a year of service, my pay was doubled again. But it was still miles from a living wage. Those developments put an end to my illusion that I could somehow save enough from my earnings to finance a university education in America. My hopes rapidly dwindled.

My spirits were given a lift in the autumn of 1948 when Hon-Kit told me he was marrying his fiancée Frances and asked if I would be his best man. I felt immensely honoured and immediately agreed, before I realised I did not have any appropriate attire for the occasion. As usual, my grandaunt came to the rescue.

My joy was short-lived, however, because Hon-Kit and Frances decided to head for China not long after the wedding in order, in their words, "to do some good". I was sorely tempted to join them by pulling up stakes in the colony. But they dissuaded me in the strongest terms possible. One pair of hands more or less in China was not going to make any difference, they argued. The country's greatest need was for well-trained minds and for that reason I ought to stick to my original plan for studying in America.

I sent them off by going by train with them as far as Lowu. I then watched them walking across Lowu Bridge with a heavy heart. I was not to see either of them again for another 40 years.

* * *

After the departure of Hon-Kit and Frances, my pessimism about my future took a nosedive. My work exposed me to the poorer sections of the community and it struck me that many of them and I were in the same predicament. It was as if we had all been placed into treading wheels inside a cage and no matter how fast we pedalled our dreams would remain forever out of reach. I had been working for two years and I was getting nowhere.

My grandaunt must have noticed the shift in my mood, for she said to me one day quite out of the blue: "Tzi-Ki, why don't you talk to your granduncle and ask him to give you a loan for studying in America?"

"I'm against loans, Grandaunt," I replied. "Loans have to be repaid and I don't want to start life saddled with debts or obligations. If I were not afraid of taking on obligations, I could have gone off under my father's proposal two years ago."

"What a silly boy, you are! Asking for a loan from a relative just falls better on the ear than asking for a gift. Do you think your granduncle will really demand that you repay a loan if he sees you are in financial difficulties?"

"It's not so much what others might or might not do but what I myself would feel obligated to do."

My grandaunt shook her head and chuckled. "You're a good boy," she said, "one with backbone."

*   *   *

After that conversation with my grandaunt, I did some research and made some precise calculations. I discovered that the cost of a four-year undergraduate degree course at Stanford was so enormous that I could never in good conscience ask my granduncle for such a sum. At the same time I uncovered that many American universities had scholarships which they routinely offered to students with outstanding grades.

Over the next two or three weeks following my researches, the desire to get started on a university education niggled me like an itch which I could not quite reach to scratch. In the end, I formulated a strategy I was determined to stick to, come hell or high water. I arrived at a sum sufficient to pay for my passage to San Francisco by steerage on the American President Lines and the cost of the first year of studies at Stanford. I took it as read that I would secure grades good enough to land a scholarship for the following years.

Should I fail, then I would have had my chance to prove my worth and I would deserve whatever fate which might befall me. America, after all, was supposed to be a land of opportunity. I was confident it would be easier to make a living there than in China.

On that basis I asked my granduncle for a loan. He agreed to my request quite readily. "Are you sure that's enough?" was all he said. I assured him it was more than enough and thanked him.

I did not begin to repay his loan fully till after I had joined the Hong Kong civil service in 1961 and before he passed away in 1965.

* * *

When the time came for me to set out for America, I became very conscious that I would be heading for a strange country without any family members or relatives to fall back on in times of need. It would be either sink or swim.

I remembered the years in Australia after the death of my grandmother when I had no one to go to for advice or guidance, After all the care and affection lavished on me by my grandaunt, I dreaded the possibility of having to be on my own again.

In 1949, it was quite common for young people to possess an autograph album into which they would ask friends and elders to write a message. I had one too. So I asked my granduncle and grandaunt to offer me instructions to guide my life abroad.

My granduncle wrote me a Chinese maxim in English, as follows:

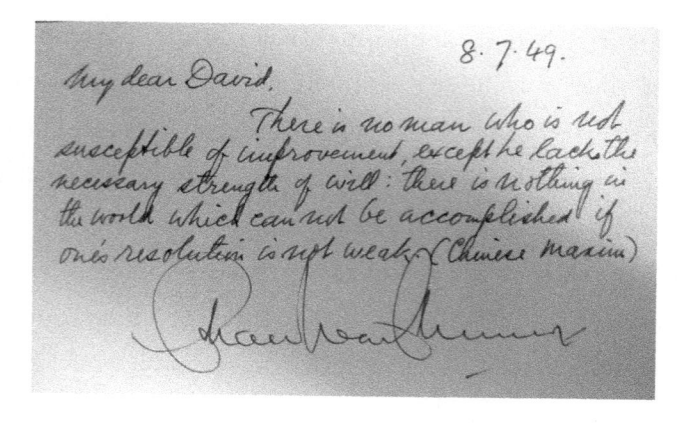

> My dear David, 8.7.49.
> There is no man who is not susceptible of improvement, except he lack the necessary strength of will: there is nothing in the world which cannot be accomplished if one's resolution is not weak. (Chinese Maxim)

My grandaunt wrote me a couple of lines in Chinese taken from Mencius. Mencius held that the Superior Man was blessed with three delights, though becoming the ruler of a kingdom was not one of them. His first delight would be that his father and mother were both alive and that the conditions of his brothers afforded no cause for anxiety.

His second delight would be the ability to look up at Heaven with no cause for shame and to move among his fellow men with no occasion to blush.

His third delight would be to secure from the entire kingdom the most talented individuals to teach and nourish them.

Through her writing as follows my grandaunt wished that I would enjoy the second blessing of the Superior Man:

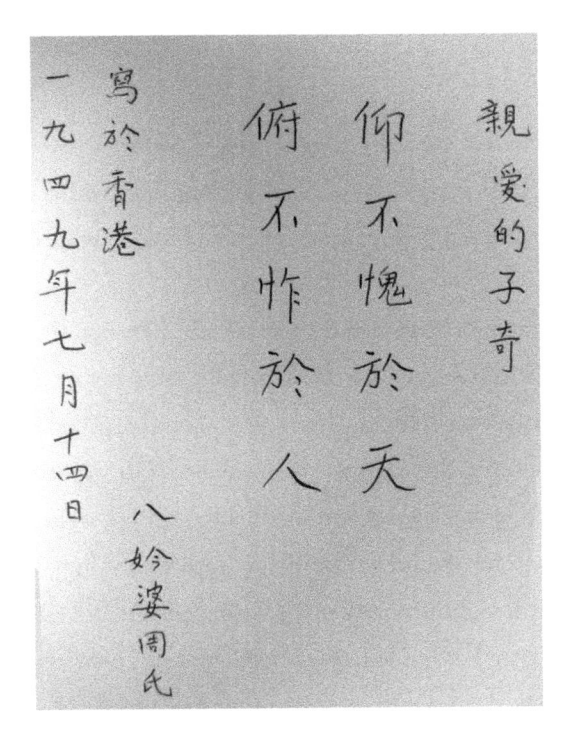

親愛的子奇

仰不愧於天

俯不怍於人

寫於香港

一九四九年七月十四日

八姈婆周氏

Sadly, after I left for America in July of 1949, I never saw my grandaunt again. She passed away from a heart attack in Hong Kong in the middle of 1952, just as I was completing my first degree at Stanford. She was only 55.

Because of my great love and affection for her, I have tried throughout my entire life to live up to the expectations she had wished for me. It would be idle to claim I had always succeeded. But at least I did sincerely try my best.

CHAPTER 2

Terms of Engagement

WHILE I WAS SERVING OUT my year of notice before early retirement from the Hong Kong civil service, I was also holding discussions with Li & Fung Limited on the detailed terms under which I would work for that publicly listed company.

The broad parameters had already been agreed between the then Chairman of Li & Fung, Fung Hon-Chu, and myself, well before I submitted my application for early retirement. There was something endearingly Chinese and traditional about the way we had reached our agreement. We relied essentially on each other's word, with virtually nothing written down. In any case, how would one reduce some of our understandings into enforceable legalese? For example, how would one acknowledge that I was not a respecter of persons and that I intended to give no special consideration to anyone under my command simply by virtue of his or her surname being Fung?

That meeting of minds had been a landmark for both of us. It had flowed from a friendship which had been developing since 1962. On H.C.'s part, filling a key post in a tightly held family concern with an outsider, was a big departure from normal practice. On my part, I required an arrangement stable enough for me to count on seeing my children through university. For these reasons, our commitment to each other had to be for an extended period, possibly for as long as ten years.

It was also agreed that my initial salary and perks would not be less than those I was enjoying as the head of a major government department. Such a package would in fact mean a modest boost in my income because Li & Fung, in common with other private sector enterprises, paid an extra month's salary at the Lunar New Year, a practice not followed by the government.

In addition, salaries at Li & Fung would be adjusted annually, whereas salaries for Staff Grade civil servants would only be revised once every few years. On top of that, there was also the prospect of an annual bonus which, if the business prospered, would more than make up for any loss in the size of my government pension.

That package took into calculation the fact that I would be able to draw a monthly pension of a few thousand dollars immediately upon retirement. That sum would comfortably cover the North American educational costs of my children without impacting upon my existing standard of living.

Other less important details, however, still had to be ironed out between myself and Dr. Victor Fung Kwok-King, the elder of H.C. Fung's two sons.

Victor, when I got to meet him, turned out to be short and dumpy, taking after his mother, the ever-hospitable Charity Fung. He had recently returned to Hong Kong to join the family business, after securing a doctorate at Harvard and teaching there for a spell. He had assumed the post of Managing Director of the parent company.

But before proceeding further, a little background on Li & Fung might be helpful. The firm was originally formed in Canton in 1906, as a partnership between Li To-Ming, a merchant in the porcelain trade, and Fung Pak-Liu, an English teacher and father of Fung Hon-Chu. The partnership exported mainly porcelain, fireworks and Chinese handicraft to America. In 1937, it opened a branch in Hong Kong, after acquiring a property on Connaught Road Central. In 1946, Li sold his share of the enterprise to the Fung family.

With the outbreak of civil war in China, however, the Fungs decided to relocate the firm's headquarters to Hong Kong. Following that move, the company was headed by Fung Mo-Ying, another son of Fung Pak-Liu and the elder brother of H.C. Fung.

Over the years, in reading between H.C.'s words, I had gained the impression that he and his elder brother had not always seen eye to eye on business or family matters. H.C. had remarked wistfully to me once that while his elder brother was alive he always deferred to his brother's wishes.

The company remained true to its trading roots after its relocation. But as the colony industrialised, it soon branched out into additional product ranges, like textiles, toys and footwear. It continued to trade as a principal in some of the traditional lines but for most of the new lines it operated as an agent. In other words, in acting as an agent it earned a commission on each transaction, just like the compradores in the large Western trading *hongs*, that is, by identifying suitable suppliers, providing a linguistic bridge between buyers and sellers, and overseeing the quality and timely delivery of goods ordered.

As the company expanded, it took advantage of Western corporate laws to spawn a number of subsidiaries to ring-fence the risks inherent in the different types of trading activities. By 1973 it had grown sufficiently to become listed on one of the colony's four stock exchanges.

But its culture remained largely that of a paternalistic Chinese enterprise, with Fung family members holding most of the equity and making all the major decisions. Employees were generally considered more or less to be just *fokis*, there to carry out the instructions of the proprietors.

A *foki* was an early Chinese version of the 20th century wage-slave. His pay would be meagre in the extreme but his employer would provide him with his meals and he could bed down in some nook at the place of business. Such arrangements probably evidenced a degree of low cunning on the part of the employer, for it ensured during all exigencies at every unholy hour a ready supply of elbow grease. But that sort of indentured servitude became less fashionable over time, due to the availability in Hong Kong of more job opportunities, the incipient growth of trade union activism and the passage of some poorly thought-out labour legislation.

In 1989, after I had left the trading arm of Li & Fung, its Board of Directors once again utilised the provisions of Western corporate law to privatise the concern. That had been during the à *gogo* era in America, when the "junk bond king" Michael Milken and Ivan Boesky, the author of *Merger Mania*, epitomised Wall Street greed and "greenmailers" engaged in ruthless leveraged buyouts, asset-stripping and insider trading to enrich themselves.

Li & Fung went in for a public listing again some time later and, in 1991, changed its official domicile from Hong Kong to Bermuda, presumably as a hedge against the perceived risks associated with the projected return of the colony to Chinese sovereignty in 1997.

* * *

The detailed discussions with Victor Fung went without too much difficulty, although his approach to tidying up the details of the deal seemed too extravagantly clean-cut and Americanised. He displayed his understanding of what his father had already agreed but he did not leave sufficient scope for the interplay of Eastern subtleties. Nonetheless, we managed to conclude most of the subsidiary agreements on an oral basis.

Victor informed me the intention was to appoint me as the Managing Director of its main subsidiary, Li & Fung (Trading) Limited, of which he was the Chairman. Trading activities represented at that time the overwhelming bulk of the company's business and accounted for most of its headcount of around 200. I would not be required to sit on the main board, he added, or to become involved with other activities of the group, such as, investments or property development. That limited remit suited me just fine. I figured I would have my hands full just getting to grips with the trading business and adjusting to its family-oriented organisational structure and ethos.

Apart from Fung Hon-Chu as the Chairman of the group, one of his sisters sat on the board of the parent company, as did Victor as Group Managing Director. H.C.'s had a younger brother, Dr. Joseph Fung, a well-known surgeon, and he operated the staff medical scheme for the company's employees. H.C.'s other son, William, was in charge of the textile divisions as well as heading the properties subsidiary. His nephew, Fung Kwok-Hong, was in charge of the handicraft and fireworks division, assisted by Kwok-Hong's wife, Rosetta. H.C.'s eldest daughter, Angela, oversaw for a time a branch office in San Francisco while the husband of his second daughter, Belinda, worked for a spell in the finance section of the parent company. His third daughter, Clara, a very sweet and pleasant girl, worked in one of the textile divisions.

The gossip doing the rounds within the organisation was that any person whose surname was not Fung could not be expected to carry much weight. I did not know whether that gossip was an oblique hint for me to watch my step. That kind of situation was not uncommon in Chinese family businesses; I was waiting to discover the reality.

One of the first items to be settled with Victor was housing. I told him that the government was providing me with a fully furnished luxury apartment of 3,500 square feet at Palm Court. To provide me something similar over ten years would cost Li & Fung a bomb and there would be nothing for either of us to show at the end of the day. I did not need so much space once my sons had gone off to university. Both parties would therefore benefit if I were to be paid a sum sufficient to purchase a much more modest apartment and to furnish it, so long as I would end up owning it at the end of my employment.

To include in that lump sum deal, I would be willing to forego another government perk — the use of a chauffeur-driven car. That was a perk I did not relish, for I much preferred walking or taking public transport, since some 90% of motorised journeys within the colony were being done on public transport. I felt I would be in closer touch with the rest of the population that way.

Victor thought my propositions workable and we decided that each would go away to do the sums so that a suitable amount could be agreed upon at our next meeting.

*   *   *

A payment of X millions was eventually settled upon, in return for ten years of service. Then it was a matter of sorting out the detailed conditions and contingencies. I suggested that ten years might be too long a time and perhaps there ought to be some provision for an earlier break. After all, I might turn out to be inept at making money for the company. If so, Li & Fung would probably not wish to be lumbered with me for so long.

I, of course, had my own calculations. I thought six years should be long enough to see my sons through university. I never could work up much enthusiasm for the soulless activity of making money as an end in itself. There was a wide range of other activities I would much rather devote my time to. So I suggested that there should be a break clause after five years, with each party giving a year's notice to the other. An appropriate portion of the lump sum would then be returned for any unserved period below ten years. That arrangement was readily agreed but with one proviso — that in the event of my sudden death or incapacity for whatever reason, no repayment for the unserved time would be required.

We then went on to discuss other perks. My leave entitlement in government service was 48 days per annum, with a maximum accumulation limit of six months. I asked for the same terms and Victor agreed. I realised it must have been a big departure for the firm because most Chinese companies granted only 14 days leave per annum to employees. Neither did private sector firms allow for any accumulation for leave not taken within a specified year or for any payment in lieu. Leave not taken by the end of the year was usually forfeited.

Workers generally accepted such mean-spirited terms because of the hardworking culture of the Chinese and their realisation that life was tough. The harshness of the Japanese occupation was still fresh in many minds and the continuing influx of poor mainlanders into the colony reminded them that plenty of other people were anxious to replace them in their jobs. Trade unionism and collective bargaining had also been slow to develop in the white-collar sectors of the private sector. Where labour was concerned, it remained persistently a buyers' market, though unemployment remained low.

Annual holiday passages were another perk senior expatriate officers and their dependents enjoyed in government service. This came about as a hangover from the pre-war days, when expatriate officers went on what was known as "home leave" after every three-year tour. Back then, there were no air services and the journeys had to be made by sea, which could take as much as a month's travelling each way. Coupled with several months of leave an officer could be away from his desk for a protracted period.

With the expansion of air travel, the government switched to providing holiday air passages on an annual basis instead, except for those who wished to retain their grandfather rights. With localisation, that benefit was anomalously conferred upon senior local officers who usually took their "home leave" far away from their real homes.

I pointed out to Victor that I was now unmarried and that once my sons had gone off to North America I would have no immediate family members to take on holiday. Assuming that I would be required to do a fair amount of travelling to Europe and North America for business purposes, I said I would be willing to forego holiday passages as such, so long as I remained single. I would simply tag my holidays onto the beginning or the end of business trips. In any case, I had had more than my fair share of travelling in government service and I was beginning to suffer from jet-lag. So I no longer relished travelling more than necessary. Thus the provisions for leave entitlements were agreed.

There were one or two minor government perks I did not pursue. For example, since I was an official Justice of the Peace and a senior official, it was sometimes necessary to contact me on official business out of office hours. For that reason, the administration paid for the installation and usage of a telephone at my home. Although it had been agreed that my package would include all civil service perks, I did not feel I should demand every last ounce of flesh from my new employer.

*   *   *

A snag soon emerged, however, over the agreed lump sum payment. It occurred to me that the money paid might be construed by the tax authorities as part of my salary and hence liable for tax. If so construed, then a hefty chunk would be eaten up. Moreover, that tax would be payable for the year in which I received the payment, although the benefits would only accrue over a ten-year period. If either party disengaged in less than ten years, it was unlikely I could secure a refund of tax from government.

I thought that in fairness Li & Fung ought to compensate me somehow. On that line of reasoning, I sought another meeting with Victor.

We mulled the matter over for a bit and then Victor said there might be a more effective way of solving the problem. He said he would get Coopers & Lybrand, the auditors of Li & Fung, to look at the issue and come to me with a solution.

Two accountants from Coopers & Lybrand duly called. They explained that the best solution would be for Li & Fung not to give me the lump sum but to set up a Panamanian company and make an interest-free loan to that company. The Panamanian company could then utilise the money to buy whatever apartment I wanted and rent it to me at a nominal rent, just like I was paying for my government quarters. My rent would pay for the running costs of the company.

The company would issue bearer bonds and whoever held those bonds would be the legal owner of the entity and of all its assets and liabilities. Li & Fung would write off 10% of its loan every year, while the shelf company would similarly write off 10% of its assets. Theoretically, at the end of ten years, both assets and liabilities would be completely written off. The company would technically and legally have no debt and no assets. The bearer bonds could then be passed to me or sold to me for a token sum and nobody would have to pay taxes or conveyancing fees.

What the Coopers accountants described reminded me of the way an old business friend and his family had arranged for their personal affairs. The rich were truly different from those of common clay; they had means of protecting their wealth not available to ordinary sods.

My bureaucratic training left me uneasy, however. I asked whether the proposal was really kosher and legally above board. They assured me the arrangement was absolutely legit, openly used by many Hong Kong corporations.

I was mindful that should an accounting firm for a client work for both accounting and auditing purposes, then there had to be a "Chinese wall" separating the two functions, so that there would be no conflict of interest. I supposed that professional arrangement would be on a par with barristers belonging to the same chambers taking briefs for opposing sides in a legal dispute.

Besides, the Chairman of Coopers & Lybrand in Hong Kong at the time was Sanford Yung, with whom I was fairly well acquainted. We were fellow horse-racing enthusiasts and racehorse owners. Besides, Sanford was the brother of the late Lorraine Sung and brother-in-law to Leslie Sung, with both of whom I had been playing bridge with since 1953.

Sanford did not appear to me as a person likely to allow his firm to stray beyond professional standards and the purlieus of the law. On that basis, I accepted the proposal.

Sanford Yung, Chairman of Coopers & Lybrand, and the author

I did require, however, that the Panamanian company be structured with three equal bearer bonds, so that each of my three sons could be handed one bond should anything untoward happen to me.

* * *

Following the establishment of the Panamanian company, I set about hunting for a suitable apartment. I eventually found one agreeably laid out with two fair-sized bedrooms. It was in a 20-year-old building at the junction of Seymour Road and Robinson Road, almost directly opposite Palm Court. The apartment covered a total floor area of a little over 1,200 square feet, which was more than sufficient for a single person.

Both bedrooms had windows on two sides. There were also two balconies, one outside the sitting room overlooking Seymour Road, and the other, accessed through the kitchen, facing the harbour. The latter offered a quite respectable view of the city and harbour. A cubby room of about four feet square sat at one end of that balcony. It was presumably intended as a laundry room, for it had a large metal wash basin inside.

However, some previous owner had glassed in that balcony to turn it into a servant's room. It had obviously been one of those illegal conversions so common in a city with an insatiable lust for additional living space. In theory, any prospective purchaser should verify with the building authorities whether permission had been granted for that conversion. If not, then regulations required that the balcony be restored to its original state.

But then, who was the prospective purchaser? Surely not I. I would be merely a tenant renting the premises from a Panama company. That company had purchased the apartment and its accounts were being handled by an internationally renowned firm of chartered accountants. As a tenant, I could not possibly be responsible for any structural changes. It was all an arm's length deal, legally and meticulously arranged. On that dicey rationalisation, I neatly sidestepped the sleeping dogs lying across the path to my future home.

The unvarnished truth, however, still niggled me. Too much knowledge was sometimes an unsettling thing. Small wonder why some wise ancients had declared ignorance to be bliss. I could not help being aware that a hundred years of British Companies Law, a prolonged insouciance by colonial authorities over infractions of building codes and the all too widespread proclivity by locals to cut corners had all combined to create an insidious grey area of public irresponsibility. An unfathomable number of citizens had been gleefully playing ducks and drakes with their colonial masters and the law! A time of reckoning had to come, sooner or later. But like St. Augustine facing the need for continence, I prayed that any reckoning would not come until after my time.

After the apartment had been purchased, I set about arranging for its renovation, upgrading and furnishing, before "renting" it from a Panamanian company. The electrical wiring and water piping systems were relaid; built-in wardrobes and bookcases were installed; the two bathrooms and the kitchen were re-tiled and fitted with the latest accessories. Furniture to my liking was also ordered to be custom made. This included a sturdy teakwood bed of my own special design.

I was then still living at Palm Court because I was technically on my six months of pre-retirement leave. It was therefore quite convenient for me to nip across the road to oversee the work being done.

* * *

Wong's new gamble

by Catherine Lewes

WHY does a top government official give up his influence in public life for a behind-the-scenes post in the private sector?

"In many ways I regret leaving government service," says former Deputy Secretary for Economic Services David TK Wong, 52, who takes the managing director's chair at Li and Fung (Trading) this week.

"But there are problems involved in being a local officer. You get a decent salary, and housing, but only so long as you work in the government. I can't afford to buy a place when I retire."

The choice then was either to emigrate to a place where real estate was cheaper, or go into business.

Starting a new career in mid stream doesn't affect Wong's life. Behind the glasses and crew cut is a boy-adventurer, teenage idealist and now an aspiring writer.

He speaks very slowly, with a British accent, taking long pauses between each phrase. He recalls with apparent satisfaction the whims of his youth, folding his arms and pulling on a cigar.

"I was a stowaway on the last ship to leave Singapore before it fell to the Japanese in the Second World War," he says, remembering women and children who clambered on board with no idea of where the boat was going.

He just tagged along with an uncle. They landed in Freemantle, Western Australia, where the 12-year old boy started his working life as a dishwasher.

Later he found his way to China, where he vainly looked for his very first post in government.

"I thought I would go back to do something for my country,' (he was 17). I tried to get a job in the government but in those days you got to know somebody."

"My family knew many influential people, but I was against using influence to get where I wanted to go."

Finally running out of money, he came back to Hongkong where he settled for a lowly post as a cub reporter, earning $150 a month.

He later saved up enough money to buy a one-way ticket to the United States and a term's tuition at Stanford University.

"My friends and relatives thought I was crazy." Now he has the masters degree in journalism to prove they were wrong.

The next reckless move to bemuse his relatives was a decision to "go away and write in a London garrett".

"I wrote a number of short stories and had a few published."

Although he returned to Hongkong and finally joined the government in 1960, the desire to write has stayed with him all these years.

For the last ten years he has been hammering out page by page his first novel, called *The Summer of the Dispossessed*.

It is now finished and with his agent Harold Ober in New York, who is looking for a publisher.

MR WONG . . . . new adventure from tomorrow.

Meanwhile, Li & Fung issued a press release announcing that I had assumed the post of Managing Director of Li & Fung (Trading) Limited with effect from 1 March 1981. That led to a flurry of newspaper items. The

Hong Kong Standard asked in addition for an interview; and that came out under the questionable headline of "Wong's new gamble".

The press accounts caused a number of friends and acquaintances to offer me non-executive directorships in their companies. They said I could earn my director's fees by simply agreeing to have my name appear on their letterheads and in their companies' publicity.

Those offers sounded far too much like those legendary free lunches for me to accept. I fended them off as best I could, saying I was new to the commercial world and until I had found my feet I did not wish to stumble into conflicts of interest. I also reminded them that my being a director on their boards was a two-edged sword. My directorship on both the local bus companies had not been universally welcomed. I was prone to asking too many inconvenient questions.

The newspaper headlines and the accompanying offers set me wondering if I had indeed embarked upon a monumental gamble. I had needed the extra money before I could meet the wishes of my sons to be educated in North America.

I could be gambling with the future and wellbeing of my sons as well. Their adolescent wishes had struck me as another of those potent but questionable middle-class fads. Their roots in their own culture had not yet been firmly planted. They had little idea of what being transplanted into an alien culture would involve. Without proper parental or educational guidance, they might well turn into half-baked philistines. They would only discover long after the event the loneliness, the racial prejudices, the cultural disorientations and the ready temptations of foreign habits and choices.

It was natural for most fathers to want to protect those under their care from harm. My own childhood and youth had left me with clear impressions of what lay in store. I too had been deprived of the attentions of a mother from a tender age and so had to find my own way through the snares of life in foreign climes.

But I had never been much good at explaining such things to the young. What could I do in the face of their misplaced teenage preferences? Perhaps I ought simply to allow them to learn their truths from the university of hard knocks. They should be carrying some of my genes. With luck, they might — like myself — re-discover their true identities in some far-off place.

On the other hand, the means for meeting their wishes required submitting myself to activities patently repugnant to me, to the unsavoury dog-eat-dog ethos of the private sector. Such work would be far from my first, second or even third choice. Chinese culture for thousands of years had relegated traders to the lowest level of society, for they were engaged in mere exchanges for profit rather than producing anything useful or beneficial to society. Even the Communists lambasted them as "skimmers in the middle".

I could visualise with dread the necessity of getting on and off planes to chase after deals, sweet-talking to pliable customers and over-selling my services at trade fairs. Nothing less than a modern-day purgatory arrived at through a Faustian pact between my intellect and my self-deceptions for the sake of quick money.

Could I fake sufficient enthusiasm to discharge such a pact? I was within a whisker of turning 52, though most people — probably because of my crew-cut — took me for being a decade younger. But there was no denying I was middle-aged. Could an old dog still learn new tricks? Or even pretend to learn them?

H.C. had, out of friendship, taken a risk in bringing me into his company. The least I could do to repay him would be to gain him a respectable return on his investment.

* * *

Li & Fung had prepared an impressive suite of offices for me at Lifung House on Cameron Road in Tsim Sha Tsui. The building was not owned by the company. It had merely exercised the naming rights extended by some Hong Kong developers when a tenant leased a significant number of floors in a new building. This Li & Fung did. The head office of the parent company, however, remained at Fung House in Connaught Road Central, where both H.C. and Victor had their offices.

The location of the office was quite conveniently situated for me. I could continue to walk or take a bus to the centre of town before catching the underground for two stops to cross the harbour to the Tsim Sha Tsui Station. One of the exits of the station was directly in front of Lifung House.

My office consisted of a spacious room, complete with a comfortable long sofa on which I could sometimes catch a short nap after lunch. There was an open-planned ante-room to my office, with enough space to accommodate an administrative assistant and two personal secretaries. One of the secretaries was for William Fung, who had a much more modest office next to mine.

I did not recruit my administrative assistant and personal secretary till much later, until after I had got acquainted with the existing senior staff and their current product ranges. The administrative assistant I eventually recruited was a smart female graduate from the University of Hong Kong by the name of Gloria. If she had chosen to apply, she would have made a fine candidate for appointment as an Administrative Officer in government.

The personal secretary I engaged was a petite and energetic young wife of a police superintendent. Her name was Mrs. Gina Cheung and she worked faithfully for me for most of the period I was at Li & Fung.

Attached to my office was a fair-sized conference room which I could access from either a private door in my office or through its main entrance farther along a corridor.

* * *

After the Seymour Road property had been purchased and as the renovations were progressing, I did a rough calculation and discovered that a sizeable amount would still be left from the lump sum payment after all the bills had been settled. What should happen to that surplus money? Should it be left with the Panamanian company or passed over to me? If the latter, would I still not be liable for taxes?

Being uncertain, I contacted the two accountants from Coopers & Lybrand.

"That issue can be easily solved," they said. "Do you have any artefacts, antiques or the like?"

"Yes, I have some paintings and calligraphies," I said. "Also a collection of antique Chinese stone seals, some given me by my father and others collected by myself. In addition, a couple of old Ching Dynasty porcelain vases and some hand-knotted Tientsin carpets."

"Splendid! They'll do," one of them replied. "The Panamanian company'll buy them from you and pay you whatever sum that's left over from the lump sum. All the items will be left in your possession, of course, for your continued enjoyment, though they would be technically owned by the Panama corporation. Since the payment would be for the purchase of personal possessions, it would not be considered as part of your salary. So no tax of any kind will be involved. The company will in due course write off those purchases like its other assets."

"But antiques can only increase in value over time. How can they be written off as valueless?"

"That's the way the system works," they reassured me.

Thus I dipped my toes deeper into the murky waters of the Hong Kong commercial world, an opaque and ill-defined way of getting business done that Western neoliberal politicians and economic gurus extravagantly and mistakenly touted by as the freest of free markets under the sun.

* * *

I had hardly settled into the job at Li & Fung when I fell seriously ill. My ailment came all of a sudden, on a Thursday evening, while I was having one of my regular weekly *mah-jong* game with friends.

There was a group of seven or eight of us. The two more or less permanent fixtures were myself and a senior liaison officer in the Home Affairs Department by the name of Chia Chi-Pui. The rest were almost entirely civil servants who had become friends after working together at either Home Affairs or in the Secretariat. They participated as and when their family, social and official duties permitted and when everybody was free, we would have two tables.

Included among the regulars was my relative Chau Yiu-Hung who had spent most of his life in the clerical service, though he had never worked for me. He was an exceptionally gifted *mah-jong* player and I had learnt a great deal from him when I first took up the game in 1948.

Once in a while, when there was a desperate need for a leg to make up a table of four, the services of my ex-South China Morning Post colleague from the late 1940s, Auyeung Ming, would also be roped in.

No civil servant senior to myself had ever participated in the group. The simple reason was because those senior to me would virtually all be expatriates and none of them was a serious *mah-jong* player who had skills worth a brass farthing.

On the evening I fell ill, we had met as usual after work at the Hong Kong University Alumni Association club at D'Aguilar Street. We customarily started as soon as we were gathered, only to be interrupted for dinner at around 7.30 pm, before resuming play till about midnight.

About an hour after dinner that evening, however, I began experiencing a growing discomfort in the middle of my chest. The discomfort intensified quickly into pain. By 9.30 the pain had become so severe that I could no longer play. I was also beginning to feel nauseous. The symptoms reminded me of what I had experienced some ten years earlier when I was suffering from gallstones. But those gallstones had been removed. Could new ones have developed in their place?

Before my friends could even get out of the building, I was in such excruciating pain that I could no longer stand up. They had to carry me out to find a taxi. They decided that the quickest way to get help would be to send me to the private Yeung Wo Hospital at Happy Valley rather than to the government Queen Mary Hospital at Pokfulam.

It happened to be a quiet night at the Yeung Wo. There was no queue at the emergency reception. The law in Hong Kong required that everyone had to carry an Identity Card, to be produced on demand by any authorised officer or for identification purposes. So I produced my I.D. from my wallet and my friends helped me to register.

The doctor manning the emergency service saw me quickly and asked what my problem was. I said I did not know. I had been suddenly seized by a great pain in the middle of my chest after dinner, similar to what I had previously experienced when I had gallstones, only more sharp and intense. It might be a case of food poisoning. My friends and I had all eaten the same meal but none of them seemed to have had any ill-effects.

The doctor did a check of my pulse, temperature and blood pressure. He then applied his stethoscope to my chest and back. When he was satisfied I was not suffering from a heart attack, he gave me an injection while I was still on his medical examination bed. He said that if it was a case of food poisoning I should be feeling better in about 30 or 40 minutes. I could then go home.

My friends had waited during my examination. They now continued to wait for me to recover. Sure enough, the pain went completely after about 30 minutes. But I had a sneaky premonition that whatever was ailing me might return. If it did after I had gone home, the two teenage boys and an old servant there would not know what to do. So I asked the doctor if I could stay at the hospital for the night.

"It's all right by me if you want to spend a thousand dollars just to sleep here," the doctor said.

My three friends then started to tease me. They had all previously worked for me at either the Home Affairs Department or at the Secretariat. Though we had long since become friends, few of them ever addressed me by my name. They usually expressed their respect by addressing me only as "Ah Sir."

So one of them said teasingly: "We can all figure out why Ah Sir would want to spend a thousand bucks to sleep here, can't we? Some pretty nurse must have caught his eye."

With that they laughed and ribbed me furiously before leaving. Notwithstanding that most of my entanglements with the opposite sex had been part of a legitimate search for a replacement wife, facile society gossip had ended up painting me as a Don Juan. If even close friends who should know better gave credence to such gossip, what could any man do?

I asked Chia Chi-Pui to call my sons to say I would not be returning for the night. He belonged to a very selected group of friends and relatives who occasionally came up to Palm Court on weekends for *mah-jong*, notwithstanding Ah Duen's unexciting food. They would usually bring along a roasted duck or a soy sauce chicken to supplement the bland meals on offer. For them and for me, the challenge of a well-contested game was the thing.

Chia had also taught my sons *tai ch*i exercises on and off, so he was well known to them.

* * *

I fell asleep shortly after my friends had left. But at around three in the morning, I felt the sharp pain in my chest coming back. I pressed the emergency bell for the doctor.

"You shouldn't be getting any pain again," the doctor said, sounding puzzled. "I'd better test your blood." He extracted a blood sample and then gave me another shot of pain-killer.

The doctor returned about 40 minutes later and said: "Mr. Wong, there is something seriously wrong with you. I'll have to transfer you right away into intensive care. Your amylase is going through the roof."

I was not sure what amylase was and what a high level of it meant. But intensive care sounded alarming, from both the medical and financial points of view. If I had to pay a thousand bucks for an overnight bed, heaven only knew what a period in intensive care would cost. Though Li & Fung had a medical insurance scheme, I had not been with the company long enough to discover what its terms were. But I was fully aware I was still technically a senior civil servant on leave and hence entitled to free first class medical attention at any government hospital.

Through the skein of my apprehensions, I asked tentatively: "If I'm seriously ill, doctor, could you wait till morning to transfer me by ambulance to Queen Mary Hospital? I'm a civil servant, entitled to free treatment there."

"Unless you go into intensive care right away, Mr. Wong, you're unlikely to be around by morning," the doctor said gravely. "Your pancreas seems very busy devouring itself. A very dangerous case of acute pancreatitis, I reckon."

I was completely thrown by the dire situation conveyed by the doctor. His words sounded surreal and ominous. How could my life suddenly be dangling by so slender a thread? Could life and death be decided in a matter of a few short hours?

"All right," I said, stunned and bathed with uncomprehending alarm. I gave him Chia Chi-Pui's phone number and beseeched him to get someone to ring Chia and tell him what had happened to me. Chia would know what needed to be done.

*　*　*

What happened exactly after I had been pushed into intensive care had been largely lost to me. My mind was too clouded by the real and present possibility of death. How could one die before even beginning to untangle the baffling puzzle of life, with all its random joys and its abiding regrets? And how to leave with so many loose ends?

But reflection had itself suddenly become a luxury I could neither enjoy nor afford. I was completely in the hands of others; things were happening to me over which I had no say at all. A tube was being pushed through my mouth into my stomach, another into my nostrils to help me breathe. An intravenous drip found its way into my arm and some kind of ventilation equipment was installed next to me. I had no idea of what kind of substances were being pumped into me.

Through a haze I recalled dimly overhearing talk about the risks of hypovolemic shock, without the faintest notion of what that meant or its lethal possibilities. I simply drifted from semi-consciousness into hallucinations and then periods of erratic sleep.

*　*　*

The next morning, H.C. Fung appeared at my bedside. I felt weak and half-drugged but I tried to apologise for landing myself into such an awful mess.

H.C. told me to take things easy and to just concentrate on getting well again. He said he had already asked his brother, Dr. Joseph Fung, to take over my care. Costs would all be covered by the company's medical insurance scheme, so there was no cause for worry, he added.

Dr. Joseph Fung turned up shortly afterwards. He looked at my charts and asked the nurses a few questions. He then told me it appeared I might have some problem with my pancreas but that could be gone into more thoroughly after I had recovered from my present condition. For the moment I would only be fed intravenously. He would call again to check on me in the evening.

In the afternoon Chia Chi-Pui brought my two sons to the hospital. By then I was feeling weak, exhausted and dull-witted. The pharmaceutical cocktails I had been subjected to might have produced that effect.

"I've brought your sons to see you," Chia Chi-Pui began brightly, after he had led them into the intensive care ward.

"Thank you," I mumbled, over the stomach tube sticking out of my mouth and the oxygen feed in my nostrils.

As I peered at Tien-Kay and Tien-Kit, their faces appeared uncomprehending and expressionless. I must have been a grotesque sight, lying there limp and vulnerable, drained of vitality and at the mercy of strangers, with unfamiliar tubes and accessories protruding from different parts of my body. My attempts at speech must have sounded wan and bronchial too.

Then, through the fog of my stupor, a flash of intuition came. It occurred to me that the possibility of my demise was confounding them, not so much in itself but in its implications for their pending travels abroad! That impression was strengthened when they spoke. Their voices sounded flat and devoid of compassion and warmth.

My heart felt a pang of disappointment. It was almost like a fresh wound I had to endure. How badly I must have distanced myself from them! Their teenage needs had been lost by default; their aspirations and dreams left unmet. All those exhausting years I had restrained myself, so that no cutting words between myself and my wife would ever be uttered within the hearing of our children had earned no credit with them.

Even if I pulled through my current crisis, it would be too late to explain or to make amends. We would be on the cusp of separation. And when they leave, they would carry with them an image of myself as a Great Negator who had diminished their lives in a thousand ways, by always holding them in check. I consoled myself with the thought that — regardless of what might happen to me — I had at least ensured their education. I had not had the opportunity to tell them of the arrangements I had made for the Panamanian corporation to pass them each a bearer bond for the Seymour Road property in the event of my demise. That should at least see them through university.

But it was now too complicated and difficult to explain any of that from a hospital bed. So I left them their unspoken anxieties undisturbed and unassuaged.

* * *

Dr. Joseph Fung discharged me from the Yeung Wo Hospital after about a week. He said my attack of acute pancreatitis had taken a lot out of me; I should stay home and rest for the next two or three weeks. He had as yet not identified the cause of my malady. Once I had fully recovered, however, he would arrange for an endoscopy and some ultrasound tests to be conducted.

I rested at home for a week before I started getting bored and restless. I felt well enough to get back to work but Fung Hon-Chu deterred me. He was a great believer in *fung shui*. He wanted my office to be first surveyed by Mr. Choy Park-Lai, the foremost Hong Kong geomancer of that time, to ensure there was nothing in it that could conflict with my horoscope and the Eight Trigrams.

I was touched by his concern, although I was myself fairly agnostic about *fung shui* and those types of beliefs. I had already gone through that rigmarole once before, in respect of the spooky office I had to occupy at the Central Secretariat. I had not been of much help to Mr. Choy that first time around because I had no idea what my precise hour of birth had been. My mother never told me and I had never been interested enough to ask. But somehow I managed to survive for five years in that office after various interventions by friends and most particularly by wearing around my neck the miniature jade sword given by Mrs. Q.W. Lee, who was later elevated to Lady Lee after her husband's knighthood.

H.C.'s faith in *fung shui* originated many years ago, after he had moved into a luxury apartment in a Magazine Gap Road building owned by Li & Fung. He soon began having recurring nightmares of being attacked by hordes of demons. In order to fight them off, he began repeatedly raining blows all over the place during his troubled sleep. Unfortunately, a goodly number landed on his poor wife, Charity, instead.

Eventually he consulted a master in geomancy. He was told he was having nightmares because the doorway to his bedroom was in the wrong place. A new doorway at a different location was suggested. When a new doorway was opened and the old one blocked off, his nightmares miraculously vanished.

When H.C. told that story to his friends in support of his trust in geomancy, they all ribbed him wickedly, accusing him of being a natural-born wife-beater. His alleged nightmares, they said, were nothing more than fabrications to cover up his habitual assaults upon poor Charity.

In any case, H.C. insisted that my office be inspected by Mr. Choy before I returned to work. The geomancer duly surveyed the premises to establish its polarities with the universe. He did so with all the solemnity of a high priest of an occult order. In the end, he pronounced that the physical layout of my office was not inconsistent with the requirements of my horoscope, though he suggested moving my desk about three inches to the right of its existing position to improve natural flow of the mystic *chi* or energy.

Since I saw no harm in following his advice, I acted accordingly. Then I tried to settle back into my new job, leaving behind the initial inauspicious hiccup.

The following month, Dr. Joseph Fung arranged for me to undergo an endoscopy and an ultrasound test. Neither uncovered anything amiss with my pancreas. The only conclusion that both Dr. Fung and I drew was that my ailment must have been just one of those inexplicable one-off events.

* * *

Towards the end of June, the refurbishing of the Seymour Road apartment had been completed and the new furniture delivered. The wife of a friend helped me to select and order curtains for the various rooms while I engaged an electrician to take down a couple of chandeliers from Palm Court to reinstall them across the road.

My two sons then assisted me in a leisurely process of transferring various possessions not in immediate use over to the new apartment. No heavy lifting was initially involved because all the furniture at Palm Court belonged to the government and could be left in situ.

The first items of importance to be carried over in manageable lots were naturally my books. I gathered them together into handy lots, according to subjects or authors. They more than filled the built-in bookshelves covering one entire wall I had made in the room intended as a study cum guest room. So additional shelf space had to be found in the sitting room.

The next consignment to be moved across the road consisted largely of glassware — sherry and port glasses, brandy snifters, beer tankards, water tumblers and the like. Accompanying them was a medley of partially-consumed bottles of alcohol — more than a dozen bottles made up of sweet and dry sherry, gin, brandy, armagnac, vodka, whiskey, bourbon, rum, *crème de menthe*, Drambuie and a half decanter of port. An altogether respectable reserve for extending and promoting good cheer among friends and for lubricating those solitary nocturnal conversations I occasionally had with myself.

The third lot of items under consideration for evacuation, however, brought forth an entirely different mood in me, one reflective of human thoughtlessness and absurdities. The items involved were things left inside various cupboards for more than two decades and which no one had ever used. They were for the most part wedding presents bestowed upon my ex-wife, Man-Ying, and myself, including such gems as pairs of crystal candleholders, two Royal Doulton English tea sets and boxes of polished Sheffield steel cutlery.

One's mind could only boggle over how people obliged to give wedding presents had arrived at their choices. Did they really expect a newly wedded couple, forced by stricken financial circumstances to live with in-laws, would sit down each evening to dine by candlelight on, say, Chateaubriand steaks or a Beef Wellington? And all somehow magically produced by a "one-foot-kick" servant who had never in her entire life set foot inside a European kitchen?

But the *pièce de résistance* among the hoarded presents was a hand-painted Chinese dining set for 16 people presented by one of Man-Ying's richer relatives. It was complete with oval-shaped plates for serving up whole steamed fishes, deep round dishes for other foods, soup and rice bowls, spoons, small condiment dishes, chopstick rests and traditional Chinese teacups. Each item had an attractive turquoise and gold design, painted against a white background. No part of that elaborate set had even been put to service.

Two traditional Chinese teacups forming part of the dinner set

Given the cramped state of most domestic accommodations in Hong Kong, was that dinner set meant as an expensive joke? Who — except for multi-millionaires — would have a dining room spacious enough to fit in a round banquet table for 16? Certainly I could not have found room for more than a table for eight in my luxury 3,500-square-feet quarters at Palm Court. Or had Man-Ying's relatives expected me to rise to some dizzying height of wealth in a glorious future?

When I moved in with my in-laws in 1959, they already had the use of a much more modest and traditional set of Chinese eating utensils. So there was no call for trying out any part of that elaborate wedding gift. It so happened that when my in-laws migrated to America in 1971, I inherited their old eating utensils. I was entirely content to continue using them till I myself migrated to Britain in 1991.

Throughout those decades, no one in my family entertained any fear of being poisoned by lead or cadmium in using the old utensils. Those materials had been used for thousands of years for improving colour fastness before porcelain was fired. There was certainly no significant evidence of Chinese dying off *en masse* because of leaching from their traditional eating utensils.

Given that background, my initial reaction was to donate all those unused wedding presents to charity raffles. There seemed not the slightest point in my hanging onto them for another 20 years.

But as I set about making arrangements for their disposal, a perverse and irrational feeling slowly came over me about the dining set with the turquoise and gold design. The people who had made the gift must have entertained great expectations for our marriage. What a damp squib we must have been! And I had been more responsible than anybody else for that mess!

It seemed only fitting that I should live with that failure, caring for that dining set for the rest of my life as a penance but also as a reminder that I should not behave so rashly again. Besides, I found the set quite impressive to look at even though I could not possibly put it to proper use.

Under the influence of those thoughts, I packed the plates, bowls and various accessories carefully and got my sons to help me carry the lot across to Seymour Road.

*   *   *

By the end of July, most of the items which required moving over to the new apartment had been transferred. The only three items needing assistance from professional removers were the large hand-knotted Tientsin carpets. Once the carpets and the paintings and calligraphies had been transferred, the faint or dusty markings left by them at Palm Court gave the place a very abandoned and desolate air.

By then, it was also time for Tien-Kay and Tien-Kit to leave for North America, where they could enjoy reunions with both their mother and their maternal grandparents before they began their studies.

It transpired that the boarding school that Tien-Kit wanted to attend in Canada was located on Victoria Island in British Columbia, quite close to Vancouver where my mother and my sister, Mabel, were living. Mabel was then working for the Canadian Imperial Bank of Canada. So I asked her to help him get settled and to assume the fiduciary duty of doling out to him at the appropriate times his school fees, living expenses and pocket money.

Mabel duly picked Tien-Kit up at the airport when he arrived and offered him hospitality at her home for a couple of weeks. When he was ready to start school, my mother told him he was welcome to visit at any time he wished, but particularly during his holidays. But for reasons I have never been able to get to the bottom of, the lad seemed to have deliberately tried to minimise contact with his grandmother and aunt throughout his years in Canada.

In the meantime, I had assumed that Tien-Kay was still trying to pursue his stated desire of studying chemical engineering at an appropriate institution when he left for North America. It turned out that he eventually enrolled at Gonzaga University, a private Jesuit university located at Spokane in Washington State, where he chose to study psychology. He did not seek my advice on either his choice of subject or university. If he had done so I would have suggested that his temperament was not quite suited to psychology. But since I had always held the view that a first degree was not a matter of moment, I kept silent on his choices.

Gonzaga was also quite close to Vancouver, just across the border in fact. So I asked Tien-Kay to find opportunities to pay his respects to his grandmother and aunt. Though his contacts with them had been very limited over the years because of geography, they were nonetheless important family elders. Appropriate Chinese proprieties ought to be observed. But it transpired that he did not follow my advice, unless I asked for his presence because I happened to be visiting my mother.

The failure of my sons to show due and proper respect towards those elders in spite of living so close to them was a great disappointment to me. My guess was that they both preferred spending time with each other than with elders because the two brothers had always been quite close. Nonetheless, it did make me regret that I had allowed them to venture abroad before I had instilled in them the essential Chinese etiquette for dealing with family members and with society at large.

* * *

Notwithstanding the departure of my sons, I did not move over to Seymour Road right away. Since I held the tenancy at Palm Court till the end of my pre-retirement leave till August, I wanted to take over the remnants of whatever remained at my own pace.

The most important of the remaining tasks was the culling of a vast accumulation of old magazines, press clippings, personal papers, miscellaneous working notes and the tomes of civil service regulations with convoluted and sometimes absurd provisions I was no longer bound to observe. It was amazing how much excess baggage a person could squirrel away over time.

There was also a number of mundane practical items like pots and *wok*s, the porcelain holder for chopsticks, my shirts and underwear and other oddments which had to be moved.

In addition, I wanted to explore quietly with Ah Duen her inclinations for the future. Although I would no longer need a full-time live-in maid after my sons had gone, I was quite prepared to retain her for a while longer if she so wished. After all, she had served me faithfully for ten years. But Ah Duen told me she preferred returning to help her relatives with farming in the New Territories. I therefore gave her a reasonable severance package.

So it was towards the end of August before I returned the keys to the Palm Court apartment to the people in charge of government quarters.

CHAPTER 3

Transition

WHEN MY OLD FRIEND and *mah-jong* partner, Ip Yeuk-Lam, learnt I had moved out of Palm Court to formally end my 20-year tenure as a civil servant, he immediately asked if he could drop by my new home to deliver a house-warming present.

"Oh, that's very thoughtful of you!" I responded in Cantonese, the normal language we communicate in. "But why stand on formalities when we're such old friends? Just the thought would be more than sufficient. Besides, although I've been a rolling stone, I think I've got most of the household essentials I need."

"Certain social conventions ought to be followed," Yeuk-Lam rejoined. "They provide social glue. I'm not saying we should stick to all the rites specified in the *Book of Rites*, but being conscious of them has given our nation a high degree of cultural cohesion. Imagine where we would be if we had long ago stopped sweeping the tombs of our ancestors at Ching Ming or gathering for family dinners during the Spring Festival. We would all be reduced to rootless and unconnected atoms, unlinked to our ancestors and unmindful of the generations to come."

"I take your point; but social niceties ought to be capable of reciprocity. There you have me at a disadvantage. You and Suze have settled so nicely at Bowen Road that you're unlikely to move again. So how can I ever give a house-warming present in return?"

"Don't worry, my dear boy. I've got reciprocity fully planned. You'd be giving me plenty in return. You see, I intend arranging a *mah-jong* game with our usual chums after delivering the present. That should give ample opportunity for cleaning out the wallets of weaker players like your good self."

"Hah, what an absolute fantasy! My father taught me from an early age that kinships count for nothing at the *mah-jong* table. That goes for friendships too, I surmise. So don't expect any quarter just because you've given me a gift. We'll soon see whose wallet's going to be emptied. I'm almost beside myself at the prospect of receiving two presents in a single day!"

"Your esteemed forebear has taught you well. I presume he has also alerted you to the fact that neophytes must pay hefty tuition fees before they can master even the most elementary points of the game. So you shouldn't count chickens before they're hatched."

With that, we broke out laughing. During our long friendship we had got used to ribbing each other relentlessly whenever the subject of *mah-jong* skills cropped up.

In my heart of hearts, I had to admit that Yeuk-Lam was indeed a superior player in defensive techniques compared with myself and the other intimates. But none of us would ever concede as much to him — even under extreme torture!

* * *

And so it was that Yeuk-Lam duly called on me one Sunday morning. But he did not come alone. Accompanying him were two hefty workmen carrying between them a magnificently sculptured horse set on an intricately carved ebony base. The fact that two men were needed to carry the object suggested it was probably made of stone. The carved animal was dark brown and captured in a rearing posture, with its mane flying and its muscles superbly defined.

The size and stunning nature of the gift took me by utter surprise. The rearing horse stood about 20 inches tall. It left me completely lost for words.

"Well, where would you like to put your present?" Yeuk-Lam asked nonchalantly, as his workmen stood on my threshold with the gift.

"There," I stammered, pointing to the only place that came to mind. It was the top of a large teakwood cabinet I had installed in my sitting room to house my collection of alcoholic beverages, glasses, cocktail shakers and ice buckets.

Ip Yeuk-Lam's gift of a stone horse set on an ebony base

The top of that cabinet was already substantially occupied. A column of shelves rose from both its ends to reach the ceiling. They had been designed for displaying the few Chinese artefacts I possessed, as well as the collection of silver cups and trophies won by my race horses. Two of the shelves in both columns had already been requisitioned by the overflow of books from my study.

A four-foot gap of wall stood between the two columns upon which I had hung a large lithograph of a woman in a state of semi-undress. The lithograph was done by the modern French artist Bernard Cathelin. I had acquired it during a visit to Paris in the mid-1960s.

The spot beneath the picture was where I had directed the workmen to place the horse.

"Is that the right position, boss?" one of the workmen asked, after depositing the sculpture.

"Oh yes, precisely. Thank you," I said.

Yeuk-Lam then released his workmen.

After they had left, we both stepped back a couple of paces to assess the sculpture in its new setting.

"Your gift is magnificent," I blurted out, seeing how well it fitted in juxtaposition to the Cathelin lithograph. "I don't know how to thank you."

"You must have been very prescient," Yeuk-Lam remarked, "leaving that most suitable space for my humble gift. Yet, I see a pewter Tang horse already present in this room. Why didn't you put the Tang horse there?"

"I did try; but it didn't look quite right. It was too small for the space. Besides, the Tang horse's only a replica, cheap enough for me to afford but not magnificent enough to take pride of place. Your gift's far more suitable. I had no notion of what you had in mind so there was no question of reserving that space for it."

"Now your association with horses is unmistakably stamped in your new abode. It's a pity that the worthy citizens of our city can only regard horses as vehicles for racing wagers or, if they happened to be fortunate enough to own one or two, as status symbols. They've completely forgotten the importance of horses in the formation and protection of our nation against the marauding nomadic tribes from the north. It was only when we repeatedly overlooked the importance of horses that barbarians managed to invade and overrun our country."

"Ah, yes, the Tang Dynasty represented the glory days of equestrian skills and horse husbandry. The dynasty had started with only a few thousand horses, you know, having lost many during various wars. But it soon created a special department for importing and breeding all types of horses — for war, transportation, sports and even for dancing. It set aside royal pastures for them and their number soon soared to over 700,000. Those who oversaw those programmes all got elevated to high offices. The most popular sports at that time were hunting on horseback and polo. I think I wouldn't have minded living in the Tang era."

"It takes a history buff like you to have such esoteric facts at your fingertips. I was never taught any of that in my colonial school."

"Mine neither. I had to dig them out for myself much later, at an American university of all places."

"Well, with your attachment to horses I guess you would fit in rather well in Tang China. Look at where urbanisation has left us today. Most of us can't even mount a horse without falling flat on our faces. And if we wanted to see a decent horse race, we have to hire a bunch of foreign jockeys to put it on for us!"

"Let's mourn the passing of our ancient equestrian skills with a stiff drink. I can then also thank you properly for your spectacular gift. What's your poison? As we imbibe, you'll have to tell me where on earth you've discovered the gem you've brought. Surely not in Cat Street."

But as I made for the liquor cabinet, Yeuk-Lam put an arm out to restrain me.

"My dear fellow," he said. "This is Sunday morning, in case you've forgotten, and lunch is still a fair way off. If you're trying to ply me with drink to befuddle me during the game to follow, I'm not biting, although drunk or sober, I reckon I can more than handle players of your ilk. But for now, I'd rather have tea."

"Okay, if you think tea would sharpen your game any. I'm not a connoisseur and can't offer much variety. Only Dragon's Well and Iron Goddess of Mercy. And don't ask whether they're from fine pluckings or coarse or whether they're fermented, semi-fermented or not fermented. I'm now hooked on coffee because Chinese teas had been rarely available in foreign restaurants during my travels."

"Whatever you've got would be excellent."

"In that case, I'd better go and boil some water. I haven't quite settled in yet, as you can see. Why don't you have a look around and tell me what deficiencies I still have unattended."

* * *

The Chinese tea cups from the long-unused banqueting set came in handy. By the time tea was ready, I found Yeuk-Lam sitting in one of the two Queen Anne armchairs with winged headrests and cabriole legs in the sitting room. They had been placed at an angle to each other, each accompanied by a lacquered Chinese teapoy.

"Tea is served, sir," I announced. "I've selected Dragon's Well but I fear it has been brewed with ordinary Hong Kong tap water rather rather than spring water from the Tiger Running Spring that connoisseurs would prefer."

Yeuk-Lam half-rose to receive the cup before setting it down on his teapoy.

"Your armchair's very comfortable, just right for someone who wants to nod off after reading the morning or evening papers," he said. "Perhaps I ought to get a couple for my home. Where did you buy them?"

"They're fake Queen Annes, I fear, copied to order. You may not believe it, Yeuk-Lam, but they represent the first time in my entire life I've had a say over my choice of furniture. For the last ten years, for instance, I've had to put up with stolid government-issued armchairs in my quarters, manufactured by our local penal system. Before that, I had lived with my ex-in-laws and had to use their furniture. And so it has been ever since I can remember."

"Yes, I can see your character coming through in your new home. Books galore in every room. I see you have equipped yourself with the most basic necessity of life in your study — a folding *mah-jong* table! This place is obviously a pad for a well-read gentleman. There's something unusual about your bed, however, that I can't quite put my finger on."

A bed of the author's own design which he still uses today in Malaysia

"Ah, my bed of solid teak," I chortled. "You know, I've slept in beds all over the world but I've yet to find one which entirely satisfies my needs. Myths circulate endlessly about market forces responding to demand. But there must be thousands of singletons like myself who prefer the type of bed I've designed for myself. Yet no one is meeting that demand. Can anyone find a bed similar to mine on the market?"

"Your bed certainly appears unusual. Is it its width? What are its special features?"

"Well, first of all I dislike beds with springs. They do not wear well and springs are probably quite bad for the spine. Secondly, given the premium on domestic space locally, my bed has four large drawers built underneath, for storing bed linen, towels and the like.

"Thirdly, my bed is wide enough to accommodate a bedmate comfortably for the night and yet not be over-spacious when sleeping alone. I've therefore made the width of my bed half way between that of a single and a normal double bed.

"There's bound to be a host of items an average person would wish to have within reach in bed. For instance, items like books and other reading materials, an alarm clock, a cassette player, a box of tissues and the inevitable glass of water to quench the late night thirst. Possibly room for the odd bottle of medication. For me, space also to safely deposit my spectacles before turning in.

"In case anyone should seek to copy my design, let me sound a note of caution. It's far easier to find a furniture maker to make a bed to specification than to find a mattress-maker to produce a mattress of the appropriate size."

Warming to my exposition, I continued expansively: "Lastly, I cannot abide by the absolute impracticality of most standard headboards. Some are nothing more than decorative panels hung on walls. Where they are fixed to beds, they are often very shakily attached, for no real functional purpose. In my experience, there are inevitable moments during sexual congress when those engaged in it would wish to grab hold of something more solid than just each other's bodies. Hence the headboard to my bed is firmly bolted to the rest of the bed, with stout but artistically fashioned wooden bars, each strong enough to take many forms of stress.

"The Tang Dynasty, apart from being a golden age for poetry and equine husbandry, was also notable for its plethora of sex manuals. Frankly, I've found some of their instructions and their descriptions of positions for congress quite impossible to replicate. For the avoidance of doubt, I should state clearly that neither I nor any of the ladies who have shared my bed have been bizarre in our sexual habits. None had any yen for those weird indulgences in the form of bondage, sado-masochism or asphyxiation.

"You know, I've nonetheless discovered that women are fascinating creatures if men would only talk and listen to them more, rather than being in a hurry to bed them. Each of them may have very moving tales of joy or woe to tell. After a couple of nights with such a woman, one might find the bed of roses one had climbed into turning out to be a bed of neuroses."

"I defer to your expertise on such matters," Yeuk-Lam said, tartly. There was an insinuation of disapproval in his voice. "We've known each other long enough, David, so I hope you won't take it amiss if I were to speak like an elder brother. Suze and I often worry about you. She and a number of your other friends have introduced you to many matrimonial prospects. Unfortunately, none has really clicked. Isn't it about time you settled down?"

"Most of my friends know I've genuinely been trying for some time to find a wife for my children's sake. But it hasn't been easy at all. Someone suitable for my children might be unsuitable for me, and vice versa. There are simply too many conflicting issues to resolve among too many individuals — temperament, chemistry, ambition and so forth."

Yeuk-Lam made an ambivalent sound. "Have you seriously thought of marrying again, if the right woman came along? You can't keep escorting an endless parade of girls around, especially when many are young enough to be your daughters. This is a town filled with wagging tongues. You're already acquiring something of a reputation as a libertine, trifling with the affections of the innocent and taking advantage of them."

"Yes, there are risks all right. Idlers make up the most amazing stories. But every liaison I've had has been absolutely consensual, with eyes wide open on both sides. How much lower can I sink in Chinese esteem? I used to be a teacher. Then I traded that to become a running dog for foreign imperialists. Now I've surrendered myself to money-grubbing commerce, skimming a living off the labour of others, just for the sake of my children. Only the criminal classes remain below the level I'm at now.

"As for marriage, it seems utter ill luck that a right woman never presents herself at the right time and under the right circumstances. It has usually been the opposite. Now that my sons are finally off my hands, all the women I had previously been attracted to have also disappeared. That's fate, I suppose. How can anyone fight against it? It has to be one of life's crueller paradoxes that so much of what a person regards as precious often slips away between the cracks."

Yeuk-Lam nodded, shifting into a more empathic mood. He picked up his cup of tea and took a sip.

I did likewise. As I did so, the torrents of memory concerning missed opportunities came rushing back — the stimulating evenings with Barbara, that sensual Canadian diplomat, and the stolen moments of adulterous love with C. Other times and other engagements also returned. Sharlee in Holland and the Jewish girl I had once danced with on a star-spangled Californian night. Those bygone events all seemed so real, so freshly minted that they did not appear at all to belong to a distant past. The old extravagant dreams I had woven around many women had in fact all been dispersed, like morning mists under the harshness of sunlight.

Suddenly, I heard Yeuk-Lam's voice calling me back from my ruminations. "It's not good for a man to live too long alone," he said. "The ancients have consistently stressed the importance of getting one's *Yin* and *Yang* in balance. I think the Bible also has a reference to it being better to marry than to burn, although on present evidence you do not appear to be burning very much."

"Let's forget about my problems. They're insoluble, my friend. Just tell me where you found the sculpture and why you decided to acquire it for me."

"Aren't the answers quite simple?" Yeuk-Lam replied. "All your friends know how much you are attached to horses. You get up at the crack of dawn to clock your own gee-gees at training and you regularly visit them at their stables, bringing them carrots and lumps of sugar.

"For most owners, their animals represent no more than status symbols, something to show off. But you have real affection for them. So when I saw the sculpture at a national exhibition of Chinese arts and craft in Canton, I knew it would be just the gift for you. So I bought it, especially after the sculptor told me it had taken him two years to carve it and he intended never to carve another."

"You know my weaknesses, all right. When was this exhibition? Recently? You should have told me about it; I would have loved going to see it with you."

"Actually I bought the horse three years ago."

"What! Three years ago? Yet you haven't breathed a word about it till now! Where has the sculpture been all this time? Why did you wait three years before giving it to me?"

Yeuk-Lam chuckled. "Just think for a moment, my dear chap, before getting excited. Aren't the answers obvious? Three years ago you were still a hidebound civil servant, punctilious over regulations governing receiving personal 'advantages'. You've always been so fearful of conflicts of interest that you've consistently refused to touch any of the local stocks and shares friends have recommended to you. Or enter into our highly speculative property market either. Would you have accepted a gift from me which your British masters would be bound to question? Certainly not. If you liked the gift, as I felt sure you would, you would have demanded to buy it from me. But such a breach of the etiquettes of friendship would have been unacceptable to me.

"What recourse would have been open to you then, except the one specified in civil service regulations? You would have to apply to the government for permission to accept a gift from none other than the Vice-President of the left-wing Hong Kong Chinese General Chamber of Commerce. How do you think the administration would have reacted? All kinds of alarm bells might go off. That would not have done your standing as a senior Chinese civil servant any good, would it?"

"No, I guess not. But I wouldn't have given a damn about that."

"Well, you had told me previously that the government had refused, allegedly on political grounds, to grant you permission to go to Taiwan for a holiday with a prospective bride. You swallowed that refusal. Could you swallow another should the British bar you from accepting my gift?

"What if the British authorities were to go a step further? They could not have been entirely ignorant of your being a regular *mah-jong* player at the General Chamber, playing with politically questionable characters like myself. What if they were to advance some security consideration for you to cease consorting with people like me? Could you have swallowed that as well? If not, you would have to deal with a crisis of identity, friendship, conscience and a whole lot of other issues. It was precisely because I did not want to put you in that position that I've stored the horse in Canton till now, before offering it to you after you had shed your civil service ties."

I nodded in reluctant agreement as Yeuk-Lam set out his analysis and reasoning. He was of course spot on about the situation I would have had to face.

"You know me too well," I muttered. "If you had offered me the horse three years ago, I might well have left the civil service that much earlier."

"That would have been a great loss to the community. Even now, your being with Li & Fung, represents a serious loss for the community."

"How so? I never had much power to influence fundamental issues; I was just a small cog in a great big machine. Now I am at least trying to generate some wealth for the community, if you subscribe to the economic myth of trickle-down effects. I fear in reality I might have merely sold out while in financial need, for thirty pieces of silver. In truth, I had always suspected I might just be creating wealth mainly for Li & Fung shareholders and its top executives rather than for society at large."

"Don't sell yourself short. You've many friends who believe you would always act in the best interests of the community."

"Alas, the same point of view did not exist in many of my colonial superiors."

"Not much can be kept under wraps in this place, you know. News gets around. People know you'd been a burr under British saddles and they're delighted. As a senior official, you did manage to do things your British superiors ought to have done but did not.

"The British, for instance, promised an expansion of the Western wholesale market right after the war, to cope with growing demand, but nothing happened till you intervened. You stuck your neck out to argue for the right of citizens to hold peaceful demonstrations, like during the Diaoyu Tai dispute. You laid the groundwork for the land-for-oil deal with Chinese interests during the OPEC oil embargo. You fought Whitehall for fair sharing of air traffic right for our local airline, Cathay Pacific. You scuppered the plot to build an expensive reverse osmosis plant instead of simply buying more water from Kwangtung. Need I go on?"

"But you don't know of the other occasions I have banged my head against stone walls to no avail. Such successes I had would not have been possible without help from people like yourself."

Yeuk-Lam took another sip of tea. "Come to think of it," he reflected, "our relationship must be quite baffling for people who do not know either of us very well, because we were obviously standing on different sides of a significant political fence. That goes as much for the British elite as for some General Chamber members. Such people probably regard you as either a British stooge or some kind of back channel fixer."

"That's the trouble with this fractured town of ours. There are too many people around with secret allegiances, fabricated loyalties and hidden enmities, living within their own private bubbles and cliques and seeking their own self-interest. Many cannot recognise a genuine friendship even when it hits them in the face."

"Part of the reason is that you confuse them by being too open and straightforward. You've got moral red lines but not political ones. You'd talk to whoever's sensible, even if he doesn't share your point of view. That makes people suspicious. They figure there has to be an ulterior motive somewhere, some personal benefit in cash or kind. Take for example your attempt to bring H.C. Fung and myself together. How did you go about it? You invited us to lunch at the Owners' Box at the Jockey Club on a crowded race day. It took place in front of half of Hong Kong's business bigwigs. People had to wonder what was in it for you to act as a middleman."

I sighed. "I was just trying to bring together two friends with different political persuasions but who could also pursue mutually beneficial economic interests. Chinese history tells us that whenever we are divided among ourselves, outsiders are bound to take advantage. I was just trying to frustrate that customary British tactic of divide and rule here."

"I'm sorry it didn't work between me and H.C.," Yeuk-Lam said. "As you saw, we were civil and courteous to each other, but the chemistry just wasn't there. I guess H.C had too much invested with the Kuomintang in Taiwan. If it had not been for your effort, H.C. and I would probably never have sat down at the same table to share a meal."

"Well, I'm not giving up on cementing relationships between friends. Better times may yet come."

"You're no doubt aware that what you're trying to do coincides neatly with the mainland's United Front slogan that those who loved their country should not be divided between the Left and the Right."

"Slogans are more easily shouted than given reality," I remarked dryly.

* * *

Thus that morning chit-chatting with Yeuk-Lam passed swiftly and agreeably, as time usually did when bosom friends sipped tea and engaged in open-hearted exchanges of views. We both turned a little wistful at times when we touched upon matters beyond our power to amend.

After a leisurely lunch, we settled down to the pre-arranged *mah-jong* game with our favoured partners, Uncle Lau and Sixth Eldest Brother. By the end of the evening, both Yeuk-Lam and I left with our honour more or less intact, both managing to win a little while the others lost.

* * *

In the week following Yeuk-Lam's delivery of his gift, I could not help mulling over the changes in life I would henceforth have to accommodate. My children were gone; I was all alone. In theory, I ought to be footloose and fancy free. But reality was quite different.

With the departure of my sons, I no longer had any need for a live-in maid. I therefore engaged only a part-time replacement for Ah Duen. She happened to be a chubby woman of about 40 by the name of Ah Seam. She only had to come three times a week, for a couple of hours each time to do cleaning and to take care of my laundry. I had decided to eat my meals out, so that she would not be involved in marketing or cooking. On the rare occasion I might be forced to eat at home because of, say, an approaching typhoon, I could simply make do with a cheese sandwich, a couple of boiled eggs or a bowl of instant noodles.

In respect of romantic affairs, I found myself in an invidious position. Although I could now initiate a relationship with whoever I fancied, without having to take account of the needs and proclivities of my children, what was there to choose from?

Unattached women looking for a long-term relationship were likely to be successful executives with lonely hearts, ageing spinsters, divorcees seeking a father-figure for their children, and the prematurely widowed, wanting a man to cuddle instead of a fidelity arch to be erected in her honour. And of course there would always be those liberated and street-smart young things of Ping's generation, probably playing the dual roles of innocent victim as well as predator, out either to snare a sugar daddy or get noticed by some movie or television talent scout. Not a very promising field.

I had told Yeuk-Lam during our Sunday conversation that my life had been plagued by the right woman always appearing at the wrong time and under the wrong circumstances. I might have claimed with a semblance of truth that our karma happened never to have been properly aligned. But that too would have constituted only a partial truth. Indeed, I might as readily try some hackneyed tale of star-crossed lovers as a face-saving evasion. When has the path to love ever been straight and smooth? Another partial truth might be my unwillingness to take tough decisions over responsibilities, either those already assumed or potential ones to come. Or perhaps it was simply a matter of cold funk. I could not really be sure.

Yeuk-Lam was a bosom friend of long standing, from whom I had no need to hold back personal secrets. Yet how could a person unfold his life before another, like a bolt of fabric, to point out the patterns and uniqueness in the cloth or to highlight its shifting colours when viewed under light or in the shade? What was more concerning were the insecurities, doubts, frustrations and other hang-ups buried inside myself.

If I were prepared to submit myself to the tender mercies of a latter-day Freud or Jung, I might perhaps, through the fog of their pseudo-scientific jargon and double-talk, gain an insight or two. But would any such diagnosis be meaningful or reliable? Headshrinkers had a penchant for ascribing present emotional problems to past childhood events. Some, like Freud and his followers, went in for interpreting dreams, believing that dreams would reveal repressed trends and wishes in the individual.

My own childhood had certainly been unconventional and unsettling. I had also been prey to an odd recurring dream too, lasting throughout my boyhood until well after I had finished university. What could any headshrinker make of that?

Perhaps the best approach might be to summarise here some of my more salient experiences of my childhood, so that readers can draw their own conclusions as to whether any psychological kinks, fixations, prejudices, phobias or resentments might be attributable to those events.

* * *

I shall begin my summary from about the age of three or four, when my parents' marriage collapsed spectacularly amidst much ado. Shortly afterwards, my mother took me and my younger brother by train from Hong Kong to Canton, where she had a job with the British-run Chinese Maritime Custom Service. My understanding was that she had to work in order to support herself and my brother and myself.

We went to live at the home of her father, an Anglican archdeacon who had some years earlier been responsible for founding the Church of Our Saviour at Wanfu Road in Canton. He was a humble, kindly and frugal man, though in my eyes he appeared rather serious and dour. His name was Mok Shau-Tsang and he was already 67 when we arrived. He had eight children of whom my mother was the fourth. He was, naturally, a fervent Christian and he, together with his wife and my mother, did their best to turn me into one as well.

They all seemed to hold the belief that people were born inherently bad and loaded down with sins. They explained that was why everybody needed the grace of their Christian God to save their souls from everlasting hell-fires. Their belief puzzled me. I could grasp neither the concept of hell-fires nor of people's souls roasting in them. What was a soul? I also did not feel I was really bad, just because I preferred playing games with other children rather than attending church and singing hymns.

Things came to a head one day when I hit one of my cousins on his head with a piece of wood, for taking a toy from me and refusing to give it back. He did suffer a scratch which drew blood but he wailed like a pig being slaughtered.

According to the Christian virtues taught to me by both my maternal grandparents and my mother, someone who had suffered at the hands of another ought to turn the other cheek. My cousin should therefore have allowed me to hit him again instead of kicking up such a fuss. Otherwise what did that teaching mean? He was in any case bigger than me. Moreover, I thought it right I should defend what was mine.

None of the adults who quickly gathered at the scene of the incident saw things my way, however. I was roundly scolded for being naughty and for using violence to settle disputes. Nobody tried to explain another way of getting my toy back.

Because my mother had to go to work and my grandparents were always too busy to keep an eye on me, I was soon passed into the care of a kindergarten. It was one administered by the church. I was put into a class run by a nice teacher whose name I have forgotten. But I remembered her well and gave her the name of Miss Nice.

Contrary to my adult family members, Miss Nice was quite willing to explain things. But I quickly got into trouble nonetheless. I got punished for disrupting her class by asking too many questions. After a while, it came to me that I was in a situation where I could not win. Adults must have thought processes entirely different from mine. Moreover, they often did not follow the logic of what they taught children.

In 1934, when a new South China diocese was created by the Anglican Church Missionary Society, my maternal grandfather was unanimously elected as the first Bishop of Canton. His religious teachings and his devotion to helping the poor, the sick and the dispossessed must have gone down well for so many to choose him to lead the flock. It was then that I began worrying more about the possibility that I might actually have some unaccountable form of badness or evil festering inside me.

*　*　*

Soon after I had turned five, a dispute arose between my parents' respective families over who should have custody of my younger brother and myself. Some to-and-fro bargaining took place among adults. My mother, to my chagrin, decided in the end that she would keep my younger brother but surrender me to my paternal grandmother, who would take me to Singapore, to a father I had hardly ever seen.

My mother did not explain why she had made that choice. She had never been much good at giving explanations, as I was subsequently to find out. But neither did anybody else explain why I should be the one to be given up. Neither did anybody ask for my preference. It did not seem fair that I should be disposed of in that way, like some inanimate object. I suspected the decision must have turned upon my alleged badness.

Once I had been handed over, it was to be more than 12 years before I saw either my mother or my brother again. In 1947, when I did meet up with them again in Canton, one of the first questions I asked my mother was why she had given me up but kept my younger brother.

Her reply was that it was a case of being pragmatic. The Wong family had wanted both of us but she was unwilling to agree to that. At the same time, she realised she was in no financial position to support and bring up two children. Since the Wong family insisted on having at least the firstborn, she thought that I, being three and a half years older than my brother, would be able to cope better without a mother. Thus a bargain was struck to split up my younger brother and myself between the two families.

*　*　*

After my arrival in Singapore, I discovered that my father was a journalist and was living with his parents in the old Chinese extended family tradition. The family home was at No. 10 Blair Road, a quiet and sleepy street. My father did not appear particularly pleased with my arrival, however. He struck me as more than a little aloof and distant. I put that down to my reputation of being bad and troublesome.

My paternal grandfather, the head of the household, was more welcoming, presumably because I happened to be the firstborn son of my generation. His name was Wong Wan-On. He was nominally a Christian too; but he had none of my maternal grandfather's fervour or adherence to Christian practices and doctrines.

He was born in Hong Kong in 1876 and studied at the Diocesan Boys' School before enrolling in the then Hong Kong College of Medicine, graduating in 1900. He then immediately took up a position as a Medical Officer with the British Colonial Service and was posted to Singapore. By the time I arrived at his home at Blair Road, he was already 59 and had long retired with a generous pension.

He was a man of many puzzling parts. It took me a while to suss out the stories and characteristics associated with him. First of all, he was a polygamist, for he was said to have had a total of nine wives. The grandmother who had brought me to Singapore had been his principal wife. One of the implications of that polygamous condition was brought to my notice shortly after my arrival, when one of his concubines or subsidiary wives dramatically gave birth to a child who was to be my uncle!

What was more amazing still was to discover that the lady who had just given birth was also considered to be one of my grandmothers! She was living only a few doors away — at No. 38 Blair Road to be precise! I was subsequently also introduced to a gaggle of married aunts whom I never knew existed, all of whom were living in different parts of Singapore.

The second unusual feature about my grandfather was that he was a revolutionary. I had no idea what that meant or what a revolutionary ought to look like.

My grandfather was tall and thin. When I first saw him, he was dressed in a loose-fitting Chinese suit. He spent much of his time reading newspapers and smoking a variety of pipes. He came over more like an aged but genial school teacher rather than someone plotting to topple governments. Soon after my arrival, my grandfather began to grow a scraggy beard and to wear spectacles.

My grandfather Wong Wan-On, at the age of 81, taken at his home in Serangoon Gardens Estate in Singapore

It was only later, through photos hanging on the wall next to his bed and in the photo albums shown by my grandmother, that I discovered he was a friend of Dr. Sun Yat-Sen, the father of the Chinese Republic. He had spent years not fighting as a revolutionary but raising funds among overseas Chinese to finance the overthrow the Ching Dynasty in China. It was not till 1911 that the revolutionaries met with significant success.

After my grandfather had retired as a Medical Officer from the British Colonial Service in 1920, he began work as a ship's surgeon on vessels plying throughout the Far East. He did this for about ten years. I was told that he was accompanied on some of those voyages by another of his subsidiary wives. It could not be established, however, whether he had continued to support Dr. Sun's political activities after Dr. Sun had set up a government in South China after the revolution of 1911.

My grandfather was also an opium-smoker. That activity was quite legal back in those days. Indeed, he used to take me with him to a nearby police station to buy the opium, after which he would then take to the home of one of his many Chinese friends for it to be smoked while they engaged in congenial conversations.

From snatches of their conversations, I gathered that they considered the five ideal conditions for smoking opium to be a dark room, with a bright opium lamp, a pipe that could sing, rain on the window and a loquacious friend. All those strange refinements were quite beyond me.

So was much of their conversations. They seemed to centre largely upon a longing for China and developments there, both past and current, which also left me in the dark. My own recollections of China were merely those of my mother, my maternal grandparents and Miss Nice, my kindergarten teacher.

No one sent me so much as a postcard to Singapore after I had been given up. I had retained some vague impressions of a younger brother but I did not even have a photograph of him to remember him by. I could not help wondering once in a while why my mother and my folks in Canton did not fight harder to keep me there. The only reason I could come up with was my supposed badness.

When my paternal grandfather and his friends talked, I could sometimes detect a certain wistful longing in their voices, over being in a foreign place. Their mood triggered something similar in me. I too longed to be back at my native home with my mother, instead of being thousands of miles away in a sun-drenched tropical place. Why my mother did not cling to me more forcefully remained a disturbing puzzle.

Unexpectedly, hanging around the smoking sessions of my grandfather and his friends, I soon grew to love the pungent aroma given off by the burning drug. It was a smell I found attractive and I fantasised over puffing opium myself as soon as I was old enough. Unfortunately, well before I could attain adulthood, the world had declared opium an illegal substance to be prohibited from use on pains of fines or imprisonment.

* * *

While I was getting to know the nature of my grandfather and his exotic life, my father was busy raising an illicit second family with a beautiful woman named Anna. He and Anna had already created a sister and a brother for me by the time I reached Singapore. They were to produce two more siblings in the years ahead.

I had used the word "illicit" deliberately, because my father and Anna did not formally marry till late in the 1950s, about three decades after they had become lovers. And then only because Anna had threatened to leave him unless they got formally married.

How the two of them ever got together was a tangled tale of incredible naivety and outrageous innocence. Anna had in fact been my mother's best friend and bridesmaid. When I was born, my paternal grandparents had a home in Hong Kong as well as Singapore, because my father was a student at the University of Hong Kong and my grandmother wanted to be close to her only son. My father was living in a university hostel and came home only on weekends.

My mother was apparently restless and bored with living with her mother-in-law, where household decisions, including those concerning my care and welfare, were in the hands of my grandmother. She therefore decided to return to Canton to resume work with the Chinese Maritime Customs and to help her own father in some of his charitable church activities.

But she was conscious at the same time that after her departure my father might be at a loose end during weekends. So she asked her best friend, Anna, to have an occasional meal with him and possibly to take him to the cinema. Given my father's charm, good looks and romantic inclinations, the inevitable happened. He and Anna became lovers.

When my mother found out, there was hell to pay. A council of elders was convened and my father was ordered to apologise to my mother and to end his extramarital liaison. But their affair did not end. In fact, they continued furtively and Anna soon became pregnant.

My father's explanation for disobeying elders was that he loved both the women. My paternal grandfather, given his own approach to matrimony, was relaxed over the whole thing. He suggested that his son should marry both. But my mother, having been brought up as a Christian, would not hear of it. She forced my father to choose between herself and Anna.

Meanwhile, my grandfather took Anna to Singapore to wait out her confinement. For a while, relatives there thought my grandfather had brought home another wife!

As soon as my father graduated from university, he chose to decamp for Singapore. Thus the marriage of my parents came to an end.

* * *

After my arrival in Singapore, Anna was no more welcoming of my presence than my father had been. I gained an immediate impression she wanted to have as little to do with me as possible, preferring to keep me at arm's length.

I assumed my presence must have reminded her of things she would rather forget. I had no problem with her approach and we remained for years on hardly speaking terms.

Staying out of her way was easy because she was a working woman, initially employed by Nestle and later by the British Special Branch. I did envy my siblings, however, whenever I saw them playing with their mother, whereas I had no memories of ever having played with my own.

Anna's career at the Special Branch eventually got her assigned to work in its Safe Care Registry, where all confidential and secret files were kept. That fact, in a roundabout way, led to my being evacuated from Singapore when the Pacific War reached Singapore. It was a last minute thing, being evacuated on the deck of a British minesweeper called the *Gorgon*.

My escape in 1942 was due entirely to the stubbornness of two strong-willed women — Anna and my paternal grandmother.

The circumstances, in a nutshell, were as follows: When the Pacific War broke out with the Japanese attack in December of 1941, the British severely underestimated the capabilities of their enemies. Because of that flawed assessment, they suffered one military defeat after another. They maintained that illusion even after the Japanese had sliced through British defences in Malaya like a knife through jelly. They did not seem able to abandon their mistaken notion that Singapore was impregnable.

The Japanese shattered that belief too, when they made a successful amphibious landing in Singapore on February 8 of 1942. By then it dawned on Anna's superiors that the city would fall and that all British personnel would quickly become Japanese captives. Anna was a person privy to many secrets. They feared she might spill them under torture. So they decided to send her out of harm's way.

But Anna was greatly devoted to her children. She refused to leave without them. Her superiors were forced to agree to evacuating her children as well.

My father then entered the picture. He knew there was no chance of any adult male member of the family being evacuated. But, being a filial son, he was anxious for the safety of his mother, then aged 68 and in failing health. He therefore asked Anna to persuade her superiors to provide for my grandmother to leave also, on the grounds that Anna, being an office worker, would be incapable of looking after so many children on her own. Anna's superiors, with other more important things on their minds, readily agreed.

It now became the turn of my grandmother to dig her heels in. The fortunes of war were uncertain, she declared. The continuation of the family was paramount. If she were to flee without the menfolk, then she had at least to take the firstborn of the next generation with her. Otherwise she would rather stay and share whatever fate was in store. In the confusion, panic and urgency spawned by war, I somehow got included as one of Anna's children.

While the adults wrangled over the composition of the family group to be evacuated, hostilities swept steadily closer to Blair Road and the heart of the city. Late on the afternoon of February 14, orders suddenly came for those earmarked for evacuation to go immediately to the quayside. No time was allowed even for packing daily essentials. Everyone had to go at once, in the clothes they stood in.

A permit of some sort was produced which allowed our party to board a waiting launch. It then took us alongside the grey hulk of the *Gorgon* in the harbour. The minesweeper, on loan from America under a lend-lease agreement, normally had a complement of 40. But by the time we boarded, it was additionally packed with some 280 expatriate women and children. Only a sprinkling of Asians were among them. Since all the comfortable spots on the ship had already been occupied, our family members had to split up at different locations on the deck, fully exposed to sun, wind, surf and possible enemy attack.

Under the cover of darkness on the night of February 14, the *Gorgon* set sail. No member of my family knew its destination. On the following day, the British surrendered Singapore.

* * *

After a six-day journey, the *Gorgon* reached Fremantle in Western Australia. By then everyone in my family stank, for we had to live throughout the trip in the same clothes we had on when we boarded. There was not even a toothbrush or a piece of soap between us. We disembarked at Fremantle and were then quickly transported as refugees to Perth, the capital of Western Australia. A number of the other evacuees continued on the *Gorgon* to Sydney, where they presumably had friends or relatives. I was then 12 years' old while my youngest brother, Tzi Seng — Anna's favourite child — was only two.

Finding ourselves filthy and almost penniless in a strange land was quite disconcerting. The fact that we had to deal essentially with white folk added to our discomfiture. Our former comfortable middle-class mode of life seemed to have evaporated for good. We had no idea how we would survive.

Happily, the people and the charitable organisations which helped us settle into our new environment were friendly and helpful. They took us in hand, got us kitted out with donated second-hand clothing and shoes and saw to our registration with various relief agencies.

The apparel we thus acquired looked outlandish on us, for we were not accustomed to having different clothes for different seasons. But the assurance of receiving a modest cash grant on a regular basis for food, housing and incidentals came as a great relief. We were also told that the law required all children above kindergarten age and below 16 to undergo compulsory schooling. That meant that all my siblings except Tzi Seng had to attend school. It proved a trial for my sister Helen to cope in a class of her appropriate age because her education had hitherto been largely in Chinese, which left her less than proficient in English.

Another problem soon manifested itself. The cash grants turned out to be insufficient to cover all our basic needs. Renting a house took out a big chunk. That meant we had to skimp on food.

It soon became apparent to me that my grandmother and Anna were both eating very sparingly, to leave more food for the children. Although I was thin as a reed, I had a voracious appetite. But I was now "the man of the house" as it were and I could not bring myself to devour a greater share of the limited food than my siblings. That left me feeling hungry and ravenous most of the time.

Since necessity was the mother of invention, I soon found a solution. I approached the owner of a Chinese restaurant, a Mr. Wong Sue, to ask if I could do odd jobs for him after school in return for food. He readily accepted, for he was shorthanded because of the war. Thus I began illegally washing dishes and doing odd jobs for him at the age of 13. I did that for a couple of hours each day, in return for all the food I could eat. Later on, Mr. Wong Sue also allowed me to retain any tips I found while clearing tables. I kept working for him for almost four years, until transportation could be arranged after the war to repatriate the family to Singapore. Before then, however, my grandmother had passed away.

Before I started work at the restaurant, I had volunteered for training as an Air Raid Warden because I wanted to help in the war effort. After completing the training, I was certified as an official warden and was sent out in the evenings with adult wardens to enforce the blackout regulations. I was also 13 when I began those unpaid nocturnal rounds of duty.

I have never figured out why it should be legal for governments to use a child for unpaid civic and community duties but illegal for that child to work for food to feed himself.

* * *

To round off these recollections of things past, it might be as well for me to record the recurring dream which had dogged me for more than 20 years. I first had that dream soon after my grandmother had taken me from Canton to Singapore.

The dream was an extremely simple one. It involved an encounter with an aged lady resembling my grandmother but not actually my grandmother. She held out to me a needle with a long thread running through its eye. I reached out to receive the proffered needle. But in the fraction of a second before I could capture the needle between my thumb and forefinger, she released it. The needle naturally fell to the ground, whereupon the old lady said: "There, you've dropped it."

That was all there was to the dream. Yet it kept coming back to me over the years, until well after I had graduated from Stanford. Then it stopped and did not recur again.

I never managed to divine what my sub-conscious mind was trying to tell me. No doubt psychologists and psychiatrists could offer up all manner of amusing interpretations and theories. But psychology and psychiatry are relatively recent disciplines and I would regard any analysis or theory advanced with a healthy degree of scepticism.

If the needle and thread had been symbols, then I supposed my failure to take hold of them must imply some self-assumed deficiency on my part. Or was my inner practical self trying to tell me to start repairing that ravelled sleeve of self-pity over my dispossession and want of care? Life had to have its ups and downs and one should just get on with it. I fear I shall never know for sure.

It had to remain largely a matter of speculation whether my boyhood experiences and my recurring dream contributed to shaping my habits of mind and heart. And if so, to what degree and to what end?

If I were later in life to be charged with some serious criminal offence, for example, a wily defence counsel could well draw upon those episodes to soften the hearts of both the judge and the jury hearing my case. To mitigate my wrong-doing further, he might also draw upon the mental and emotional scar left upon me by the public humiliation of being caned at a Chinese primary school at the age of six.

But that would not come remotely close to the whole picture. Human beings are complicated creatures. They are meant to be tested in the crucible of life, to see if they could rise in the face of adversity or merely sink into the depths of despondency and despair.

That is where the more positive influences in one's life come into play. Could it really be said that the love my paternal grandmother lavished upon me for years had left no effect on my character, that the food, shelter and care given to me by elders from both sides of my family evoked no gratitude, that my excursions with my paternal grandfather to Sunday *dim sum* lunches, to catch grasshoppers to feed his canary, to eavesdrop on conversations with his *confrères* while breathing in the fumes of opium had all been just water off a duck's back?

And what about that succession of exceptional teachers I had been privileged to encounter — Miss Nice in Canton, Miss Fox and Tutor Tam in Singapore, and Mr. Harold Lewis and Mr. Maurice Zines in Perth. Mr. Lewis had instilled in me the notion that libraries were "warehouses of ideas" from where everyone could draw intellectual nourishment for free while Mr. Zines taught me not only the French language but a variety of folksongs like *Ma Normandie* and *Auprès de ma Blonde*.

It was simply not possible that all those experiences left no effect upon my character. Every individual must choose what he or she wishes to take on the journey through life.

Now, 75 years after I had first begun learning French folksongs from Mr. Zines, I am still prone when taking my evening shower after a satisfactory day of writing to belt out in my cracked voice — to the consternation of my neighbours — a stanza or two of one of those French folksongs.

Dans les jardins de mon père,
Les lilacs sont fleuris.
Dans les jardins de mon père,
Les lilacs sont fleuris.
Tout les oiseaux du monde,
Viennent y faire leurs nids.
Après de ma blonde
Qu'il fait bon, fait bon, fait bon,
Après de ma blonde,
Qu'il fait bon dormir.

The lyrics would inevitably bring back memories of France, of Paris and of the blondes who had once entered my life before slipping away like shadows.

* * *

The second transition I had to face after leaving public service was to turn myself into a hustler for profits based on the labour of others. It was an activity which filled me with apprehension. It was not that I had not previously sold my services like a mercenary, out of sheer financial necessity. But this time it would be on an unprecedented scale, to justify the large payment I had already received in advance, and with myself deeply involved in calling the shots.

My first experience of the effects of a dominantly profit-driven system in Hong Kong was in 1947, when I was on the receiving end of it, upon taking up a job as a cub reporter with the *South China Morning Post*. My starting pay was HK$150 per month, which was less than 10 pounds sterling at the then prevailing rate of exchange.

HK$150 per month worked out at five dollars per day, a sum hardly sufficient for two reasonable meals. I was 18, however, and had only a

Cambridge School Leaving Certificate to my name. But still, a workman ought to be worthy of his hire. Although I had not made any comparative study, I suspected that my wage must be pretty close to what convicts got for prison work. But convicts at least had the advantage of free food and lodging.

I managed to survive on that unsatisfactory sum only because the Right Reverent Victor Halward, the Anglican Assistant Bishop of Hong Kong, and a colleague of my maternal grandfather's, had invited me to stay as his guest at Bishop's House. Later, my Eighth Grandaunt came to the rescue by offering me the hospitality of her home at No. 33 Leighton Hill Road.

It did not take me long to discover that fellow scribes working for other newspapers were drawing wages as derisory as my own. Virtually all of them, particularly if they happened to be married, had to take on additional jobs to make ends meet, selling advertisements or insurance, ghost-writing speeches, giving private tuition or doing some other evening chores. It seemed that the starvation wages in "grub street" commented upon by Samuel Johnson in the 18th century were still very much alive in Hong Kong in the middle of the 20th century. And still being ladled out!

Admittedly, my own pay might have been geared to my lack of experience and my being on probation. When the probationary period was over, my pay was doubled to the magnificent sum of HK$300 per month or ten dollars per day.

It was natural that when journalistic hacks gathered for a drink after work, they would bemoan the inadequacy and unfairness of their wages compared with the contracts given to expatriate journalists, complete with housing and other perks. Many felt they were as good as the expatriates or even better. At least they spoke the local language and knew the local customs and practices in greater depth. But there was little that they could do to alter their plight. They were all locals, on month-to-month terms, and all expendable. Plenty of other job-seekers were anxious to join the ranks of the supposedly glorious Fourth Estate.

After a while, someone suggested the formation of a journalistic association so that some collective bargaining for better terms could be initiated with newspaper publishers. The spark of rebellion was thus lit. But countervailing forces soon came to the fore. No threat of any sort was ever openly made, no ultimatum ever delivered, but word quickly got around that should a journalist association come into existence then some of its prime movers were likely to lose their jobs.

A pall of helplessness and despondency descended upon the frustrated locals in the profession. Those with other options mulled them seriously. One of my closest friends and mentor, Chan Hon-Kit, left Hong Kong to pursue his calling in China. I was not to meet up with him again for close to 40 years.

Another colleague, Raymond Chow, abandoned journalism to take on a job with a film-maker named Run-Run Shaw. Later he was to set up his own film company, Golden Harvest, to launch the *kung fu* star Bruce Lee upon the world. A number of others settled for the iron rice bowl of the civil service, to become government press officers or other bureaucratic executives.

As for myself, I chanced at that time upon a copy of the *Book of Mencius*. Its opening pages, which described a meeting between that famous disciple of Confucius and King Hui of Liang, captivated me. When the king asked Mencius what suggestions he had for profiting his kingdom, the sage answered with a rhetorical question. "Why must Your Majesty speak of profit when there are issues such as benevolence and justice?" The sage then went on to argue the futility and danger of relying on profit-seeking.

That exchange got me thinking in a fresh direction. All enterprises had to make a profit to survive. But surely it must be self-defeating for the owners of newspapers to put the survival of their reporting staff at risk for the sake of enhancing their own profits? And where did benevolence and justice come into that essential relationship? There had to be a contradiction somewhere.

There was another aspect of the teachings of Mencius that pleased me enormously. He held that the nature of man was good, being born with a sense of compassion, righteousness and modesty. That inherent goodness needed to be cultivated through education. Only a bad environment or bad company could pervert his original good nature.

However, Confucius also had another celebrated disciple by the name of Hsun Tze who took a different view. Hsun Tze believed, like my maternal grandfather, that man's nature was evil, filled with greed, jealousy and sensual desires. Left to their own devices, men would soon become enemies of one another. They therefore needed a strong rule of law to curb their evil nature. But Hsun Tze also believed that education and training could turn them into good men.

Regardless of whether I had been born good or evil, those ancient sages indicated clearly a path to goodness. My eagerness to rush along that path, however, was stymied by my lack of resources. I therefore had to continue working for the *South China Morning Post* for two and a half years before I could embark upon further education. But that period turned out to be a valuable form of education in itself.

My formal education at Stanford was eventually made possible by my Eighth Granduncle, Dr. Chau Wai-Cheung, who noted my restless desire to soak up knowledge. He therefore kindly granted me an interest-free seeding loan.

And I have been on a never-ending quest ever since to learn as much as I possibly could about the many paradoxes and contradictions besetting an unstable world.

CHAPTER 4

Exits a Bureaucrat

ANY PERSON WHO HAS SPENT 20 years in that dull, plodding, paper-pushing world of the civil service ought to find it easier than falling off a log to find his feet in Hong Kong's hustling mercantilistic snake-pit. After all, the poor man has now been abruptly liberated from all the legal, social, political and other institutionalised restraints that had hitherto inhibited his freedom of action, not to mention those bewildering provisions detailed in paragraph after turgid paragraph of the Establishment and Security Regulations.

In theory, he has been rendered at one stroke entirely free to indulge all his baser and possibly hitherto suppressed instincts, to plumb the depths of his own meanness, guile and greed for profit, like every other person in the cut-throat and self-seeking arena of commerce. But in reality life seldom pans out in such a neat and simplistic way.

After all, 20 years have to be a very long time. Over such a period, a civil servant has to become conditioned, whether he has been fully conscious of it or not, in much the same way as Pavlov's dogs or Skinner's rats or Kohler's chimpanzees.

If he has had the good fortune of working for fair-minded and enlightened mentors, he would in all probability have acquired certain habits of mind when approaching any given problem. He would view propositions from a broader and more objective perspective, as if by second nature, weighing whether each was in the public interest, good value for money, in keeping with existing legal, social, political, environmental and requirements, being largely neutral in its effects upon different segments of the population, and so on and so forth.

A public servant's career in essence offers only two broad paths to follow. If he were ambitious, he would usually seek a staff position in the air-conditioned ivory tower of the Central Secretariat. That was where one could more easily catch the eye of the great and the powerful and, with either luck or guile, be rewarded with accelerated advancement. The Secretariat also happens to be a place where the competition for promotion would be at its keenest and the tradition of backstabbing almost *de rigueur*.

Secretariat life would in itself be a kind of unreal and desiccated existence. Yet it would suit individuals of a certain bent and disposition. It was a life wedded to clever abstractions, playing with numbers, extrapolating from dubious statistics to formulate suggested courses of action. Without doubt policies always seemed to sound more convincing and digestible once the unpredictability of human nature had been factored out of equations.

The second great sphere in civil service endeavour lay in the more messy work of frontline departments, that is, in departments dealing with problems generated by those living closer to the sharper edges of human existence. Examples of such work would be in squatter clearances, hawker control, enforcing the rules and regulations governing "industrial undertakings" or under the Buildings Ordinance.

Anyone who has ever stepped inside a squatter encampment or through the former legally disputed Kowloon Walled City could not help being struck by the festoons of electric wires tapping electricity illegally from the overhead mains cables. Such activities, apart from being crimes, also represented serious public hazards.

A public servant stumbling upon such a situation would have a clear duty to act. He could, to some extent, sidestep the issue by reporting the problem to one of the two franchised power generation companies. After all it was their electricity that was being stolen and it had to be in their own self-interest to put a stop to it.

On the other hand, if he were a factory inspector coming across half a dozen housewives in a flat making garments as piecework to supplement their family incomes, his duty would be more immediate. He would have the sticky business of deciding whether the place constituted an industrial undertaking within the terms of the relevant rules and regulations. If so, the problem would hoist him into an uncomfortable position because it would be an issue he could hardly meaningfully resolve.

He could warn the housewives they might be breaking the law and that if they did not desist he would have to issue a summons against whoever might be in charge of the place. Thereupon the housewives would probably meekly move their sewing machines elsewhere to continue earning their pittance. If he were to decide that the enterprise was not strictly speaking an industrial undertaking within the terms of the law, he immediately exposes himself to the risk of being accused later of not doing his duty. Worse still, he might even be accused of having taken a bribe to turn a blind eye to a clear infraction of the law.

The lot of officials on the frontline was seldom a happy one. They faced invidious decisions almost on a daily basis. Sometimes they would be blamed even without doing nothing wrong.

Imagine for a moment the following scenario: The government, after due study and public consultation, decides to build a new highway linking two townships through the suburban areas in between. The only snag in the project was a small cluster of illegal squatters camped somewhere along the route of the proposed highway. Someone would have to remove them and some official in squatter clearance would have to do that thankless job.

Such a clearance official would be depressingly aware that he would always be a convenient Aunt Sally for disgruntled citizens of all shapes and sizes. The countless thousands of motorists, commuters, goods hauliers and others who would benefit from improved traffic flows and the enhanced connectivity between the various parts of a city could not be counted on to openly support his clearance work. He and his demolition team would have to face alone the placard-carrying squatters, loud in their complaints about relocation packages being inadequate, temporary accommodation being sub-standard and alternative resettlement sites too remotely located.

And the mass media, always striving for a "human interest" angle to stories to boost readership, would avidly photograph some withered widow scheduled for removal, with her miserable possessions piled next to her, or some tearful single mother with a brood of children complaining about the disruption to their schooling. Such photographs would imply an obvious cold-bloodedness in officials handling their evictions. In that fug of emotion the fact that the squatters had been illegally occupying Crown land for umpteen years would be entirely lost.

Frontline officials are also human. They are not deprived of natural empathy. But their hands are tied. They are utterly incapable of offering succour. They are not allowed to deal with unfortunates as individuals, each with his or her own different set of personal circumstances. They are bound by precedence, by rules and regulations, by well established compensation packages, as if every victim of misfortune had been produced by an identical mould in some infernal machine. and had to be processed in the same way.

The more reflective of those in the frontline must ponder their predicament in having disagreeable duties over which they had little flexibility to alter or amend. They might vent their frustrations with colleagues, commiserate with one another over their common fate. The more conscientious might trawl through old files to see if there had been flaws in the original decisions or whether changed circumstances would merit a review.

If the frontline officers happened to be Chinese, their discomfiture might be even greater. First, they would feel the prick of racial discrimination against them *vis-à-vis* their European colleagues being paid better for carrying out the same kind of tasks. Then, in spite of the consistent attempt to de-emphasise the teaching of Chinese history and culture in the colonial educational system, they would recall the millennia-honoured Chinese ideal of officials treating common people under their care as if they were children and they their very own fathers and mothers.

But no amount of anguish and no number of initiatives at reform would be of much avail. Every bureaucracy has its own steadfastness. The high-fliers in the Secretariat would be quick to label all colleagues challenging the status quo disparagingly as "bleeding hearts" or, collectively, as "the wets".

* * *

Strange as it may sound, there had been a period in the colony's history when "the wets" had appeared to be in the ascendant.

The origins of that ascendency could reasonably be traced to the start of the governorship of Sir Geoffrey Northcote in September of 1937. His appointment happened to follow hot on the heels of the Marco Polo Bridge incident in China which ignited the long-running Second Sino-Japanese War.

As fighting erupted all over China, refugees began streaming towards the colony. The situation turned particularly dire after the fall of Canton and Northcote quickly declared Hong Kong a neutral zone. But with the arrival of refugees, he saw that additional housing and social services had to be provided for the growing numbers of poor. He appointed an Administrative Officer as the first "Labour Officer" to oversee the working and living conditions of workers as the colony willy-nilly started to industrialise.

Matters like an income tax to pay for increased social services and the possibility of encouraging the development of trade unions began to be mooted. By the time his term of office ended in 1941, he had been overtaken by poor health. So he retired.

He was succeeded by Sir Mark Young in September of 1941. Sir Mark, like Northcote, had a progressive cast of mind. But early in December Japan suddenly attacked Hong Kong and Pearl Harbour simultaneously to create their great co-prosperity sphere. Since the Japanese had long had seasoned troops well positioned in Kwangtung, they made short work of British defences. By December 25, Hong Kong had no alternative but to surrender.

Sir Mark was thus taken as a prisoner of war and held till August of 1945. In spite of his high rank, he was not spared many of the normal brutalities of the Japanese. After a period of recuperation in England, he resumed his duties as governor in May of 1946.

He saw at once that the Japanese had punctured the comforting myth of white superiority which had hitherto cocooned much of the expatriate community. He pressed ahead with a programme for reform which echoed some of the ideas of Northcote. Within three months of his return he removed the bar against Chinese taking up residence on Victoria Peak and on the hills of the island of Cheung Chau. He also appointed the first Chinese to the elite Administrative Service.

In the political sphere, he proposed a 30-member Legislative Council to be chosen by Hong Kong residents with its decisions immune to the Governor's veto. He felt that if Chinese residents were given a greater say over their affairs they might develop a sense of belonging to Hong Kong and thus become more inclined to be loyal British subjects, as a sort of local antidote to the irredentist sentiments growing in other parts of China.

Sir Mark was fortunate in having a similarly progressive-minded Administrative Officer by the name of David MacDougall to support his programme. Indeed, MacDougall had anticipated some of the possible reforms even before Sir Mark had resumed duty as governor in May of 1946.

MacDougall had been working in Hong Kong since 1928 and he had harboured a dim view of some of his expatriate colleagues. He thought many of them pompous and too inward-looking and provincial in their attitudes. It would not be surprising if he had thought of them in terms of Kipling's lines about "the flannelled fools at the wicket and the muddied oafs at the goal".

After the Japanese had captured the colony, MacDougall managed to escape and find his way back to Britain. There he rose to become the head of the Hong Kong planning unit in the Colonial Office.

Because of that experience, he was appointed the chief civil affairs officer when Rear Admiral Ceil Harcourt and his flotilla came to Hong Kong to set up a military administration after World War II. During that eight-month period before civil government could be restored, MacDougall and his small team did whatever was necessary to get the city back on its feet, without too much regard for pre-war bureaucratic protocols.

After Sir Mark had resumed the governorship, MacDougall was appointed Colonial Secretary. The reforming zeal of the duo, however, produced an unexpected response from the bulk of the Chinese population. Most were not much interested in abstractions like being represented in the councils of government; they desired more to be left alone to make a living as best they could. Nonetheless, many took their initiatives as manifestations that they were trying to live up to the Chinese ideal of being "*fu-mo-guans*" who had their best interests, as would their own fathers and mothers. From such a mistaken perspective, the Chinese inhabitants were content to leave political and social affairs largely in the hands of such enlightened British rulers.

* * *

The impetus for reforms came to a shuddering halt when Sir Mark retired and an arch-conservative colonial bureaucrat, Sir Alexander Grantham, took over as governor in July of 1947.

Grantham had spent a period of service in Hong Kong in the 1920s. But much of it had been in the Secretariat where he had little contact with the people he ruled over.

The 1920s had been a fractured and turbulent period in China. The country had entered into the Allied Triple Entente in 1917 to participate in the First

World War, on the understanding that the spheres of influence the Germans had in Shantung Province, which Germany had already surrendered after the Siege of Tsingtao, would be returned to China. As part of that agreement, China sent 140,000 labourers to France to assist in the common cause.

But during the negotiations leading up to the Treaty of Versailles in 1919, Britain and France went back on their word and allowed Japan to take over the former German possessions.

The entire Chinese nation was outraged by that betrayal and demanded that its weak government should refuse to sign the treaty. Intellectuals, students, the media, magazines, chambers of commerce, workers and other sectors of society then joined forces to launch an anti-imperialist cultural and political movement which came to be known as the May Fourth Movement.

The movement represented a very significant turning point in Chinese history. The Russian Revolution had taken place in 1917 which suggested new possibilities for organising society. However, much of the country remained parcelled out among warlords and their militias, each seeking only power for themselves.

The Revolution of 1911 might have overthrown the Manchu Dynasty but it still failed to deliver the national unity and pride people had longed for. The masses were almost past the point of endurance after so many decades of humiliations at the hands of foreign powers and so much corruption practised by their own rulers. Many came to regard the movement as a carrying forward of the yet uncompleted Revolution of 1911.

Yet among the leaders of the movement, the old Chinese disease of disunity was still virulent. Some blamed the old Confucian culture for the weakness of the country and suggested that the Western emphasis on science and liberal democracy was the right road to follow. Others advocated Marxism.

Still others charged that the Western notions of individualism, materialism and utilitarianism were corrupting the young and advocated Confucian teachings of traditional virtues be brought up to date so that those virtues might remain the foundation of the nation. Among those advocates were General Chiang Kai-Shek and Dr. Sun Yat-Sen of the Kuomintang.

In the near term, the more conservative voices prevailed and the government began purging foreign ideas and books from the educational system.

But however political leaders and intellectuals might bicker among themselves over political theories, the genie of Chinese nationalism had been released from the bottle and there was no putting it back. The masses expressed their anti-foreign sentiments spontaneously through boycotts, strikes and demonstrations. They were aimed primarily at British, French and Japanese interests.

* * *

For reasons which were not readily explicable, the British officers who commanded armed policemen or soldiers seemed unduly trigger-happy whenever confronted by Chinese demonstrators. What had happened to the legendary British phlegm and stiff upper lips? They opened fire prematurely on demonstrators in the Shanghai International Settlement on May 20th in 1925 and killed nine of them while injuring many others. Again at Shameen on June 23rd they killed 50 more while the number injured ran into triple figures. Those shootings added fuel to an already raging fire.

The Chinese authorities in Canton, responding to popular outrage and being advised by a number of Comintern agents from Russia, decided to call a boycott of British goods and a general strike in Hong Kong. British interests there presented obvious targets for retaliation. Pamphlets were distributed all over the colony to incite anti-British sentiments and to call upon Chinese to abandon the colony and to return to the mainland. Free rail and steamer passages were offered as a further inducement.

By the end of the first week of that retaliation strategy, 50,000 Chinese had left the colony; by the end of July that number had increased to a quarter of a million. That sudden loss of essential workers paralysed the city. Trade declined by half. Rumours circulated that the water supplies might be poisoned. The city quickly turned itself into almost a ghost town

Since the colony was hugely dependent upon China for food supplies, prices sky-rocketed, Those in need had to draw upon their savings to make purchases and that in turn triggered a bank run. To prevent a total collapse of the economy, London had to make an emergency loan of three million pounds to stave off that eventuality.

The Governor of the time was Sir Reginald Stubbs. He initiated forceful emergency measures, which included the deployment of triad thugs to intimidate those who supported or encouraged either the strike or the boycott. But he was criticised for being out of touch with Chinese sentiments and was shunted out of office. Stubbs Road stands today as a monument to his very mediocre governorship.

Stubbs was to land himself in another maladministration scandal in Ceylon some years later, after he had been appointed Governor of that island.

The strike in Hong Kong eventually fizzled out, after strike funds became exhausted and when those who had not returned to China found it necessary to accept whatever work they could get. But the strike revealed the potency of what united Chinese action could achieve. It also sounded a warning to the British that the mood of their colonial subjects had to be taken seriously.

The French writer André Malraux used those events of 1925-6 as the backdrop to his novel *The Conquerors*.

* * *

Alexander Grantham had been a young administrator in Hong Kong when those events unfolded. But he drew quite a different conclusion from them and he subsequently wrote about them in his memoirs. They also affected his approach to running the colony after he had been made Governor of Hong

Kong in 1947.

Grantham had noted the havoc which could be inflicted on British interests once the Chinese decided to act in concert. The British had shot them in Shanghai and again in greater numbers at Shameen. But such measures brought no change in their behaviour. He might therefore have concluded that they were an irascible and irredeemable race. He began regarding the notion advanced by Sir Mark Young and the Colonial Secretary David MacDougall that such people could somehow be turned into loyal British subjects through constitutional and other reforms as totally misguided. And he told Whitehall and the Colonial Office so.

Grantham had not actually been a die-hard imperialist. He was not out to plunder the place as the leading lights in the East India Company had done in India. But he certainly governed with more of an eye on the broader United Kingdom interest than the more focused interests of the people of Hong Kong.

No doubt he was fully aware of the chronic balance of payments of Britain and the recurring pressures on sterling. He was aware also of the dark arts practised in the Colonial Office and the City of London. He therefore thought that by maintaining the city as a secure and stable hub for profitable trade the home country would benefit from the invisible contributions from banking, insurance and corporate dividends.

He set out to realise that vision, keeping a wary eye out for whoever might turn out to be victorious in the civil war then raging in China. He felt he had to keep the city on an even keel for there were many supporters of both factions in the colony. And a lot of fickle fence-sitters too.

He did not encourage the social intermingling between rulers and the ruled and he kept some of the racist and discriminatory colonial policies in place. But his ability to maintain reasonable stability during unsettled times made him popular with the local elites, for stability offered enhanced opportunities for wheeling and dealing and making money.

* * *

With the retirement of Sir Mark Young and his replacement by Sir Alexander Grantham, the Colonial Secretary David MacDougall found his ability to initiate reforms on the wane. Moreover, apart from philosophical differences with Grantham, there had also been personality differences.

MacDougall's family was in Britain and he fell in love with a woman in Hong Kong. He engaged in an extramarital affair which Grantham did not approve of. Grantham thought it an unbecoming lapse for someone in such a senior position, as if those high up in the social order should all have atrophied hearts and be incapable of romantic impulses and sins of the flesh. Other more reprehensible types of human sins, however, appeared less objectionable.

In the end, MacDougall sought early retirement in 1949 at the age of 45, making use of a civil service provision which he, ironically, had himself introduced to get rid of deadwood infesting the bureaucracy. With his departure, the Administrative Service lost one of its most talented and farsighted members.

But MacDougall was not to be the last Colonial Secretary hounded out of the service for an extramarital indiscretion. That testified to the narrow-minded social attitude still infecting the colonial hierarchy.

* * *

The first Chinese to be appointed into the elite Administrative Service had been brought about by Sir Mark Young in 1947. But it would be the 1950s before another Chinese was admitted into that magic circle.

The official explanation for that hiatus was that most of the graduates from the University of Hong Kong had studied medicine and the sciences and only very few graduated with Arts degrees. And among those few, most went after the better paying jobs in the private sector than enter government service. Hence the government had a very limited pool of suitable candidates to choose from.

That official narrative was disingenuous in at least three respects.

First, it ignored the fact that in the early 1950s a growing number of Hong Kong students were returning to the colony with degrees in the Humanities from foreign universities. Therefore there had been a much larger pool of suitable candidates than had been made out.

Secondly, the aspersion cast upon the civic mindedness of the young was quite uncalled for. The real reason why some locals did not put themselves forward was because they could not abide the more generous pay scale offered to Europeans than the one offered to locals.

Thirdly, a secret protocol was in place which rendered it more difficult for a Chinese candidate to be admitted to the service because no matter how many vacancies there might be and how many suitable Chinese candidates might be available, the admission of a Chinese was restricted to no more than one a year.

All those discriminatory and atavistic policies had been in place and in practice during the Grantham governorship.

* * *

When I returned from Stanford in 1953, a friend suggested I should apply to become an Administrative Officer. I had been very much in two minds. I was not a fan of the recurring hypocrisies of British colonialism. But since I was in urgent need of employment, I decided to give it a try.

I turned up for the preliminary interviews and took all the written tests. The final hurdle was to appear before the Public Services Commission. On the appointed day, two other Chinese candidates and myself turned up. I thought all of us did fairly well and I had expected all three to be offered appointments.

In retrospect, I might have blotted my copybook somewhat by answering a question too truthfully from a rather supercilious looking British Chairman of the Public Services Commission who went by the rather commonplace surname of Jones.

He had asked me to name the last book I had read. I replied unhesitating and truthfully that it had been Oswald Spengler's *Decline of the West*. Maybe I should have lied a little to ingratiate myself to a haughtily inclined Britisher. I could have said it had been a volume of Churchill's wartime speeches, which incidentally had just been handsomely published around that time by Cassell. But I was not quick-witted enough.

I had no idea whether Mr. Jones had an aversion to German writers. I would now never know because he merely raised an eyebrow, looked down his nondescript nose and did not pursue the subject further. Neither did any other member of the Commission.

It transpired eventually that only one of us was given an appointment and that person was not I. It was then that I become aware of the secret protocol limiting the appointment of Chinese candidates to no more than one a year.

* * *

Having failed to secure a post in the civil service, I reverted to my previous profession of journalism. I landed a job as night sub-editor with the *Hong Kong Standard,* which formed part of the strongly pro-Kuomintang Sing Tao Newspaper Group. I was not particularly concerned by the political orientation of the newspaper; I was just there to edit other people's reports.

The Editor-in-Chief of the paper at the time was a Eurasian by the name of Leslie Sung. He was a graduate of the University of Hong Kong and was several years older than myself. His father was Chinese and his mother a

Swede. He had worked as a journalist in Shanghai before coming to Hong Kong after the Communists came to power in 1949. He was a six-footer, though he carried himself with a slight stoop, probably because his wife, Lorraine, a jolly and dainty lady, was barely five feet tall.

Leslie and Lorraine were avid bridge players and the three of us soon fell into the habit of meeting up at the Craigengower Cricket Club for a few rubbers before Leslie and I turned up for work early in the evening. Lorraine would continue her game at the club till we picked her up after work at around 2.30 in the morning. We would then repair for a snack at an eatery in North Point which served up a very succulent duck congee before making our separate ways home.

After I had been with the *Standard* for a few months, I offered to write an occasional editorial page article for free, just to keep my hand in. Leslie accepted my offer and a few of my pieces began to appear. They were for the most part anodyne stuff for I was not out to bruise colonial sensitivities or to ruffle the political feathers of the owners of the newspaper. However I did take an occasional swipe at what I regarded as misguided American foreign policies.

* * *

One day, a few months later, when Leslie and I turned up for our evening stint of work, Leslie was asked to go and see Miss Aw Sian, the Chief Executive of the Sing Tao Group.

When Leslie returned to his office, his mouth was set in a grim line and his face was black as doom.

"What's the matter?" I asked.

"I've been told to pay you a month's salary in lieu of notice and to ask you to leave."

"Why?" I cried, staggered by his answer. "What have I done?"

"Those were the very questions I had asked. It appears that the government Press Relations Officer, a chap by the name of Jock Murray, had called on Miss Aw Sian and indicated that the government did not like the tone of some of your articles. He suggested it would be better if you were no longer on the *Standard*'s payroll."

"But Jock Murray is just a low-level functionary," I said. "He would have neither the authority nor the guts to advance such a proposition unless he has already got a nod from someone much farther up the Grantham administration."

"My reading of the situation precisely. I argued against your dismissal, stating it was clearly an underhanded attack on freedom of speech and the independence of the press. But Miss Aw Sian was adamant you should go. I'm very sorry."

"Don't worry, Les. I'll survive. I'm employed here on a strictly month-to-month basis in any case, like the overwhelming majority of salary-earners in Hong Kong. I'm being paid off. I can't quarrel with the right of bosses to hire and fire as they like. That *is* the prevailing custom here. It's too bad that there's not even a union of journalists for anyone to go to. Some of us did try to form what we called 'an association of journalists' back in 1948. The elites did not like the idea and it came to nothing."

Leslie sighed. "I can't just let you go like that. It impacts on my own position. If the government does not like the tone of your articles, then I am also implicated because I approved all of your articles before publication. The least I should do is to resign in protest."

"Don't do anything quite so silly, Les! Why allow them to silence two voices instead of one? I'm a bachelor but you've a family to support. Impartial journalism is a fight worth sticking around for. Just continue doing whatever you think is right."

That unexpected episode must have made Leslie realise that he could never count on job security in journalism. So he began studying law. After he had qualified, he left newspaper work and became a partner in the venerable legal firm of Lo & Lo. But long before that, Lorraine had passed away, leaving behind a daughter named Elaine to be raised by Leslie.

As for myself, I did a number of odd jobs to keep change in my pocket. It was fortunate that during that financially unstable period, I had an amazing run of good luck at the bridge table. Eventually I had to settle into two years of teaching English and European history at secondary schools.

* * *

It came as no surprise to me that after the return of Hong Kong to Chinese sovereignty in 1997, the Sing Tao Group of newspapers quickly abandoned its longstanding pro-Kuomintang stance and switched support to Peking. It was about par for the course for those fond of extolling the virtues of Hong Kong "pragmatism".

What I derived a certain degree of malicious satisfaction from, however, was an event which occurred the following year. In 1998, members of the management of the Sing Tao Group were found guilty of falsifying the circulation figures of the *Standard* in order to charge higher advertising rates. The government of the day, however, decided not to prosecute the spineless Miss Aw Sian for reasons of "public benefit". No doubt this had been a decision made in keeping with the slipperiness and selectiveness of the great British tradition of allegedly following the rule of law.

Miss Aw Sian, however, was required to give up her substantial holdings in the Sing Tao Group.

* * *

To be fair to Sir Alexander Grantham, the city had always been a place wide open to the influences of events occurring elsewhere in its neighbourhood, to the petty squabbles and misguided conflicts waged between others. His tenure overlapped a tumultuous period not only in Asian history but also in world history and in social and economic developments within his own country. For him to have maintained peace and stability in a tiny slice of alienated soil on the underbelly of China — and to do so with fairness and justice — would have tested the wisdom of Solomon.

A number of altered realities ought to be kept in mind in assessing the Grantham administration. Or perhaps they should be more appropriately described as "shattered illusions".

I remember clearly some of the propaganda during World War II. The Japanese had been routinely depicted in cartoons as having buckteeth and wearing thick glasses. I imagined that had been partly the reason why Churchill had failed to consider the Japanese air force a serious threat when Japan entered World War II. Well, Japanese pilots made very short work of the British warships *The Prince of Wales* and the *Repulse* once hostilities began.

But the Japanese also did something far more important to the psychology of Asians living as colonial subjects. They shattered once and for all the long-cultivated myth of white superiority. People under British colonial rule woke up to the fact that their white masters had feet of clay. Grantham could no longer expect the deference previously granted to some of his predecessors.

Furthermore, he was ruling from a position of metropolitan weakness rather than of strength. World War II had virtually bankrupted Britain. Strict rationing of food and other essential goods was being enforced. Recurring balance of payments problems were destabilising the pound, leading it to be devalued in 1949. Since the Hong Kong dollar was linked to sterling, that provided another headache. Grantham knew that if Hong Kong ever got into serious economic trouble, he could not count on the kind of financial help granted during 1925-6.

The first of the many great tests of his mettle came when Chairman Mao's forces drove the remnants of the Kuomintang armies to their island redoubt of Taiwan, where they could be protected from further defeat by the naval might of the United States Seventh Fleet.

Meanwhile, Chairman Mao proclaimed the establishment of the People's Republic of China on October 1st of 1949. It was fairly touch and go for a while whether the People's Liberation Army, filled with irredentist fervour, would respect the borders of the colony. In the event the borders were respected. But within those borders lived large numbers of supporters of both factions in the civil war. How to deter them from extending their fights to the streets of Hong Kong called for considerable finesse.

But another international development farther afield also posed an unexpected challenge to Grantham's instincts.

The end of World War II had left the Korean peninsula divided into two regimes, both of which claimed to be the legitimate government of the whole country which had previously been under Japanese colonial rule. In June of 1950, the regime in the north invaded the south to assert its claim. Being better prepared, the northern troops soon had the southern forces on the run.

America and its allies then intervened militarily to help the south. That aroused the concern of China for its own national security. It conveyed a warning to the Americans that their forces should not move north of the 38th parallel dividing the two regimes nor move towards the Yalu River bordering China.

But General Douglas MacArthur, directing the allied armies from the comfort of his office in Tokyo, paid little attention. He dismissed the possibility of a Chinese intervention and even contemplated the use of nuclear weapons against them and the North Koreans.

When American forces went above the 38th parallel, China made good its promise by entering the conflict in October of 1950.

America responded by placing, via the United Nations, an embargo on all trade with China. But how could such an embargo be enforced in Hong Kong, whose very *raison d'être* had been and remained to facilitate *entrepôt* trade with China?

At the beginning of the 1950s, virtually every Chinese family in the colony had close relatives on the mainland. On average, about 5,000 Hong Kong residents travel to China every day for family or business purposes. How would junior civil servants on the frontline determine whether a traveller carrying, say, a quantity of insulin for his diabetic wife or several tins of milk powder for his newborn grandchild, was engaging in embargoed "trade"?

Or should the extreme option of closing the entire land border with China be considered? But the city was highly dependent upon China for its food. Could it endure another 1925-6 type of food scarcity? Any notion of replicating the 1948 Berlin airlift was totally impractical. Quite apart from the enormous financial costs, planes taking off or landing at the Kai Tak International Airport would have to overfly Chinese airspace.

And what about the sea boundaries? For centuries, the myth of Britannia ruling the waves had been assiduously cultivated and uncritically accepted. But during the 19th century, when British naval power was at its height, the British never managed to impose their will on the smugglers and pirates operating around Hong Kong. Indeed, at times they had to cooperate with those lawless elements to get the better of the Chinese authorities in the opium trade. And of course, during World War II, British naval might counted for little against the modernised Japanese.

The Grantham administration also had to contend with the emotional, psychological and commercial resistance of a significant section of the domestic population towards the UN embargo. Many Chinese saw the embargo as a fresh attempt by foreign powers to bully and humiliate their country again. Determined bands of patriots were soon formed to supply China with a whole range of strategic supplies essential for prosecuting the war in Korea. High on the lists of required items were sulphur drugs, antibiotics and other medicines needed to treat those wounded or maimed in Korea.

A more disreputable element in the colony's money-grubbing society soon entered the picture. Taking advantage of the Chinese lack of sophistication over pharmaceuticals, they began manufacturing fake drugs to sell to them. Both stages in that enterprise constituted criminal offences under colonial law but that did not deter the rascals who regarded money as thicker than blood or human life.

The kind of policies pursued by the Grantham administration in the light of such political cross-currents and countervailing circumstances was by no means clear. I was not in Hong Kong during the Korean War. So I cannot speak with any first-hand knowledge. What I had subsequently heard from others who had been there at the time indicated that there had been neither consistent interdictions of junks breaking the embargo by smuggling strategic supplies to China nor any serious clampdown on the manufacture of fake drugs.

It would appear that Grantham and his administration had resorted to the old dodge adopted by Lord Nelson at the Battle of Copenhagen in 1801 — holding his telescope to his blind eye to avoid seeing what he had no wish to see.

To an extent this represented another grand example of the triumph of British colonial non-management. Under it a number of Chinese patriots grew exceedingly rich and won great kudos and rewards from Peking. The producers of fake drugs which harmed those who had fought to defend the nation's security were left to be eventually dealt with by patriots in their own way.

If similar acts of wickedness were to take place today and the local authorities failed to prosecute the perpetrators to the full extent of the local law, then I see no objection to their being extradited to face justice in the jurisdictions where their products had caused harm.

Not all the crises befalling Hong Kong could be solved through benign neglect. For example, the 1953 Christmas fire at the Shek Kip Mei squatter area left two dead and 53,000 homeless overnight and immediately tested the capabilities of the bureaucracy to respond to emergencies. It resulted in the start of a massive public housing programme.

Regrettably, six and a half decades after Shek Kip Mei and after the touting of several Ten-Year Housing Plans by successive administrations, affordable housing in Hong Kong remains a lively and critical public issue.

CHAPTER 5

Enters a Trader

WHEN THE PUBLICLY LISTED trading firm known as Li & Fung, originally established in Canton in 1906, offered me a package worth substantially more than 30 pieces of silver, I duly retired prematurely from my job as a colonial civil servant to become a corporate buccaneer.

I had to make that decision with very mixed feelings. It was not that being a civil servant in a British administration was in any sense the most ideal employment choice for a reasonably educated Chinese. The colonial bureaucracy was not only riddled with racism and assumptions of white superiority but, like the society it was supposed to serve, it was much given over to petty jealousies and spites, to blatant back-stabbings and naked ambition.

As the New Territories lease loomed ever closer to its expiration at the midnight hour of June 30, 1997, the fundamental defects in the society were magnified by widespread political uncertainties. Among the expatriate elites in the bureaucracy, there began at first some mumblings about their roles not being fully appreciated and adequately rewarded. Soon those mumblings morphed into an almost indecent form of "thinking out loud". Invidious comparisons were made with packages believed available at the top of major private sector corporations.

The line of argument appeared to be that the policy secretaries in the Central Secretariat and the heads of major government departments fulfilled functions every bit as onerous as those of corporate executives. After all, had they not to handle thousands of employees, often acrimoniously supported by radical unions? And was there any guarantee they would ever receive their full pension should the Chinese make a hash of the city's finances after they had recovered sovereignty over the ingeniously created "Pearl of the Orient"?

What had been conveniently overlooked in such "thinking out loud" was that corporate executives could be turfed out on an instant should they fail to produce the profits expected by shareholders, whereas civil servants had jobs for life, plus perks, pension and usually a metal gong to boot.

Naturally, there were very few Chinese in the upper reaches of the bureaucracy. And locals within spitting distance of attaining such elevated offices must have thought it prudent not to be so self-serving as to "think out loud".

My own position on the issue had always been reasonably clear. If a person had chosen a civil service under foreign rule as a career, then he had to be reconciled to a fairly plain mode of living and to accept the implied humiliation of belonging to an inferior breed. In return, if he were a family man, he would be assured of steady employment for life and a modest pension afterwards — that so-called highly cherished iron rice bowl. He might or might not also have small opportunities to nudge public policies closer to outcomes he preferred. That would mainly be a function of chance, being in the right place at the right time and having a sympathetic superior.

If a person required more in the way of material benefits or intellectual or emotional satisfactions, then the fervid dog-eat-dog commercialism of the private sector would always be available to him if it suited his temperament. Like many others, he would have to weigh that decision against a variety of other personal considerations like status and face.

Until one had reached the highest levels in the civil service, being in officialdom conferred little in the way of actual power but it did confer a degree of status and face. There was a general deference in Chinese culture for anyone occupying an official position, even if only a minor one. In addition, little British gimmicks like badges, medals and titles could be had along the way to reinforce those small human vanities and to create the illusive trappings of power.

For example, if one were assigned to a sphere of activity which merited representation on the Legislative Council, one could expect to be appointed as one of its members, enabling one to prefix one's name with "The Honourable". Again, if one were appointed an official Justice of the Peace to boot, one could add the initials "JP" after one's moniker.

Towards the end of one's career, bureaucratic convention dictated that a senior civil servant who had been consistently obedient and docile might be rewarded — theoretically by the British monarch — with some medal attached to a colourful piece of ribbon.

Such an award would entitle one to attach further letters after one's name, like "OBE" or "CBE" or some similar combination of initials. A certain section among the Chinese, who made up 98% of the city's population, had derisively characterised such a development as analogous to someone "growing a tail".

Of course, it has been well known throughout British parliamentary history that "honours" could sometimes also be bought with cold hard political cash. But since most folks are born into the world without any ornamentation, it might be safer to leave life unsullied by too many artificially created appurtenances.

However, at the beginning of the 1980s, a palpable mood of self-seeking for honours and other benefits crept in among certain expatriate circles in the bureaucracy. They even started "thinking out loud" about an enhanced salary package for themselves and the best means of securing their objective. The move met little resistance, because everybody knew instinctively that a rising tide lifted all boats. It was only after I had retired that the initiators of thinking out loud achieved their goal.

It had an inflationary effect in many different directions. For example, service on the Legislative Council used to be entirely voluntary and members went without the payment of fees. Service in the legislature soon began attracting a hefty salary plus equally hefty expenses. That had resulted in many fresh and utterly unimpressive university graduates and other assorted nonentities putting themselves forward for political office!

Of course, those working for public-funded institutions like universities jumped onto the bandwagon and professors and lecturers got substantial increases in pay as well. It seemed everybody had a wonderful time except John Q. Taxpayer.

Before leaving the subject, I think it would be appropriate for me to state that I had found the 20 years I had served as an Administrative Officer in the Hong Kong government to be, on the whole, both exhilarating and rewarding. The main reason for that outcome was because I had the extreme good fortune to have worked for a succession of very decent, honourable and highly intelligent superior officers. They collectively taught me a great deal about the art of public administration and the human dimensions which must always be taken into account.

* * *

Fortuitously, as fate would have it, the educational requirements of my children forced me to consider a change in my career. They, like many local youngsters of their generation, had been brainwashed by the grossly inadequate colonial educational system which not only denied Chinese historical training and culture but also exerted peer pressures among classmates in seeking a so-called "superior" education in North America. Europe or elsewhere.

It had been fashionable for some years for the better-off and social-climbing parents in Hong Kong to enrol their offspring in one of the international secondary schools for a start and then in one of the more prestigious universities in Britain or America.

In so doing, they must have believed that such an approach would confer upon themselves certain bragging rights. After all, for a child to enter a famous institution like Oxford or Stanford, even by hook or by crook, must be some sort of feather in the caps of parents. Such parents seemed not to have critically examined whether it was really in the best interests of their children to be cut loose in an alien land and be exposed to an alien and uninhibited culture at a tender age.

My own experience had been disorientating. World War II had tossed me, as a 12-year-old Chinese refugee, upon the shores of a hitherto unknown Australia, a country with a firmly established "white Australia policy".

On the other hand, Hollywood films had created such potent images of Western individual freedoms that they were difficult to ignore or forget, such as, young girls speeding along in an open convertible with the wind rushing through their long hair, or youngsters throwing their limbs around in all directions while they jived or jitterbugged to some infectious foot-stomping music. Likewise the precociousness among Western teenagers to experiment with alcohol, drugs and sex.

Finding accommodation between what I had seen on the silver screen and what I had found in reality had left me feeling lost, misplaced and unbalanced, especially when I had insufficient understanding of Chinese history or culture to offer any ballast. It had taken me a great deal of time and effort in later life to find my bearings and to rediscover my own true identity and culture.

I did not want my children to have to go through that kind of emotional displacement and trauma. I wanted them to spend their teens in a Chinese environment, to be exposed to references to Chinese maxims and fables which formed part of the currency in everyday conversation. If they could only absorb and reflect enough upon some of them, they might yet arrive at a better understanding of their own identities.

The colonial education system they had gone through had been deliberately designed to de-emphasise Chinese history and identity. The British rulers had an instinctive hunch that cultivating Chinese cohesion of any kind would make for less pliant clerks and subjects to support their mercantile agendas.

In any case, my sons had already been over-conditioned by Western films, fashions, music and modes of behaviour into a muddled psychological and emotional state. They might have cultivated a more Confucian community-focused outlook if I had often been around them more. But as a single parent, I had often been absent, sent away on civil aviation negotiations or to attend meetings of the Asian Development Bank or the United Nations Economic Commission for Asia and the Far East.

My failure to explain what my life had been all about had been near total. In the minds of my children, I might have come over as just another deadbeat civil servant following the orders of white masters. My belated attempts to draw attention to their being members of the Chinese nation and to the alienating drawbacks in their proposal to study abroad simply cut no ice with them.

I therefore changed tack and suggested there might be other practical educational options instead of going abroad right away. Perhaps that could be left for post-graduate studies. For example, many of our family elders, including their own grandfather and their own great-grandfather, had first attended humbler and more economical local institutions of higher learning; and they had all subsequently led entirely satisfactory and fulfilling lives.

"You went to Stanford, didn't you?" was the tart interjection I got during my not entirely convincing spiel.

I reminded them, trying as best I could to keep my irritation in check, that I had gone to Stanford on a loan from a relative which I had to repay entirely myself. I had not gone away expecting my expenses to be underwritten by my father.

"So it's all an issue of money, is it?" one of them observed blandly.

"Well, I am only a civil servant earning a very limited salary and not as well-heeled as many of the parents of your classmates."

My statement was met with expressions of sheer astonishment. Only the most mean-spirited of fathers, they had inferred, would deploy economic arguments against his own children. Besides, why should a man bring children into the world if he was incapable of providing for their education and their needs?

The deadliness in their logic had me stymied. Rather than waste my breath on a lost argument, I told them I would finance their studies in North America, if they so wished, and I would expect nothing in return. However, once they had graduated, I could not be expected to entertain further requests for financial subsidies.

It was against such a background that I accepted the package offered by my old friend, Mr. Fung Hon-Chu, Chairman of Li & Fung, to work for the trading arm of his publicly-listed corporation.

* * *

As I have said, being a colonial civil servant was no great shakes. Nevertheless Chinese culture did cultivate a certain class system and a degree of deference towards those holding official positions, not so much because he was in an official position *per se* but because — since the time of Confucius —officials had been largely selected from among scholars, through a regular series of imperial examinations opened to all.

To abandon a public office to join the rough and tumble of commercial life, therefore, must appear to many as a strange and incomprehensible descent from the perceived superior social status among scholars to drop to the ranks of traders and merchants. That class had long been relegated to the bottom of the social heap, beneath scholars, warriors, farmers and artisans.

The historical perception was that traders and merchants were corrupt, treacherous, selfish and non-productive, merely seeking to gain from exchanging the fruits of the labour of others. They were also considered disruptive to the existing social order due to the frequent changes in the price of the goods they sold. Nowadays, under the neoliberal capitalism running rampant around the world, their activities have taken on an almost praiseworthy complexion, for "maximising profit" or "responding efficiently to the market forces of supply and demand".

In times past, traders and merchants operated in pretty much the way a modern capitalist would when they required labour. They provided the capital and directed their employees or *foki*s to do their bidding, such as, the warehousing of goods or their delivery to customers. *Foki*s had no security of employment or contractual terms. They could be hired or fired at the whim of employers. They were not expected to be creative or innovative in any way, just honest and obedient.

Merchants used to be a very cagey and wary lot. They kept trading records to themselves, sometimes several sets for use under different circumstances. This had developed long before chartered accountants and tax consultants had appeared to advise them on shell companies, tax shelters, off balance sheet accounting and the rest of the dodges currently employed by international corporations.

They were forever fearful of employees or competitors learning their secrets and stealing a competitive edge over them. There was also a fear of tax-collectors and local officials demanding exactions should they be perceived to be doing too well.

To deal with some of those problems, they previously used to wear jackets with very wide sleeves so that they could negotiate business deals by slipping their arms inside each other's sleeves to send finger signals.

In dealings among themselves, however, the traders and merchants of old were not without a certain recognisable code of conduct. Since they generally disliked setting agreements down in written contracts, they placed considerable reliance upon the spoken word being as good as a bond.

That development was somewhat linked to the quintessentially Chinese concept of "face". Reputation within their own circle was important to them. Should some disagreement occur between merchants, they would probably try to settle it by giving "face" to each other through dialogue, rather than to resort to arbitration by a third party or to head for an official's *yamen*.

"Face" as a concept is rather difficult to explain to a non-Chinese. In 1933, in his book *My Country and My People*, the learned Dr. Lin Yu-Tang tried to explain it in the following way:

"Face cannot be translated or defined. It is like honour and is not honour. It cannot be purchased with money, and yet gives a man or woman a material pride. It is hollow and is what men fight for and women die for. It is invisible and yet by definition exists by being shown to the public. It exists in the ether and yet can be heard, and sounds eminently respectable and solid. It is amenable, not to reason but to social convention. It protects lawsuits, breaks up family fortunes, causes murders and suicides, and yet it often makes a man out of a renegade who has been insulted by his fellow townsmen, and it is prized above all earthly possessions. It is more powerful than fate or favour, and more respected than the constitution. It often decides a military victory or a defeat, and can demolish a whole government ministry. It is that hollow thing which men in China live by."

Dr. Lin elaborated further. He held that not to give a man "face" was the utmost height of rudeness, tantamount in the West to throwing down a gauntlet. It was nevertheless a goad to ambition and about the only thing to overcome the Chinese love of money.

While I cannot subscribe entirely to all of Dr, Lin's descriptions, I have to admit that many of the qualities he described had existed and do continue to exist in the present time. Certainly many Asian societies have in place social codes not dissimilar to "face".

With the increase in urbanisation and commerce in the last couple of centuries, some merchants have become enormously wealthy, some more so than many of the old landed gentry. Some have therefore tried to move up the social scale by marrying their children into the landed gentry.

To round off this brief reference to the ancient Chinese class structure, I should perhaps add that there had once been a stratum ranked lower than traders and merchants. That category, known as "mean people" or outcasts, encompassed the likes of street entertainers, prostitutes, beggars and others in dubious callings.

With the modern proliferation of callings, professions and white collar criminals, it is difficult to determine who should now be classified into that category. Possibly reckless money-printing central bankers, price-gouging pharmaceutical manufacturers, mean-spirited reality television producers and their unhinged participants, media moguls waxing rich on publishing tabloids filled by salacious stories and fake news, and the like? Modern neoliberal society seemed to have spawned too many types eminently suitable for inclusion in the lowest reaches of traditional Chinese society.

* * *

I first met Mr. Fung Hon-Chu of Li & Fung at the beginning of 1963 when we were both appointed members of a four-member delegation to represent Hong Kong at a three-week-long ministerial meeting of the United Nations Economic Commission for Asia and the Far East to be held in Manila.

Mr. Fung was at that time a member of the Hong Kong Legislative Council and he was named the head of the delegation, whereas I, a relatively new Administrative Officer attached to the Social Welfare Department, was appointed "secretary" to the delegation. That was in effect a polite way of saying I was a dogsbody. Sandwiched between the two Chinese at the top and bottom were two expatriate members — a British professor of economics at the University of Hong Kong and a more senior European Administrative Officer.

For some inexplicable reason, Mr. Fung took a shine to me right away and suggested that I should consider quitting the civil service to work for Li & Fung instead. He assured me that I would in commerce soon be making multiple times my existing civil service salary.

I thanked him for his offer but stated that since I had a young family I could not put their livelihoods in any jeopardy. A modest but assured income was far safer than some pot of gold at the end of an uncertain commercial rainbow.

Nonetheless a friendship developed steadily between us in the years that followed. Mr. Fung, or "H.C." as I came to call him, persuaded me to join some of the dinners he hosted for potential foreign customers. I was apprehensive over being wined and dined by business people in case it was interpreted as receiving "an advantage" from them.

But H.C. insisted that I had a duty as a public servant to help promote the colony's export trade. I pointed out that the government had set up the Trade Development Council for that purpose, so he did not need me. He stressed, however, that my education in foreign countries, my fluency with the English language and my position within the bureaucracy made me a more persuasive promoter of the local interest. So I reluctantly accepted some of his invitations.

Years later, when I needed a larger income to meet the demands of my sons for overseas education, I naturally approached H.C before anybody else and asked if he still wanted me to work for Li & Fung. When the answer came back in the affirmative, a deal was quickly struck between us.

In entering the service of Li & Fung, I had little idea of its corporate structure. All I knew was that I would be responsible for the trading arm, which constituted the biggest part of the company, both in terms of the number of staff employed and in profitability.

Because of my long association with H.C., I did not want any misunderstanding to arise between us. Since its inception in Canton in 1906, the company had been a family business and for H.C. his whole life had been woven around it as a proprietor. I, on the other hand, was only an employee, a professional manager with nothing else besides my package at stake.

I was, of course, conscious that capitalism was in essence an exploitative business and that it was entering the terminal stages of its decline. But it suited my immediate needs and I had to produce sufficiently enhanced profits to justify the hefty salary package I was receiving.

But I never felt any inclination to transgress the letter of the law to achieve that result or to act against the dictates of my own conscience. Indeed, I was often mindful of Buddha's observation that wealth made in a moral way was praiseworthy but if attained in an immoral way was blameworthy.

So before I signed up for the job, I had to agree a mutually acceptable *modus operandi* with H.C. Over the years, in attending his dinners with Western buyers and customers, I had noticed how far he was prepared to go to butter them up and to put them into an amenable deal-making mood.

He had been an extremely shrewd businessman. He had concluded from his long trading experiences that Western men were generally fond of their drinks. He therefore saw to it that Westerners were always plied with fine liquors. He was not a drinker himself, but he made sure that some hard-drinking subordinate would always be on hand to jolly things along.

In addition, he had detected in Westerners some quite unfounded fantasies about Oriental women. He did little to disabuse them, however. Indeed, he fanned those fantasies, by keeping a little black book with telephone numbers of available Chinese escorts in Hong Kong and in Taiwan, who would — for a fee — be willing to entertain foreign men at dinners or drinking parties. Whatever other arrangements the two sides might arrive at subsequently were none of his business.

Given that background, I told H.C. that I would be happy to take potential customers and buyers to lunch in the Owners' Box of the Jockey Club should one of our horses be running. Otherwise, I would restrict my sales pitches and my praises for trading with Hong Kong to the confines of my or their offices, over cups of tea or coffee. Outside entertainment, if needed, would have to be done by subordinates.

Furthermore, there was no shortage of topless bars and nightclubs with hostesses in the city and I did not think there was a case for anyone in the company to pimp for potential foreign customers.

H.C. accepted my philosophical and other limitations with a minimum of argument. It was as if he had calculated that experience, the prevailing capitalist system and the general human greed would soon combine to force me to recognise the error of my ways.

I thought — rather naively with hindsight — that that was that.

* * *

When I started work at the trading arm of Li & Fung, I discovered that it consisted of a collection of fiefdoms specialising in a diverse range of mass consumer products — garments, shoes, toys, bags, handicraft, fireworks and so forth.

There appeared to be little interaction between those disparate entities, even though they were all housed within a single building, let alone interactions between other parts of the corporation, like the subsidiaries dealing with property or investments, which were located in other buildings, or indeed, with branch offices in other territories unless they happened to be involved in their own product ranges.

Each unit was generally regarded as a "division" under the trading umbrella, with each headed by an individual manager whose terms of service had been individually negotiated. Some were on a straight salary plus bonus basis while others might have a profit-sharing element based on equity holding. It was all rather messy and *ad hoc*.

Each unit comprised a staff ranging from around a dozen to more than

20, depending on its own workload. All the more junior staff, like product managers, merchandisers, shipping clerks and so forth, were engaged purely on a month-to-month basis, with fringe benefits trending towards the minimum levels required under the law.

Their main channel of communication was upwards, ultimately towards the divisional head who had a great deal of autonomy over their own divisions. And each unit was considered too small and disparate to merit union representation of any kind or any collective bargaining across different divisions. That left me rather isolated from most of the junior employees.

If the purchases of a particular regular customer were substantial enough, like those of the American toy giant, Toys R Us, or the popular Californian garment retailer, Gap, then a whole division might be devoted exclusively to dealing with their requirements and protecting such stylistic innovations each might have designed for its customer base for the following season. For example, a pair of denim jeans might be cut looser or tighter the following season or might be made more faded through stone-washing or incorporating tears and patches to give it a different seasonal look.

It was obvious from the very start there was a vast amount I had to learn about the various products I was responsible for selling. The stitching requirements for a shoe or a garment or a wig were all different. A shoulder bag with a strap had to be "drop-tested" to ensure the strap being serviceable when bearing substantial weight. It had to be tested for colour-fastness too. A product produced in one country had to vary from another produced in a different country and so on. The safety of users had also to be an issue, as with firecrackers and toys for children, and serviceability and value for money had to be considered for other customers.

One of the first things I instituted after my arrival was a 45-minute meeting every Monday of all the divisional managers to pull the organisation together, to give it some form of unity. I wanted to know exactly what work each division had in hand, whether any snags had been encountered, when fresh orders were expected and when buyers would be visiting. A check-list of things to be done would be issued immediately after the meeting — usually within an hour of the end of the meeting — and the list would be reviewed and up-dated the following Monday.

I invited H.C. and Victor Fung to attend those meetings if they wished. In any case, both would be on the distribution list of the check-lists. But during the entire eight years I was the Managing Director of the trading arm, neither of them attended a single Monday morning meeting. Part of the reason might be that their offices were located on the other side of the harbour.

In addition, I had copies of all out-going and in-coming telexes of the past 24 hours placed on my desk at the start of every working day. Should there be any obscurities in any of them, then they would be queried and my Administrative Assistant would produce an appropriate answer within hours.

* * *

In trading activities, Li & Fung operated as either a principal in products where it possessed proprietary brands, as in the case of fireworks, or as a general agent for most other products. In the latter case, it operated pretty much along the lines of the compradores of the old foreign trading firms, providing contacts with suitable suppliers and offering a linguistic and a secure and reliable financial bridge between the parties.

In serving as an agent, it would charge a percentage of orders placed as a commission. In earning the commission, Li & Fung would inspect the goods during the various stages of production to ensure that they conformed with specifications, that they be shipped out on time, and that it acted as an intermediary in effecting payments.

The percentage levied as a commission would vary, depending on the size of the order and the complexity of production. But as a general rule, the percentage sought would be in the order of around 6%.

The terms of trade were usually by irrevocable letters of credit made out to Li & Fung, denominated in US dollars for American customers or European national currencies for European ones. Sometimes D/A (Documents against Acceptance) and D/P (Documents against Payment) terms would also be used. Since payments to local factories would be made usually in Hong Kong dollars, monies received could be converted forward in order to guard against fluctuations in foreign exchange rates, unless Li & Fung itself happened to want a punt on making an exchange gain.

* * *

It soon became apparent that, in spite of some modern trappings and usage of elements of management-speak, the culture of the trading arm of the company was pretty much that of traditional Chinese family businesses. In other words, employees were regarded as disposable *fokis* who were to be used to execute orders and to perform the more menial tasks. Apart from heads of divisions, they were not expected to offer creative inputs on designs or to make suggestions on work habits.

Those employees had neither unions to represent their interests nor any established channel to communicate with top management. From my experiences in the public sector, I knew that to be both an unwise and an untenable position.

When I was in the Post Office, for example, I had a staff of over 5,000, but there had been at least a Staff Forum with various union representatives to voice grievances. And even then, improper things would be happening right under my nose without my being aware of any of them!

Since I was now in name and in actual fact the head of the trading arm, I could not remain ignorant of what was taking place at the lower levels, as some corporate heads had tried to do when mistakes were uncovered. If they were to try and pass the buck lower down, how could they justify their enormous pay packages?

Although the number of staff at the trading arm of Li & Fung was much reduced compared with the Post Office and not at all unionised, I felt I had a pastoral duty towards all staff, to hear their problems and misgivings, both about work and about their private lives. I also believed that people could be more motivated and committed as a team. After all, Napoleon was reputed to have visited his troops on the eve of some battles.

Therefore, what I did immediately was to declare that I kept an open door and any staff member would be free — subject to securing an appointment with my secretary — to call on me to discuss whatever they wished.

As things turned out, only one staff member ever complained about a difference of opinion with a divisional head during the eight years I was in charge. I had interviewed the head of division concerned subsequently and it appeared there was a personality clash between them. I had offered the complainant a transfer to another department but she declined and resigned instead.

On the whole, though many called on me, no one was looking for a long-term career at Li & Fung. Many were in fact hoping they would get a quick salary boost by hopping to a rival trading outfit which would appreciate their talents and connections more than their present employer. But I was unable to intervene more directly because wages were a province left in the hands of divisional heads and I was ignorant of the strengths and weaknesses of individual employees. The staff were nevertheless glad that someone in top management was prepared to see them and treat them as individuals.

This was consistent with the talk around town, of Li & Fung staff being competent but under-valued. Most regarded the company and Hong Kong itself as a mere transitional point, a stepping stone to whatever might happen after 1997 — or sooner, if the Chinese authorities so demanded.

They were largely ignorant of what was happening between the British and the Chinese authorities but they were generally distrustful about their British overlords. They thought the British might sell out their wider interests in exchange for some minor benefit to British trade or some other less tangible advantage for the United Kingdom, as the British had done to others in so many parts of the world.

Because I had been for so long within the colonial government, many thought I should have a better insight into 1997 and thereafter. Many therefore sought my advice about their future plans. In truth, my insight was no better than their own. I had no inside track, though I had my own suspicions. I knew, for example, there would never be any large-scaled migration of Hong Kong people to the United Kingdom. Racism and insularity were too virile in Britain for Chinese migration to be politically acceptable.

So long as people accepted Chinese sovereignty, I felt, there was no reason why the city should not continue to thrive under Chinese rule as it had done under the existing British one. There might be a few bumps along the transitional road but they would be relatively minor.

* * *

As was highly popular at the time, many thought seriously of pulling up stakes altogether and migrating once and for all, to Australia or Canada or elsewhere. Most would prefer a stable life and a steady means of making a living than to live from moment to moment with uncertainty and on edge. A large number wanted to become what came to be termed "aeronautical" families, constantly flying across the Pacific Ocean. But after some years, many of the menfolk returned to Hong Kong because the city still offered them the best opportunities for their careers.

One attractive, youngish and unmarried girl, had been among those who had consulted me. She had arrived in the city with her Chinese widowed mother. They had both been quite well-to-do refugees from a war-torn Laos and she herself had a fairly good command of both English and Chinese.

She was loath to pull up roots again later; she would rather apply for a Green Card to migrate to America right away than wait for things to slowly turn sour.

I told her, as I did to others, that each would have to make a decision based on his or her own personal circumstances, balancing security with an overhanging uncertainty. I did not expect things to be much changed with the exit of the British, though I could not foretell the future. There was no one simple decision applicable to everyone facing a dilemma. In the end, after years of hesitation, she decided to migrate to Los Angeles in any case.

* * *

It was after I had joined Li & Fung for more than a year, and after that interview with the young lady from Laos, that I received a surprise one day. I had turned up for work that day, quite forgetting that it happened to be my birthday. I had long passed the age when I kept count.

I subsequently heard a noise in the adjoining conference room, where I usually held my Monday morning meetings, and then the connecting door flew open. A group of staff members whom I worked closely with as my personal staff and some in the Administration Division then came in and ushered me into the conference room.

Upon my appearance, the staff gathered there broke into the "Happy Birthday" song. There was a birthday cake with a single candle on top of it. The female staff members then took turns to plant kisses on me.

So far as I have been able to establish, it was the first occasion that a surprise party had been thrown for anyone in the top management by junior staff since the company was founded in Canton in 1906.

* * *

Enters a Trader

I have often wondered over the intervening decades — now that feminism has finally taken off in many parts of the world and it is fashionable to resuscitate ancient flings and old indiscretions — whether it would still be possible for me to sue Li & Fung for exposing me to sexual harassment in my workplace and in placing me in such an agreeable position so many years ago?

*   *   *

When I took over the administration of Li & Fung (Trading), I simplified one set of rules governing reimbursements for overseas expenditures. The change was generally welcomed by junior staff but opposed by some heads of divisions.

The background to the issue was as follows: One of the primary functions of a trading company, when acting as an agent for others, would be to identify for its customers the cheapest sources for products which customers might wish to purchase.

In the normal course of industrialisation and globalisation of commerce, the cheapest sources would usually go from the more developed countries to the less developed ones. For example, Japan started out producing grey cloth after World War II. But when Japanese labour costs went up, the country began producing more sophisticated items and grey cloth production devolved upon South Korea and Hong Kong. A similar pattern followed in other mass consumer product ranges, be they garments, toys, shoes, handicraft or whatever.

A trading company, when acting as an agent for a customer, had to provide certain services in order to earn its commission. One of those services was to send merchandisers and inspectors to the foreign countries producing the ordered goods to ensure that the goods were being produced to specifications and on time.

In the normal order of things, the cheapest producers were likely to be in the less developed and poorer countries where factories would be located on the periphery of large cities, in newly established industrial zones or perhaps even among squatter areas.

For those employed by Li & Fung to undertake such inspection trips, it was part of their conditions of service. They would be reimbursed for their out-of-pocket expenses but not earn any overtime payment for being away from their families for two or three days or for however long it might take for them to complete their duties.

For those directly involved, they faced an immediate choice — they could either stay at more comfortable centre-of-town hotels and eat at better restaurants but take time journeying every day between the factory to do their work and returning to their hotels for rest or else stay at a less modern hotel in the vicinity of the factory and eat street hawker food in the hope of finishing their tasks quicker and returning home earlier.

The operating regime when I entered Li & Fung was that those on inspection duties would submit claims for expenses, together with receipts where appropriate, to their heads of division for reimbursement.

When I examined the system, I spotted a number of flaws immediately. Since British parliamentarians had been caught out repeatedly over exaggerated claims in expenses, how could poorly paid wage-earners be expected to behave differently? Why should any individual have to explain why he had taken two glasses of imported Asahi beer with a meal instead of two glasses of water? It was an infringement of personal liberty, especially when the person had to work extra hours away from his home without any extra pay. Besides, it was an invidious use of a head of division's time to examine relatively minor items of expenses.

Moreover, I remembered the many occasions I had been sent to London on official duty as a civil servant. I had preferred to stay at one of those modest bed-and-breakfast establishments along Sussex Gardens so that I could spend more of my per diem allowance on slap-up meals.

Actually, when I was sent on a duty trip to Singapore, I stayed at the home of my brother, Francis, and spent my per diem taking him and his family out for fancy meals.

In line with such thinking, I suggested that employees sent on inspection trips should be paid a fairly generous per diem to compensate for their longer periods of work, so that they do not have to submit detailed claims for reimbursement after their return.

Surprisingly, a number of heads of divisions opposed my suggested change. Among them were those who had a profit-sharing arrangement with Li & Fung. It then became abundantly apparent to me that the profit-centred free market ideology had an insidious hold on everybody. Not only was I and others putting a squeeze on factories to gain higher profit margins for our customers but some of us were also squeezing our own staff so that they could gain some extra advantage for themselves!

It was an unending game played by the more powerful against the more vulnerable and desperate. Those who wore bespoke suits and displayed clean fingernails might call it greater efficiency, improved productivity or enhancing staff morale. But at bottom it was the same old miserable game.

Once in a while, when dozens of factory workers perished because a badly constructed building had collapsed or a fire had occurred in a place with inadequate fire escapes, corporate representatives of world-famous brands would always appear to wring their hands and cry crocodile tears. But I have never heard of such representatives admitting complicity in such tragedies, for squeezing production costs so that they could make larger profit margins.

I therefore pushed through the change in spite of its impact on profits. I never discovered whether that rule change endured after I had left the company. Not knowing sometimes niggled me a little. But that did not really matter.

It was just another slice of corporate life, I told myself. One could toast it, smear it with butter and marmalade, or simply swallow it down with a gulp of coffee. But I could not overlook the fact that I had taken 30 pieces of silver and must now deliver my side of the bargain.

CHAPTER 6

Fireworks

ONE OF THE FIRST CONVERSATIONS I had with H.C. after joining the trading arm of Li & Fung was about the performance of the Handicraft Division. The division was headed by Fung Kwok-Hong, the nephew of H.C. and the eldest son of H.C.'s long deceased elder brother Fung Mo-Ying.

Fung Kwok-Hong was a sober, middle-aged man who was rather hesitant and halting of speech. He did not strike me immediately as an impressive mind in the same category as Albert Einstein might have been but rather as a hard-working plodder.

His wife, Rosetta, served as his deputy. Her own speciality was the sale and handling of Christmas decorations, wigs, earthenware, plastic flowers and handicraft. She was a woman who was much smarter and more talkative than her husband. The two of them nonetheless formed a good team and between them they shared a teenaged daughter.

The main income of the division derived largely from the sale of fireworks throughout the southern American states and in particular from the sale of a proprietary brand known as the Black Cat.

Whoever began the fireworks business in the early part of the 20th century operated very smartly. He recognised America as a promising market because its people celebrated the Fourth of July and Halloween by discharging vast quantities of fireworks. He not only registered the brand in the United States in 1952 but promoted it assiduously among young customers by slogans such as "The Best You Can Get". T-shirts with a Black Cat logo and other small gifts were handed out from time to time and myths about Black Cat products giving more "bang for the buck" soon took root.

Today Black Cat fireworks are not only favoured by the younger users but they also command a premium of about 10% in the market over all other brands of fireworks in the southern states of America.

Li & Fung joined the American Pyrotechnics Association at around the same time as the registration of the trademark. The Association was the main lobbying organisation for manufacturers, importers, retailers, distributors and others involved in the fireworks trade in America.

For reasons which were not very clear to me, H.C. had always retained a close oversight over the fireworks business and had ever since been working directly with Fung Kwok-Hong. Part of the reason could have been because H.C. had been involved in that business from way back and so retained a sentimental attachment to it.

But another reason might have forced itself upon him because of politics. Most of the supplies came from a large factory in Kwangsi Province, one of the five provinces designated by the Chinese for producing and exporting fireworks when the country began its export drive in the 1980s. H.C.'s political connections with Taiwan might have rendered it awkward for him to go directly to the mainland himself. So he sent his nephew there to negotiate, even though Li & Fung retained some fireworks connections with Taiwan as well.

What was curious about the factory at Kwangsi was that it produced fireworks for a number of different brands, both from China, Hong Kong and elsewhere. They were in reality identical products. The only difference between them was that the factory stuck on different labels according to the wishes of each individual customer. In that sense, it was a little disingenuous for Li & Fung to claim that the Black Cat fireworks were "The Best You Can Get".

* * *

When H.C. spoke to me about his nephew soon after I had joined the company, he asked me to keep a close eye on Kwok-Hong. He said he had heard rumours that Kwok-Hong intended to leave Li & Fung to set up a trading business for himself.

"That's par for the course, isn't it?" I replied. "In the neoliberal capitalist world we're operating in, it's every man looking after and promoting himself. Mrs. Thatcher says there's no such thing as society. It's dog eat dog. Can't blame anyone for wanting to better himself or herself."

"But if Kwok-Hong goes, so would Rosetta. That could spell a wholesale reconstruction of the Handicraft Division."

"That's a possibility we will have to face should it arise. Unless you have solid evidence of some wrong-doing on Kwok-Hong's part, I don't know the man at all. If you have more than rumours, you could take action directly against him. You have been working directly with him for years. You don't need me to deliver the *coup de grâce*."

"It's not so easy for me; he's part of the family," H.C. replied.

All at once it occurred to me that I might have been invited into the company for an ulterior purpose. Was my role to be a buffer in an old family feud, the roots of which had been lost in the mists of generational relationships?

I recalled that years ago, when I first met H.C., he had hinted at differences of opinion with his eldest brother, Mo-Ying, who was at that time the chairman of the company. He had always been submissive and obedient, he told me.

His brother was now dead and H.C. had inherited the running of the family firm and its chairmanship. Was he trying to rid all remnants of his brother's progeny within the company in the interests of his own children?

Was he attempting the proverbial Chinese gambit of "borrowing a knife in order to kill someone else"? I did not want to serve as another man's hired knife.

In theory, Kwok-Hong was under my wing and I owed him — just as I owed everyone else under my charge — a duty of care and protection. I recalled that I myself had been fired in 1954 from the *Hong Kong Standard* just because someone in the colonial government of the time did not like what I had written.

I was helpless then and without resources and had to accept my fate, notwithstanding that a principled friend, Leslie Sung, the Editor-in-Chief at the time, was willing to stand with me in my downfall. But I had deterred him from it as being only a pointless gesture.

Now, however, I could stand on my own two feet and I was not convinced that anybody should be fired just on somebody else's say-so. I needed proof of serious misdeeds before I would act against a person under my command.

So I said: "Well, you know the way I tend to think, H.C. We've been friends a long time and we trust each other. That's why we've had such a good horse-owning partnership. I will keep a close watch on Kwok-Hong's division and his activities in general. But I would need concrete proof of wrong-doing against Li & Fung before I can act against him. It will be no small matter, because Rosetta will have to become a casualty too. Perhaps also others in his division."

"Of course there must be unambiguous proof, if he is going to be sacked," H.C. said. But the tone of his voice and the way he expressed himself implied that I was failing in my first test of loyalty and obedience. I dreaded to think that our friendship might be under threat.

* * *

Perhaps it is appropriate at this stage to make a small diversion, in order to explain through history why we Chinese are such a noisy people, addicted to the use of drums, gongs, cymbals and firecrackers on every conceivable occasion — at weddings, anniversaries, inaugurations of new businesses, festivals and even at funerals.

Our love for noise and clamour is rooted in a widely held Chinese superstition that evil spirits could be frightened away by noise. Hence, since ancient times, the discharge of firecrackers has been seen as a means of preventing evil spirits from marring auspicious occasions.

Originally, this was done by the throwing of segments of bamboo into fires. The oxygen trapped inside bamboo segments would heat up and explode, making a frightening sound. After the invention of gunpowder in the ninth century, firecrackers eventually took over that noise-making role.

It took the Chinese quite some time to stumble upon gunpowder, even though they had been familiar for centuries with three of its most important elements, namely, saltpetre or potassium nitrate, sulphur and carbon.

Saltpetre was in fact in great abundance in China from the earliest time, though it was completely unknown in the West till the Middle Ages. The Chinese, however, did not recognise it for what it was. It took quite some time for them to differentiate it from a number of other similar-looking chemical salts. Although the ability to liquefy potassium nitrate for use in dissolving otherwise indissoluble minerals had been apparent for some centuries, it was not till around 300 AD that a reliable way was found to identify genuine saltpetre from other ores.

It likewise took some time to purify sulphur, another important ingredient in the making of gunpowder. On the other hand, the carbon of charcoal had been to hand since ancient times.

Once the three basic elements had been brought together, it was only a matter of time before someone mixed them in the appropriate portions to produce gunpowder. Thereafter, its evolutionary use into fireworks came fast and furious. But, sadly, so too did its military applications.

The invention of gunpowder was a historical irony. It emerged not out of any desire by anyone to seek a better means of waging war or killing off one's enemies but rather out of experiments carried out by a bunch of old Taoists codgers seeking to find an elixir to immortality.

That search itself had been a fascinating one, involving a number of jolly mishaps and the singeing of some quite venerable beards. But those tales have already been amply and exhaustively told elsewhere so I will not recapitulate them here.

I mention this in the present narrative only to draw attention to one of the many unintended consequences that can flow from all kinds of human endeavours. How could those early Taoist alchemists have foreseen that the repeated mixing of chemical elements to find some life-extending potion would unleash upon the world a substance capable of killing and maiming millions of people ever afterwards?

The West knew nothing about gunpowder nor its uses until late in the twelve century. That knowledge reached Europe via the Arabs trading with China. But the European nations were not much interested in using gunpowder for making fireworks and firecrackers. Their enthusiasm for the substance stemmed from its military applications.

A great many scientific and technological advances have been made since the invention of gunpowder. Unfortunately, man's ethical and emotional maturity have not developed apace with man's mastery of the sciences.

As a consequence, terrifying new weapons of mass destruction are constantly being unleashed upon a sleep-walking world. Political leaders have apparently been unable to curb such developments, let alone prohibit them. Some have even been egging them on, with reckless bravado and oblivious of the possibility for self-annihilation and total human extinction.

Even at my present age of 91, it is not the kind of possibility that can earn me a good night's sleep.

*   *   *

Since I had promised H.C. I would keep a close watch on Kwok-Hong and his crew, I had to find a fair and unprovocative way of discharging my mission. H.C. had made no bones about his antipathies under the long rule of his brother, Mo-Ying, and I was well known in many circles as a horse-racing partner of H.C.'s long before joining the company. It did not take a genius to put two and two together and for rumours to circulate. Therefore I had to step warily.

After a while, I invited Kwok-Hong and Rosetta for a bite after work, on the basis it was all part of my getting to know divisional heads and their responsibilities.

The meal naturally got off to a shaky start. The air was thick with uncertainty and apprehension. I could not blame Kwok-Hong and Rosetta for thinking I might have an ulterior motive in inviting them out or suspecting that I might be working against their interests. In actual fact, I was only trying to determine how well their division had been doing and whether H.C.'s instructions were being complied with.

I began by enquiring what H.C.'s instructions had actually been in general and regarding Black Cat products in particular.

According to Kwok-Hong, he had been asked to explore with the Kwangsi manufacturer the possibility of adding a little more gunpowder to Black Cat products being manufactured, so that they would go off with significantly louder than other brands.

But that proved impossible to do, Kwok-Hong explained, because the production lines were massive and the factory had no idea where its standard products would go until it started slapping designated labels onto them. If every customer specified his own requirements, production would be in chaos.

Nonetheless, notwithstanding reporting his failure, Kwok-Hong was told by H.C. to keep promoting Black Cat items as superior to anything else comparable on the market.

This turn of events had me worried. I had not bargained for any systematic misrepresentation to customers when I opted for a business life, even though such misleading promotion had been going on within the company for decades before my arrival.

Li & Fung had built up a brand and was charging a premium for the stuff. Its youthful consumers were also more than happy to pay extra for the goods they were getting. Like everyone else, they were free to spend their money any way they pleased, even if they were acting foolishly. Who was I to stand in their way of going about their enjoyment?

The tobacco barons had been lying about the potential health effects of smoking cigarettes for decades; big international banks had been consistently misleading their clients over their various financial packages; and car manufacturers had been fiddling for ages with the readings of the pollution gauges in their vehicles.

All governments, in any case, were accustomed to misleading their citizens every other day of the week by spewing forth a plethora of indigestible statistics over a whole range of everyday subjects. What would a little exaggeration about fireworks matter, especially when there was good money to be made? It was all bluff and advertising and sales pitches, standard practice accepted by all and sundry in neoliberal capitalist societies.

The trouble with knowledge and experience is that once a person has discovered a truth it becomes very difficult for that person to unlearn it and feign ignorance. Truths somehow seep into his character and become part of his personality. He can neither plead ignorance nor turn a blind eye to them. Truths would remain there, just beneath his consciousness. I suppose I could behave like Pontius Pilate in the New Testament, by asking for a bowl of water to wash my hands. After all, it was really H.C. who called the shots where fireworks were concerned.

Faced with such alarming thoughts, I nudged Rosetta temporarily onto the more anodyne terrain of her relationships with her customers and their products. By the end of the meal, the atmosphere had begun to become more relaxed.

A week or so later, Kwok-Hong and Rosetta returned the compliment by inviting me for a meal after work. I accepted, because I thought it wise and prudent to build up an on-going and harmonious relationship with divisional heads. I was also uncomfortable about the not altogether straightforward role I would have to play.

The meal went more smoothly than the previous one and Kwok-Hong gradually unburdened himself during the course of dinner. He said someone had been circulating a false rumour about his intending to start out on his own and that was doing him no good. The gossip was completely without foundation. He was contented with his work at Li & Fung and he had every intention of sticking with it, if allowed. Likewise, his wife.

I could tell that he felt under a degree of unspecified pressure. I replied soothingly that the city was full of rumours and most people were too busy to pay much attention to any of them. Nonetheless, I accepted in my own mind he was sincere in his declaration of loyalty to the company from the way he had expressed himself. He did not appear to me at all the go-getter type. He came over instead as an honest and uncomplicated plodder caught in a situation that was way above his head.

I doubted privately if he would ever become a conspicuous success in running his own company, even if he tried, so it was better for him to stay where he was. He was certainly not as astute a businessman as his uncle, H.C. Fung, had been. Nor did he possess a fraction of the hustling gift of the gab commanded by his cousin, Victor Fung.

So I tried to put him at ease. I volunteered that, so far as I was concerned, I would be quite happy to have him continue as head of the Handicraft

Division and working directly with H.C. on fireworks as heretofore.

* * *

Based on my conversations at the two dinners and a series of other observations on the culture and prejudices within the company, I told H.C. he might be quite mistaken about the veracity of the rumours he had heard about Kwok-Hong.

His nephew did not look to me a venturesome type. Moreover, he had no obvious motive for deserting his old family concern to start afresh elsewhere, unless he were pushed. He would, in any case, have to continue to get supplies of Black Cat from Li & Fung if he wanted to continue in the fireworks trade. An awkward prospect at best. By everything I had picked up, he appeared contented to stick with his existing position in the company.

After I had given my assessment, H.C. smiled knowingly and observed: "My dear friend, while a person can always listen to what people may say about themselves, he cannot actually look into the corners of their hearts. You must be more cautious if you want to succeed in business. Rumours don't circulate for no reason at all. There's no smoke without something smouldering somewhere. Continue to keep your eye open on Kwok-Hong and his outfit."

I reluctantly agreed to do so, though I remained unconvinced I would really find any misdeed of sufficient gravity to warrant recommending Kwok-Hong's dismissal. Indeed, I was beginning to feel sorry for a simple man facing forces arraigned against him by members of his own family.

* * *

In 1983, after I had taken an extended holiday to many Chinese cities with Ip Yeuk-Lam and his family the previous year, H.C. asked me to join him and Kwok-Hong at an annual meeting of the the American Pyrotechnics Association. It was to be held that year at Scottsdale in Arizona, a town I had never visited before.

I met the request with a degree of ambivalence, however, since I had hitherto kept myself aloof from major fireworks customers, more than happy to let them be handled between H.C. and Kwok-Hong. But on the other hand, H.C. might also have other more deeply-laid plans in mind. Was H.C. trying to tell me I ought to step up to the firing line and assume my full responsibilities in the trading arm? It was a fair enough request to make; I could only wait and see.

At Scottsdale, as Managing Director of Li & Fung (Trading), I was naturally treated as a new boy on the block. A great many members of the American Pyrotechnics Association wanted to make my acquaintance and to discuss means of augmenting our business relationships, little realising that it was H.C. who really called the shots where fireworks were concerned.

One of those who invited me for a cup of coffee was the chief buyer of a company in a southern American state. He was a regular customer of Black Cat products and was well known to Li & Fung. But he also bought other brands made by the Kwangsi manufacturer from other local dealers. He said he wanted to discuss some business matter with me. When he approached the substance of the discussion, however, he did so sideways, like a crab.

He began by saying what a fabulous city Hong Kong was. He simply could not get over the profusion of luxury items during his annual buying visits. French designer shoes, lovely jewellery, perfumes and other up-market stuff.

"My wife would go crazy over the luxury items available in your home town; armed with my credit card, of course," he said. "She has asked me a dozen times to take her with me on my next buying trip but I've never found the guts."

"Hong Kong's not the kind of place any man ought to cut his wife loose with a credit card," I observed. "When I had a wife, I never allowed her to use my credit card anywhere, and particularly not in Hong Kong. So I suppose that explains why I've become a bachelor again."

"Things could be different if a man had some money tucked away somewhere, like some of the other traders I know. I understand juicy deals can be arrived at in your town."

I supposed the chief buyer was referring to some of the shadier deals occurring in the trading business. Sometimes, when either an agent or a supplier was too anxious for new customers, they might arrive together at some kick-back arrangement for money to be passed back underhandedly to a buyer without the knowledge of his employer.

"Well, that depends on whom you are in contact with. We do have a free port and what is commonly called a free market system; we are a top global financial centre as well. So there's no foreign exchange control and our taxes are extraordinarily modest. That means people can bring whatever money in or out of the place and both visitors and locals can play whatever markets they wish, stock and shares, commodities, foreign exchange or whatever, taking their winnings or losses with them when they leave."

"I hear your city also has friendly bankers who do not ask too many questions."

"You could say that. We remain a relatively open and tolerant society nonetheless, though — once in a while and against the odds — we do produce some real sticklers for the rule of law."

"I hear people can open bank accounts with whatever name they choose and money can go in and out of those accounts without any fuss at all."

"That is indeed a possibility. Banks don't much mind if you want to call yourself 'Miss Susie Wong' or 'Mr. Joe Blow' or indeed, 'Captain Hook' for that matter. Our British colonial regulators also seem fairly lackadaisical over the whole process. Most of what they've left us are lovely bits of Latin like *'quid pro quo'* and *'caveat emptor'*, over which our tongues sometimes trip over their proper pronunciations and their meanings.

"Some of our masters have even picked up the old Nelsonian knack of putting their telescopes to blind eyes. So that does mean we get away with a few things which might otherwise be frowned upon other administrations.

"For example, we have a number of stock exchanges, which make the people here the most obsessed of inhabitants over stock and shares anywhere in the world. They are attended by some 1,400 traders. The up-to-the-second stock prices are flashed on screens all over our town.

"Those facts are wonderful for corporations which want to cook their books or do some other kind of funny business, like share-price manipulation or some unobtrusive insider trading. This is also the ideal place for asset strippers, dawn raiders, vulture capitalists and pyramid sellers. And if anyone entertains the illusion that there is no linkage or collusion between our go-getting Hong Kong and the prim and proper Square Mile in London or the cocaine-snorting masters of the universe making hay on Wall Street, he should think again."

"Wow! No wonder some Western politicians have held up your free market system as a model for solving problems in their own societies. It sounds as if your town is not only famous for its custom-made suits but also for its made-to-order financial wet dreams."

"What Western politicians have often overlooked is that free markets only work because the ordinary Joes here have also a certain kind of work ethic and a certain attitude towards hard slogs. Sure, quite a lot of foreign scammers and chancers do head our way. But we have some pretty smart local cookies as well."

"To change the subject slightly, your Black Cat products are rather pricey, you know, when compared with some other available brands," he said. He then rattled off the names of a few brands, including two being produced at the same Kwangsi factory which made Black Cat products.

I did not have the heart to reveal that Black Cat firecrackers were in fact no better in quality than some of the other brands he had mentioned, even though people had been willing over the years to pay a premium for Black Cat items.

"Well, we did invest a mint into brand identification," I observed, rather smugly and with barely a sigh.

"Yes, our kids sure seem to keep asking for Black Cat bangers."

"Good! That shows that our efforts have paid off. Get them while they're young enough and they'll stick with you forever."

"Look, could we work out some kind of deal that would be beneficial to both of us? I could, for example, consider consolidating my purchases of Black Cat with Li & Fung together with those of other brands. It would make financial sense to deal with one party as both principal and agent instead of spreading things among so many different parties."

"Consolidation will certainly bring greater efficiency," I replied, pretending not to have grasped at all the full import of what he was driving at. "Li & Fung is always ready to accommodate your boss or yourself, in any way we can," I added, leaving the next move completely up to him.

In actual fact, I knew precisely what the man was hinting at. He was a buyer, a mere employee and an agent of his master. He was indirectly seeking something on the side for himself, so that his wife could indulge herself on some long-postponed visit to Hong Kong.

The only trouble with that proposition was that it was quite illegal. Li & Fung had a long-established relationship with his employer, that of one principal dealing with another principal. It was not the business of one principal to question another about how he might wish to conduct his affairs. If he wanted to dispose of his resources in a particular way, so that he could, for example, not have to disclose them to his own tax authorities or to his wife, that was his own business for which he would have to assume responsibility. No one could be expected to play his brother's keeper.

For an agent to attempt to dispose of his principal's assets in a questionable way was quite a different proposition for Li & Fung. His employer must first make his intentions clear. There was a duty of care on us. At least a confirmation of the other principal's intentions was needed to begin with.

That was where I had left the chief buyer. His boss had to first signify his agreement to what was being hinted at by his employee. Therefore the ball was in the buyer's court; it was up to him to get his employer to endorse what he wanted. Otherwise it could not be done legally. I was also averse to being suckered into a commitment on fireworks when I was not entirely familiar with the ins and outs of the subject.

* * *

Since the chief buyer had approached me and his dubious proposition had an effect on the fortunes of Li & Fung, I thought I ought to report the conversation to H.C. When I did so, I gave the view that the only course open to the company was to seek the confirmation of the principal before proceeding.

But H.C. reacted more cautiously. "It's an excellent opportunity for growing our business," he said. "No need to formally test the ground on relationships yet; let's explore things a bit more first, to see what exactly is involved."

"But the ball is in the buyer's court," I said. "There is a wrong smell about the deal. We should not appear too keen to go along."

"I understand the technicalities," H.C. replied. "Just pass the matter over to Kwok-Hong. He has experience and a further conversation with the buyer might clarify exactly what he is after before we decide on what to do."

"All right, if that's the way you want to play it," I said, feeling disappointed.

But even as those words left my mouth, I already knew I was adamant against bringing Kwok-Hong into the picture. An entire cascade of conflicting considerations was already rushing through my head.

For a start, we were all physically gathered in America, a country where the legal system was complex and confusing. Secondly, Kwok-Hong was part of my staff and I had a duty to protect him and not to steer him legally into harm's way. I knew that his English was less than fluent and that his choice of words far from subtle. I did not want him saying anything which might compromise or incriminate him. In bribery cases, it always took two to tango; there always had to be an offerer as well as a taker of a bribe. Kwok-Hong, in my view, ought not to be on the receiving end of any stick.

Besides, the benefits to accrue to the company, so far as I could make out, were quite limited, so the game was not worth the risks. It might all merely be an entrapment for a better deal. I was quite content to leave Kwok-Hong out of it and wait for the buyer to make a further approach if he was not merely fishing.

In the event, no further approach from him came during the rest of the conference and there the matter appeared to rest.

* * *

After we had all returned to Hong Kong, I received a telephone call from H.C.

"Kwok-Hong tells me that you did not give him the information concerning the buyer's initiative at Scottsdale," H.C. said. He sounded a little out of humour.

"Oh, yes, I'm so sorry," I replied quickly, trying to pacify him. "It has been entirely my fault, not Kwok-Hong's. I met so many new faces at Scottsdale and had so many conversations that the matter quite slipped my mind. I'll send a telex immediately to the buyer as a follow-up."

"No need for that. I'll follow through myself."

I was thus left with the distinct impression that our friendship was under strain and that I had earned myself another black mark in the eyes of my employer.

* * *

For about three years after the Scottsdale conference, Kwok-Hong and Rosetta continued to work satisfactorily at Li & Fung. H.C. seemed anxious to continue to call all the shots on fireworks and I happily left things to him. He did not speak to me again about rumours of Kwok-Hong's departure.

I therefore thought the animosities and tensions within the Fung family had run their course and that there would be no further talk of the couple leaving to start out on their own.

I got along quite well with Kwok-Hong and Rosetta as colleagues, although we shared little in common outside of work. Nonetheless, we got into a habit of going out for a meal together after work every so often.

Meanwhile the turnover of Li & Fung (Trading) was growing steadily. Indeed, during the eight years I was its managing director, the turnover multiplied roughly tenfold. However, much of the credit for that improvement depended mainly on the hard work of the staff in ensuring that the goods ordered by customers had been made to specifications and delivered on time.

A contributing factor was the sound marketing sense of the customers themselves in designing and distributing the type of goods desired by their mass consumers at reasonable and affordable prices. Their chains of stores grew apace and so did the size of their orders.

There has long been a maxim in the trading business that there is no accounting for taste. We were not out to elevate the world or to make it a better place. We were out to sell what people wanted to buy. If people wanted to buy rubbish, then we supplied rubbish.

The only claim I could make for myself was that I started a branch of Li & Fung (Trading) as a joint venture in Seoul of South Korea. I had met a Korean leather goods manufacturer by the name of Chung during a visit there with a British customer.

Chung and I had a conversation and both of us were struck by a ridiculous idea simultaneously. We were both Asians and close neighbours; yet we could not communicate with each other except through a borrowed European language! Out of that observation, the idea for a joint venture was eventually born. That project was successful initially but it also led some years later to my departure from Li & Fung. I shall deal with the circumstances of that move in a later chapter.

In the meantime, let me round off the events concerning Kwok-Hong and fireworks.

One day I got another irate telephone call from H.C. "Why did you deliberately put Kwok-Hong in contact with garment buyers?" he demanded to know.

"I can't recall having done so," I replied, perplexed.

"He will try to snatch those buyers away with him when he leaves," he thundered.

"You're not on that old chestnut again, are you? I did not put him in touch with any garment buyer and there is no indication at all that Kwok-Hong is intending to leave."

"You're overlooking some facts in betraying the company."

"If *that* is what you really think, then perhaps it's time I consider leaving the company too." I rejoined, because I had become irritated by the allegation made and the intemperate tone of H.C.'s voice.

There the conversation ended.

But on calmer reflection, I realised there might be — in a roundabout way — a little substance to H.C.'s accusations.

The facts were as follows: Li & Fung (Trading) owned a fully crewed pleasure craft which was used to entertain potential and actual buyers travelling around the many islands and isolated beaches in the neighbourhood of Hong Kong. I was in charge of allocating the craft to divisional heads. The cost for its use would be borne by the corporate entertainment budget and not be charged to individual divisions. It was a corporate perk and hence people had to apply to me.

When the craft was free, senior officers could also apply for its private use. I myself had never used the vessel because I usually preferred my pleasures at the *mah-jong* table or else in bed.

In any case, Kwok-Hong asked me if he could use the craft to entertain a single fireworks buyer who was in town one Sunday. I told him that the boat had already been booked by a garment divisional head for that day. However, since the boat was quite large and only two persons were involved from the Handicraft Division, I suggested that Kwok-Hong might have a word with the head of the said garment division. If the garment group was not large, perhaps two additional persons would not present a problem. That was how I had left it.

Apparently the garment people accommodated Kwok-Hong and H.C. got to hear about it. Hence his complaint.

Just for the record, Kwok-Hong and Rosetta remained with Li & Fung long after I had left the company. And Kwok-Hong and Rosetta continued to be friends with me for years afterwards. It was from them that I subsequently learnt that Fung family elders had years ago, when H.C. was young, bestowed on him the nickname of "The Cripple" because of the limp occasioned by his boyhood polio. I presumed it must have been the over-use of that nickname by Mo-Ying that had partly given rise to the sensitivities and animosities between the brothers.

Kwok-Hong and Rosetta and I continued to have an occasional meal together whenever convenient. It was for me a useful means of picking up titbits of gossip about the Fung family.

CHAPTER 7

China, My China

IN THE SUMMER OF 1982, Ip Yeuk-Lam told me he intended in the autumn to take some members of his family on an extended and privately-arranged holiday in China. He asked if I would care to join. I naturally jumped at the chance. Yeuk-Lam had wide connections and considerable standing in the mainland and, if there were interesting parts not yet fully opened to outsiders, I felt sure he could somehow arrange access.

Besides, I had not been inside China itself since 1948, when I visited my aunt, Chau Miu-Yee, in Swatow after she had married a Chinese businessman there. What had been happening in my homeland since had tantalised me. I was more than keen to see for myself what had been achieved after Deng Xiao-Ping announced the opening up of the country to economic reforms at the end of 1978.

There had been so many conflicting narratives of what was actually happening inside the country by both pro-China and anti-China elements that I did not know what to believe. Some of the attempts at social and economic restructuring, like the Great Leap Forward and the Cultural Revolution, had gone awry and must assuredly have had implications and unintended consequences for the country.

Inside myself, however, I had long felt a niggling sense of guilt. In 1949, my close friend and mentor, Chan Hon-Kit, had gone back to China with his newly wedded wife, Frances, to participate in the post-war reconstruction of the country. I had toyed with the idea of going back but got sidetracked by the more selfish ambition of university studies in America. That decision had left me psychologically and emotionally divided ever since.

After completing two degrees at Stanford by 1953, I made my way back to Hong Kong on an American Presidential Lines vessel. On board were also a fair number of Chinese graduates from other American universities, all heading back to different parts of China to help in the modernisation of their country. Their decisions to return reawakened my sense of guilt again.

It was clear that China was inviting Chinese from all over the world to contribute to the rebirth of the nation. I could have, though belatedly, still answered the call. But I had been troubled by too many reports of killings, imprisonments and suicides during the course of the Three Antis Campaign against the evils of corruption, waste and bureaucracy in 1951 and the subsequent Five Antis Campaign in 1952. Travellers moving between Hong Kong and China every day also brought back tales of privations, hardships and the loss of personal freedoms. So I hesitated again.

At the same time, I began arguing mentally with myself. What would a person expect during a revolution? I remembered the chaos and the corruption and the stratospheric inflation I had found in Canton in 1947 when I was staying briefly with my mother. The last had wiped out my mother's modest savings. A revolution was not a tea party, Chairman Mao had asserted. It seemed right that a citizen should make sacrifices for the good of the nation and for future generations.

I thought the best way to cut through my indecision was to get an objective assessment from people I could really trust. Chan Hon-Kit and Frances seemed the obvious candidates. They had lived through changes from the very start. So I tried to contact them. But nobody knew where they could be found in China. During that interim, destiny took over and sent me in quite a different direction.

In 1958, when I was working for the *Straits Times* in Singapore, I met in the home of a friend a Malayan Chinese woman slightly older than myself who had actually answered China's call to return to develop the nation. She might be described as a liberated bourgeois woman of respectable means, who was also rather voluptuously configured.

When I met her she was dressed in one of those casual cotton suits worn by Chinese women in the tropics known as a *sam-fu*. But the outfit had been custom-made, to show to advantage her physical attributes. She had been sent by her family during her teens to study at a boarding school in England, after which she — in rapid succession — got married, gave birth to a daughter and secured a divorce.

She then took her daughter, together with her fur coats and her fashionable high-heels, to China to participate in the country's modernisation. I imagine she might have thought naively that, after having grown up under British colonialism, she would have the chance simply to continue a bourgeois Bohemian lifestyle under a Chinese flag.

It was unclear whether she realised that her mode of living constituted the very "yellow culture" China was trying to eradicate from the brave new world being created for socialist heroes. Apart from being bilingual, she had no other qualification or skill. It should come as no surprise that, only after a short and unhappy stay, she should leave the country disillusioned. Her name was Liao San.

One day, shortly after I had met San, she favoured me with a vampish "come hither" look and the gift of a copy of a book she had written called *Peking Blues*. It was about her disappointing China interlude. I accepted the latter but I played at being too obtuse to respond to the former.

At 29, I had never been slow in accepting a dalliance with a woman of experience. I was, however, at that time engaged to be married later that year and I was acutely conscious that the lady who had introduced San to me was a bosom friend of my prospective mother-in-law. Any untoward deed by me would inevitably be transmitted in whispers to her ears. Under the circumstances, discretion trumped the inclinations of the male libido.

Peking Blues was an eminently forgettable book. It detailed San's efforts to take care of her ailing daughter, to unsuccessfully badger officials into allocating her a suitable job, and to conduct a rather banal affair with a married Chinese official.

San's book, nevertheless, did ease my feelings of guilt over not having rushed back to China much earlier. On reflection, I realised I had no real contribution to make either. My Stanford degrees were pretty worthless in China. What the country needed were agronomists, bio-chemists, engineers, architects, scientists, doctors, seasoned administrators and the like. What I could offer were merely footnotes to certain aspects of history and philosophy. And China already had far too much of both.

From that point onwards, I reined in my desire to become part of the forces for change in my country. It was just as well, for what could I ever have contributed during the Great Leap Forward in 1959 or the three-year long Great Famine which followed hot in its heels? And later still, the utter turbulence of the Cultural Revolution?

At the same time, I recalled the report of an interview that Arthur Waley, the eminent British translator of Chinese and Japanese classics, had given to a journalist shortly after World War II. Waley had taught himself Chinese and Japanese though he could speak neither language. Neither had he ever visited either country.

But he had done fine translations of the *Analects* of Confucius, the *Tao Te Ching*, the *Journey to the West* — under the title *Monkey* — and the *Book of Songs*, besides writing books on the lives and times of the Tang poets Li Po and Po Chu-I. He had also popularised Chinese poetry among the general British public — and particularly among the then Bloomsbury literary set — by publishing in 1918 a book titled *A Hundred and Seventy Chinese Poems*.

When the journalist asked whether he was ever tempted to visit China to see what the country was really like, he replied unhesitatingly in the negative.

He said the China he knew through its literature, painting, music, innovations and crafts had been one of perfection. Why spoil all that with reality?

That gave me the idea that I could also create in my mind and heart a China to my own liking, a China without any of its ruder and more jarring realities. So I pieced together elements from Chinese history, literature and the arts as building blocks, selecting my favourite poems, epigrams and proverbs and such random samples of landscape paintings, Sung celadon, Ming stem cups and jade artefacts I had the good fortune to admire in some of the greatest museums in the world.

I would add as part of that imaginary world a few realities that I had to hand, like the antique seal stones my father had given me. Whenever I handled one of them, I would marvel over being in possession of something once owned by somebody three or four hundred years ago. And those ancient seals, with or without a *niou*, with or without a side inscription to indicate provenance, and engraved with characters in either relief or intaglio, would also enrich the secret world I was constructing.

Over time, further elements accrued. For example, when my photographer friend, Patricia Fok Lai-Ping, presented me with copies of her books of pictures filled with evocative images of China, they too became included in my imaginary world.

Patricia, who described herself as "a Chinese girl with a camera" was in fact the eldest daughter of Fok Ying-Tung, a Chinese patriot and a Hong Kong billionaire. Her father was a member of the Standing Committee of the National People's Congress and a Vice-Chairman of the National Committee of the Chinese People's Political Consultative Conference. His political status enabled Patricia to gain access to parts of the country at the time closed to outsiders.

Patricia and I shared a few things in common. We both had received significant parts of our early education in foreign lands but had something indubitably Chinese in our blood which we could not shake off.

Patricia's handiwork often featured the misty beauty of Chinese landscapes, like the Yellow Mountain or the hills of Kweilin. It has been said that Picasso got his inspiration for cubism after seeing a series of photographs of Kweilin's hills at an exhibition, with individual hills taken from different angles and perspectives.

Her photographs affected me differently, however. They stirred in me ancient lines of Chinese poetry and memories of how, during my rebellious boyhood, Tutor Tam had tried to drill me into remembering the names of China's five sacred mountains and its four crucial rivers.

Once I had begun creating my idealised China, a place inhabited by benevolent rulers and contented citizens, with each trying to cultivate the inherent goodness in himself or herself, the actualities in the real China slipped away from the centre of my attention. The Five-Year Plans, the targets they set, the endless slogans and the mischievous disinformation pumped out by the propaganda machines of the Cold War, all largely ceased to engage my interest.

Another reason for my indifference to such matters was my more pressing need to extricate myself from a disastrous marriage and its unhappy consequences.

Thus when Yeuk-Lam asked me to join his family on a holiday in China, the invitation came at a very opportune moment. I had not only been divorced but my children had all gone off for education overseas. Indeed, my eldest son was then about to graduate. I was, in addition, retired from the trammels of public service and at the start of a new career in commerce.

But what was the most crucial spur for me to see the real China was a further severe attack of acute pancreatitis. I had gone on a visit to the Li & Fung branch office in Taipei early in 1982 when, on my way back, I suffered another sudden attack, causing me to collapse in agony at the Chiang Kai-Shek Airport. That brought home to me that human beings were mortal and that if I did not engage with the real China soon I might well quit the world with only my imaginary China accompanying me to the beyond.

That was why Yeuk-Lam's invitation was so timely. So I quickly applied for one of those "home visit" passes for returning to China.

When my ex-colleague in the Home Affairs Department, Chia Chi-Pui, heard that I was heading for China with Yeuk-Lam, he quickly asked whether he could join in as well. Since his Mandarin was much better than that of the rest of us, his participation was welcomed with alacrity.

* * *

And so it was that a group of a dozen of us headed into China in the autumn of 1982. The group comprised Yeuk-Lam and Suze, their eldest son Shing-Ki, who was a Federal Canadian Immigration official, their youngest son Shing-Kwan, a doctor, and his wife Maureen, a nurse, Chia Chi-Pui and myself, with some predominantly female friends and relatives making up the rest.

Yeuk-Lam was never a man to do things by halves. For the first half of our trip he had secured as our official guide the services of a Cantonese in his fifties. The man had a slightly melancholy look but once he started performing his duties it became clear he was learned in Chinese architecture, landscaping, social customs and history. My guess was that he must have been at one time an intellectual of the old school, before political imperatives reduced him to a more humble mode of earning a living as a tourist guide.

Yeuk-Lam also had great foresight in another important matter. He saw to it that our itinerary placed the group on the banks of the Chientang River, close to Hangchow, around the Mid-autumn Festival so that its members could witness the tidal bore rushing into the narrowing bay from the sea.

The tidal bore was reputed to be the largest in the world, sometimes rising as high as 12 metres. And daredevils would set out to sea in small boats beforehand, in order to ride the surf in. For centuries, people from all over the country had been gathering there each year to watch those spectacular sights.

Ip Yeuk-Lam and the author, together with Shing-Kwan and his wife, Maureen, waiting with the crowds on the banks of the Chientang River for the tidal bore to arrive

* * *

The next destination for the group was the ancient fabled garden city of Hangchow, described by centuries of writers as a paradise on earth. The pliant beauty of the place, ringed by hills and forests hosting temples by the hundreds and blessed by the presence of the West Lake with its strategically located islets, appeared to wear its antiquity with an astonishing air of dignified insouciance. The beauty and the mellowness of the setting took my breath away. They exceeded all that I had ever imagined that a 2,100-year-old city to be. They brought to mind the lines by the great Sung poet Su Tung-Po:

The light of water sparkles on a sunny day;
And misty mountains lend excitement to the rain.
I like to compare the West Lake to 'Miss West',
Pretty in a gay dress, and pretty in simple again.

Hangchow had indeed been fortunate to have had Su living there after he had been Governor of West Chekiang Province in 1089, at the age of 52. He took an intimate interest in all the affairs of the city.

Two and a half centuries before him, another great poet, Po Chu-I of the Tang Dynasty, had also served as its Governor. Po Chu-I was one of the most prolific poets of that dynasty and was noted for poems depicting the sufferings of the common people and satirising greedy officials.

Both those poets had enhanced the natural loveliness of the city without disfiguring it, like planting willows along a lakeside park. The pathway along the park soon acquired the poetic name of "Listening to orioles among the willows".

The Chinese have such a pleasing way of naming things, always with a nod to nature or mythology. In Hong Kong, when left to their own devices, the Chinese had given streets names like "Spring Garden Lane" or "Tin Hau Temple Road". After Western colonisers came, however, their rampant individualism and egocentric ways caused many thoroughfares to be slapped with the names of inconsequential — and sometimes even undeserving — colonial bureaucrats.

The West Lake had a circumference of approximately ten miles. Po Chu-I constructed a causeway promenade running east and west near the northern shore of the lake, complete with pavilions and hump-back bridges, to provide for more convenient access between the two sides.

Su Tung-Po was to construct another promenade running north and south, near the western shore of the lake, two and a half centuries later. Those two promenades were named by the city's citizens after their respective creators. Both embankments have been boons to pleasure-seekers ever since.

But apart from being a poet and an administrator, Su Tung-Po was also an outstanding engineer. Two canals had been cut through the city to provide for barge traffic. But the seawalls built to prevent seawater from bringing mud and silt into the canals were in disrepair. That necessitated dredging the canals every three to five years at great expense and to considerable disruption to residents. Su Tung-Po devised a way of building a third canal and some locks to shut off the seawater at high tide but released it at low tide. Thus the seawater needed for the canal could be brought in without so much silt. Additionally, that arrangement increased the depth of the canals and improved navigation.

He then turned his attention to securing fresh water supplies for the city. The fresh water came from mountain springs, which was then brought by bamboo pipes to six reservoirs and to the West Lake. But those bamboo pipes were easily damaged, compromising the quality of the water.

Su Tung-Po remedied that by replacing them with strong clay pipes which were in turn protected top and bottom by flag-stones. But there was yet another major problem. He noticed that the capacity of the West Lake was steadily being reduced by a fast-growing weed. The weed was already covering almost half the lake. The remedy was to marshal enough labour to remove the weed, a simple though costly exercise. Yet none of his immediately preceding governors had attempted the task. He sought funds from the central government and the job was completed in four months.

He then hit upon an idea for preventing the weed from returning — by leasing out sections of the lake shore to farmers to grow water chestnuts. Those holding the leases would then automatically see to weeds not interfering with their crops. The income from the leases could then be used for the upkeep of the lake and its promenades.

It would be a mistake to think that Su Tung-Po's contributions to Hangchow were limited to the foregoing. In fact, he did a great deal more. He established in that city what was probably the first public hospital in all of China. He was indefatigable in pursuing famine relief measures, human-hearted in dealing with law-breakers brought before him, and stubbornly opposed to unreasonable taxes being imposed by the imperial court.

It was no surprise, therefore, that he should be thoroughly admired and loved by ordinary inhabitants of the city during his time. Although he was a native of Szechuan Province, many citizens of Hangchow — even today — insist on regarding him as their own.

* * *

After entering Hangchow itself, our Cantonese guide's knowledge of Chinese history and folklore splendidly manifested itself. He explained that the city's landmark Broken Bridge had never been broken at all. People in ancient times gave the bridge that name because in winter snow often completely covered the balusters of the bridge, so that viewed from a distance the bridge appeared broken.

The bridge gained further prominence because it was featured in one of the four greatest Ming Dynasty romances and folktales called *Madame White Snake*. According to the story, the spirit of a white female snake had been meditating earnestly for a thousand years. As a result of that effort, it had gained the ability to transform itself into human form.

One day, after taking on the form of a beautiful young woman, the snake spirit encountered on Broken Bridge an orphaned shop assistant working for a herbalist. The two fell hopelessly in love and duly got married.

A Buddhist monk, discovering that unholy union, tried to break it up by revealing to the young man that his wife was actually the spirit of a white snake. But the two by then had become so enamoured of each other that the revelation did not deter them from continuing as man and wife. They eventually gave birth to a son who distinguished himself at the Imperial Examinations.

Likewise, when our Cantonese guide led us to the Ngok Fei Temple, he regaled us with many of the legends surrounding the life of that Southern Sung Dynasty general. Ngok Fei had been leading Sung forces against the invading Jurchens from the north but, when he was on the brink of success, corrupt and treacherous court officials caused him to be recalled and charged with treason.

During his denial of the charges, he removed his clothes to display four characters tattooed on his back which meant "serve the country with utmost loyalty". One version of the story had it that his mother had caused those characters to be tattooed when he was young to remind him of his duty. But the four characters were not enough to save him from being tortured and executed in Hangchow.

Subsequently, when the truth became known, high posthumous titles were conferred on Ngok Fei and, when the temple in his honour was built, kneeling effigies of the officials who had betrayed him were placed in the courtyard for future generations to mock. Thereafter, Ngok Fei came to be regarded as the epitome of loyalty in Chinese culture.

Our guide was well up on the lore of tea and tea drinking as well. He took the group to the Tiger Running Spring close to the city and told us that the quality of the water from that spring was reputed to be one of the best in all China. Connoisseurs of the local Dragon's Well tea, therefore always insisted upon its use when brewing tea.

* * *

For myself, the highlight of the visit to Hangchow came when our group visited the Sai Ling Seal Engravers' Society located on the western side of Solitary Hill. The Society was an organisation I had heard my father mentioned when I was young and again a couple of decades later when he bestowed upon me his entire collection of personal and leisure seals.

Seal carving was popularised by the first Ch'in Emperor when he had the Heirloom Seal of the Realm made to symbolise he had received the Mandate of Heaven. That heirloom seal was handed down through the subsequent dynasties for more than one and a half millennia until it got lost at the beginning of the Ming Dynasty. That caused some of the Ching emperors who followed to have numerous imperial seals made.

The Engravers' Society at Sai Ling had roots dating back to the Ming Dynasty, although it was not formally established till 1904, to devote itself to the seal-carving art. My father must have become acquainted with it upon going to China after finishing his secondary education at St. Joseph's Institute in Singapore in 1919.

His disappearance to China for a period of six years has remained something of a family mystery. Elders had said he had gone there to seek work. But upon my own belated introduction to Hangchow, it came to me that it had to be just the kind of scenic and agreeable place to captivate my father and keep him lingering there. In any case, he did not show up for further education at the University of Hong Kong till 1925.

The Society occupied spacious gardens and grounds studded with museums displaying calligraphies, stone rubbings and ancient seal imprints and kiosks selling seal stones, the oil-based vermilion cinnabar seal paste in lacquer containers and other paraphernalia associated with seal engraving. The superb "field yellow" and "chicken blood" seals on display in the kiosks, at a fraction of the prices prevailing in Hong Kong, simply blew my mind. Obviously, even at those bargain basement prices, the seal stones were beyond the purses of the locals.

I became suddenly afraid of admiring and coveting them for too long, for

I understood at that instance the irresistible impulses that could sometimes overtake housewives in the midst of sales!

I therefore deliberately turned my attention to the small number of local people visiting the gardens and grounds of the Society. They were dressed uniformly in baggy clothes of blue, grey or green. But they appeared relaxed and contented as they went about smoking cigarettes, reading newspapers, taking in the scenery or playing chess. Should children accompany the adults, then dashes of red were likely to be added through their wearing the red neck scarves of the Young Pioneers.

Although the local people had a far more modest standard of living than the citizens of Hong Kong, young and old alike seemed to carry themselves with quiet dignity and confidence in the future.

The same could not be said of the citizens of the British colony at that time, however. 1982 was the time when Britain and China began seriously locking wills on the return of the territory to Chinese sovereignty. Scary rumours of dire outcomes emerging from those exchanges — some maliciously generated for short term advantage by one side or the other — were buzzing around the city more thickly than bluebottles around a rotting carcass. They so disturbed local sentiments that many of the more faint-hearted started pulling up roots and seeking foreign visas.

The tranquil views of the West Lake from the gardens came as a very pleasant diversion from those ill-informed rumours back home. As I took in those magnificent sights, it came to me they must have been the same sights that had captivated my father. Indeed, those very sights had probably remained largely unchanged for the last two thousand years!

On a more contemporary note, Chairman Mao was also fond of watching the play of the water on the West Lake from nearby gardens. He visited Hangchow often when he retreated from the bitter cold of the Peking winter, staying in Shanghai at a residence converted for his use at the former French Club.

The only detail obviously absent from the dappled waters of the lake after the Communist Revolution was the presence of the former flower boats, which used to be filled with courtesans plying the intelligentsia and officialdom not only with drink, music and dance but also with their ability to match couplets or to discuss philosophy and religion with the best of them. It was through such carousing with well-read courtesans that Su Tung-Po gradually perfected and popularised the *tse* form of poetry.

What has happened in our modern world that we should now have descended into the crudities of topless bars and naked pole-dancing joints? In eras past, fun and entertainment came with more imagination and greater erudition. I could only lament that I had been born too late to enjoy those bygone pleasures!

* * *

The next city on our itinerary was Soochow, in the neighbouring province of Kiangsu. Soochow, having been founded in 514 BC, was a much older and bigger than Hangchow but it was equally celebrated for its beauty. It was pleasantly located on the banks of Lake Tai, one of the largest fresh water lakes in China, covering 869 square miles. The city was also connected to the Yangtse River. A criss-cross of canals and ancient bridges ran inside the city, causing it to be known as the Venice of Asia. It was also linked to many other towns and cities by means of the 1,104-mile-long Grand Canal.

Soochow benefited enormously from the trade generated by the completion of the Grand Canal during the Sui Dynasty. That project was achieved by connecting up a number of local canals along its route, some of which dated back to the fifth century BC.

Because of Yeuk-Lam's political connections, the top officials of Soochow hosted our entire tour group to a sumptuous meal on board a large launch as it cruised around the 90 islands in Lake Tai.

Because of the city's great age, it was only natural that it should boast a great many ancient monuments. Among them were two of the best preserved classical Chinese gardens in all of China — the Humble Administrator's Garden and the Lingering Garden.

At each our learned Cantonese guide was able to dilate upon the finer points of Chinese landscaping, on why there should be none of the sweeping views and grand vistas of Western gardening and why there was a need for diffused crooked walks and rhythmic curves. The aim was to reflect the simple harmonies of natural things and to offer as many arresting views as possible as a person strolled through the garden. To that end, objects outside a garden, like distant mountains or pagodas, might be incorporated to form part of a scene.

He also explained that some of the fantastically shaped limestone formations dredged up from the bottom of Lake Tai were much sought after by people keen to install rockeries in their gardens.

Wonderful as Soochow gardens were, the city had been associated in my mind ever since childhood with the atmospheric poem by the Tang poet, Cheung Gai, which had been anthologised in the standard primer *Three Hundred Tang Poems*. It was about a scholar passing through Soochow by boat and stopping near the Cold Mountain Temple while *en route* home after failing in the Imperial Examinations.

When I first learnt the poem as a child in Canton, it had been little more than mastering by rote a series of rhythmic sounds, with no real understanding of the actual meaning of the words being recited. It was only some years later, when I was studying under Tutor Tam in Singapore, that he explained the meaning of the words.

Still more years later, I tried to clarify with my father the precise imagery Cheung Gai was trying to convey in the last line of his poem. I wanted to pin down whether the poet sought to convey the impression of the failed scholar being in the boat in the middle of the night, unable to sleep, when he heard the bells of the Cold Mountain Temple or whether he had been out drowning his sorrows and only upon returning to the boat in the middle of the night did he hear the temple bells. On my reading, both seemed plausible.

"That's the beauty of Chinese poetry," my father replied. "Its terseness engages the imagination of the reader. Each line can be pregnant with allusions. What a reader brings to a verse would depend on his imagination and the breadth of his scholarship."

It was inevitable, therefore, that after the group's arrival in Soochow a visit to the Cold Mountain Temple had to be included. We strolled through its grounds and ran our hands in wonder over its ancient bronze bells. Outside the temple, we gazed contemplatively upon the two bridges mentioned in Cheung Gai's poem and studied the fishing boats still moored between them.

It so happened that after our temple visit, while ambling through the venerable streets of the city, I spotted a shop selling writing brushes, sticks of ink and stone ink slabs. My eyes lit up when I saw on display an ink slab with a cover engraved with Cheung Gai's poem in archaic small seal characters. I could not resist buying it there and then. That ink slab is still with me today and being used.

Writing about events which had taken place decades ago, I could not help wondering if engravers still carved Cheung Gai's poem on ink slabs today. If so, do tourists still buy them? Or would they settle for one of those ubiquitous T-shirts with the Chinese characters for Soochow emblazoned across it or a plastic or plaster cast replica of the city's leaning Cloud Rock Pagoda?

* * *

The next place for the tour group to head for was Yangchow, another ancient city on the north bank of the Yangtze River which was in many ways similar to Soochow. It was founded around 485 BC and was filled with canals and blessed with many lakes and well-tended gardens.

The ink slab, with Cheung Gai's poem carved in small seal script

The attractiveness of its surroundings have been widely praised in literature. The romantic Tang poet, Tu Mu, had written the following lines about the city:

After ten years, I awake from my Yangchow dream,
All I gained was a fickle reputation in the green mansions.

The "green mansions" was a reference to the green tiled roofs in the city's pleasure districts. Alas, those pleasure districts no longer existed.

The most famous of the many lakes in Yangchow was called Slender West Lake. There was a garden next to it with a number of historical features, one of the most notable was a fishing platform called Diaoyu Tai. It was a spot favoured by the Ching Emperor, Chien Lung. He was partial to it because he always landed abundant catches there.

What the emperor did not know was that local officials, seeking to please him, had arranged on each occasion for divers to go beneath the waters to surreptitiously attach fishes to the imperial hooks! It appeared that emperors, like the common man, also had to be fed with a few illusions and dreams.

Yangchow, connected to other parts of the country by the Grand Canal and by the Yangtze River, thrived through being a centre for the salt, rice and silk trades. The city also had a reputation for its lacquerware, embroidery and its cuisine. Its gardens, like those at Soochow, exuded a Taoist air. They would feature pathways and nooks with eccentric names like "The place for cultivating friendship with the moon" or "The path and the bamboos lead to a place of mystery".

During the rule of the Mongols, Marco Polo claimed he had been appointed its governor, though later historians have speculated that his office was of a lower order.

The city had also seen its share of hard times. After the Manchus invaded China, the Ming Dynasty set up a short-lived capital there. But when the Manchu forces took the city in 1645, they went on a ten-day killing spree during which 800,000 of its inhabitants were said to have lost their lives.

During my various travels around the world, I had often eaten in Chinese restaurants in places as far apart as New York and Sydney, Barcelona and Rio de Janeiro, Toronto and Karlsruhe. In all of them, I had found on their menus an item called "Yangchow Fried Rice". Whenever I had ordered the dish, however, I discovered that the ingredients used in its preparation varied slightly from place to place. Therefore, finding myself in Yangchow, I was determine to establish what the genuine article tasted like.

But to my great chagrin, when I tried to order that dish at a couple of restaurants in that city, I was told that the dish was completely unheard of. The only fried rice dish that both places could offer was something called "Cantonese Fried Rice". I nevertheless ordered the local fried rice for comparative purposes and — lo and behold — each tasted pretty much like the Yangchow Fried Rice served up elsewhere.

Well, I suppose that showed what cunning marketing could achieve. Fried rice by any name had to taste just as fried. What an exotic world of illusions, brandings and self-deceptions we are increasingly creating for ourselves.

* * *

At the end of our group's stay in Yangchow, we had to bid farewell to our learned tour guide, for he had not been authorised to travel with us to Peking for the next stage of our holiday.

That proved a great disappointment for all of us, because most of us benefited enormously from his comprehensive recitals of Chinese history and legends. So long as people like him continued to narrate orally the tales of the country's past and the notables who had emerged over the centuries, there was little danger that anything as ephemeral as Chairman Mao's Great Proletarian Cultural Revolution could ever erase those stories from thousands of years ago from the hearts and minds of the common people.

Most members of our group had lived through the overspill of the Cultural Revolution into Hong Kong in 1967 and the disturbances it brought. We had got a sight of mob psychology at work and the human propensity for violence. Inside China the turmoil or *luan* had been more extreme. We had heard horrific stories of mass struggle meetings, accompanied by torture and deaths, fierce sectarian fighting, factories and cities brought to a standstill and indiscriminate destruction of cultural icons and relics.

Many of us had been left wondering just how tough a membrane had been developed for civil and considerate behaviour over five thousand years of Chinese civilisation. Was it strong enough to hold in check our enduring discontents and our secretive paranoia and madness? If that membrane were to rupture or be punctured, would a regression back to the laws of the jungle possess us again?

Modern Chinese history has not been very reassuring on that score, especially when the masses remained superstitious and not adequately educated. In 1850, a scholar who had repeatedly failed in the Imperial Examinations decided to reinvent himself as the younger brother of Jesus and to lead an uprising known as the Taiping Rebellion. Before it was put down with the aid of foreign powers in about 1864, it had cost somewhere between 20 and 25 million lives.

A serious drought in North China towards the end of the 19th century was followed by floods. Those natural calamities saw the rise of a little known secret society called the Society of Righteous Harmonious Fists. Its members believed that if the country got rid of foreigners, their Christian religion and their Chinese converts then the problems of the country would disappear. Moreover, those practitioners of martial arts claimed they had arrived at a stage of their training where they would be immune to the bullets of foreign guns. So they began killing foreigners and Chinese Christians.

Some of the officials in the Manchu Court unfortunately subscribed to their misplaced ideas and supported them. That set the scene for the bloodbaths of the Boxer Rebellion. The Boxers laid siege to the Legation Quarters for 55 days, causing eight foreign powers to join in sending an expeditionary force to free their diplomats.

The upshot of that demented episode was that several hundreds of foreigners and in excess of 30,000 Chinese Christians were slaughtered by the Boxers. In vengeance, the troops of foreign powers relieving the Legation Quarters unleashed fresh orgies of murder upon suspected Boxers as well as upon totally innocent peasants whom they took to be Boxers.

Another aspect of the bloodlust was that the foreign powers making up the expeditionary force demanded the execution of all court officials who had supported the Boxers. It was noteworthy that none of those officials sought to escape their responsibility. Having chosen a stand, they accepted their fate stoically. Some committed suicide while the rest turned up for their executions. If only modern officials and politicians were as ready to admit responsibility for their mistakes!

During the Cultural Revolution, there were many instances of demented activities as well. For instance, a detachment of Tsinghua University students broke into a lunatic asylum in Peking in the autumn of 1966 and found an inmate by the name of Chen Li-Ming.

Chen somehow convinced them that he had been locked up for criticising Liu Shao-Chi, Chairman Mao, Marx and Lenin. The students soon hailed him as a revolutionary martyr, wrote a play about him and sent him to address mass meetings from one end of the country to another. It was only in 1968 that Chen was finally sent back to the asylum. That showed that university students could go off the rails as spectacularly as the more poorly educated in a time of chaos and paranoia.

* * *

Since our group happened to be in China long after such ghastly events, we naturally wanted to learn at first-hand details of how those who had lived through that "lost decade" of the Cultural Revolution had been affected.

But we had no opportunity to talk to ordinary people. We were, after all, not a group of social scientists or behavioural psychologists out to dissect the social structure of an emerging China. We were only a group of rather privileged tourists trying to escape for a while from the quotidian pressures of the get-rich-quick environment in Hong Kong.

On the face of things, we found nothing worryingly disturbing or regimented in the cities we had visited. The only mass activity we had spotted were gatherings of citizens in the parks, practising *tai chi* exercises.

But, of course, changes had indeed occurred. Urban life was far cleaner and the traffic more orderly than I had seen in Canton back in 1947. There were no beggars, mendicants and pickpockets in the streets and there was no air of impending doom of that time, when nerves were being jangled daily by runaway inflation.

In addition, the people of the cities we visited seemed quite relaxed as they went about their daily business. There was little motor traffic on the roads except for buses and lorries. Private cars hardly existed except for the odd Red Flag limousine conveying high-ranking officials on their missions. The ordinary citizen went about among the endless streams of bicycles. The tinkling of their bells were far more pleasing on the ear than the agitated blaring of horns in Hong Kong, when cars got snarled in traffic jams.

The demographics also seemed to have changed. There appeared to be more younger people around, with their faces eager yet relaxed, confident about their future. I would not use Chairman Mao's description that their faces shone like "the sun at eight o'clock in the morning" but they certainly did not carry the shut, harried look of many of the Hong Kong young, burdened with excessive homework or with overlong hours of underpaid employment.

When the Communist Party came to power in 1949, the literacy rate in the country was probably only about 15%. Illiteracy must have been virtually wiped out by 1982, for everywhere young and old alike could be seen reading newspapers or books to while away their leisure.

People were not by any means affluent, measured by Western standards, but they seemed contented with their simple lives and there was not any obvious sign of hunger and malnutrition.

I remembered that during the years of the Great Famine the post office in Hong Kong had to work round-the-clock to cope with all the food parcels residents were sending to relatives inside China. That had become a thing of the past.

During our tour, our Cantonese guide took the opportunity to brief us about the efforts made by China to create a more egalitarian society. The social and legal equality between men and women had been written into the Chinese Constitution in 1954, he said. In 1965, all insignias of rank had been removed from members of the People's Liberation Army. A general was supposed to wear the same uniform as a private.

Then how would anyone know who was an officer and who was a common foot soldier, one of our group asked.

The guide smiled. There were in fact subtle indications for those in the know, he explained. One could draw inferences, for example, from the number of fountain pens a person had clipped to his breast pocket or whether his sandals were made of leather or plastic or the quality of the watch he wore.

"Wages are egalitarian too," he added. "I draw exactly the same pay as the driver of your coach. What does pay matter, when we are both working for the Revolution?"

I remain unsure to this day whether he had intended to reveal the slight wryness in his tone of voice.

As for myself, the tour we had had so far had lifted my spirits considerably. It was with a secret delight that I found that much of the material I had put together to form my imaginary China still existed in reality. I could relate to what I had seen and genuinely felt that a part of myself still belonged there, in spite of the sometimes erratic actions of its Communist rulers.

* * *

I have noticed that Western journalists who have visited China nearly always make some play of the large number of slogans they found plastered everywhere. They inevitably point to them as an attempt by an authoritarian government to brainwash the populace. I therefore made an effort to note down the kind of slogans I had encountered.

Among the slogans I had seen during the tour of the three ancient cities were the following:

"Build the nation on thrift and industry."

"Love science, love hygiene, love labour."

"Protect the Motherland."

"Serve the Revolution."

"Strike down Imperialism."

"Fight Cultural Pollution."

"Struggle hard to implement the Five-Year Economic Plan."

I myself could not see much that was wrong with such exhortations. They seemed infinitely more sensible than the advertisements blazoned in Times Square in New York and Piccadilly Circus in London, urging people to guzzle more sugary or alcoholic beverages, to supersize their greasy hamburgers or to buy another fancy designer garment or a pair of shoes or a jar of alleged beautifying goo. Would such conspicuous consumption really dull the gnawing hollowness within the soul of the ordinary urbanite?

It was true that other slogans like "Long Live the Chinese Communist Party" and "Long Live the People's Republic of China" existed aplenty. They could be regarded as a form of indoctrination. But should they be considered more reprehensible than my being made to learn songs like "Onward Christian Soldier" and "Rule, Britannia" when I was a boy in a British colonial missionary school?

By the end of the first part of our tour, a sense of apprehension did creep into my thoughts, however. It was all very well to open China up to the outside world but would the country learn the right things from the outside world? Human greed was infinite. If a get-rich-quick mentality took hold and ran riot, would much that was fine and precious in Chinese culture not be severely compromised?

It was a frightening thought to imagine that one might one day enter a Soochow or Yangchow garden to seek communion with nature only to find oneself hemmed in by an overbearing forest of high-rises, complete with neon signs touting all the latest mass consumables and electronic gadgets. It might then be too late to regret what had been gained through modernisation and what had been lost.

CHAPTER 8

Karma at the Great Wall

PEKING, AFTER HAVING SERVED as the capital for a total of six Chinese dynasties, is a city weighed down by history and crowded with ancient monuments. If I were to attempt to describe every temple, pagoda, *hutong*, bridge and human construction visited by the tour group and explain their individual backgrounds, I would have to fill another book. I therefore propose to mention only those places which are germane to the current narrative.

However, having said that — and with the benefit of hindsight — I should like to record one observation. When I visited Peking, the air had been fresh and clean. Apart from buses and goods vehicles and an occasional official limousine — the Red Flag — there was little in the way of motorised traffic. The citizenry went about largely on bicycles, massive and seemingly endless flows of them.

How could one imagine that within a few short decades the air would become almost unbreathable because of pollution and that the streets would be gridlocked on an almost a daily basis with private cars.

As other major cities around the world — like London and Paris — try to persuade their citizens to revert to bicycles, one must wonder why the human psyche is so hopelessly prone to following fads and novelties that, without first thinking through and appreciating what it was already enjoying. So far as I can judge, far too many urban centres around the world, both those which are new and developing as well as those of ancient vintage, are repeating the same mistakes. And what seems even more absurd is that the hordes of *nouveaux riches* would be prepared to lay out good money to join expensive gyms in order to pedal furiously on cycling machines which would take them nowhere.

* * *

Upon arrival, the group was assigned a new tour guide, an officious northerner, aged around 30, who behaved as if he had been assigned to instruct a bunch of unruly country bumpkins. The fact that he could only speak Mandarin was another immediate minus from our point of view. Several of us could not fully understand his commentaries without the help of fellow group members. He made us wish we had our former Cantonese guide back.

As was customary with Peking tours, we began our exploration of the city at Tiananmen — the Gate of Heavenly Peace. The monumental gate was first built in 1420, during the Ming Dynasty, as one of the main entrances to the imperial palace behind. It had been destroyed and rebuilt several times since, the last occasion having taken place after the Communist victory in 1949, when a lift was installed inside.

Over the gate, a large portrait of Chairman Mao occupied pride of place. The practice of placing a portrait of a national leader there originated after the Revolution of 1911 when a portrait of Dr. Sun Yat-Sen went up. Later, under the rule of the Kuomintang, a portrait of General Chiang Kai-Shek was put there.

But Chairman Mao had died in September of 1976 and, after a brief spell under Mao's designated successor, the benign but uncharismatic Hua Guo-Feng, Deng Xiao-Ping became the Paramount Ruler in 1978. Deng never occupied any of the main Communist Party or government positions after attaining power. He died in 1997 and subsequently other leaders took over. Yet, in spite of those changes, Mao's portrait remained on display.

Ip Yeuk-Lam and myself at Tiananmen Square

What did that mean? It had to become a topic for speculation, even though Deng Xiao-Ping had said Chairman Mao's portrait should be kept there forever as a symbol of the country because of his contributions to China and the Chinese Communist Party. Did it signal that the later leaders had moved decidedly away from supporting any cult of the personality and towards a more collective leadership? Or did it simply imply that no leader had yet emerged with sufficient gravitas and stature to oust Mao from his perch? Only time will tell.

The Gate of Heavenly Peace, with its august Ming Dynasty pedigree, bestowed its name upon the vast square in front of it. Tiananmen Square is probably the largest city square in the world. At 880 metres long and 500 metres wide, it is suitable for the most grandiose of celebrations and parades. It had been consistently used for those purposes. Our party all busily took photographs to mark the occasion, before exploring the many other features in the square.

One of the most outstanding was the mausoleum dedicated to Chairman Mao. Its presence was something of a puzzle because Chairman Mao had expressed a wish for his remains to be cremated. But somehow a decision was arrived at to embalm him instead. A vast army of builders were recruited to build the mausoleum, to be completed before the first anniversary of his death. A simple yet select ceremony was then held to put his embalmed body on public display.

* * *

After spending a couple of days visiting some of the central landmarks like the Summer Palace, the Temple of Heaven and the Palace Museum, the group set out in a private bus for the roughly 50-mile journey to the Badaling section of the Great Wall on a pleasant autumnal morning. The sky was cloudless; a slight nip in the air promised a delightful day.

En route, our new guide briefed us on the history of the Badaling section of the Great Wall. His delivery, however, was dry and unanimated, as if he were just going through a spiel to fulfil his duty. He made all of us miss our former guide even more.

The section we were visiting used to be considered of great strategic importance, the guide said, because it historically commanded a number of routes with access to the capital. The full stretch consisted of several miles but the part we were visiting was only approximately two-and-a-third-miles long. It had been opened to visitors only since 1957, after it had been restored for that purpose. The section included watch towers, signal stations and troop barracks.

Boundary and protection walls had a long history in China, he added. Some parts of the Great Wall could be traced back to the Spring and Autumn period when a collection of feudal rulers lorded it over different parts of the country. That period would be from 700 to 476 BC. They had built walls to mark out their respective domains.

But all that changed after the First Emperor of Ch'in defeated all his rivals in 221 BC to unify the nation. He ordered some of the old walls to be knocked down, to signify that everything now belonged to him. But he also ordered some of the existing walls to be linked up to guard against attacks from the nomadic tribes inhabiting the northern steppes.

Thus the grand engineering project began along the northern edge of a unified China, for a wall which would ultimately run for approximately 13,170 miles across 15 provinces and regions. Such a massive task, naturally, could not be completed within the short-lived Ch'in reign. It was left to succeeding dynasties, notably the Han, Sui and Ming Dynasties, to complete the job.

Over the centuries, time, weather, neglect and vandalism had taken their tolls on the structure. It is estimated today that about a tenth of the wall had already disappeared. Some of the earliest parts were made of stamped earth which did not stand up well against sand storms and desert winds. Bricks and stones were later used. However, that merely invited villagers in the remoter areas to help themselves to those materials whenever they needed them for their own purposes.

The section at Badaling was of Ming origin, probably built around 1504. That dynasty had contributed about 5,500 miles to the total length of the

Great Wall. On average the wall stood 26 feet tall and 20 feet wide, sufficient for ten men to march along abreast.

* * *

On arrival at our destination we were pleased to note that mass tourism had not yet fully taken hold. Visitors to the Great Wall were few and far between. There was a number of kiosks selling the usual souvenirs but custom was slow.

The guide announced that we were now free to do whatever we wished so long as we reassembled at the tour bus at a certain hour to proceed to our next destination — the 13 Ming tombs.

Some of the group tarried momentarily at the shopping kiosks; others went looking for latrines.

Chia Chi-Pui and I decided to walk along as much of the wall as we could within the time given, to take in the view from every vantage point. We wanted to get some sense of the vastness of the inhospitable steppes and to imagine what it might have been like trying to defend the wall against hordes of fierce and outlandishly-clad barbarians. And to give a thought too to the countless thousands who had sacrificed their lives more passively, building the wall to protect a cultural and governmental system which nowadays so many took for granted or even openly ridiculed.

As Chia and I strode along, we noticed a small plateau on one side the wall, On it, a man was tending two mangy camels. On one of the animals was a young girl with bobbed hair and a large pair of dark glasses striking a pose. Another girl in a purple and beige vest and a pair of light grey slacks was snapping her picture. They both appeared to be teenagers.

That tableau struck me as slightly incongruous. The girls appeared modishly dressed and yet not quite in keeping with other mainland girls I had seen earlier during the trip. Could they be a couple of overseas Chinese on a visit like ourselves? But then, overseas Chinese usually moved in larger groups.

At a distance, the girl on the camel had a resemblance to Audrey Hepburn. She had the same sort of gamine air that the British actress had projected in the film *My Fair Lady*.

Then I noticed that the girl using the camera had two long plaited queues dangling half-way down to her thighs. That form of hairdo had long been out of fashion with Chinese girls living outside China. My curiosity was aroused. I suggested to Chia that we go down to the plateau to have a closer look — at the girls, that is, not the camels.

By the time Chia and I found our way down there, the girl with the sunglasses had dismounted and the other was fiddling with an old Rolleiflex camera. Apparently something had gone amiss. Thinking that our arrival was because we wanted to take photographs astride the camels as well, the girl who had just dismounted said: "Please go ahead, uncles. We're having problems with our camera."

"Perhaps I can help," Chia said. "We're Hong Kong compatriots here to see for ourselves what the new China is like."

"Hong Kong compatriots are always welcomed," the other girl said, with an easy laugh. "Our country is opening up to learn from the outside world. Maybe you can show us how to fix our camera."

With that, she passed the Rolleiflex to Chia.

Seeing the girls up close, I was staggered by how beautiful they were. Both were indeed teenagers and neither had any make-up. Yet their cheeks glowed with the rosy tinge of rude health; their lips were shapely and red; their youthful voices resounded like music in the still autumnal air. In addition, they carried themselves with an open confidence that seemed quite remarkable for their ages. If they were representative of the younger generation in China, had they the moral and intellectual underpinnings to develop into leaders? Being good-looking was not enough.

Hong Kong was certainly not producing youngsters who carried themselves like them. But would the opening up of the country ultimately affect them adversely? They seemed, so far as fashion was concerned, already a couple of steps ahead of most of the girls in their country. Would they be up to the task of reshaping the nation or would they become corrupted by the materialism of the outside world? How long would it take before they, too, would have painted nails, mascaraed eyes, Shiseido-ed faces and hennaed hair like their older sisters in Hong Kong?

Meanwhile, Chia had finished examining the camera and had found himself unable to fix whatever was at fault. "I think the film advance crank is stuck," he said. "But I have a Nikon; I can take whatever pictures you want and send them to you afterwards."

"Thank you very much," the girl with the dark glasses said. "No need to trouble you, uncle. My camera is very old. We can always come back after we have fixed the camera."

"Are you both Peking residents?" I asked.

"I am," the girl replied. "But my friend's from Nantong."

"Nantong? Where's that?"

"In Kiangsu Province, on the Yangtse River," the girl with the pigtails replied, with a slight note of surprise at my ignorance.

"Oh, we have just come from Kiangsu," I said, trying to redeem myself for both my less than adequate geographic knowledge and my clumsy Mandarin. "We've been visiting Soochow and Yangchow. Is Nantong just as beautiful? If so, we should have visited it before coming up here."

I noticed then that the form-fitting purple and beige vest the girl was wearing was hand-knitted and that it hugged her well-shaped figure very fetchingly. However, the two long braided pigtails she had conferred an air of guilelessness and innocence.

"Afraid not," the girl said. "Nantong's noted mainly for textiles and ship-building."

"So you're like us, just a visitor to Peking. What made you choose Peking for a visit? It's a long way from Nantong. Had you been here before?"

"I didn't choose." The girl gave another of her cheerful laughs. "Coming here was a prize for demonstrating sound leadership qualities in my unit of the Communist Youth League at home."

My ears pricked up immediately. Here I was, face to face with two agreeable children of the Revolution, Communists in the making, inheritors of China's ancient culture! Or at least what was left of it after the whole-scale destruction of the Cultural Revolution. It seemed too good an opportunity to miss. I wanted to discover what had animated them so far in their lives and what vision they had for their country in the new but uncertain quest for modernisation.

"Congratulations!" I cried. "Does the Youth League have a full programme for you here? Or are you free to do whatever you like?" The thought came to me that our entire group would be delighted to invite them for dinner for the chance of talking to them.

"No, I've no fixed programme. I'm staying with my eldest sister and her husband. They're stationed here; with the People's Liberation Army. She's a dancer and he's an actor and film director."

"A dancer and a film director, in the People's Liberation Army?" The situation seemed more and more pregnant with possibilities.

"Yes. They're both in the Cultural Division."

"I don't suppose it's against the rules, is it, for a bunch of visiting Hong Kong compatriots to invite you and your sister and her husband to a casual meal with us? We're keen to know more about our motherland."

"I'm not sure."

The Audrey Hepburn lookalike then intervened.

"Please excuse us, uncle, but we're running behind schedule," she said. "The wretched animals took so long to do what we wanted that we haven't explored the Great Wall yet. We had better get going. Hope you have better luck with the camels."

It sounded like a polite brush-off. It was on the tip of my tongue to persist, to suggest exploring the Great Wall with them. But it would appear too unseemly for two middle-aged men to be running after two teenaged girls and importuning them. So we said our farewells and watched the girls making their way back onto the Great Wall.

Chia and I really had no interest in taking pictures with camels. We gave the girls a few minutes' head start before returning to the Great Wall ourselves. When we got there, we saw them going in one direction. We headed in the opposite direction.

As we gazed far into the steppes and its empty silences, I could not help being humbled by the insignificance of man and his puny works. One could detect something elemental in that emptiness, as if it were a glimpse of nature in the raw, free, infinite and eternal. It was a feeling I had never encountered within the confines of any city.

* * *

After Chia and I had reached the limits of our section of the wall and had soaked in the atmosphere, we headed back to where our tour bus had been parked. On the way back, we met Ip Shing-Ki — Yeuk-Lam's eldest son — and a couple of others in our party coming our way.

"Come quickly, David," Shing-Ki cried excitedly. "We've been searching for you. My mother has made friends with a couple of very beautiful Chinese girls. Since you're the only bachelor in our group, this is your chance."

"Ah, I've already met them," I replied nonchalantly. "One of them's from Peking and the other from Nantong, right? My reputation with women hasn't been built on thin air, you know."

"But the girls are heading to the Ming tombs with us; and to have lunch with us as well."

"Oh! That puts a slightly different complexion on things."

When we got back to the gathering place for our group, I noticed that the girls were already getting on like a house on fire with several women members of the group. Suze's outgoing and matronly presence must have reassured the girls. They had already exchanged names and were taking pictures together. The girl with the dark glasses was known as Liu Hung while the one with the braids was called Chiu Kit.

I surmised that the quick warming of relations was not solely due to their all being females. There might have been aberrations during the Cultural Revolution but the two girls had clearly reverted to the age-old deference given to those older than themselves. No doubt they addressed the ladies in our group as aunties. Their openness in answering questions had been impressive as well. The women in our group must have made mental comparisons of how less considerate of elders the young in Hong Kong were.

On approaching, Chia and I introduced ourselves and expressed our delight that we would all be lunching together at the Ming tombs. The girls respectfully addressed us as uncles and asked if we had managed to get satisfactory photographs with the camels. I lied outrageously, pretending we got some marvellous snapshots.

We then all straggled our way to our waiting tourist bus.

*   *   *

But, as the womenfolk tried to usher the pair of young girls onto our bus, our tour guide asked the girls to step aside with him to exchange a few words.

I immediately smelt trouble and indicated quickly to Yeuk-Lam and Chia in Cantonese that we should stick to the girls like glue.

The guide moved a few steps away from the bus and the girls followed him. But the three of us trailed closely behind as well. The guide's inability to talk with the girls without witnesses disconcerted him. In the end, he elected to address us instead of the girls.

"The two girls are not allowed to travel with us on our bus," he said. "It is against the rules for local citizens to travel on tourist buses meant for outsiders."

"But we're not outsiders," I declared. "We're compatriots from Hong Kong, part of the Chinese nation, of the same flesh and blood. We're here to strengthen our bonds with our motherland. Why should you stand in the way?"

"We don't want to cause any embarrassment, uncle," one of the girls said quickly. "We can take a public bus."

"No, you're welcome to come with us and you should," Yeuk-Lam interjected. "We've paid for this bus to take us to the Ming tombs. There's plenty of spare room in it."

Then turning to the guide, he added: "These two young comrades want to go to the Ming tombs as well. It would be a waste of money and scarce resources if we were to force them to take public transport. It is only common courtesy that we offer them a lift and it should be quite in order for them to accept such an offer."

"I didn't make the rules," the guide retorted. "My job is to obey them."

It was now Chia's turn to intervene. "Do you realise that the gentleman who has just spoken is a member of the Kwangtung Provincial People's Congress?" he said. "If you would like him to speak to your superior, that can easily be done. The central government has directed the country be open to the world, to learn more efficient ways of doing things. If your work unit wishes to contradict directives from the central authorities, then that would appear to be a matter which ought to be brought to the attention of those higher authorities."

It took a moment or two for the guide to weigh Chia's bluff. Meanwhile, the women in our group had also grown curious over what was delaying our departure. So a number of them got off the bus to find the reason.

Seeing himself outnumbered and the tone of the exchanges slipping onto dangerous political terrain, the guide gave in. With poor grace, he allowed the girls to board the bus.

En route, much of the chit-chat was conducted only by the women who happened to be sitting next to the two girls. The guide sulked.

* * *

The physical shape of the Ming tombs in the form of a burial mound, and their individual locations in compliance with the accepted principles of *fung shui* or geomancy, were set by the first Ming Emperor, Chu Yuan-Chang. His mausoleum was located in Nanking, however, where his capital had been.

By the time the third Ming Emperor, Yongle, came along, he chose to move his capital to Peking, a place he had been familiar with. While he adhered to the fundamental principles of *fung shui* set down by his father, he chose for his own tomb a peaceful and pristine valley by the side of Tianshou Mountain, approximately 26 miles from the centre of Peking.

Yongle was probably the most visionary and ambitious of all the Ming Emperors. When he eventually came to the throne as the third Ming Emperor, he saw the need to restore the confidence of the nation in its own illustrious history after being subjugated by the Mongols. He therefore began a massive programme of construction, beginning with the Temple of Heaven where the annual ceremonies the emperor, as the Son of Heaven, was required to perform. Then he tore down the palace built by the Mongols to build his own magnificent Forbidden City.

He was not forgetful of the security of his own people against the ravages from the northern barbaric tribes. So he embarked upon repairing the Great Wall and extending it by a further third of its original length. Such constructions required the feeding of millions of builders and artisans, which meant having to ship sufficient food and other building materials from the south of the country. This in turn necessitated the dredging and upgrading of the Grant Canal with 36 new locks to facilitate transportation.

Not satisfied with those projects, Yongle also wanted to expand trade and gather to China more tributary states so that the country could be acknowledged as the dominant power in the world. He therefore caused a massive expansion in naval power, under the command of an Islamic admiral named Cheng Ho. Under Cheng were many brave and daring seafarers like Hong Pao, Chau Man, Chau Wen and Yang Ching.

The vast armada that came to be built plied the oceans of the world under their leadership and mapped the distant corners of the globe long before Columbus, Magellan, Cook and other European mariners came on the scene.

Another important feature about their missions was that they were ordered by their emperor "to treat distant people with kindness". This was in marked contrast to some accounts left on the wanton cruelties inflicted on native peoples after the arrival of later Western navigators and explorers.

And, if one had been given a mainly Eurocentric colonial education — as I had been — one could pass through the whole system without ever hearing a whisper of the exploits of Cheng Ho and his fellow Chinese explorers.

When Yongle hosted a Lunar New Year banquet in Peking in 1421, no fewer than 28 heads of state had been there to *kowtow* before him. The kings of England, France, Castile and Portugal were not invited, however, because the emperor had thought that their countries had nothing worthwhile to contribute to China.

In 1420, Yongle began designing his own mausoleum in the valley he had chosen. He died in 1424 and was buried there with an extravagant ceremony.

With his passing, however, China turned inward. The Ming emperors who succeeded him considered that too much resources had been spent on the foreign expeditionary and scientific missions which could be better spent at home in the best Confucian traditions - on improving the lives of ordinary people.

The voyages by Cheng Ho and his commanders were therefore brought to an end and their logs and observations largely expunged from official records.

Foreign trade and travel were banned. The Chinese settlements, which had been established in Africa, Australia, New Zealand and North and South America, were abandoned to their own devices.

Two fascinating accounts of what Cheng Ho and his illustrious companions had achieved during Yongle's reign were subsequently to be popularised for Western audiences in the early 2000s by two scholarly and well-received books written by Gavin Menzies, namely, *1421* and *1434*.

After Yongle's passing, 12 other Ming Emperors followed his lead and were buried in adjacent mausoleums. Each mausoleum had two or three courtyards in front of the burial mound. Before reaching a mausoleum, a person would have to pass through a four-mile long Spirit Way, which was supposed to be the path the spirits of the departed emperors would have to follow to enter the afterlife after shedding their mortal coils.

The Spirit Way was lined with huge larger-than-life statues of guardian animals and stout officials to safeguard the tombs. During the Ming Dynasty, a "death zone" of one or two miles surrounded each of the mausoleums. Any unauthorised person found within that zone was liable to be punished by death.

The centuries thus rolled by. By about the mid-1950s, there was some demand in certain quarters of the new Communist government for the tomb of Emperor Yongle, which was naturally the oldest and largest one in the valley, to be excavated. Many archaeologists argued against it, however, fearing that the available scientists, technicians, support staff and financial resources would be insufficient for the undertaking.

Eventually, as a compromise, it was decided that a smaller tomb might be opened on a trial basis. The tomb of the Thirteenth Ming Emperor, Wanli, who reigned from 1602 to 1612, was selected. Excavations began in 1956 and thousands of silk, textile, porcelain and wooden objects were found among the artefacts. But, as feared, proper storage, preservation and recording facilities proved inadequate and many of those relics quickly deteriorated.

A worse fate was to befall the remains of Emperor Wanli and his two concubines about a decade later, however. During the Cultural Revolution, rampaging Red Guards broke into the tomb and burnt the remains of the emperor and his concubines. They then went on to destroy most of the artefacts they found.

Consequently, most of the items currently on display in museums relating to Emperor Wanli's tomb are in fact reproductions.

Today, ten of the Ming tombs in that valley have remained intact and unopened. Public access therefore has been limited to only the three that have been opened so far.

* * *

By the time the bus got to the Ming tombs, the lunch hour was already upon us. So we repaired to the dining facilities right away, leaving the exploration of the Spirit Way and the tombs for after the meal.

Two long rectangular tables, seating about four on either side and placed within speaking distance of each other, had been prepared for us. I was seated between Yeuk-Lam and Chia on one side of the table while on the opposite side Suze played the welcoming hostess with Liu Hung and Chiu Kit on either side of her.

I fear I have no recollection of exactly who else sat where. I was mesmerised by the beauty the two girls present. Liu Hung had taken off her sunglasses and I was pleased to note how without artifice they both were in the presence of a group of total strangers. Their out-going and almost naive way in replying to personal questions flowed as fluently and as unguardedly the kisses of virgins.

The conversation naturally dwelled on the circumstances of the two young girls, who their parents were and what they had been doing in Peking. Apart from Yeuk-Lam and Suze, none of the group had set foot in China for decades. Therefore there was great curiosity over how people in the mainland approached life under a Communist regime. The two girls represented the first opportunity for getting close to any ordinary mainlander.

From the answers given by the girls, we learnt that they were both 18 and had just completed their secondary education. They had met because Liu Hung's father was, like Chiu Kit's eldest sister and her husband, also in the Cultural Division of the People's Liberation Army. Moreover, the three service personnel were all neighbours as well, sharing adjacent homes in one of those traditional Peking courtyard residences known as a *siheyuan*. Since the two girls were both on holiday from school, they soon became friends.

Liu Hung was an only child, while her father was an expert *erhu* player. An erhu was a versatile two-stringed musical instrument of Mongolian origins first introduced into China more than a thousand years ago. The strings were originally made of python skin and the bow of horse hair. It was a sort of Chinese fiddle or violin. However, with an *erhu*, the bow and the instrument were never separated.

Liu Hung had already been selected for admission into the People's Liberation Army, though it was doubtful whether she would follow in her father's musical footsteps. The medical corps might be more likely. Nonetheless, having been selected for admission into the People's Liberation Army was considered an envious achievement by many, for it provided a secure and satisfactory career.

Chiu Kit, on the other hand, was the youngest of four children. Her father was a sub-manager in a government organisation responsible for allocating fuel oil quotas to factories and other public bodies. Her mother was a housewife.

She told us she had seen very little of her eldest sister, Chiu Shu-Ching, because around the time she was born her sister left home to study at the Peking Dance Academy. Back then, Chairman Mao's wife was in charge of developing the socialist culture of the country. Madam Mao therefore had sent spotters all over the land to find youngsters firm of limb and pleasant of visage for training to become dancers. Her eldest sister was thus identified and chosen.

"My sister turned out to be a very accomplished dancer," Chiu Kit elaborated. "She danced so exquisitely that she was asked to do a solo number for Chairman Mao himself. Later, she got inducted into the People's Liberation Army."

A murmur of approbation rippled among her listeners.

"Wow!" somebody said. "That performance for Chairman Mao must have been a great source of pride for your family."

Chiu Kit smiled shyly and gave a tentative nod.

As to her other two siblings, she continued, she had an elder brother who was married to a girl from Nanking, after which he moved there to work as a civil servant. Her remaining elder sister, Siu Wah, married a deck hand working on one of the cargo boats plying up and down the Yangtse River. When liberalisation was announced and after the Paramount Ruler had declared that getting rich was no crime, Siu Wah took that advice and started a small provision store. She was so far doing quite well.

"And what about you?" Suze asked, smiling, apparently much taken by the girl's beauty and her winning ways. "Are you going to join the People's Liberation Army or are you going to start your own business?"

"Neither, auntie," Chiu Kit said. "When my holiday is over, I will return home and wait for a 'work assignment'."

"What does that mean? You've been awarded a prize by the Communist Youth League. Doesn't that confer some kind of advantage? Couldn't you ask to go for further studies?"

"Not really, auntie. To get into a university a person needs to secure very good grades in the national examinations. Mine were not good enough. The competition is fierce and the number of places very limited. But we must all serve the nation in whatever capacity the authorities consider best. After I get home, I will be assured of an appropriate job assignment in any case."

"What kind of job is that likely to be?"

"I'm not sure, auntie. Most probably work in a textile factory. That's what my home town is noted for."

Suze's brow knitted. "You don't mind that?"

"Of course, not, auntie. During school, we've all been often sent to work in the fields and in factories. That is to teach us to value the dignity of labour."

The way in which Chiu Kit accepted whatever fate being arranged for her by others bothered me. I had no idea what the textile industry in Nantong might be like and I doubted whether the girl fully knew either. Textiles had become a major industry the world over, as each nation tried to industrialise. That sector involved many different processes, some of which were far from pleasant. I had been exposed to some of them when I headed the Factory Inspectorate in the Labour Department.

For example, a person might have to work in a blowing room as a bale breaker or in a carding room to separate and assemble loose cotton fibres into yarn for spinning. Or to put yarn through a series of Bunsen burners to rid it of any projecting fibres before turning yarn into grey cloth.

Thereafter, there would be the additional processes of singeing to improve smoothness, scouring with a chemical wash to remove impurities, bleaching to improve whiteness, Sanforising to deal with shrinkage, mercerising to improve lustre and dye affinity, before actually dyeing and printing.

As I cast my mind over the various processes, I heard Suze continuing to quiz Chiu Kit over other options. "Isn't there some other choice you might prefer, like going overseas to study? There must be plenty of universities overseas which would be easier to get into."

"But they are all quite expensive," Chiu Kit replied. "My family will not be able to afford their fees."

Fortuitously, the luncheon dishes began arriving and that put a halt to further discussion on the subject. The gathering thus began eating with relish, but in relative silence.

* * *

Towards the end of the meal, Suze turned to me and asked: "David, universities in Hong Kong are not all that expensive, are they?"

I could visualise at once what must be going through Suze's mind. She was a woman always ready to extend a helping hand to others. She must have taken an instant liking to a girl as bright and intelligent as Chiu Kit. She had mentioned to me once that she had missed not having a daughter of her own. The thought of any girl spending the rest of her life in a textile factory must have been disconcerting for her. I felt sorry for the limited choices available to the young people in China. I wished they were more plentiful. But what alternatives were there, at that particular historical moment?

The young in China had been brought up in an entirely different world. Just as many ordinary Russians after their revolution had been brought up to make sacrifices for the good of their country, to subordinate their individual needs to the more pressing requirements of the nation, so it had been in China after 1949. The young seemed to have adjusted cheerfully to their lot. Was it wise for outsiders to intervene and disturb the equilibrium they had achieved?

They might have been taught to determine right from wrong too simplistically, in hues of black or white. They were bound to shed their innocence in their own good time, to discover that life came mostly in unpredictable shades of grey. During that inevitable journey they would at least have the whole of Chinese history and culture to guide them, whereas their contemporaries in Hong Kong would have to struggle to find their identities after a century and a half of foreign occupation.

"A Hong Kong university would be cheaper than one in Europe or North America," I allowed at last, rather blandly. "But a candidate would still need a reasonable command of English to be admitted."

Turning to Chiu Kit, Suze asked: "Do you know any English?"

The girl shook her head.

"Would you like to learn?"

"Yes, auntie, if I had the chance. Knowing another language is always an accomplishment. But I can't see how I can. English is taught mainly in universities but I have failed to earn myself a place."

"Isn't there any private English tuition you can sign up to in Nantong?"

"None that I know of. Besides, I'll have to be assigned for work. I don't yet know whether I will be assigned a day or a night shift."

Chiu Kit's statement at once renewed my disquiet over her lack of choice. Apart from the rest of my concerns about the repetitive drudgeries in front of some textile machine, a year or two of night shifts would in all probability put an end to her youthful beauty and her rosy cheeks. What would also happen to the *joie de vivre* reflected in her spontaneous laughter? Youth and beauty were such transient things. Petals must inevitably fall from even the most lovely of flowers. My heart felt touched.

Suze's voice cut into my private brooding.

"What would you and your parents say if I were to propose adopting you as my god-daughter? If everybody is agreeable, I can sponsor you to come to Hong Kong to study English. You can then enter a university, if you wish, to study whatever you like. You'd make a wonderful god-daughter, you know. What do you say? I promise you living with me and Uncle Ip will be quite comfortable."

"You are very kind and considerate, auntie, but that would not be possible," Chiu Kit replied. "The government is very strict over granting exit visas to unmarried girls. That's not any reflection on your good intentions. It is just for protection of Chinese girls in general. The government does not want girls to be taken out of our country to be exploited by bad elements on the outside."

"What about a married Chinese girl?" I interjected. "Could she leave?

Would she be granted an exit visa easier?"

"Of course. A married girl has the care and protection of a husband."

"Then the solution is quite simple. If you wish to study abroad, you and I can get married," I declared in a rush of braggadocio. "Then you'll be free to go and study wherever you like."

"But I cannot possibly marry you just like that, uncle," Chiu Kit said. "Girls in China are not allowed to marry till they've reached 20."

"Ah! Another brilliant idea bites the dust, laid low by bureaucratic nannies!" I exclaimed.

A look of perplexity came into Chiu Kit's eyes. Possibly my inadequate Mandarin gummed up my attempt at irony. But I was spared the embarrassment of having to explain further by the timely arrival of the guide, to announce that the post-prandial walk down the Spirit Way was about to begin.

* * *

Since the Rolleiflex brought by the girls was out of order, Chia offered to take whatever photographs they wanted and send the pictures back to them from Hong Kong once they have been developed. The girls happily accepted the offer and Chia began taking snaps as they posed with the various giant statues along the Spirit Way.

I tagged along and, like other members of the group, I took a few pictures with the girls too before we engaged in desultory conversation.

The longer I strolled along with them, the more I became filled with misgivings. My impromptu proposal of marriage, though uttered half in jest, seemed to have washed over Chiu Kit and her friend like water off a duck's back. Could they not see enough absurdity in the whole proposition even to remark upon it? A huge gap obviously existed between our ages. But Chiu Kit chose to refer only to some rule against underaged marriages for girls.

Indeed, she was younger than two of my boys. Had the Communist Youth League trained her not to react to insinuations smacking even of the mildest hint of flirtation?

From left: Liu Hung, Chiu Kit and the author next to one of the guardian officials along the Spirit Way in 1983

She was certainly a beautiful girl, one bound to attract plenty of male attention. Yet she seemed friendly and open even before a group of outside strangers. What kind of young people had China been producing? Too innocent and open-hearted ones? If so, how could they cope with the dog-eat-dog capitalist world that was about to descend upon the country?

In the middle of the 19th century, under the barrels of foreign gunboats, China had been forced to open its territory to foreigners. And they came rushing in with their extraterritorial rights, spheres of influence, most favoured nation clauses, arrogant envoys, military detachments, evangelical Christian sects, drug-dealing merchants, soldiers of fortune, charlatans and mountebanks.

Today, when foreign gunboats and armies were no longer of much account, the country was openly inviting a new wave of foreigners to come in with their latest commercial gimmicks and legalistic tricks.

How could the ordinary Chinese — whose labour and hopes were bound to be cruelly exploited — cope with pyramid selling, Ponzi schemes, counterfeit goods, *caveat emptor*, limited liability, off-balance sheet accounting, manipulations in stock and share prices, rampant insider trading, off-shore shelf companies and tax havens, rigged markets, leveraged buy-outs, asset stripping, trading naked put and call options, fabricated wants through slick advertising and whole farrago of commercial sleights of hand in a frenzied hunger for profits at whatever human cost?

Chinese leaders were doubtless looking to Hong Kong's perverted and mixed economic model for replication in the mainland. But the folks in the mainland were much less wary and sophisticated compared with the people in Hong Kong.

Innocent people would inevitably get hurt. So too would the traditional Chinese instincts towards frugality and thrift. Every crack and crevice opened up in the established mainland order through Western commercial machinations would provide fertile nooks for the weeds of corruption to sprout and flourish.

But on the other hand, the Chinese leadership was faced with an invidious dilemma. Its experiments with austerity and egalitarianism had failed to produce the capital formation needed for the country to push forward with its programmes. Should another experiment be made, to loosen the ideological constraints placed by Marxism, Leninism and Mao Tse-Tung Thought?

The Paramount Ruler Deng Xiao-Ping had posed the question of whether a cat was black or white mattered, so long as it could catch mice. He had further declared that no matter to what degree the country opened up to the outside and admitted foreign capital, the relative effect on the country would be small. Neither of those developments would affect the socialist ownership of the means of production.

Presumably, the Chinese leadership must have given sufficient weight to the uncontrollable nature of human greed. It was like a genie in a bottle. Once released, it could never be put back inside. Had Marx not warned of what he called contradictions in certain aspects of the capitalistic economic system? Could any the system be adopted without also embracing some of its more obvious flaws as well?

Whatever might be in the minds of the country's leadership, the hopelessly innocent like Chiu Kit and Liu Hung would be heading for rough rides. It would be futile to attempt to warn them, to put them on their guard. Their ears were untuned to the confusing cacophony of capitalistic duplicities.

It would be like trying to explain Planck's Constant or the Copenhagen interpretation of quantum theory to schoolgirls who had yet to begin their elementary physics. In the final analysis, the citizens of every nation had to rely on the wisdom of their leaders to advance their lot. Or else to suffer the consequences of their lack of wisdom and foresight.

Suze's notion of bringing Chiu Kit to study in Hong Kong would serve little practical purpose. The maladies of the neoliberal economic order had heavily infected the entire commercial life of the colony. Neither its sophisticated inhabitants nor its current colonial masters had sufficient foresight to try and find effective remedies. Those who could make a positive difference had largely disappeared from the scene.

The cut-throat situation evidently suited the existing elite. The knavishly inclined would simply exploit legal loopholes for their own enrichment while the mediocrities shrugged their shoulders and claimed — quite falsely — that defects were inherent in every laissez-faire or open market system.

As I watched the rest of the party strolling happily along the lengthy Spirit Way, snapping camera shutters, I slowly became alarmed and depressed. The thoughts I had been entertaining did not appear to have entered their consciousness at all. The path we were trundling along was supposed to be the one spirits of departed emperors had to take to enter their afterlife. Had it not occurred to any of them that the path we were all blithely taking might also lead us to another kind of doom?

After striding along in my own silence for a while, I heard Chiu Kit addressing me out of the blue: "Uncle, are you in the same business as Uncle Ip?"

"No, Uncle Ip imports Chinese fruits, vegetables and eggs for sale in Hong Kong," I replied. "He has an export monopoly, granted by Kwangtung provincial authorities. A monopoly is always something everybody tries to get, by hook or by crook, under every form of economic system. I'm not half as fortunate, I fear, for I'm in the much more competitive exporting business. Many others are all trying to sell the same Hong Kong mass consumer goods to Europe and North America."

"What sort of goods are those, Uncle? Can't other countries make such goods for themselves?"

"Yes, but not as cheaply and as profitably. I sell things like toys, shoes, handbags, fireworks, garments and the like. For example, the denim shirt and trousers I'm wearing now are very popular in America. So they buy them from us because we can make them faster and cheaper."

"I see. Those clothes look nice on you, Uncle."

"Thank you. Your knitted vest looks very nice too. Did you knit it yourself?"

"Yes."

"Splendid! No doubt you selected the colour combination as well. I'd say you have the makings of a good fashion designer."

Suddenly, in the midst of that banal conversation, a revelation struck me like a slap across the face. All that internal agonising about the fate of the two girls was just a subconscious pose, an elaborate masquerade, to evade facing up to the truth. What was really at issue was the utter futility of the life I had lived so far!

When I had been their age, I was filled not only with the same foolish optimism about the future they displayed. At least their ambitions were modest. They merely wanted to serve their country in whatever capacity assigned to them, whereas I had at their age entertained an overweening conceit about my own abilities.

I had told my mother in Canton that I was minded to enrol in the Whampoa Military Academy so that I could one day put an end to the chaos and civil wars plaguing China. I would, with gun or pen, right the injustices in the world.

My mother had reacted to my outpouring of hot air with ridicule. She told me I had best learn some shorthand and typing and get a job clerking for the Chinese Maritime Customs or some foreign trading hong. My pride had been woundingly crushed by her low assessment of my capabilities.

Now, at the age of 53, it seemed my mother had been right after all. My ambitions had faded like mirages. All the promises I had made to myself and to others had remained unfulfilled. What had I actually achieved after seven years as a journalist, two as a teacher, 20 as a bureaucrat and a year in the commercial swamp? A fatter bank account but otherwise only a handful of dust! And what lay ahead for me was only more years of indentured money-grubbing servitude. It seemed like a form of torture that was almost worse than death.

An unbearable combination of anguish and self-pity filled my heart. Man, from the moment he was born, was destined to die. But why must circumstances be so often stacked against him, so that he ended up being squashed like some gnat against the sky? At this belated stage, my own future looked depressingly bleak. Was there still any remote chance for redemption?

I sensed Chiu Kit saying something I could not catch. I reached desperately for the lifeline of that totally pointless conversation. I told myself I needed to keep talking to prevent myself from slipping further into even darker realms.

So I asked carelessly: "How many more days do you have in Peking?"

"Ten, Uncle," she replied. "And you?"

"Only two more, I'm afraid. We'll be visiting that 800-year-old Lukou Bridge made of stone tomorrow morning."

I had it on the tip of my tongue to invite her and her friend to join our excursion. Their gaiety and optimism would provide a counterpoint to my own gathering gloom. But then I remembered we had a lunch to attend with Peking officials.

The meal was initially meant as an official welcome for Yeuk-Lam. But when the officials discovered that Yeuk-Lam had arrived with many family members and relatives, the whole group got invited.

If the girls were to come, it would be too awkward to disentangle them at the end of the morning, not to mention the risk of another confrontation with the guide. So I said instead: "Have you been to that old bridge yet?"

"No, Uncle, not yet."

"Oh, you must see it before you return home. I've read that throughout its 870-odd feet length, it is covered on both sides with hundreds of sculptured lions, in different sizes and poses. The exact number appears to be in dispute but the consensus is in the low 400s. I'm looking forward to seeing it myself. Marco Polo was so mightily impressed when he saw it that he praised it extravagantly in his book. That's why many foreigners keep referring to it as the Marco Polo Bridge."

"I didn't know what Marco Polo said. But I've been taught that the Lukou

Bridge was where the war of resistance against the Japanese started on July 7th in 1937."

"Yes, it's important to learn from history. Otherwise we run the risk of repeating past mistakes."

*　　*　　*

After the group had visited one of the Ming tombs, the bus took us back to Peking. During the journey, Suze promised the girls she would collect all the photographs group members had taken with them and would forward them from Hong Kong once they were ready.

The girls were dropped off close to their homes. When the moment of parting came, Chiu Kit offered me a smile of radiant ignorance and a respectful handshake. They struck me oddly, like unexpected thrusts of a dagger. Oh, to be so young and so blissfully ignorant again, with most of life waiting ahead, still to unfold!

Then it came to me that I had never really enjoyed that joyful state of expectancy and innocence. I had always felt as if I had emerged from my mother's placenta already tainted with wariness and distrustfulness of the world I was being released into.

I sighed quietly over my reflections, as our bus headed back to our hotel.

CHAPTER 9

Suze the Matchmaker

A COUPLE OF WEEKS after returning from the China holiday, I handed Suze copies of all the photographs Chia Chi-Pui had taken of Chiu Kit and Liu Hung, for onward transmission to the girls concerned. Then I left for one of those periodic palm-pressing pilgrimages to the corporate shrines of Li & Fung's major customers in North America and Europe. En route, I managed to squeeze in a couple of days for a side-trip to Vancouver, to visit my mother and my sister Mabel.

By the time I had finished my commercial rituals, I had been deprived of a decently-cooked Chinese meal for so long that upon arriving home I immediately availed myself of Ip Yeuk-Lam's standing invitation to lunch with his family on Sundays at the Hong Kong Chinese General Chamber of Commerce club.

Yeuk-Lam, being an understanding friend, was also well acquainted with some of my other weaknesses. He had thus arranged a *mah-jong* game with our favourite partners for after lunch to assuage my other deprivation.

During the course of the meal, Suze reported that she had received a letter from Chiu Kit, thanking the various members of the tour group for the photographs taken with herself and Liu Hung.

"It was a very well-written letter," Suze remarked. "Surprising too, for it was couched in some of the pre-revolutionary formalities used by the young when addressing their elders. Showed good breeding. I had not expected that from someone born and brought up in the mainland after the revolution."

"Perhaps she was just making allowances for our backward and unenlightened condition," I chuckled. "How has her work assignment worked out?"

"Not terribly well, I fear. She's been sent to a weaving factory, working a night shift, from midnight till whenever the day shift was supposed to come on."

"Oh, dear, what rotten luck! But then, I suppose that's a normal assignment for neophytes. Somebody has to work the unsociable hours."

"Such a pity," Suze said. "Such a pretty girl too."

"Yes, a great pity," I concurred.

"She'd make someone a very good and attractive wife one day," Suze observed, with a sigh.

* * *

After the meal was over, the other participants, young and old alike, dispersed for their different Sunday programmes, leaving Suze, Yeuk-Lam and myself to chat among ourselves pending the arrival of the *mah-jong* partners.

Suddenly, apropos nothing at all, Suze said: "I feel so sorry for Chiu Kit. Such a bright and delightful girl. I wish there was something I could do, to give her a wider choice in life, rather than spending the best part of it in a weaving factory."

"When we met her, she had appeared satisfied with her assigned lot," I said. "She's from an entirely different world. If she were here, I'm not sure she would relish the uncertainties and risks associated with our choices."

"All the same, it seems such a terrible waste of her potential. Can't you think of some means of helping her?"

"What? How can I alter her situation?"

"Well, you did offer to marry her. You must have liked her enough at first sight to make such an offer . . . ."

I interjected at once. "Remember it was *you* who started out on the business of adopting her as a 'dry' daughter and bringing her to study in Hong Kong."

"Yes, I was taken by her beauty, her youth and her general cheerfulness. She was quite shapely too, you must have noticed."

"Suze, my offer of marriage was just a facile boast, made on the spur of the moment. By the time we got to the Ming Tombs she had forgotten all about it.

"Besides, I'm not a cradle-snatcher, you know. The last time I got involved with an 18-year-old, I ended up with a terrible marriage and the responsibility for bringing up three kids on my own. I'm not going to head down that path again. That girl's younger than two of my boys. If we were back in the age when parents selected mates for their children, I might have considered her for one of my sons. But for myself? No. I've only met her that one time, over a few short hours. To pursue a woman on so fleeting an impression would be almost as silly as chasing after someone whom one had just caught sight of crossing a road."

"In marriage, it is compatibility that really counts, not differences in age," Suze asserted. "As a teenager, she would be exactly like freshly prepared clay, to be shaped into whatever form you might fancy. There's no time to be lost. You're single and on your own now, and you're not getting any younger. A lonely middle age is not a happy state to find yourself. You'll soon need someone to take care of you."

I shook my head. "I'm neither a potter nor a sculptor; and I'm far from being adventurous enough for such a lark. None of us knows anything much about the girl, apart from her being a leading light in her unit of the Communist Youth League. And you've all heard her say that girls in China are not allowed to marry till they've reached 20."

"That would fit in perfectly; it'll give you time to get to know each other better and to avoid any rash or precipitous moves. If you're so minded, Yeuk-

Lam and I should be able to find a way for the two of you to meet again. What do you say?"

I shook my head again. Yeuk-Lam had a look of pure amusement on his face. What a rascally friend he was, I thought, finding delight in my discomfiture. He should have come to my rescue, damn it! I shall certainly exact my revenge at the *mah-jong* table!

Fortuitously, at that point Lo Yuk-Chuen, alias Sixth Eldest Brother, turned up for the *mah-jong* game. An exchange of salutations duly followed, causing the conversation to veer in a different direction.

* * *

It was amazing, in retrospect, how innocent conversations with well-intentioned friends could play such havoc with one's disposition and sentiments. I understood their concerns well and appreciated them. They were fearful that my erratic playing-the-field style of romantic engagements might lead me into an empty and lonely old age. That was a prospect that I had not really pondered; my life had been too filled with more pressing exigencies.

After that day, both Yeuk-Lam and Suze had continued to nudge me about my precarious situation. Suze, in particular, mentioned Chiu Kit's potential as a suitable mate and sang her praises whenever given the opportunity. The two had apparently been engaged in a lively correspondence, like pen pals of old.

Life had certainly not turned out to be easy for the poor girl. She reportedly had to cycle for miles in the dark, under all weather conditions, to get to and from work. But why should that misfortune be any of my business?

Suze's references to her youth and malleability triggered an echo of the arguments that had been put forward by my ex-in-laws when I told them after a year of marriage to their daughter that it would be best if we both sought a divorce and went our separate ways. Our personalities had been so constructed as to clash.

But they had pleaded that Man-Ying was their only daughter. She was young and immature; I ought to give her another chance. I was much older than she and there was much that I could teach her. I had kicked around the world and was familiar with its devious ways. Their daughter, on the other hand, had led a sheltered and pampered existence. She should come to her senses once she had matured further, through assuming more family responsibilities. Why not try having another child, they suggested.

I had given way to their entreaties; very much against my own better judgement. And what did I get in return? A ten-year marital sentence with no hope for parole.

Every counsel of reason now was set against any involvement with another teenaged girl. Chiu Kit might be young and beautiful but I had not felt that spontaneous intellectual or spiritual fizz with her that I had experienced with Sharlee and Barbara and the Stanford girl with whom I had once danced on a certain Californian moon-night long ago. The memory of having written a poem to her in exchange for a gift of two volumes of plays by Sartre still loomed as fresh in my mind as if it had been yesterday.

Compared with them, what lay behind the youth and beauty of Chiu Kit? A barely formed personality that was impenetrable and unknown. She might well be just a Socialist version of Ping. At least with Ping, her terms of trade were open and up front. A budding paragon in the Communist Youth League was a different matter. Such a one sent forth only question marks.

And yet, there was something about Suze's urgings which appealed to my vanity. What if I could pull it off something like Professor Higgins in Shaw's *Pygmalion*? It would be interesting and challenging to discover how a product of a new Chinese Communist system would react to the material blandishments of a consumerist society.

Doing a Professor Higgins would be a tall order, however, going well beyond a simple matter of linguistics. What kind of Chinese history and culture had the girl been taught? Probably not much before the Long March and Chairman Mao's proclamation of 1949. And her exposure to Western thinking would be in all probability quite limited, to just a few choice quotes from Marx and Lenin.

That would be par for the course for the younger generation in both China and Hong Kong. They had been so thoroughly blinded by unsatisfactory educational systems they must be almost beyond redemption. Could they recognise any truth adumbrated by Chuang Tzu or Mencius or Thomas à Kempis even if it hit them full in the face? Hardly. To expect them to develop a contempt for the vanities of the world and its ephemeral joys had to be too much to expect.

Lying beyond my own vanity were also certain middle-aged insecurities. It was one thing to go hunting for a wife in the 1970s for the sake of my children. But now that I was utterly unattached to children, a wife had to be a woman suited to my own temperament. Even if Chiu Kit proved malleable, getting her up to speed emotionally and intellectually would take far more time and effort than I had at my disposal.

Perhaps, buried deeper in my psyche, I also shared Suze's yearning for a daughter. I never had one. I had been quite disappointed I had never managed to build up much rapport with any of my sons. They had sibling rivalries and I had to play a disciplinarian during those conflicts.

It was also possible that I had absorbed too idealised a version from those ancient legends of daughters selling themselves into slavery or prostitution for the sake of giving a deceased parent a decent burial. Filial piety was becoming an endangered concept in these modern individualistic times.

In that context, having Chiu Kit as an adoptive daughter and carer — rather than as a wife — might make a little sense, if only it could somehow be worked through the bureaucracies on both sides of the border. Someone with her cheerful disposition would be a great plus should either my mother or my father decide to spend a spell in Hong Kong during the autumn of their lives. She could attend to them much better than I ever could. She would be a boon for myself too, should I suddenly be struck by another of those bouts of acute pancreatitis.

Her lively disposition would, in addition, provide some relief for my soul-destroying commercial preoccupations. Serving a colonial bureaucracy had previously enabled me to pretend to myself that I was working towards some larger social purpose. Now I had become just another money-grubber in a sterile and alienated city, it was disheartening to face the reality of serving only Mammon. Having someone to vent my frustrations to would be quite comforting.

And, at the end of the day, when time came for me to shed my mortal coil, having someone sympathetic on hand would at least spare me the fate of passing on to the next world entirely alone. I could not visualise any of my sons being filial enough to return to fulfil that role.

Thus I tottered mentally through all those muddled motives and conflicting sentiments as I considered Suze's suggestion for engaging further with Chiu Kit.

But to cut a long story short, let me just state simply that at the first blush of spring in 1983 Suze, Yeuk-Lam and myself boarded a plane in Hong Kong to spend a long weekend in Shanghai.

* * *

As the crow flies, the distance between Shanghai and Nantong, the home of Chiu Kit, was not very far. The two towns just happened to lie on opposite sides of the Yangtze River estuary. But the transportation infrastructure back then was such that it required at least a three-hour journey to travel between the two places.

During the first decades of the 20th century the people living in the two cities were also deeply separated by their histories, mindsets, culture, aspirations and attitudes towards life. The inhabitants of Nantong were generally stolid and conservative; those of Shanghai tended to be flamboyant, prone to taking risks and greedy for gain.

The origins of Nantong went back to the Spring and Autumn period in Chinese history, around 500 BC. Its minor city status was only upgraded in 958, to that of an independent prefecture. Its deep water port and its connection to internal navigation channels made it a vital centre for trade. Its inhabitants had long engaged themselves in agriculture, mainly rice and cotton. As a consequence they also had a thriving industry in textiles, particularly in its blue calico.

It became the birthplace of modern Chinese industrialisation late in the Ching Dynasty because of one of its local sons by the name of Chang Jian. Chang was the first scholar from the town to ever secure the top position in the National Imperial Examinations. He thus gained high office.

He was a sentimental and philanthropic man by nature. After acquiring fame and fortune, he never forgot his home town. He founded in 1899 the first cotton mills in Nantong. Thereafter he formed an industrial complex which included the production of oil, flour, silk and wine. He also started schools and orphanages and homes for the aged.

His home town never forgot him either. By the time of the Revolution of 1911, the locals already commonly referred to their city as "Chang Jian's Kingdom". Some of his descendants had remained very much a power in that city ever since.

* * *

Compared with Nantong, Shanghai was a Johnny-come-lately. Its history as a small fishing and agricultural village went back only about a thousand years. It was recognised as a city only in 1291, under the Yuan Dynasty, and it had no city wall till the Ming Dynasty, when raids by Japanese pirates forced it to build one.

It was only after the First Opium War with Britain and the subsequent establishment of foreign concessions that the city began to develop into an economic and financial powerhouse. At its height, the city was responsible for handling half the imports and exports of China.

Chinese weakness in the mid-19th century caused foreign powers to demand territorial concessions to further their trade in opium, silk, tea and other commodities. The British led the charge in 1845, demanding to establish themselves in an area south of the Soochow Creek, an old outlet for the overflow of seasonal waters from Lake Tai, and bounded on the right by the Whampoa River, one of the tributaries of the Yangtze River. The United States did likewise in 1848, seeking a slice north of Soochow Creek. France followed in 1849, securing an area squeezed between the British concession to the north and the old Chinese walled city on the south. Other powers made their own land grabs.

Although all the concessions remained technically under Chinese sovereignty — for the foreign powers continued to pay ground rent to the Chinese — none of those enclaves subjected themselves to Chinese law. They ran their own administrations using their own laws. Military detachments were brought in to demonstrate their power. Their merchants and priestly classes soon followed.

The protracted Taiping Rebellion between 1850 and 1864, and the bloodlust it engendered, complicated the situation and had enduring consequences. While the British and the Americans initially remained neutral, the French supported the Ching government. Although the foreign occupied territories around Shanghai had been left relatively untouched by the fighting, they nevertheless had to accept the presence among them of a criminal and triad offshoot known as the Small Swords Society.

In 1861, the United States and most of the other foreign powers agreed to a British initiative to join their concessions together to form an International Settlement, to be administered by a Municipal Council. The French, however, preferred to retain control over their own concession.

By the 1880s, the British-dominated Municipal Council had secured monopolistic powers to supply gas, electricity and water in the International Settlement, in addition to powers over taxation, road repairs and refuse disposal. It also regulated the sale of opium and the running of brothels.

But with growing prosperity, entrepreneurs, investors, refugees, chancers, fraudsters, criminals and soldiers of fortune flooded in. The size of the city grew rapidly, till it became about four times the size of the original walled city. By 1936 Shanghai — divided in rule and poorly run as it was — had become one of the largest cities in the world, with a population of about three million.

During the course of the city's expansion, refugees and immigrants from other Chinese provinces rushed in for a share of the perceived cake. They formed themselves into "native place" associations or guilds, both for their own protection and to exercise their collective power. This sometimes led to bloody results.

Immigration over all parts of the city operated haphazardly at best. That enabled another significant group of outsiders to flood in — the White Russians following the Bolshevik Revolution of 1917. They numbered around 35,000, rendering them the largest group of Europeans in Shanghai. They were relatively poor, however, and were looked down upon by the more imperialistic Europeans. Nonetheless, the Russian refugees did introduce to the emerging Chinese petty bourgeoisie certain aspects of Western culture, in music and ballet. A significant number of their women, however, had to end up as kept mistresses or courtesans.

Chinese intellectuals, revolutionaries, reformers and rebels also sought to pursue their individual agendas in the city, for they — like the criminal triads — saw jurisdictional grey areas suited to their purposes. They could settle scores with political enemies by whatever nefarious means they might choose.

The activities of the worst of those coming into the city, however, soon turned it into a grotesque and dystopian entity, where human lives were cheap, assassinations and murders commonplace, bribery and corruption a given, and group loyalties as changeable as socks. Hand in hand with such developments were the rise of racism, narcissism, hedonism, debauchery, class struggles and the catering for every conceivable form of human vice.

For example, the highest ranking Chinese detective in the French Concession was a man known as Pockmarked Huang. He ran on the side an establishment called the Great World Amusement Palace, where opium-smoking, gambling and prostitution were freely available. He used as his enforcers members of the notorious Green Gang, a latter day triad offshoot of the Small Swords Society.

The head of the Municipal Police in the International Settlement admitted that triad members had infiltrated his force, so much so that he was powerless to intervene when mobsters stormed the Shanghai Stock Exchange and suspended trading till their demands for dues or protection money were fully met.

Following the Japanese victory in the First Sino-Japanese War in 1894-5, Japan also muscled into Shanghai, sending the largest military contingent among the great powers to be stationed in the International Settlement.

That development not only upset the political equations within the Municipal Council but also portended the arrival of the economic might of Japanese investors and industrialists. That, in turn, created new flash-points of tension between two ancient enemies, between the Japanese setting up new enterprises in China and the Chinese working in them.

Concurrently, Chinese patriots of various persuasions began using the city to propagate their differing versions for rejuvenating their country. The May 4th Movement had already erupted following the perceived unfairness under the Treaty of Versailles of handing over to Japan certain of the former

German privileges and possessions in China.

While some Chinese advocated reforms, others sought a more radical Marxist solution for the ails of the nation. The Chinese Communist Party was formed in Shanghai in 1921 and their activists set about forming trade unions for the inevitable proletarian revolution to come.

In May of 1925, for example, a strike was called by Chinese workers at a Japanese cotton mill in Shanghai. Eight worker representatives were sent to negotiate with the management. Somehow a fracas occurred and one of the worker representatives was killed by the Japanese. When the Municipal Council failed to prosecute the Japanese, mass demonstrations broke out. The Municipal Council police initially tried to dampen the demonstrations by arresting 15 of their leaders and holding them for trial.

That move only infuriated the wider Chinese community. There was no Chinese representation on the Municipal Council at that time; representation did not actually come till 1928. When the number of protestors increased and the atmosphere became more hostile, the British-led police panicked and opened fire, killing nine and wounding many others. Afterwards, the two British officers who had ordered firing on the demonstrators suffered no greater penalty than being asked to resign.

Those killings ignited the first major anti-imperialist movement in China, sparking strikes, boycotts of British and Japanese goods and large demonstrations in towns and cities all over the land. Shooting of demonstrators occurred in other places too, most notably in Canton, where 50 students and cadets from the Whampoa Military Academy were slaughtered by British and French forces when they tried to storm the British and French Concessions on Shameen. About 120 others were wounded.

Strikes and demonstrations against the British also took place in Hong Kong and those dislocations lasted for almost a year. Within the first week, some 50,000 Chinese left the colony to return to Kwangtung Province in protest, almost turning the city into a ghost town. Trade and commerce fell by half and rents by 60%.

Meanwhile, the death of Dr. Sun Yat-Sen in March of 1925 caused General Chiang Kai-Shek to assume the leadership of the Kuomintang. General Chiang had his own plans for bringing the various warlords in China under control. He ended the cooperation between the Kuomintang and the Communist Party and embarked upon his Northern Expedition to unify China in 1926.

Upon reaching Shanghai, he made an agreement with the Green Gang to massacre every Communist they could find. Thus began the White Terror of 1927, during which untold numbers of left-inclined people were summarily killed. It did not matter whether they were in the walled city or in the International Settlement, they were hunted down and murdered. Some were even barbarically boiled alive. Chou En-Lai, one of the leading Communists in the city at the time, escaped only by the skin of his teeth.

Many notable writers had tried to bear witness to some of those raw, greed-driven and demented segments of life in that sprawling and fractured metropolis. Lu Hsun, the author of *The True Story of Ah Q*, had for a time headed a League of Left-Wing Writers and had declared that lies written in ink could not disguise facts written in blood. André Malraux had penned *Man's Estate* to reflect on some aspects of the White Terror. Later, Vicki Baum came along to write *Nanking Road* about another catastrophic episode which befell the city.

But the Kuomintang had a ready answer to the publication of material it considered unwanted. It passed a new censorship law in January of 1931 threatening to punish with life imprisonment or execution anyone producing literature deemed to "endanger the public" or to "disturb public order". By February, 24 Chinese writers had been arrested and executed. For many Chinese at least, writing has turned into a very lethal occupation.

Today, there probably remains ten thousand haunting but untold stories about life during that turbulent period of Shanghai's history. Sadly, those who could recount them at first hand have long since vanished from the scene. Whatever might emerge in the future would only be reconstructions, done by academics and others at third or fourth hand. As Hu Shih, one of the leading intellectuals of the time, had observed: "You cannot write my poems just as I cannot dream your dreams."

Meanwhile in Europe, the rise of Hitler brought tens of thousands of European Jews to seek refuge in Shanghai. The city's lax or almost non-existent immigration rules facilitated their move.

That exodus merely echoed the influx of Sephardic Jews centuries earlier. The timing of their arrival was a matter of some debate but the majority opinion seemed to indicate they settled in Kaifeng in Henan Province as early as the Tang Dynasty, for they had already built a synagogue there by 1163.

Indeed, those early Jews had become so well integrated by 1603 that one of them went to Peking to sit for the Imperial Examinations. While he was there he met the Jesuit missionary Matteo Ricci and that was the first time Westerners became aware of the existence of a Jewish community in China.

Those Jewish settlers progressively married with the local population and today their descendants have been absorbed into Chinese society. They now go by Chinese names and follow a paternal line of descent rather than the Jewish matrilineal one. They have also become physically indistinguishable from the Chinese. The only thing which set them apart was their non-consumption of pork.

Such periodic infusions of alien peoples into Shanghai brought about not only the emergence of a Chinese class of compradores, financiers and bourgeoisie but also a thriving Eurasian community.

By the time of the outbreak of the Second Sino-Japanese War in 1937, Shanghai had already earned such a notorious reputation for decadence in the form of its Art Deco nightclubs, its shopping excesses, its gangsters overseeing drug-trafficking, prostitution, gambling and other human indulgences that the intervention of something as trifling as a war hardly altered its pattern of high octane living and sudden deaths.

*   *   *

Given Shanghai's appalling reputation, Suze had to tread carefully in trying to arrange a rendezvous with Chiu Kit in that town. This was particularly so when Hong Kong itself was being destabilised by wild rumours over the return of the city to Chinese sovereignty.

Suze had initiated her reunion plan by suggesting in a letter to Chiu Kit early in 1983 that they might get together again after the Spring Festival. She indicated that her husband — and possibly one or two of the uncles the girl had already met in Peking — might be going to Shanghai on business. She would accompany her husband there for two or three days if it were convenient for Chiu Kit to join her.

Of course, neither Yeuk-Lam nor Suze had any real need to go to Shanghai. They were simply, for the sake of friendship, trying to prevent my middle-aged bachelorhood from deteriorating into a solitary and lonely old age. No doubt the possibly of giving a bright and endearing young girl from China more options in life had also entered their calculations. Suze had made no reference to me in her correspondence, except for that anonymous reference to "one or two of the uncles" previously encountered in Peking. She had left it to fate to determine whether anything would come from a further meeting between myself and the girl.

She had been quick to add in her letter to Chiu Kit, however, that she would never dream of asking a teenaged girl to visit Shanghai on her own. Therefore her invitation naturally extended to anyone she might wish to accompany her, possibly her elder sister and her husband.

The invitation was duly accepted and a timing agreed. Thus it came about that on a spring afternoon Suze, Yeuk-Lam and myself arrived in Shanghai to register ourselves into the Peace Hotel. Chiu Kit, her sister, Siu Wah, and her husband, Yam Kwan-Lam, arrived shortly thereafter and similarly signed in.

Two inexpensive Japanese wrist watches Suze had brought for the Chiu sisters and a bottle of Chivas Regal whisky for their father set off the reunion on a high note.

The Peace Hotel, located on the Bund in a Western-designed building of 1920s vintage, was run on foreign management lines to cater mainly for tourists and outsiders. In one of its previous incarnations during the Cultural Revolution, it had served as the headquarters of the Shanghai Commune.

* * *

Seeing Chiu Kit again, after the lapse of half a year, turned out a little disappointing for me at first. Although the girl was as cheerful and outgoing as she had been in Peking, her appearance had altered drastically. Her two long braided queues had disappeared and had been replaced by a rather stiff and unfashionable perm. The loss of the queues somehow robbed her of her former allure of innocence. She explained later that she had to cut her braids because they got in the way of her duties at the factory.

Chiu Kit's sister and her husband made a very pleasant but otherwise unremarkable couple. Siu Wah was an attractive woman in her mid-20s who had a disposition as cheerful as her sister's. She was, however, more reserved and less outgoing. She had also begun to thicken around the waist following her birth of a son. Her husband was every bit the stereotype assigned to his peasant pedigree. He projected the dull endurance and persistence of an ox, combined with the docility and submissiveness of a cow.

After the Nantong trio had put their hand luggage away in their rooms, Yeuk-Lam suggested some refreshments in one of the restaurants in the Peace Hotel.

The restaurant exuded a distinctly Western ambience. Once we had been seated, the uniformed waiter handed us an afternoon tea menu featuring

English goodies like scones with clotted cream. I realised at once the Nantong trio would be hopelessly out of their depth.

So I intervened to explain that foreigners had an outlandish way of ruining tea by adding milk and sugar. Unless they wished to give it a try, it might be better for them to go for a soft drink, a fruit juice or a cup of coffee.

They asked what I was having. I said I would settle for coffee. When Yeuk-Lam and Suze indicated likewise, the Nantong guests said they would also follow suit. I said I would order some finger sandwiches and cakes which we could all share.

When the coffee came, it was served up in the small cups customary in Europe. Each cup came with a small spoon for stirring the milk and sugar offered in separate containers. After adding milk and sugar, Yam and Chiu Kit began taking their coffee using their small spoons, as if they were helping themselves to bowls of soup. Yam happened to be sitting next to me; so I put an arm out to deter him, saying that coffee could conveniently be drunk straight from the cup. He did so and the two girls duly followed.

It occurred to me then that the three of them had probably never tried coffee before. How ignorant many Chinese were of the ways of the outside world; years of self-imposed isolation had left them behind. I felt sorry for them and wanted to show them how the rest of mankind had changed — for better or for worse — during their country's determination to become self-reliant.

After our refreshments, we went for a stroll along the Bund. The long row of buildings following European and American designs stood as unhappy relics of a bygone imperialistic age. Shanghai remained a mere shadow of its glitzy pre-war self, however. Its former wickedness was no longer blatantly touted as before. On the other hand, its old air of menace and riskiness was also no longer apparent.

The pedestrians and the cycling traffic on the roads now consisted largely of Chinese, mainly garbed in their ill-shaped boiler suits of blue, grey or green.

The Huangpu River flowing beside the Bund presented its usual miscellany of busy water-borne vessels.

The stroll enabled me to engage Chiu Kit in conversation. I asked how she was settling at work and she said the job was not onerous except for having to cycle in the dark to get to work. But there was the prospect of being able to apply for a change in shift after a year. The only other complaint she had was that her cotton gloves were too inadequate to protect her hands from cold while gripping the handle-bars of her bike during winter.

I promised to secure a pair of fur-lined leather gloves from Canada to send to her.

Later, I asked if she still had an interest in learning English. When she answered in the affirmative, I also promised to send her a Linguaphone set for learning English so that she could familiarise herself with some of the basics in her spare time.

The group thus explored the streets of Shanghai till it found a suitable place for a Chinese dinner.

* * *

We began the next morning's activities by visiting the splendid Yu Garden, one of the largest and most prestigious constructions of its kind in Shanghai. The property was originally owned by the Pan family. One of its patriarchs had been a minister during the Ming Dynasty. When he was about to retire from public life, one of his filial sons decided to build the garden for his father's enjoyment during retirement. Thus its construction begun in 1559.

But the building work got delayed for one reason or another. In the end, the costs for its elaborate features spiralled so much out of control that they ruined the family financially. The property subsequently fell into other hands. Eventually, the garden was opened to the public in 1961 and in 1982 was declared a national monument.

At the Yu Garden, from right: Siu Wah, her husband Yam Kwan-Lam, Ip Yeuk-Lam, Chiu Kit and Suze Ip

After visiting the Yu Garden, I suggested seeing the small Huangpu Park established in 1886 in the International Settlement by the British, because it had been the subject of repeated but not entirely accurate stories designed to stir up Chinese hatred against the British. It was alleged that the park had a sign specifying that dogs and Chinese were not allowed.

When I first heard such stories, I knew they could not be completely accurate. I had grown up among British people and I had no doubt that a strong streak of racism existed in some of them, for I had been a victim of it on a number of occasions. But I also knew that the British were capable of greater subtlety and would not express racism in such crude and blatant terms.

So I investigated the historical facts and discovered that they had been deliberately skewed for emotional impact. The park was originally simply called "Public Gardens" with the racism neatly disguised in the meaning of the word "public".

The use of the park was governed by a set of ten regulations posted at the entrance. The first regulation stated: "The Gardens are reserved for the Foreign Community." That effectively excluded all Chinese and no Chinese was indeed allowed in until 1928.

The secondary insult was delivered underhandedly in the fourth regulation which stated: "Dogs and bicycles are not admitted." The overall effect was that dogs, bicycles and Chinese were all considered by the British of the time as belonging to the same category of things. But no sign had ever existed specifying unequivocally that dogs and Chinese were not allowed into the park, though the intention was abundantly clear.

Yet that fact did not prevent those with ulterior motives from repeating and propagating that inaccurate story, both orally and in print. Perhaps it had been from such incidents that governments and corporations learnt that the precise facts in any situation did not really matter. So long as an assertion was repeated often enough, some segment of the population would accept it as the gospel truth.

Because of the unfortunate associations of the Public Gardens with racism, its name was later changed to Huangpu Park.

* * *

We ended the day with a leisurely meal in a Chinese restaurant that evening, when most of the talk turned on the efforts by Siu Wah and her husband to experiments with the wonders of capitalism. Siu Wah's provision store appeared to be flourishing, depending on a customer base made up largely of friends and neighbours.

Her husband's job working on a river boat enabled him to spot products like ginkgo nuts, edible fungi, dried mushrooms, dehydrated cole and varieties of wine available more cheaply in the remoter towns along the Yangtze River than in Nantong itself. He saw the advantage of buying such products and hauling them home for his wife to sell at a higher profit. Being a member of the crew, he could transport the purchases without cost.

Siu Wah expressed bewilderment over the evening of some of the changes brought about by the government's liberation policy and the seemingly endless ways for citizens to become rich. She said she had often been approached by others to invest her profits from the store into surefire ways of multiplying her gains. But she often could not fully understand how some of the suggested investments could make money more easily than she could with her provision store.

Yeuk-Lam and I took pains to urge her to be very careful over parting with her hard-earned money. Capitalist societies were filled with confidence tricksters with a smooth line of patter offering ingenious ways of getting rich quick. With the opening up to a more market-orientated economy in China, Hong Kong fraudsters were bound to prey upon the innocence of mainland investors. Scammers would be setting up Ponzi schemes or using some form of pyramid selling. We urged Siu Wah to be on her guard.

The next day, we spent the morning exploring some of the older parts of Shanghai. After lunch, we brought our reunion to an end by making our separate journeys back to our respective homes. It was one of the oddities of the technological age that a journey to Nantong, 65 miles away, should take longer than to reach Hong Kong 1,223 miles away.

* * *

After I had sent Chiu Kit a pair of fur-lined leather gloves and her Linguaphone set, we engaged in a steady exchange of letters. The missives were totally pedestrian and banal in nature. Mine enquired about the chances of changing her shift, the progress in her English studies and how Siu Wah's provision store was thriving.

She answered at greater length than I had expected. I sometimes told her of encounters I had with Yeuk-Lam and Suze, whom I had teasingly referred to as her "dry" or adoptive parents. I also mentioned some of the destinations I had to visit during my various business trips.

In spite of the ordinariness of our exchanges, I could detect a warming friendship and a growing respect between the two of us. For my part, my interest rested more on my being an elder overseeing the progress of a likeable member of the younger generation. I had little inclination at that time towards any romantic conquest. My overall feeling was that I still did not know enough about her inner configuration to speculate on whether any meaningful future existed.

I had no idea of the contents of the letters being exchanged between Suze and Chiu Kit. I suspected that Suze must have sensed from them some warming in our relationship because one day, several months after the Shanghai visit, Suze casually suggested: "How about another get-together with Chiu Kit?"

To my own surprise, I replied: "Sure. Why not?"

And so it came about that Suze invited Chiu Kit for another long weekend rendezvous in the ancient town of Wushi, located only a short distance from Nantong. Chiu Kit accepted enthusiastically. She had been to that town before, though it had usually played second fiddle to the more celebrated Yangtze River towns like Soochow and Yangchow. Its dull and rather laid-back reputation, coupled with the enhanced familiarity and confidence in Suze and myself, caused the need for a chaperon for Chiu Kit to be dispensed with.

Wushi nested on the shores of Lake Tai, the second-largest freshwater lake in China. It was founded in 202 BC, allegedly because there used to be a lot of tin in the neighbourhood. Over time, however, the tin got mined to exhaustion and the town then took on a name which literally meant "No Tin".

But the town was crisscrossed with canals — including the Grand Canal — and its population continued to make a living through fishing, agriculture, silk production and as a water transportation hub for domestic trade.

* * *

Suze made arrangements for accommodation at a good lake-side hotel and then accompanied me on her own to Wushi. After meeting up with Chiu Kit, we spent the first day exploring the many delights of the Li Yuen Gardens. Their lotus ponds, rockeries, pavilions and winding walks lined with a wide variety of flowering plants and trees provided endless excitement for the senses as well as balm for the soul.

We had planned to walk along some of the shorefront paths hugging Lake Tai the following day. But right after breakfast, Suze suddenly developed a diplomatic indisposition. It required her to rest, she said. Through that device she created the opportunity for Chiu Kit and myself to spend more private time together.

We chatted in a desultory fashion as we strolled along some paths alongside the lake. Apart from the odd cluster of people practising slow motion *tai chi* exercises, the paths were quite sparingly used. As I gazed upon the vast stretches of the lake, seemingly infinite, I reflected on how difficult it was to gain what the Buddhists have called "the wisdom of the other shore".

For the sake of making conversation as we walked along, I asked how Chiu Kit was getting along with her Linguaphone lessons. She readily confessed she was hardly making any headway. She was too shy, she explained. She did not want her neighbours to laugh at her for making those strange foreign sounds, especially when there was no one handy to tell her whether her pronunciations were correct or not.

Her statements alerted me to the pointlessness of encouraging her to study English in the first place. A fat lot of good that skill would do her in a weaving factory. It would only be meaningful if she were keen on further studies. She was in some ways bright as a penny; yet in others displayed no intellectual bent. However, she did express some interest in furthering her studies. But was that interest genuine? If so, she should be preparing for another crack at those university entrance exams. If she had some notion of studying abroad, how would she gain permission to leave the country and afford the expenses involved?

On the other hand, she had displayed every appearance to being reconciled to her station in contemporary Chinese life, to cycling in the dark to get to work, come fair weather or foul. Why should I disturb that almost blissful state of acceptance? To raise false hopes and unrealistic expectations for someone in her situation would be heretical or even subversive and unkind. Too much awareness of alternative modes of existence would only unsettle a girl in her situation.

An uneasy silence had descended between us because I had been distracted by my own reflections. After a while, Chiu Kit rekindled the conversation. "You told me you were in London on business last month," she said. "Did you go to the Highgate Cemetery, to pay your respects at the tomb of Marx?"

Her question took me completely by surprise. Paying homage to Marx had never crossed my mind. But I did not want to tell her that too bluntly. So I dressed it up by saying: "My schedule had been far too tight to fit that in."

"What a pity!" she said, sounding disappointed.

I tried to salvage my lapse by saying brightly: "But I did manage to visit the Père Lachaise Cemetery when I was in Paris. Loads of notables buried there — writers, musicians, artists." I then rattled off the names of Balzac, Oscar Wilde, Molière, Hugo, Gertrude Stein, Colette, Abélard and Heloise, Chopin, Rossini, Delacroix, Pissarro.

But she showed no sign of recognising any of those names. It came to me I had really wrong-footed myself again. The young in China, just like the young narrowly educated under British colonialism in Hong Kong, had been brought up on flawed doctrines and to worship false gods. How could I expect any of their generation to pay heed to thinkers or ideas which might enhance their lives when their schools had made no mention of them? Their thoughts had been too strictly channelled for far too long, their fates in one way or another had already been sealed. What a terrible waste of the human potential!

I recalled that when I had been a teenager, my own fate had been virtually sealed as well. I had been stuck in a dead-end job as a cub reporter, earning a wage totally insufficient to keep body and soul together. If my Eight Granduncle and Grandaunt had not come to my rescue by making me a loan sufficient to get myself to university at Stanford, I would not know where I might be today. In all probability, I would have ended up as an embittered hack, trying to make ends meet by ghost-writing speeches or company reports for some corporate bigwig deficient in his vocabulary.

Was there a moral in there somewhere? Was it time for me to do a good turn for some other deserving youngster? I was not enormously rich, but I was fairly comfortably off. My eldest son, Tien-Kuen, had just graduated and that ought to cut me some financial slack.

So thinking, I said: "Would you really like to see Marx's tomb? I can take you there you know; to Paris too, if you like."

"How?" Chiu Kit asked, quizzically.

"By marrying me."

Chiu Kit chuckled. "You tried that line last year at the Ming Tombs; but I knew you were only joking then."

"I'm dead serious now. But before you answer, I want you to consider all the ramifications very carefully. This is neither a joke or a simple matter. You and I belong to different generations, living in different worlds with different rules of conduct. I'm also 34 years your senior. A mighty effort will be required of you to adjust, if we were to marry."

I had to struggle more than a little to get my sentiments across because of my sub-standard Mandarin. I tried to explain that I had lived through many experiences; the lessons learnt from them were not easy ones to unlearn or to pass on to others. There were, in addition, many things about myself which others might find mystifying. If there were things about me or what I was saying which she did not understand, the best move would be to stop me and ask me to explain more fully.

"I've been married and divorced," I continued, "and I have three sons to show for it. Two of them are actually older than you and the third is only younger than you by a month. I hope that does not make you uncomfortable. They're all being educated in North America now and it's most unlikely you'd be meeting any of them any time soon.

"The rumours in China might be that everybody from Hong Kong was ruthlessly capitalistic and filthy rich. I'm not, but I do have a good income plus a Hong Kong government pension which I am entitled to for life. You can count on a reasonably comfortable life with me.

"There is something else I would like to say, although I don't quite know how to say it. It is this: If it turns out to be just a marriage of friendship and convenience, I would not mind at all, though I would wish otherwise. Should you wish to go off to university somewhere after marriage, I'd be more than happy to finance you. Do you understand what I'm saying? Do you have any questions?"

As I tried to set out my case in a halting manner in my deficient Mandarin, the pace of our steps had slackened too. By the time I paused with my questions, we were practically standing still.

Chiu Kit turned to face me to study my expression, before breaking out in a broad smile. "My adoptive mother always said you were a good uncle, reliable and responsible," she allowed.

"What do you mean by that?" I asked, perplexed. "What is your answer? Have you understood what I've said?"

"Shouldn't we go back to the hotel first, to see whether my adoptive mother's ailment has worsened or eased?"

So we made our way back to the hotel. During the journey home, Chiu Kit slipped an arm around one of mine. Her gesture seemed as ambiguous as her words. As we walked along arm in arm, I remained apprehensive and uncertain, not knowing whether our relationship had advanced or whether she had merely extended a touch of care for an elder.

When we reached the hotel, however, we discovered that Suze had gone off to do some shopping in the town.

I escorted Chiu Kit to her room. But upon reaching its threshold, we somehow clinched into our first kiss. By the time Suze got back, our futures had already been settled.

* * *

A couple of weeks later, I arrived at Nantong with two bottles of Hennessy XO cognac as a gift for Chiu Kit's parents. I felt that regardless of whatever the new socialist form might be regarding marriages, Chiu Kit was still a teenager. I would more at ease if I were to do things the old fashioned way, by formally asking her parents for her hand.

I had booked into the Wen Feng Hotel and had invited all members of the Chiu family to a meal in the hotel restaurant. I was confident none of them had eaten there before because it was one of those places where the bill had to be settled in foreign exchange certificates rather than local currency. Since Chiu Kit's elder siblings were living elsewhere in the country, only her parents and Siu Wah and her husband turned up.

Chiu Kit had briefed me before my visit that her father, Chiu Bun, was born in 1927, only two years ahead of myself, whereas her mother was three years older than her father. But her mother had come from a peasant family and had not had any formal education. She would not be able to converse with me either, for she did not know Mandarin. She could only communicate in her native village dialect.

Her mother turned out to be a very pleasant and homely woman, though showing her age more than her husband. Although we could not communicate without someone acting as interpreter, she made me feel welcomed by offering me a timid smile whenever our eyes met.

Chiu Kit's father had been born in a village near Nantong where his father had owned a rice shop. Given such a family background, I imagined his education must have been the traditional Confucian type of his time. He had worked in the family shop until he was 17, before venturing into Nantong city itself to gain wider experience. He found work in a shop selling textiles and he married shortly afterwards. The couple produced their first daughter, Shu-Ching, in 1945, followed by an only son, Bing Hsin, in 1951, another daughter, Siu Wah, in 1958, and finally Kit in 1964.

Civil war then erupted throughout the country. After the Communist victory in 1949, Chiu Bun entered the civil service in a local branch of the National Bureau of Supplies.

During the course of his career he made two futile attempts to join the Communist Party. Probably because of those failures, after some 30 years in bureaucratic service, he still occupied only the lowly position of a sub-manager in charge of processing applications for petroleum product quotas in Nantong when I called on him in 1983.

*   *   *

From the moment I met Chiu Bun I knew he was a person I could respect and relate to. There was something in the genial and courteous way he greeted me which indicated he was a man unpractised in deception and guile. He was soft-spoken but he had his own definite points of view, to which — so far as I could judge — his family members deferred.

Chiu Bun and the author, taken in Nantong in 1983

The Chinese meal at the Wen Feng Hotel proceeded with all the customary formalities of the occasion. Everybody ate heartily. Did a bit of drinking too.

After the meal, Chiu Bun suggested that we should both take a breath of air in the adjoining Wen Feng Park. It was clear he had things to say to me in private, so I accompanied him outside.

In the park, he began by saying that he was glad that his youngest daughter had chosen to marry me. He and his wife — after having heard what their daughter had told them about me and after meeting me in person — were confident that I would take good care of their daughter. I could certainly offer her a better life than she could possibly hope for within China.

But he hoped I would understand that in contemporary times, just as in periods of past history, a marriage was not just a simple matter between a man and a woman. The respective families might, willy-nilly, have also to be involved. After his daughter had left China, the rest of his family still had to remain behind. The country was in a state of political flux; nobody could tell what might happen in the future. The policy today might be the opening up to the world but tomorrow, or perhaps the day after, another political line or a new mass campaign might be launched. It could well be aimed against someone or some foreign idea.

In order to protect his family from any unforeseen turmoil or any change in policy, he had to absolve his family from any involvement in the marriage between his youngest daughter and myself. He therefore proposed that all family members would write to their work and residential units declaring for the record that they had been adamantly opposed to any marriage between Chiu Kit and a Hong Kong bourgeois capitalist.

Each would further declare that he or she had done all in their power to dissuade Chiu Kit from such an unseemly liaison with a man so much older than herself. But the girl had proved headstrong and stubborn, possibly taken in by the sweet-talk and exaggerated material promises of a decadent capitalist roué.

I heard Chiu Bun out and then immediately agreed with his prescient and prudent line of action. I did not wish anyone to suffer because of my marriage. Chiu Bun and I shook hands warmly at the end of our conversation and in due course letters of opposition to the marriage between Chiu Kit and myself were sent by every member of the Chiu family.

Little did either Chiu Bun or myself realise the furore that would later be stoked by those letters.

CHAPTER 10

The Runes of History

THE TREATY OF NANKING of 1842 ended the first of the so-called Opium Wars between China and Britain. It saw China ceding Hong Kong Island to the British in perpetuity. But Lord Palmerston, the then British Foreign Secretary, cavilled at the measly prize, declaring it "a barren island with hardly a house upon it."

Lord Palmerston's usage of the word "barren" was not entirely in keeping with more discerning use of the language because the island — at least according to contemporary Chinese records — was inhabited by 7,450 fisherfolk in a small number of villages. His reference to "hardly a house upon it" was somewhat more accurate, because most of the fisherfolk lived on their vessels rather than on shore. Such people became, in the fullness of time, to be referred to jocularly as part of the "floating" population.

They were, of course, not the only people who "floated" into the territory. That foreign-induced contusion on the underbelly of China soon became a magnet for Western drug traffickers, adventurers, missionaries, chancers, smugglers, ex-foreign servicemen, as well as Chinese seeking to escape from the long reach of their domestic bureaucracy and from the pestilences and other recurring calamities in their own localities. Those who just wanted better job opportunities for themselves or for their families also formed part of those new arrivals.

The colony thus quickly and mistakenly earned a bad reputation in Britain for itself. The *Times* of London in 1859 described it as a "noisy, bustling, quarrelsome, discontented, and insalubrious little island." Perhaps the *Times* was referring only to the expatriate community because it was doubtful if all those adjectives could aptly be applied to the majority Chinese population.

Sir John Bowring was sent there as one of the early governors, serving between 1854 and 1859. It might be difficult now to visualise what it might have been then as an essentially mixed-raced trading outpost.

The administration numbered no more than about 50 Europeans during the first ten years of its occupation. They were generally people of rather poor educational and social quality, for appointments were then often secured through patronage. Living within the bubble of a growing European commercial community offered ample scope for generating scandals, quarrels, jealousies, spites and corruption.

Sir John was an intelligent and perceptive governor, as well as a hard-working reformer. He felt alarmed that the colony's budget for the police was more than 70 times bigger than that for education. Realising the Chinese attachment to educating their young, he quickly adjusted the allocations and began expanding schools and training more teachers. Student numbers increased almost tenfold as a consequence, although part of that increase had to be attributed to the efforts of missionary organisations.

However, the question remained as to whether the Eurocentric education generally dished out — ranging from Queen Boudicca and the Romans to King John and the barons at Runnymede — was quite suitable for essentially Chinese children on the other side of the world. The Mother of Parliaments came up often enough but, of course, without mentioning the monies changing hands for buying honours or for raising suitable parliamentary questions.

Sir John did not change his reforming tack even after an anti-foreign Chinese baker had put arsenic in bread baked in 1857 to poison European settlers, including Lady Bowring.

During his administration, he quipped: "We rule in ignorance, they obey in blindness." And the "ruling in ignorance" portion of his statement became a suitable summary of the pattern of governance for his successors over the next hundred years or more. I am less certain about the "obeying in blindness" part, however.

Meanwhile, both the territory and the number of inhabitants of the Crown Colony expanded through more conflicts with China, which China lost consistently and comprehensively.

The Treaty of Tientsin of 1860 ended the Second Opium War, gaining for Britain in perpetuity the Kowloon Peninsula and Stonecutters Island and the legalisation of the opium trade, while the subsequent Boxer Rebellion of 1900 led to the Convention of Peking, conferring on Britain the lease of the New Territories for 99 years. The lease covered an area north of Kowloon Peninsula up to the Shum Chun River, though excluding the walled city of Kowloon but including some 235 islands.

In addition, the Convention specified for punishment a number of Chinese officials deemed to have sympathised with the creeds of the Boxers. So far as I could determine, not a single Chinese official thus specified attempted to make a run for it. All either committed suicide or submitted themselves for execution.

It would be salutary if at a more recent stage of world history those regarded as war criminals could be similarly dealt with under international justice, instead of further belabouring civil society with more platitudes and lies and, particularly, the obscenity of some of their book deals.

* * *

Lest anyone should accuse me of exaggeration in pointing out missed opportunities and lack of vision and wisdom in Hong Kong governance, let me admit that most people tend to become a little uncomfortable outside their own turf, due to isolation from their own language and culture. Moreover, the feeling could be compounded by the responsibility for ruling over alien peoples with different values.

For many Westerners going East, their initial contacts were likely to be domestic servants, *punkah wallahs* and toilers conveying their private rickshaws or sedan chairs between their homes and offices. Hardly the best sources for acquiring experience and local knowledge. Thus myths circulated about the all-wise white sahibs in dark or yellow-skinned communities and tall tales of the Old China or Japan hands having sussed out the thought processes of inscrutable orientals. It was an area rife with half-truths and myths.

But allow me to cite a few more facts from the runes of history to support my thesis on colonial blindness in Hong Kong.

For example, Sir Reginald Stubbs was Governor from 1919 to 1925. There had been a general strike in 1925 among workers in Canton and Hong Kong. Sir Reginald failed to control those in the colony, even though he had had a meeting with Dr. Sun Yat-Sen. He eventually used local triad members to intimidate strikers but also failed. He was removed by his superiors for being out of touch with the people and ignorant of China and its peoples. Later he got into further trouble in Ceylon but that is another story. His legacy for Hong Kong has been a road in Mid-Levels named after him.

Sir David Trench was made Governor from 1964 to 1971. He was an affable man and easy to approach but not particularly gifted intellectually. Under his watch, however, corruption flourished in several parts of the civil service.

Which middle-class family of the 1960s had not used an illegal "white-plater" taxi to convey children to school or refrained from an illegal extension or two in their homes? The current estimate is that a quarter of the buildings in Hong Kong still have illegal extensions. So much is an example of the workings of the Buildings Ordinance Office.

Sir David's administration got into trouble by mishandling a modest fare rise for the cross-harbour Star Ferry services in 1966. It resulted in a 27-year-old man by the name of So Sau-Chung staging a peaceful hunger strike in protest, by sitting outside the Star Ferry concourse on Hong Kong Island.

The protester was soon arrested and sent to gaol for two months for "obstructing a passageway". Rioting broke out in several parts of the city as a consequence and lasted for four days. Troops had to be deployed to quell them. Eventually, 258 people were each imprisoned for two years for rioting. A Commission of Inquiry naturally followed, because feelings were running high on all sides. It was held under a High Court judge who concluded, foreseeably, that the government had been out of touch with the public.

The following year, when Chairman Mao's Cultural Revolution spilled over from China in a more threatening manner, Sir David was quite out of his depth for dealing with that more serious situation.

I myself had not been directly involved in such political issues until 1971, and then over a matter of lesser importance. The police had forcefully and bloodily broken up a peaceful demonstration of about 6,000 people. The demonstration had been organised by patriotic students against the handing over of the five uninhabited Diaoyu Islands by the Americans to Japan. The islands, around which nevertheless existed rich fishing grounds, were situated between Taiwan and Okinawa.

The Hong Kong demonstrations took place on July 7th, a particularly sensitive date for Chinese people, as part of a world-wide student movement to assert Chinese national unity. Following rough police action, demonstrators got agitated and flowed over into the shopping areas of Causeway Bay. Rioting then erupted.

Sir David, fearful of things taking a turn for the worse, summonsed me to Government House and directed me to initiate a dialogue with local youth and student leaders to soothe their grievances and to dampen down their potential for making trouble. I was given authority to deal with people who might be members of illegal organisations but no authority to make any concessions.

At that time I was in the civil service and was occupying the post of City District Commissioner for Hong Kong Island. Thus I embarked upon roughly a year of interchanges with youthful activists.

In the background, among the shadows, conspiracy theorists were holding that the chessboard of *realpolitik* was being laid. The great powers had inclined towards replacing the representatives of a weakening Taiwan in the United Nations with representatives nominated by the rising economic might and money-making opportunities emerging in China. I doubted if very many of the demonstrators actually believed they might be being played as pawns in a grubby and complicated multi-national game.

When Sir David retired in 1971, he was succeeded by Sir Murray MacLehose, who automatically extended my mission for holding talks. I imagined that the conversations I had been conducting were also something of a smokescreen to obscure some larger purpose. But who was I to question the best laid plans of bigger and more important players?

Sir Murray was an entirely different kettle of fish. He had not risen through the administrative ranks of the Colonial Service but rather parachuted into the autocratic position of Hong Kong governor after serving as their British ambassador in two relatively minor territories. Perhaps he had also been picked as part of some masterplan.

He was tall, impressive, patrician and well-meaning. But he had, understandably, rather too much hubris and was over-quick and over-confident over the rightness of his own judgements.

Though Sir Murray wanted me to continue to engage with the protest leaders, he did not seem to be particularly keen on listening to what I had to report back.

After almost a year of dialogue with youth leaders and making many reports to government, I had gained a degree of rapport with the different protest leaders. They told me they intended ending the demonstrations by marching in a body from Victoria Park to the consulates-general of the United States and Japan in Central to deliver letters of protest. Thereafter they would disperse peacefully and end further protests in Hong Kong.

They wanted, however, official approval for the march, for which they had already applied to the police as the licensing authority. In order to ensure that there would be no disorder or disturbances along the route, they would appoint sufficient student marshals and would also welcome a strong escort by the police. I had, of course, only my lowly worm's eye view of events and was anxious to do what appeared right by my own bailiwick.

When the issue came up at Government House, I reported what I had heard and recommended that permission be granted for that final march. I was convinced not only by the sincerity of the youth leaders about a peaceful expression of their patriotic sentiments but also by their ability, with appropriate co-operation from the police, to maintain discipline and control during the march.

The police representatives at the meeting, on the other hand, were adamant against creating a precedent for allowing a march to go through a crowded and busy city. They would, however, arrange for a heavy police presence throughout, plus ample filming and recording of every stage of the march for future prosecution for illegal activities.

I argued that the approach suggested by the police made little practical sense. The marchers represented the best of the city's future; it would be unfortunate if so many had to begin life with a criminal record. If so much police manpower was to be devoted to escorting and recording the march, would it not be better to give official permission for the march with the same precautions?

But the decision went against me. I told the youth leaders that permission would be denied for a march and I recommended that they should call it off. Otherwise, each individual would be held responsible for taking part in an illegal activity. The police would be there to record every breach of the law and there could be consequences.

In the event, though permission was not granted, the march went ahead as planned, peacefully and without any incident along the way. The marchers dispersed quietly after handing in their letters of protest, as they said they would.

A de-briefing session was called at Government House a few days later. Every official who had been there when the decision to refuse permission was made seemed as pleased as Punch that it had gone off without any incident. Everyone was ready to write the whole thing off, except me.

When the de-briefing session was about to break up, I piped up: "Since the police have firm evidence of a mass breach of the law, isn't it the duty of the Public Prosecutor to lay charges before the courts? The rule of law should not be deterred by sheer numbers alone; otherwise the law falls into disrepute."

Everybody looked at me in silence, as if I had gone mad. Sir Murray was the first one to stand up and leave the conference table. The rest followed.

To me, the issue was a simple one of principle and logic. Those who took the original decision not to grant permission for the march must explain openly why they took that decision, in court if necessary. They had to be accountable for their decisions. Otherwise, in the longer run, governance would become unaccountable and proper governance in any crowded city in the world would become virtually impossible.

Firstly, the notion that a civilised society need not openly account for decisions taken in private on behalf of the common weal had to be anti-democratic; and secondly, the notion that the rule of law could be disobeyed with impunity by mobs claiming noble motives, however misguided or wrongly arrived at, would be a dangerous one to set.

It could well be the case that a law could become outdated or no longer in harmony with the temper of the times. But there must be constitutionally approved ways of changing the law and, until it had been changed, every person must obey it.

I surmised that my arguments did not prevail at Government House on both occasions simply because I had been the only Chinese at the meetings and I was also the most junior officer in attendance.

It would be interesting to see how future historians might speculate on whether the seeds of those two rather ugly ideas had been sown or encouraged in the city during the record-breaking tenure of Sir Murray as governor.

Recent events in Hong Kong as well as in cities elsewhere suggest that some of those baleful seeds might have unfortunately sprouted.

In the subsequent years, I have had occasion to be critical of some of Sir Murray's other decisions, or at least with their clumsy and imperfect implementation by his subordinates. Nevertheless, he had ended his tenure with high approval ratings and general popularity.

A partial explanation for this might be due to his having a very sly and efficient publicity machine. It conferred upon him fulsome credit even for things initiated by others. At the same time, it spared him blame for some of the cock-ups for which he had been ultimately responsible.

I have already challenged some of those attributions in 2018, in the third volume of these memoirs, published under the title *Hong Kong Confidential: Life as a Subversive*. I will therefore refrain from repeating my comments here. However, it is dismaying to note that lax or lazy journalists, commentators and obituary writers have kept repeating some of those erroneous attributions. I suppose in the post-truth era we are living through now, misrepresentations broadcast or repeated often enough would in the end be taken as factual and authoritatively correct. Nazi propaganda had foreseen this possibility during World War II.

* * *

When the British Prime Minister, Mrs. Margaret Thatcher, and the Chinese

Premier, Mr. Zhao Zi-Yang, sat down to begin talks on the future of Hong Kong in Peking in September of 1982, both had different aims and were subjected to different types of historical pressures.

It was significant that neither side deemed it necessary to consult the 5.2 million people in the colony on what *they* really wanted, rather than just simply using them like poker chips at a high-stakes game of chance.

Premier Zhao was apparently there to bring a fitting end to what had been commonly referred to by the Chinese as "the century of humiliation" inflicted by foreign powers. He knew, however, that there were pressures pulling in different directions within his own side.

For a start, the Chinese Communist Party was a broad church, with tens of millions applying to become members, making it possibly the largest political party anywhere in the world. It would be a far cry from the numbers wanting to join a Western political party. Yet it had to accommodate a wide range of opinions, with Leninist democratic centralism at its heart.

Premier Zhao himself had liberal inclinations but there were many conservatives favouring different approaches. There were also those tricky economic modernising and opening-up policies advocated by the Paramount Ruler, Mr. Deng Xiao-Ping, to be taken into account.

Historically and officially, the Chinese position seemed to have been made abundantly clear. As long ago as the Ching Dynasty, it had been asserted that Hong Kong was an inalienable part of China, surrendered only because of a series of unequal treaties. In time, that lost territory had to be restored. National honour demanded no less.

That position had been adhered to by successive Chinese governments. For example, General Chiang Kai-Shek, the former Kuomintang President of the Republic of China, had expressed that same sentiment in 1943, in his book *China's Destiny*.

The return to Chinese sovereignty was hence due to be negotiated after World War II. But civil war, unfortunately, erupted in the country and the issue had to be left in limbo.

The Communist government which replaced the Kuomintang in 1949 had followed the same line. The unsettled situation it inherited also prevented actual negotiations. Its premier of the time, Mr. Chou En-Lai, indicated that the future of the territory would be dealt with "when the time was ripe". Indeed, he took the further step in 1958 of informing Britain that China would regard as an unfriendly act any attempt by Britain to move the territory towards any sort of dominion status.

In 1972, right after China had replaced Taiwan in the United Nations, China went out of its way to notify the world that it did not recognise any of the three treaties pertaining to Hong Kong.

Given that background, the Chinese position at the 1982 negotiations appeared to have been fairly consistent and logical. The Chinese team held that they spoke for all Chinese in the world, knowing that at least a billion of their countrymen at home and abroad were committed to the cause for national unity. Compatriots caught in the tiny foreign-usurped enclave in China should be no different from the vast majority within China and elsewhere. To give them more say would call into question the legitimacy of the Chinese team and ferment dangerous old tendencies towards divisions and partitioning.

In any case, the cadres already stationed in Hong Kong were well-acquainted with the shifting kaleidoscope of overlapping and multiple opinions there — Kuomintang remnants, Taiwan separatists, triad societies members, faint-hearted capitalists, money-grubbing traitors, foreign spies, drug-addicts, frivolous youths, followers of bourgeois life-styles and families of those who might have suffered during the protracted civil war, as well as the irredentist forces which had surfaced in 1967 and 1971.

It was inconceivable to the Chinese leadership that the bulk of the population in the colony would prefer the humiliation of living as second or third class alien subjects than being ruled by their own kind.

After all, 92% of the inhabitants within China were of the Han stock, though recognised minorities were also living in peace there. It was also important to remember that, in the Chinese psyche and mind, the definition of being a Chinese was not just a matter of race, skin-colour, language or even the accidental location of one's birth.

From time immemorial, Chinese-ness had been considered as essentially a civilisational thing, that is, whether a person behaved in an appropriate Chinese manner, observed Chinese habits, customs, traditions and so forth. The naturalisation of foreigners in China, like in Japan, had been extremely rare in contemporary times, recording only about 1,500 cases.

For that reason, Marco Polo, Matteo Ricci and some other early Jesuits were accepted as Chinese. On the other hand, it was also true that given enough time, the Chinese had a habit of absorbing minorities within their midst. Take for example the Jews who had chosen to settle in Kaifeng, and later, the Manchu conquerors themselves. It was not for nothing that the Chinese civilisation had endured for over five thousand years, largely intact.

* * *

It was worth noting that during the negotiations for the return of Hong Kong to Chinese sovereignty, the Taiwan government, whose Kuomintang leaders had boasted repeatedly of recovering mainland China from their isolated island, had remained conspicuously silent. No talk of recapturing the mainland or any such, but rather some fake form of independence under the wings of the United States.

Apparently Taiwan politicians had no interest in gathering around themselves the Kuomintang remnants who had been so unprofessionally abandoned decades ago in Hong Kong by their officers, contrary to the ancient rules of chivalry among the warrior class of society.

Instead, the Taiwan regime had now apparently only set its sights on embracing the corrupt Hong Kong police station sergeants who had fled there with their ill-gotten loot. The fact that the two territories had no extradition arrangements was — and remained — a great legal convenience for all parties concerned.

*　*　*

The British position in the Sino-British negotiations, on the other hand, appeared all over the place, riddled with internal divisions. It was like a man desperately trying to cross a troublesome river by straddling two different boats, neither of which was amply under control.

Prominently, there was the team leader, Mrs. Thatcher, flushed after victory in her war with Argentina. Then there were her various advisors — legal, political, economics and financial, national security, *et cetera* in the form of faceless apparatchiks from the Foreign and Commonwealth Office. And finally, there was an assortment of so-called China-watchers.

Many of the advisors had been so handicapped by doctrinal, philosophical and political contradictions that they all sang slightly off-key within the ensemble, tripping over themselves concerning myths and beliefs their ancestors had sprinkled everywhere.

Mrs. Thatcher herself was a prolific myth-generator. She became a champion of that neoliberal economic and political order firmly established after World War II, together with deregulation, flexible labour markets, reducing the power of trade unions and the privatising of state enterprises. What she did not realise was that her society — and particularly its ruling elites — was actually on a downward slide and that she was taking over a sticky wicket.

Some of her advisors pandered to her proclivities while others advised forthrightly but at cross purposes. For example, some would say that the *laissez-faire* free market system Britain had put in place in Hong Kong had brought the colony bulging coffers and low inflation without recurring strikes, high unemployment, currency devaluations and balance of payments crises back in their homeland. Sound British management had been consistently demonstrated in the colony and that ought to count for something in negotiations with the Chinese.

The legal advisors, obsessed with legal minutia and the sanctity of international agreements, were quick to point out that Hong Kong island and the Kowloon peninsula had been ceded by China in perpetuity under treaty provisions, notwithstanding the firm rejection of "unequal" treaties by the Chinese. They would emphasise the rule of law and if those territories were to be given back, then they too should be worth something in return.

A few conscientious advisors, on the other hand, pointed out that provision should be made to allow the settlement of at least a number of Hong Kong residents in the United Kingdom, particularly those who had been doing the questionable work assigned to them by foreign superiors in the Special Branch, in the listening posts of the GCHQ and in other similar organisations. Without such a provision in the light of several changes in the Nationality Act, loud cries of betrayal and accusations of perfidious Albion might well arise from several quarters.

But political advisors warned at once, however, that — regardless of reasons, compelling or otherwise — the British voting public would never countenance another influx of foreigners into their already over-crowded island. It was not a matter of breed, colour or racism, just practical politics.

Then there were the China-watchers, holding forth on Chinese pragmatism, ingenuity and willingness to seek the middle ground. None of them seemed to have realised that China-watching was akin to birdwatching. It could not be meaningfully done without first ridding one's own head of accumulated prejudices and extraneous noises.

Furthermore, if done for laziness or convenience, say, within the confines of the back garden, the watcher was likely to miss a number of important indicators, like the creatures' habitat usage, their aural expressions, their migration patterns, and whether they were moulting or not. More importantly, one was likely to miss the murmuration of starlings or group flights reminiscent of the dynamics of physics rather than of the well-worn tram tracks of conventional ideas and politics.

My humble impression was that most China-watchers who had wormed their way into the establishment were still a fair distance away from the accomplishments of a Needham or a Giles.

* * *

Given the avalanche of conflicting advice received, Mrs. Thatcher decided to assume her Iron Lady persona and floated, as an opening gambit, a proposal to return both the ceded territories of Hong Kong Island and the Kowloon peninsula to Chinese sovereignty provided the British could administer the entire territory for a further period of years after the end of the New Territories lease in 1997. She felt the tested British managerial know-how could strengthen confidence in the future of the city, increase its stability as a financial centre and prevent any damaging flight of capital.

She was genuinely taken aback when Premier Zhao gave a dusty response. He said only two principles were at stake in the negotiations — Chinese sovereignty over the whole of Hong Kong and the prosperity and stability of the city. In any crunch, China would always choose sovereignty.

The following day, Mrs. Thatcher had an audience with the Paramount Ruler of China, Mr. Deng Xiao-Ping. The chain-smoking and diminutive Mr. Deng made plain the issue of Hong Kong. It had to be settled quickly, within no more than a year or two. Otherwise, China might unilaterally decide to recover the territory.

In fact, Mr. Deng had earlier passed that message informally to Mr. Edward Heath, the retired prime minister before Mrs. Thatcher, that the

Chinese deadline for settling everything was before September of 1984. He might have expected that that clear message would be percolated back to the Whitehall mandarins. But Mrs. Thatcher's opening gambit might have struck him as a deliberate British tactic to drag things out. He reacted accordingly.

The *démarche* from Mr. Deng also produced a reaction from Mrs. Thatcher. She bridled. It was not the kind of message the lady had been accustomed to receiving. She therefore ordered with hauteur that her team produce a cabinet paper on how Hong Kong might be defended militarily.

She probably would not have issued her order if she had been properly briefed by her advisors in the first place. She might then have known how many days it had taken a relatively small contingent of Japanese troops to secure the surrender of British forces in December of 1941. She might have known too how the metal border fences crumbled like match sticks in 1962 under the onslaught of Kwangtung refugees, once the People's Liberation Army had withdrawn guarding their side of the border. She might have heard also that infamous boast by Chairman Mao that Hong Kong was for the taking, with just one telephone call from him.

It did not require a military genius to tell a political leader that a territory could be defended only if the hearts of the bulk of the people of that territory were behind its leader. To have that kind of support behind a foreign leader was an unwise assumption given the history of Hong Kong.

* * *

The city has long had a reputation for being flooded with rumours and gossip, but it had an amazing ability for embellishing and exaggerating those stories as they passed from mouth to ear. So it was not in the least surprising that when leaks suggested that the talks in Peking were hitting snags, roadblocks and disagreements. Different people therefore started projecting their own fears, hopes and prejudices into widely circulated tales.

Very few individuals knew what were the actual sticking points but, in a situation of considerable secrecy, even the wildest stories were being picked up and given credence. Some things were quite understandable. For example, if a person happened to be one of the 50,000 or so members of Hong Kong triad societies at that time, he would naturally be only too conscious of the fate of such membership after Communist authorities had taken over in Shanghai, Canton and other major cities.

Again, if a person already had not got a bolthole established in Canada, Taiwan or elsewhere, he might well join one of the queues seeking visas outside the offices of consulates-general and high commissions.

Without candid statements coming from either side, some people started converting Hong Kong dollars into American dollars and liquidating fixed assets. Property prices fell. Speculators, fraudsters, demagogues and profit-seekers also jumped on the bandwagon for quick kills.

It was in that fevered and uncertain atmosphere that I too easily made many millions — but I did that out of a sense of pique and out of sheer frustration over how supposedly clever people could remain so blind to the realities under which they lived and got carried away by loose talk simply because of their own fears or greed. I shall recount how I came by my enormous windfall in a subsequent chapter.

* * *

Mrs. Thatcher might have had an easier time at the Sino-British negotiations if more of her underlings had done their jobs properly. But too many of them had fixed their sights on technicalities and legalities rather than the burgeoning of pride and nationhood among the Chinese after World War II. If they had not been smugly oblivious of the latter, they would have advised Mrs. Thatcher against the futility of her opening gambit.

No Chinese leader could have survived in the 20th century if he had made any further territorial concession in China to a foreign power. It would have violated such sense of history that most Chinese leaders of note through the ages would have been impregnated with.

As one raked through the ashes of history, it would appear that the British focus on treaties and leases caused them to overlook wider changing realities on the ground.

Since the New Territories lease did not expire till June of 1997, the assumption was that nothing much required attention till much closer to that time. But this was not the case. Some more perceptive administrators had seen that the duration of the lease of the New Territories was storing up a number of practical problems.

For example, Sir Cecil Clementi, who was the governor from 1925 to 1930, drew attention to some of the problems in 1928. He thought that the relatively short lease duration on the New Territories would be an impediment to longer-term investments in the colony. He therefore suggested to Whitehall that the territory should be made permanent like the rest of the colony. But he did not meet with success. Whitehall feared that such a move would lead to another conflict with China which the international community of the time would not support.

Another problem was that thousands of short-term renewable or non-renewable leases of various durations were being handed out for a multiplicity of purposes, like for squatter settlements, burial grounds, schools, petrol stations and so forth. Such leases had different durations. For example, leases for petrol stations were normally granted for 21 years while those for recreational purposes were for 15 years. In total there were over 30,000 leases in the New Territories.

If a lease came up for renewal with a renewal period going beyond 1997, what would happen? Both a renewal or a refusal to renew would send wild and confidence-shaking rumours flying around like bluebottles around a rotting carcass in the rumour-prone society that was Hong Kong.

A local Administrative Officer by the name of Eric Ho foresaw such a possibility in 1972 when he was serving as Director of Home Affairs. He wrote a memo classified as "Secret" to his immediate superior in the Central Secretariat, suggesting that thought should be given to a coherent policy on the issue of short-term leases in the New Territories before they became a hot issue. In due time, a "Secret" memo came back without a substantive reply but ordering him never to raise the subject of New Territories leases again.

It was not recorded who had been consulted on Eric Ho's memo or who had authorised the stern order in reply. The exchange was revealed in Eric's memoirs *Times of Change — A Memoir of Hong Kong's Governance* published in 2005.

Apparently there were some at the top of the colonial bureaucracy who preferred the good old stand-by of keeping their "heads-in-the-sand" approach when presented with difficult government problems.

* * *

In 1979, something unprecedented happened. For the first time since the Communist government came to power in China in 1949, the governor of Hong Kong, in the person of Sir Murray MacLehose, was invited to visit Peking.

The Foreign and Commonwealth Office duly instructed the governor not to raise the problems surrounding New Territories leases with Chinese officials — presumably because a British strategy had not been fully worked out.

But Sir Murray, being Sir Murray, chose to ignore the order. He must have thought that, given his cocksureness about his own diplomatic experiences and skills, he could somehow pull a difficult political rabbit out of the hat. So when he had a meeting with the Paramount Ruler, Mr. Deng Xiao-Ping, he floated the idea of the colonial government issuing short-term leases in the New Territories without a termination date, should they extend beyond June of 1997.

Mr. Deng naturally turned down that unorthodox suggestion, thinking it only a British ploy to extend the New Territories lease by stealth. But the incident alerted the Chinese to a possible British line of thinking and thereby compromised beforehand one of Mrs. Thatcher's negotiating positions.

* * *

Another handicap that Mrs. Thatcher had to face concerned some of the myths her officials had generated over the years and in which they themselves actually and honestly believed. Such myths stretched all the way back from Lord Palmerston's "barren island" remark to the latter-day narratives about British managerial genius turning that barren island and its Chinese low-life immigrants into a glitteringly prosperous and efficient modern society.

It was true, of course, that during the early days of the colony, many of the Chinese immigrants were criminals and pirates fleeing from the uncompromising reach of native laws and regulations. One of the most notorious was named Wong Ma-Chow. He somehow gained the patronage of the then British Registrar-General, a man named Daniel Caldwell, and thus was able to amass a vast fortune and considerable local power. There had been, of course, numerous lesser rascals than Wong Ma-Chow among immigrants.

But many of the early arrivals were also ordinary labourers, job-seekers, peasants, students, small time traders and plain refugees, escaping from famines and uncongenial environments. Among them were also educated people and intellectuals, particularly teachers.

However, because the British elites wanted to take full credit for the transformation of Hong Kong from its humble beginnings as fishing villages to what it has become today, they have propagated a certain narrative for a century and a half through its skewed and muddled education system. They have done it so well that many Hong Kong youngsters who had gone through that educational mill still accepted uncritically what they had been fed.

Take, for example, Mr. Steve Tsang, a person brought up in Hong Kong. He had graduated from the University of Hong Kong and later became an Oxford academic. He was commissioned to write a book about the Administrative Service which was published in 2007 under the title *Governing Hong Kong*.

In that book, he asserted that the early Kwangtung immigrants were "generally deemed to have come not from an honourable background." He added that, on the whole, respected and wealthy Chinese did not have any desire to migrate to live under alien rule.

He did not, however, provide any case histories to back up his thesis. Neither did he define what he meant by "an honourable background" or a yardstick for determining what was a "respected and wealthy Chinese".

I would, within the confines of my own kinship connections, question the validity of some of his sweeping statements. I have in Chapter One of this memoir set out in some detail the pedigree of the Chau family from which my paternal grandmother originated.

Let me now set out the background of my paternal grandfather. His name was Wong Wan-On and he was born in Hong Kong in 1876. He was the youngest of six children, consisting of three sons and three daughters, all born in Hong Kong. His father had been a teacher in the Hsin Hui District of Kwangtung before moving to the colony, but no oral history has been passed down on his precise motives for moving, except that he continued in the teaching profession after his arrival.

My grandfather studied at the Diocesan Boys' School till 1893 and then entered the then Hong Kong College of Medicine, graduating in 1900. He then became a "Registering Medical Officer" in the British Colonial Service in Singapore

While being a British Crown servant, he was also a crypto-revolutionary, raising funds among overseas Chinese to finance the revolutionary activities of his friend Dr. Sun Yat-Sen.

When I was a boy, I had seen a number of photographs of Dr. Sun taken with various elders in my family. Unfortunately, most of those photographs had been lost or destroyed during the Japanese occupation of Singapore. The only photograph surviving within the family is a copy of the one taken in Singapore in 1907 and which now is hanging in the Sun Yat-Sen Nanyang Memorial Hall at Tai Gin Road in Singapore.

As to the two older brothers of my grandfather, the eldest became a doctor and migrated to San Francisco. The second brother became a dentist and migrated to the tin mining town of Ipoh in Malaya.

A group picture taken in Singapore in 1907 of supporters of Dr. Sun Yat-Sen. The author's grandfather is seated second from the left in the centre row

*   *   *

As for the antecedents on my mother's side of the family, she was the fourth daughter in a family of nine. Her father was Mok Sau-Tseng, born in 1866 in the agricultural town of Tseng Sing, not far from Canton. His family traded in household provisions. He received a traditional education till the age of 15, when a relative suggested he should go to Hong Kong to broaden his vision and to learn some English.

He did so in 1881 and enrolled in St. Paul's Secondary School. Before he finished, however, he converted to Christianity and decided to follow a priestly calling. He therefore started to study theology.

Meanwhile, he met a Chung Shan woman named Wong Chung-Shun who had come to Hong Kong to take up a teaching post at a girls' school. She shared his religious enthusiasms and the two soon married.

Mok Sau-Tseng was ordained as a priest in 1902 and the Church Missionary Society sent him to Canton the following year to start a new ministry. He duly founded the Church of Our Saviour at Wanfu Road in Canton and the Holy Trinity Middle School a short distance away.

In 1934, when a new South China diocese was created, he was unanimously elected as the first Anglican Bishop of Canton. In that position he oversaw the work of seven churches and a number of schools and medical clinics throughout Kwangtung Province. He and his wife devoted the rest of their lives to church and charitable works.

A number of biographies, both in Chinese and English, have been published about my maternal grandfather. Today there is still a secondary school at the Tai Po area of Hong Kong, founded in 1975, named after him.

It is for others to decide whether my ancestors had come from "honourable" or "respectable" backgrounds. I think there are many in Hong Kong today who, like myself, had ancestors with similar backgrounds. For instance, I have played *mah jong* in Hong Kong with a friend surnamed Kung who traced his ancestry back to Confucius. I also know a businessman whose family originated from the great Warring State poet, Wat Yuen. If anything, some of my ancestors and those of some of my friends probably typified the complex reasons why people move from one place to another.

I cannot imagine my native city for five generations developing the way that it has without heavy doses of investment, both financial and intellectual, from China. Furthermore, the infusion of Chinese values, cultivated over many centuries, in terms of work ethics, frugality, high propensity to save, concern for future generations and respect for the aged certainly informed many sections of the city today.

After all, until the British switched to a more merit-based system of selecting civil servants in the 1930s, many of the British officials appointed to Hong Kong during the early days had been fairly mediocre. They merely continued the tradition of what Sir John Bowring had once described as "ruling in ignorance."

* * *

If Mrs. Thatcher had not been taken in to some extent by the myths that generations of her own people have created over time, she would have hardly begun her pitch at the Sino-British negotiations in the way that she had. No doubt she would have been impressed by what she could see in the thriving city. But if she thought it was entirely or even to a substantial extent due to British management, then she was greatly mistaken.

I do not know why the Chinese side had rejected out of hand her proposal for continued British management after 1997. Perhaps they could not get their heads around the contradiction between claiming credit for the success of *laissez-faire* policies and at the same time credit for displaying extraordinary management skills. Or perhaps, they judged — as I have done — that the British contribution to the overall development of Hong Kong had been not as crucial as British propaganda had made out, even without taking into account all the shambles that have occurred over one and a half centuries of British rule.

But of course it would have been contrary to the Chinese sense of decorum and politeness to spell out the unvarnished truth in so many words before a visiting lady British Prime Minister.

The curtain finally came down on the negotiations on December 19, 1984, when China and the United Kingdom signed the Sino-British Joint Declaration in Peking. The document consisted of eight paragraphs and three Annexes. Signing on behalf of China was the Chinese Premier, Mr. Zhao Zi-Yang, and on behalf of Britain, the British Prime Minister, Mrs. Margaret Thatcher.

The document provided for the return of the entire colony to Chinese sovereignty and had no provision for any British management role after 1997.

However, some Britishers with colonist mindsets still seemed fond of playing the role of back-seat drivers; in particular I refer to the Conservative politician rejected by the voters in Bath who nevertheless gained an appointment as the final British governor of the colony. It was a pity that the people of Hong Kong were never given any say over the matter.

CHAPTER 11

Making Millions

THE REVERSION OF HONG KONG to Chinese sovereignty was never a matter of doubt during and immediately after World War II. The geopolitical development of the Cold War, however, introduced a complication and gave rise to some wishful thinking. But its return remained only a question of "when" rather than "if".

Naturally, many of the 5.2 million who lived in that politically mixed society were eager to see the humiliation of "unequal treaties" being finally confined to the dustbin of history. The waiting was frustrating for them.

But they recognised that there were among them many affiliated to the defeated Kuomintang as well. They had been stuck in the colony, unable to flee or seek refuge in the still un-relinquished Taiwan or elsewhere. Intermixed with them were also possibly approximately 50,000 members of triad and other criminal societies, with their respective families. Those people could not help remembering what befell their kind after the Communists had taken over in Shanghai, Canton and in the other major cities of the mainland. They therefore were not displeased with being left in a political limbo for a while longer.

In a surprising phenomenon near the start of Sino-British negotiations, however, a substantial group of expatriate civil servants — who had claimed to have been administrating the colonial government effectively for decades — suddenly voiced a roundabout declaration of no confidence over the prospect of a city under the Chinese.

They made an unbecoming gesture by petitioning the United Kingdom government to guarantee the due payment of their pensions should Hong Kong ever run into financial trouble in the future! Their first loyalty to themselves was thus made evident. The United Kingdom, for reasons both of principle and of costs, naturally rejected their petition.

I should have thought that such a sentiment of no confidence might have led to an acceleration in the number of foreigners fleeing the city for more salubrious locations elsewhere. But instead, the opposite resulted. There was a fresh and curious increase in foreigners. The growth in non-Chinese inhabitants in fact climbed steadily, from a mere two per cent of the population to roughly eight per cent today.

It was possible that foreign chancers, ponzi schemers, vulture capitalists, spies, turncoats, provocateurs and people of that ilk had smelt opportunities and had flocked to the city for a slice of the pie. Its normally soft approach to recreational drugs, sexual orientations and other liberated lifestyles might have also provided a lure. Likewise, its growing prosperity leading to an insatiable demand for more overseas domestic workers.

The spies and foreign agents who began gathering there were not always adequately disguised as academics, journalists, publishers, missionaries or whatever. Indeed, American agents could often count on their so-called "Five Eyes" group intelligence co-conspirators to assist them in spying operations against China.

For example, the colonial Immigration Department provided American operatives with ready access to Chinese refugees to collect intelligence on the particular units of People's Liberation Army stationed at or near their former homes.

Caught up in that same prospect for change would be many sub-groups of ordinary apolitical Chinese, mainly concerned with their bowls of rice, the educational future of their children and how to turn whatever assets they might possess into ready cash.

Those with the means, skills or connections to move to a more stable place would no doubt be those forming queues for visas outside consulates-general and Commonwealth high commissions.

Trapped in a similar bind would be the more faint-hearted corporate executives who had hitherto benefited their firms and themselves from the exploitative nature of the local free market system. They now had to hedge their bets by moving their registered headquarters to more distant locations.

Therefore, when the Sino-British negotiations began in 1982, they started against a background of mistrust and volatility. That ensured that each minor hiccup affecting either side would be leaked, circulated and exaggerated. Rumours would be embellished out of all proportion and passed on to the under-informed masses as gospel truths.

Thus a slip from the lip of the British Foreign Secretary, for instance, using the word "bleak" to assess his perception of the talks, naturally sent panic circulating through society as quickly as a contagious virus. Such a slip did in fact occur. Confidence — that virtual lifeblood of any truly open capitalistic society — just sapped away with that word, with most listeners not giving the story more analysis beyond their own inclinations towards fear or flight.

Of course, whatever was "bleak" had to be a very subjective assessment, depending upon a certain point of view. If one side's expectations and arguments were sent flying like skittles, that might indeed appear quite bleak for that side. But that might not be necessarily so from the point of view of people with a different political persuasion. It might even be a cause for celebration!

Likewise, for Mrs. Margaret Thatcher to stumble on the steps of the Great Hall of the People during negotiations sent geomancers and *fung shui* masters into interpreting frenzies, as to what that misstep really portended for the two nations. Out of such frivolous stuff was history often created.

* * *

The Hong Kong dollar had a rather convoluted history. Because of the dearth of Mexican silver dollars at a certain point in time, it first got minted around 1895 in Calcutta and Bombay, for use in settling trading accounts in Hong Kong and in the Straits Settlements.

In 1866, a local mint was actually set up in Causeway Bay to mint dollars and half-dollars. But the Chinese did not take to that local coinage, so the mint was closed down a couple of years later. In 1906, however, the Straits Settlements began issuing its own dollar, fixing it at two shillings and four pence against sterling. But Hong Kong remained on the silver standard till 1935, before it introduced a crawling peg of between 15.36 to 16.45 dollars to one pound sterling. This turned into a fixed peg of 16 dollars to one pound sterling in 1939.

The devaluation of sterling in 1967, however, necessitated an adjustment and it subsequently became pegged to the rate of 5.65 dollars for one American dollar in 1972. But it soon strengthened to 5.085 for an American dollar the following year, forcing the exchange to be allowed to float within a specified currency band instead.

The strength of any currency was normally influenced by a range of political and economic factors, like the stability of the government, the level of public spending, GDP growth, the inflation rate, the state of unemployment and so forth.

In Hong Kong, public spending increased sharply after Sir Murray MacLehose took over as governor in 1971. Because he had been left with bulging coffers, he announced all sorts of populist measures. The local inflation rate rose significantly as a result, rising from 2.7% in 1975 to 15.5% in 1980. Overhanging everything was the unresolved timing for settling the political future of the city.

Although the Hong Kong dollar was backed by an Exchange Fund with one of the largest reserves in the world and was at the same time one of the most traded currencies, especially in neighbouring cities like Macau, rumours, speculations and day dreams frequently stirred uncertainty and caused fluctuations in value. The fact that the city had no exchange control mechanism to regulate the flow of funds added to volatility and likewise its attractiveness for money launderers. It also allowed those clever speculators with an eye on quick killings to enter the picture.

It would not be beyond the bounds of imagination for a few winks and nods to be given to some of the financial parasites and speculative agents inhabiting the City of London Square Mile by those intent upon testing the stated Chinese position.

Always choosing sovereignty over prosperity and stability might sound very well for political leaders. It appealed to national solidarity. But in the neoliberal order of things, chancers and cynics could easily be found who were adamant that, in the final crunch, money would always come out ahead of something as nebulous as national pride.

It would be consistent with British strategy too, to demonstrate to the Chinese beforehand that, without sure-handed British administrators in charge, things could swiftly go awry.

* * *

Meanwhile, the adherents of opposing philosophies and beliefs were playing themselves out within the rudimentary framework of the so-called free market system in the colony.

In 1981, the Hong Kong dollar was being traded at around 5.13 to the American dollar. But it soon started to ease as alarming forebodings for one part of the population gained momentum. Those rumours also affected stock market prices.

Once the Sino-British negotiations were joined in September of 1982, alarmist stories multiplied. Big speculators also entered the market. With every scare story of an impasse in the negotiations, the value of the Hong Kong dollar took a hit, stoking fear or greed in some.

I normally paid scant attention to economic forecasts. Such forecasters were largely ignorant of the real economic interconnections within the city and their wider geopolitical setting. Or else they tended to extrapolate from just one set of published statistics or some unusually narrow base.

But I supposed the city's proud tradition of freedom of speech also meant that people had the freedom to spread a lot of lies and nonsense. I placed their creditability on about the same level as those sports forecasters who pronounced the likely racing results of each race before every meeting. At least I knew from empirical knowledge that the predictions, where my own horses were concerned, were seldom right.

However, when the exchange jumped above 8.65 to an American dollar in September of 1982, I made a beeline for the office of Victor Fung at Fung House in Connaught Road Central. I wanted to discuss with him my thoughts on the speculative bubble gaining traction. If it went too far, it would endanger both trading activities and the real economy.

My view was that as Li & Fung was a publicly listed company, it should play its own modest role against the madness of fear and greed in society, especially during a difficult period of transition. The company did a lot of business in American dollars and it was cash rich besides. By releasing its American dollar earnings steadily onto the market, it could set an example for other responsible corporations to follow.

When I met Victor Fung, however, I was horrified to discover that he had actually been fuelling the panic.

"I have ordered the company's Financial Controller to convert everything into American dollars," Victor Fung said, even before I could get into my narrative. "I've been talking to some banker friends and they assured me they viewed the Hong Kong dollar would eventually weaken to 12 to one American dollar. So I am acting for the good of the company."

"Utter rubbish!" I exclaimed, possibly out of anger that he should have left me out of so important a corporate decision. And then, I quickly regained my self-control and bit my tongue.

I did not know what kind of banker friends he had been talking to. I was doubtful they were the same sober local kind whom I knew. His banking cohorts were in all probability of the same ilk as himself, people who had gone through the usual business school drill of studying the histories of corporate giants like General Electric and IBM, learning the endemic nature of cooking business books in Japan and following how greenmailers and asset strippers had made their malignant presence felt on Wall Street.

But knowing the names of the various parts of a machine was not good enough for a machine could often become more than the sum of its parts. And knowing too many machine parts could lead to a system where a machine could not function at all or only with unforeseeable flaws.

It was not good enough, for example, for a student of Adam Smith just to be able to cite a few trite quotes from *The Wealth of Nations* without also having absorbed some of the ideas in Smith's earlier and more important work *The Theory of Moral Sentiments*. So far as the underlying and complex realities of Hong Kong were concerned, the banking friends of Victor were likely not to know enough.

Victor himself had a doctorate from Harvard and I was not disposed to wasting my breath arguing with him over a *fait accompli*.

Moreover, I did not know when he had given the order to accumulate American dollars. If he had done so early enough, when the American dollar was in the six to one range, the company might well be sitting on a substantial exchange gain if he liquidated the present holdings immediately. But if he had kept on buying at the present level, on the expectation of the local dollar would fall to the 12 to one range, he could be heading for serious trouble.

It seemed to me that Victor was being carried away by the temporary mania affecting the entire city and was becoming oblivious to the fact that the government must also be reflecting on the spreading chaos in the market. The Chinese, too, must be viewing the situation with concern. The hard currency earned through Hong Kong was vital to the country's whole modernising programme. No doubt backchannel communications with Hong Kong authorities were already taking place.

* * *

The Hong Kong strategist running with the ball was Sir John Bremridge, the colony's Financial Secretary. He was in fact the first financial secretary to be appointed who had not risen from within the ranks of the civil service. I had known him well for a number of years, when he was in the private sector, as the Chairman of Cathay Pacific, and when I was responsible for civil aviation negotiations on behalf of the Hong Kong government.

Sir John was a buff but very level-headed and straight-talking individual. He had solid integrity written all over him and not the slightest hint of flamboyance. In tackling the monetary turbulence he would surely be inclined to take his own time and study all the implications, including those secret files of old containing the analysis of Sir John Cowperthwaite, one of his most celebrated predecessors, on the pros and cons of employing different types of monetary regimes. Cowperthwaite had been the economic genius who had suddenly to face, at the eleventh hour, the devaluation of sterling.

I felt confident that Bremridge would contain the market madness in whatever form he thought appropriate, perhaps by linking the local dollar again at a fresh level to the widely dominant American one. It would be imprudent to seek to restore the old level before the crisis erupted. A new peg with due allowance for a modest devaluation, at possibly around the mid-seven dollar to one range, would not be unreasonable.

I had not the slightest inclination towards delivering a dissertation about all that lengthy background to someone with a doctorate from Harvard. Let him soak up tall tales and imagine he knew what he was doing. He had made his own bed without consulting me, and he should jolly well now lie in it.

So I left his office by declaring emphatically: "I dissociate myself completely from your decision to convert the company's resources out of the Hong Kong dollar."

* * *

As I left Fung House, I still felt somewhat narked by Victor's discourtesy in not consulting me before making an important company decision. Although he was the chairman of Li & Fung (Trading), I was also its managing director.

I was not exactly sure why, but I walked almost automatically around the block to my bank at Des Voeux Road Central. Perhaps I felt that Victor had made such a bad decision that I, as an individual, was going to show him in some concrete way that he had been wrong and disrespectful in ignoring me.

I had opened an account at the bank in 1961 when I first entered the Hong Kong civil service. At that time, the bank was known as the Hong Kong Chinese Bank and its chairman had been Sir Sik-Nin Chau, who had a long record of challenging European domination in the colony. He in fact was the first Chinese to be selected to become a steward at the Jockey Club.

When I opened my account, Sir Sik-Nin, as the Chairman of the bank, had directed a junior executive by the name of Yeung to attend to all my needs.

Of course, a great deal had changed over the years. Sir Sik-Nin was no longer there and the bank had changed hands and name. But I had kept my account there and Mr. Yeung, unsurprisingly, had shifted his allegiance to the bank's new owners. He had risen now to become a senior executive of some consequence. He and I had developed a firm and cordial professional relationship over time and, notwithstanding his advancement within the bank, Mr. Yeung had retained an oversight concerning my needs.

"How can I be of service to you, Mr. Wong?" Mr. Yeung asked, immediately upon seeing me enter his office.

"I need a standby overdraft facility." I replied automatically.

"That should not be a problem. Now let me see . . . ." He then rummaged among some files and documents before continuing: "You have well over a million dollars on deposit with us — earning interest, of course — and you have a handsome monthly income from Li & Fung on top of a monthly government pension. You're at the same time clean as a whistle on our books in terms of mortgages and debts. I would say you could have whatever overdraft facility you desire. You're what we would call a very low-risk customer."

Well over a million dollars, I thought wryly and instantly to myself. The sum, made up of the remnants of the Li & Fung deal, the fortuitous dual payments of both my civil service and my Li & Fung salaries for six months, and the premature 25% commutation of my pension, had turned out not to be needed after all, now that the educational expenses for my sons had been adequately provided.

If I had been smarter at the time, I would not have commuted a quarter of my pension into a lump sum. But it was no use crying over spilt milk.

"Good," I said, returning to the matter at hand. "Just set up whatever overdraft facility you consider reasonable and appropriate and transfer my cash deposit balance to your foreign exchange department to set up an account for forward trading in foreign currencies."

"I would need signed authorisations for that."

"All right; make out the forms and I'll sign them."

He made out the forms and I signed. Afterwards, I said: "Please instruct your foreign exchange department that as soon as the exchange rate for the Hong Kong dollar goes up to nine or above against the U.S. dollar, the department should, on my behalf, start selling the American dollars forward, for settlement in six to eight weeks, to the full extent possible with my account. I believe a person could normally trade foreign currency trades on a margin of only 10%."

"What about your overdraft facilities, Mr. Wong?"

"Leave those in place, as my backup, in case there are margin calls."

"But your instructions would appear to be going against market sentiments, Mr. Wong. We're old friends. You've been a top civil servant. Do you know something that I don't?"

"I cannot answer your question, Mr. Yeung, because I don't know what you don't know."

"I mean, is there some secret information or aim which is making you leave instructions the way you have?"

"If you mean whether I have insider information, the answer is 'no'. But I have considered a number of known facts and I have arrived at my own conclusion. I do hope that I will be as spectacularly right in my judgement as Thales of Miletus had been."

"Who's Thales of Miletus?"

"Well, Mr. Yeung, I did tell you that I did not know what you do not know. But I have no time to explain at the moment. I have another pressing mission to undertake."

Mr. Yeung put on a baffled look and I, with a quick farewell, excused myself.

* * *

Upon leaving the bank, I retraced my steps back to Connaught Road Central, to the Hong Kong Chinese General Chamber of Commerce, where the office of my old friend, Mr. Ip Yeuk-Lam, could be found.

I realised while I was talking to Mr. Yeung that the money I actually had would be just a drop in the ocean in the foreign exchange market terms. So I needed much more in the way of ammunition. Yeuk-Lam had to be my first call for help.

I came straight to the point with my old friend when I entered his office. "Yeuk-Lam, have you any uncommitted cash lying around?" I asked. "I need a quick loan, for no more than two or three months at the most."

"Sure. How much do you want?" Yeuk-Lam replied.

"How much do you have?"

"I've got about two and a half million," he answered, with a quizzical look. "I presume you've got your eye on another apartment, now that property prices have fallen?"

"No, I've got my eye on a giant hoovering machine which would suck up all the money that idiots are throwing out onto our streets, right, left and centre."

"What do you mean?" Yeuk-Lam asked.

I revealed my thoughts and all the reasons I figured the current exchange of 8.65 to one American dollar was over-pricing the latter, especially after President Nixon had taken it off the gold standard back in 1971. Now that the local dollar had appreciated against the American one, that current level of exchange rate could only be sustained by continuing fear, greed and reckless speculation.

"The Financial Secretary must be working on a way to calm things down right now, I reckon, because the current level of exchange could bring real damage to the economy," I said.

"The Chinese must be worried too, but you must know more about that than I do. You know the Chinese will stand four square behind the Hong Kong dollar because the Bank of China is one of the three note-issuing banks, along with HSBC and Chartered Bank.

"I think the madness will unfortunately continue for a bit longer, with the local dollar going down perhaps some more, because the speculators and the greedy want it that way. But if the government holds its nerves, as I think it will, and then go about setting a more realistic exchange rate, at below the present level, the speculators are going to be in for a good hiding.

"So I want a loan to sell the American dollar forward against the local currency. I've already given instructions to my bank to sell forward for a duration of four to eight weeks once the figure hits nine to one or above. But my means are limited. So far as I'm concerned, any rate that the government sets below eight dollars will be sheer money for jam."

"But wait a minute," Yeuk-Lam said, "if things are going the way you have described — and I have no reason at all to doubt anything you've said — then I also want a part in the game."

"All right. Then we'll go 50:50 on what you can spare. Go to your bank and give it the same instructions I have given to mine. I can always touch other rich friends for additional loans."

"Since this sounds so sweet an opportunity, do you mind my telling relatives to do likewise?"

"You and I are like brothers, Yeuk-Lam, with mutual trust and understanding. We don't even need words. I wouldn't feel quite comfortable having other people's money on my conscience. If you think it a good idea for your relatives to get involved, I suggest you ask them to ring me first, so that I can explain to them directly and fully the basis of my thinking. If they still want to go ahead after my explanation, it would then be their own decision."

As it happened, only one of the nephews of Yeuk-Lam's rang. He was a businessman called Ip Shing-Wo. I had known him fairly well because he had stood in a few times when our normal *mah jong* quartet was short of a leg due to travel plans, illness or prior engagements. I explained my reasoning to Shing-Wo and left him to decide for himself what he intended to do.

* * *

What eventually happened in the wider world was that the exchange rate exceeded nine dollars to one American dollar a few days later in September, under high speculative pressures, and my instruction to my bank went into effect. During the last weekend of September the rate actually hit a record of 9.60 dollars for an American one.

But the joy of the speculators was short-lived. On October 15, the government threw its weight behind a new peg of 7.80 to the U.S. dollar. The currency chaos calmed down and the local dollar stabilised fairly quickly.

The net result for me and those friends who had joined in on that currency punt was that we made many tens of millions of dollars over a very short period of time — and all happily at the expense of disruptive speculators.

So far as Li & Fung was concerned, I could find no mention in the published accounts of the parent company for that year recording foreign exchange gains or losses. I assumed there must have been a loss, submerged and disguised somewhere within the other figures; if it had been a significant gain, some boast would have been made of it.

* * *

In respect of the multiple millions I had thereby gained but which I had never needed or wanted, except to prove that my view of an insane social situation was correct. I did not know what to do with the accumulated sum. It did feel amusing for a short while to have so much loose change sloshing around, especially with pressure coming from Suze Ip on the flanks nudging me towards a long-term relationship with a teenaged Chiu Kit.

But the feeling of light-headedness soon evaporated, together with all fear of taking on financial responsibilities for Kit's education should a firmer relationship occur. There were, in any case, tentative options being pushed for visiting Shanghai in the spring.

A number of other options did saunter across my mind. I could, for instance, quit work altogether and indulge my youthful fancy of writing fiction. But I could not really do that because I had given my word to my employer to work in commerce for a certain number of years.

Another complication was that, if a marriage ensued, I had also promised Kit I would show her many of the places and promises of the world. I could hardly concentrate on writing while such promises had not been kept. And all the while, the nagging need to manage excessive levels of funds stayed with me.

Eventually, a friend who worked for a leading American investment bank came to my rescue. She introduced me to that arcane world of Euroclear, zero coupons and callable and non-callable government bonds. She suggested that I open an account with her bank, park my funds there and continue doing whatever I had been doing before.

That sounded too attractive an alternative to miss. So I did as she had suggested, converted my money to pounds sterling and invested my funds into 30-year World Bank bonds with a coupon rate of 10.75% per annum. Since I had no use for extra money on top of my normal income, I asked that all interest payments on the bonds be reinvested in the same bonds.

After a while, I appreciated what Einstein meant when he described compound interest as a frightening thing. Compound interest appeared an almost obscene aspect of the capitalist system. It enabled a person with money to invest and command a high return without the slightest effort on his part! An interest rate similar to my World Bank bonds could see a person's wealth double in four years and quadruple in eight years.

* * *

I do not know whether I shall live long enough to write the fifth volume of my family memoirs. In all probability I shall not. But there is one statement I can make now which will be contrary to received opinion. In my humble experience, I have found it much more taxing and tedious to give money away meaningfully than to make it.

CHAPTER 12

Unforeseen Consequences

When the Chinese Communists came to power in 1949, after Chairman Mao had earlier declared with his usual hyperbole that women held up half of heaven, I had assumed that the subordinate position placed upon women in China since the time of Confucius would at last be brought to an end. Women of marriageable age would henceforth be expected to be completely free to indulge in the folly of matrimony on an equal basis as sillier men had been doing for ages — without the interferences of parents, relatives, religious authorities or anybody else with a sounder grasp of human frailties and life experiences.

So far as my own family had been concerned, that freedom of matrimonial choice and that readiness to indulge in the chimera of romantic love had been practised since my grandfather's generation. He had, as family legends and some of my own boyhood observations had confirmed, ended up with a *ménage* of **nine** wives — a number I could barely imagine during my adult years, let alone get to grips with during my innocent boyhood.

What became progressively clearer, however, to those of us who had subsequently made a hash of our marriages — an increasing host including my parents, myself and some of my siblings — was that we had no one but ourselves to blame for the recriminations, divorces, custody arguments over children and all the other tedious legalities and acrimonies that inevitably followed.

I was to ponder in subsequent years whether all human beings harboured a contrarian streak where love was concerned. No matter how many times we might come a cropper, hope always seemed to spring eternal. After my disastrous marriage with Man-Ying and the fruitless pursuit of other affairs, experience should have taught me to be wary of further romantic entanglements.

And yet, when I found myself increasingly drawn to Chiu Kit, I managed to persuade myself that I was falling in love again. I even convinced myself that marriage simply had to work better the second time around.

So in proposing to Chiu Kit during our meeting at Wushi, I had laid most of my cards on the table. I had led a life that had been far from exemplary, with far too many liaisons along the way with far too many women, especially when I was trying to find a suitable substitute mother for my three children from a previous marriage. But that was now all over and done with, for my children had all gone off to North America for studying subjects of their own choosing. They would be independent and on their own thereafter; and I would be free of further responsibilities.

I was comfortably off and gainfully employed. In addition, I enjoyed a civil service pension for life. I made no mention of my stash of World Bank bonds, for that money seldom came to mind. I could nonetheless afford all reasonable material, educational and travelling needs a wife might aspire to. I had already sown my wild oats, so it would all boil down to working out how best to make a companionable life together.

In order to reassure her that I was legally divorced and eligible for marriage, I sent her copies of the decrees pertaining to my divorce.

Although Chiu Kit had seemed prepared to accept my proposal unconditionally and without ado, I did not want to take advantage of her youth and inexperience. I therefore made a trip to Nantong just to meet her parents and to secure their blessing.

That meeting with her parents turned out well. They were simple and straightforward people, completely without guile. A rapport soon developed between us, especially between the father, Chiu Bun, and myself. They appeared genuinely pleased that their daughter, who had failed to secure a good enough grade in the *gaokao* or university entrance examination to qualify for higher education in China, would now have other opportunities in life besides the job on the midnight-till-morning shift in a local textile factory that had been assigned to her.

Chiu Bun and myself got onto the same wavelength very quickly, sensing that we could both be completely open with each other. He pointed out that having the right kind of social background could sometimes be just as important in socialist China as in bourgeois countries in former times.

He himself had emerged from a family of small shopkeepers and had been started with a traditional Chinese education. When he was a boy he had loved books and had dreamt of becoming a librarian so that he could always get his fill of books. But he soon realised that times were changing. Becoming a librarian might easily get him classified as an intellectual or someone with opinions to defend.

An intellectual with a shopkeeping family background might be a dangerous combination. Hence he set aside his ambition and settled for becoming just a lowly tallying clerk instead.

More than that, he foresaw that the coming age after World War II would be one where peasants and workers would be in the ascendant and more secure. He therefore sought out a healthy and agreeable peasant woman for a wife so that the family they would raise could be firmly rooted in the soil. Having taken so many precautions to shield family members from the spotlight of political controversy, it was natural that the marriage of his youngest daughter to a Hong Kong capitalist so much older than herself would not have an impact on other members of the family.

Chiu Bun therefore suggested that one means of protecting them might be for each of them to distance themselves from our marriage, by writing letters to their respective residential and work units, stating that each had tried his or her best to dissuade Chiu Kit from marrying me but she had stubbornly ignored their pleas.

The suggestion sounded more than reasonable to me. For years, Hong Kong had been represented in China as an alienated piece of the motherland, sometimes even as a foreign induced carbuncle and a den of iniquity, rife with racism, inequality and exploitation. I was part and parcel of that bourgeois set-up, now engaging in "skimming from the middle" such productive labour others might produce.

I had no desire to get anybody else into trouble because of my marriage. So I ran the suggestion past Kit for her opinion. She seemed comfortable with it. She said she had anticipated some resistance over our marriage, especially from the more puritanical apparatchiks in her town. But she believed she could hold her own against them.

She also thought we should have no difficulty securing a slot from the local equivalent of the Registrar of Marriages for a civil ceremony, once I had secured a medical certificate confirming that I was in reasonably good health and free from contagious diseases.

On that optimistic note, we set in motion the various plans for our nuptials.

* * *

One of the first things I did upon returning to the colony was to seek appointments at Queen Mary Hospital for a comprehensive medical check-up. But before I could even complete all the procedures, I received a letter from Chiu Kit informing me she had been invited for "chats" with office bearers at both her neighbourhood's residential unit and at her workplace's unit. This was a tried and tested tactic in united front work, she explained, a method for persuading someone who had strayed to return to socialist orthodoxy. However, she assured me she could adequately handle the matter.

Nantong was a relatively modest little town, though the section in which she resided had more the atmosphere and characteristics of a typical Chinese village. Everybody in it felt they had the right to poke their noses into everybody else's affairs and add their own two cents' worth. So once her father and her siblings had lodged their letters opposing her marriage, rumours and speculations circulated furiously, alleging that one of the neighbourhood's young women was intending to marry a rich but dubious Hong Kong capitalist in spite of the objections of her parents and of her entire family.

Reading between the lines, I gathered that the "chats" might range between good natured cajolery to outright threats and bribery. She was young and inexperienced in the ways of the outside world, her interlocutors would begin. Would it not be better to listen to her parents and her older siblings? They were, of course, talking to her only for her own good.

People from Hong Kong were notorious for being unscrupulous and silver-tongued; their word could hardly be trusted, no matter what they might promise. To them, money and profits were all that mattered. How could she risk marrying someone so much older than herself and whom she hardly knew? Had she not met him only two or three times? She should not be taken in by promises of wealth and luxury but seriously think again.

Information made available from Chinese official quarters suggested that the man in question already had several wives and a number of grown-up children. She would encounter all manner of complications and trouble fitting into such a family, perhaps even get rejected. What would she then do in a strange town, without kinfolk or family, should that man decide to abandon her?

The managers at her factory laid it on even thicker. They rehearsed similar arguments and expressed surprise that a young woman brought up on firm socialist principles could be so easily swayed by material blandishments from a virtual stranger. The world was filled with accounts of gullible women trafficked as prostitutes and sex slaves. They reminded her she was currently on the night shift, beginning at midnight till early the next morning. If she behaved more like a model socialist worker, it should be possible to consider changing her shift to one with more sociable hours.

Chiu Kit ended her letter by urging me to send her the results of my medical examination as soon as possible so that she could proceed with the requirements for our marriage at her end.

* * *

Kit and I had fallen into a natural pattern of writing to each other at least once a week, to update each other on what was happening in our lives. Therefore, when no letter from her had arrived for two weeks after the letter reporting on her being invited for "chats", I sensed that something was amiss.

I had thought of telephoning Chiu Bun for the latest information. But back in those days only very senior officials in Nantong had the luxury of having a private telephone in their homes. There was only a communal telephone in his neighbourhood for emergency contacts with residents but anyone relying on that instrument could be certain that the operator and everyone else in the office would be listening in avidly on all conversations and broadcasting information thus gleaned as current gossip.

By the end of the third week without a letter from Kit, I was on tenterhooks. I was almost ready to hop on a plane for Nantong, regardless of consequences.

Just then, a letter with a Shanghai postmark fortuitously arrived. It was from Kit. It appeared that the leaders of the Nantong branch of the Communist Youth League had inserted themselves into our marriage controversy, the very same leaders who had a couple of years earlier awarded her a prize of a trip to Peking for her enthusiasm and command of socialist revolutionary principles!

They now felt not only outraged but betrayed that she should have so readily abandoned her principles to seek a bourgeois life of plenty with a middle-aged Hong Kong businessman. The fact that they had so mistakenly judged her degree of reliability and "redness" previously was there on the record for the entire Nantong community to see. Those cadres risked suffering serious damage to their reputations and possibly even being called to account by their superiors.

They therefore had to use whatever influence they had with Nantong municipal officials to frustrate her marriage, while pretending to be supporting the objections of her parents and her siblings. Thus all her letters to Hong Kong and all incoming letters to her from that city had been interdicted, contrary to Article 40 of the Chinese Constitution. They had calculated that by cutting off communications between Kit and myself our relationship would soon wither and die.

But Kit had found a way to overcome their machinations. She had a good friend who had found a job in Shanghai but who returned to see her parents in Nantong every weekend. That friend had agreed to take Kit's letters to me and mailed them from Shanghai. Likewise, if I would send my letters to her friend in Shanghai she would deliver them to her personally each weekend. It would inevitably take longer for our letters to reach each other but it would overcome the blockade imposed.

The Communist Youth League leaders were also applying pressure on her father through his work and residential units to press her further into changing her mind about the marriage. This was making life awkward for her father.

A few of her former comrades in the Youth League had also been calling on her at her home for "chats". She could not foresee what other tricks the Youth League leaders might get up to. She was confident, however, that they could not legally or constitutionally stop her marriage because the freedom of marriage was protected under Article 49 of the Chinese Constitution and she was clearly of marriageable age. Therefore the sooner their marriage could be finalised the better, she said.

* * *

As I read Kit's letter from Shanghai, I felt the chill of fear entering my heart. But I simultaneously also marvelled at her initiative in setting up an alternative means of communications. The Chinese have had a long history of coping with authoritarian rulers and they had always found ways of skirting their rules and regulations.

The latter was a clear indication she was determined about our marriage and that was heartening. Having been a member of the Communist Youth League, she seemed at least to have acquired a clear understanding of her rights under the Chinese Constitution.

But how could a young woman like her, standing alone, resist indefinitely the concerted and unlawful pressures from an authoritarian bureaucracy? That somehow had to end. I wrote her immediately, via her friend, urging her to stand firm while I figured out a way of dealing with our common predicament.

The only recourse which came to mind was to seek the help of some of my many friends at the Hong Kong Chinese General Chamber of Commerce, especially those with established connections to some of the powerful political figures within China.

In approaching my friends, I was bringing my connections and *guanxi* into play, just as I would expect them to bring their *guanxi* into play on my behalf. That was a very Chinese way of solving problems and getting things done, doing it indirectly through intermediaries and behind the scenes.

I thus approached immediately Ip Yeuk-Lam and H. T. Lui, both *mah-jong* partners of long standing, and Wang Kuan-Cheng, the then serving President of the Chinese General Chamber.

Yeuk-Lam was the senior Vice-President at the General Chamber as well as a member of the Kwangtung Provincial People's Congress, while Lui was as thick as thieves with many of the political personalities surrounding Ziang Zemin, the then Mayor of Shanghai.

Ziang, a native of Yangchow and an electrical engineer by training, had by virtue of his position as Mayor of Shanghai, a seat in the Politburo of the Communist Party. He was later to rise to become the General Secretary of the Party and then President of the Chinese Republic.

Wang was, like Chiu Kit, a native of Jiangsu. Apart from his presidency of the General Chamber he was also a veteran member of the Chinese People's Political Consultative Conference, a sort of *de facto* upper advisory body made up of various political, religious, racial, economic and educational representatives from throughout the nation. The body was supposed to work in collaboration with the Chinese People's Congress in approving laws. Therefore the three I approached all carried considerable heft with parts of the political leadership in China.

The concept of *guanxi* is generally taken by outsiders as a form of corruption but that is often not at all the case. The most basic and fundamental connections are those within one's own family. The family had been firmly established as the basic unit in society since the time of Confucius. As a consequence, nepotism and a subordination of an individual's wishes to the collective interests of the family had been among its more unfortunate offshoots.

Let me illustrate what I am driving at: suppose a person has a brother who happens to be a dentist or a doctor. If he has a toothache or a stomach ache he would first seek out his brother. The brother would then naturally give him some priority in attention because of that blood connection. Other Chinese patients who might be waiting to be attended to would automatically understand and accept why that priority due to blood ties should be given.

The situation can become more clouded and less distinct if the brother happened to be a public servant, with the right to grant or withhold some scarce commodity, like a licence. Even though he might be judging all claims entirely on their merits, the perception of favouritism could unfortunately arise.

For the average Chinese, however, *guanxi* is seldom traded for cold hard cash, because it is firmly embedded in a system of family or personal relationships built up over considerable periods of time. It is also normally based on trust, reciprocity, friendship and other ties. For example, if one happened to be a member of a triad society and had sworn a blood oath with fellow members, that would represent a legitimate claim of *guanxi*.

The use of *guanxi* could lead to a never-ending series of favours being granted and received. A favour granted becomes a debt to be returned at some future time, if called upon. It would be considered in very bad taste not to treat it as an obligation which had to be honoured and repaid.

The intangible concept of face always form some element in the equation. It amounts to something more than what Westerners might merely refer to as contact, social capital or networking. In Western societies, sharing membership in the masons or a fraternity or a club might impose a similar but less compelling kind of obligation.

* * *

After I had outlined Kit's situation to my three friends, I told them I did not want to lodge a formal complaint against the unlawful deeds by those over-zealous cadres in Nantong. After all, my future in-laws would have to continue living in that town and it would be far better if things could be resolved quietly behind the scenes and out of public sight. Kit and I just wanted to be left alone so that we could get married as soon as possible.

All three friends agreed with my approach and pledged to do whatever they could to untangle the mess. However, they warned that people with influence in Peking would be unlikely to act until they had been made aware of the credentials of the person seeking their intervention. They would not be prepared to put themselves on the line just for some Hong Kong Joe smitten by some Nantong factory girl.

"I would, for example," Ip said, "have to tell my contacts what a patriotic compatriot David had been when he was working for the British colonial authorities. They would also have to know he was the one who had cut through years of delay to get a new and enlarged wholesale market built to facilitate the more efficient export of Kwangtung produce to the local market. He had also been the one who had countered the British attempt to spend money on an expensive foreign reverse osmosis sea water conversion project instead of simply buying more East River water from Kwangtung. So the authorities in Kwangtung definitely owe him some help in return now."

"I can remind my friends in Shanghai how David had initiated the dialogue during the 1973 OPEC oil crisis which led to China supplying extra fuel oil to Hong Kong in return for grants of land here for Chinese corporations to start retail petrol stations to break Western monopolies," Liu said.

"Look," Wang interjected, "we should also stress David's present position as managing director of an old established trading firm, engaged in promoting the export of a wide range of Chinese products to America and Europe. Why not get someone to put all that together in a resumé and I'll take it up with the top brass in the New China News Agency. The people there ought to be able to advise on which department or organisation in Peking we could best direct our lobbying efforts at."

"I can get one of the secretaries to attend to the resumé," Yeuk-Lam said. "But judging from what David has told us, it appears that the Nantong officials are using the letters of opposition to the marriage from Kit's parents and siblings to justify their meddling. Wouldn't things be simpler if the letters of opposition were withdrawn?"

"Those letters were intended as simply a ritual of form, to protect family members," I explained. "They were never meant to be taken literally."

"Well, the Nantong cadres seem to be taking them literally now. Can they be withdrawn? That would cut some of the ground from right under their feet."

"That should not be a problem for the parents," I replied. "They are all for our marriage. Issues might arise, however, with Kit's eldest sister, Chiu Shu-Ching, and her husband, Gao Lin-Mao. I've never met either of them. But they're both in the Cultural Division of the People's Liberation Army and are members of good standing in the Communist Party. If they were to withdraw their letters, they would need some pretty cogent reason for changing their minds."

"Can't we send someone to talk to them?" Wang asked.

"I don't have their address. But I can get it from Kit. They're living somewhere in Peking."

* * *

When I got Kit's letter giving her sister's address in Peking, it contained a pleasant surprise. She told me that Gao, her brother-in-law, was in fact at that moment in Shenzhen, just across the border from Hong Kong. He was expected to be there for several weeks, shooting a film. She also gave the name of the hotel he was staying in.

When I passed the information to Wang, he immediately sent off a message to Gao through official channels. He stated that he was the President of the Hong Kong Chinese General Chamber of Commerce and a member of the Chinese People's Political Consultative Conference. He and the General Chamber's Vice-President, Mr. Ip Yeuk-Lam, were due to visit Shenzhen presently on business and would feel obliged if they could call on Mr. Gao at his hotel for a cup of tea or a meal so as to seek Mr. Gao's assistance on a personal matter of great importance to both of them.

A reply duly came back, suggesting a time and date. So on the appointed date, I boarded a train to Shenzhen together with Wang and Ip.

* * *

Gao turned out to be a tall, handsome man of sturdy build. He displayed a distinctive military bearing, although I could not tell for sure whether it came naturally or whether he had adopted it as part of his screen persona. In any case, he met us with elaborate courtesy and politeness. He struck me as a friendly and very likeable type.

I quickly introduced myself and confessed that it was I who really needed his help because I very much wanted to marry his wife's youngest sister.

We shook hands warmly and he said he had suspected as much when his father-in-law asked his wife and himself to protect themselves by writing letters opposing our marriage.

"In uncertain times, people learn to take precautions," Gao added.

I was curious as to the precise role he might be playing in the film being made, so I asked him. But he said he was the director rather than an actor in the film being shot.

"How thrilling!" I exclaimed. "It must be very challenging to switch from acting to directing. What's the story line of the film? Is it about the People's Liberation Army or something else?"

"It's a period drama," Gao replied. He was about to elaborate on his project when Wang politely intervened and suggested that we should first offer Mr. Gao the hospitality of a cup of tea.

We therefore ordered tea in the hotel lobby and upon its arrival settled down pleasantly to discuss the matter in hand.

"You can assure your wife, Mr. Gao, that should her youngest sister decide to marry Mr. Wong she needn't have any qualms over her sister's future in Hong Kong. Both Mr. Ip and I can vouch for that. We have been friends with Mr. Wong for many years and I can stake everything I have on his good character, integrity, kindness and Chinese patriotism."

Gao let out a chuckle. "I have not the slightest doubt over the qualities described by so distinguished a gentleman as your good self. But please tell me something, Mr. Wang. A couple of years back, my sister-in-law told me that Mr Wong had proposed marriage to her on the very first day they had met at the Ming Tombs. Are all Hong Kong men as romantic and daring as that? As an actor I have been filled with admiration ever since."

"I'm not so sure that can be applied generally to Hong Kong men but that trait would be consistent with my friend's character," Wang said.

"I can also vouch wholeheartedly for my friend," Ip swiftly echoed. "It appears that some cadres in Nantong are using the letters of opposition to the marriage by family members to frustrate the marriage. If such letters were to be withdrawn, the the ground would be cut from under their feet. If it would make it simpler to withdraw the letters of opposition, by all means state that assurances about Mr. Wong's bona fides had been received from both Mr. Wang Kuan-Cheng, a member of the Chinese People's Political Consultative Conference and Mr. Ip Yeuk-Lam, a member of the Kwangtung Provincial People's Congress.

"Yes, that can be done," Gao said, with a nod. "I'll put that in hand once I've consulted my wife."

That was the first and last time I met Gao. Although I invited him and his wife to visit Kit and myself in Hong Kong in the late 1980s, he was unable to make it because he had been otherwise engaged. Only his wife came. After that Kit and I migrated to Britain. Gao passed away in 2016 at the age of 73.

* * *

Having secured Gao's agreement on withdrawing his and his wife's letters of opposition, the contacts of my friends began making representations about the unnecessary obstructions to my marriage to Kit to the United Front Work Department of the Communist Party's Central Committee.

When those representations reached a certain volume, the department decided to send an emissary to Nantong to investigate the situation and to make known the opposition to some of the extralegal initiatives resorted to by some Nantong cadres.

After the visit by the United Front Work Department emissary, the pressures on Kit and her family gradually dissipated. But some of the Nantong cadres remained resentful over being called to heel by the central authorities. They still had one or two cards to play and played them they did with great relish.

When I eventually sent Kit the report on my medical examinations at the Queen Mary Hospital to pass on to the Marriage Registry, Kit was told in no uncertain terms that a report from a colonial institution could not be relied upon as being comprehensive and unfalsified. For marriages to be performed in China, the medical examinations of the parties involved had to be carried out by an authorised Chinese medical institution. It was to be either that or no marriage at all.

CHAPTER 13

Getting Married

AND THUS IT CAME ABOUT that on a bitingly cold January morning in 1984 I presented myself at the Nantong General Hospital for the medical examinations I had to pass before I could be considered healthy and disease-free enough to marry a Chinese girl.

The hospital was at that time a squat and ugly affair of four storeys, built unmistakably to an outdated Soviet design, reflective of a time when the two countries had passionately professed eternal friendship. Creeping political differences and the growing hubris among their respective leaders, however, soon rendered that friendship somewhat less than eternal, though the hospital remained a stolid symbol of that once worthy intent.

Although Kit and I had arrived at the hospital at 5.30 a.m. a queue of half a dozen prospective patients had already been formed ahead of us, waiting for numbered tokens to admit them for attention when the hospital opened at six.

Intermittent snow flurries excited the gloomy morning air but no shelter was available for anyone except for an abbreviated and barely discernible set of eaves projecting from the top of the building. One or two of the earlier arrivals had brought along tatty quilts or worn blankets to cover themselves.

I felt immensely grateful that I was not among those who actually required medical assistance. I was dressed in a smart padded leather overcoat of iron-grey which I had acquired many years earlier during a visit to Berlin. My head was covered by one of those Russian military fur caps with earflaps which could be lowered to shield the ears from cold. I had also bought that headgear during that Berlin visit.

As for Kit herself, she appeared incongruously bundled up, almost as tightly as a glutinous rice dumpling, in her own home-made blue padded cotton garments. She had already completed her own medical examinations the previous week and was therefore merely there to keep me company. The cold had brought out fetching blooms to her cheeks which enhanced her youthful loveliness. The alien cut of my clothes and the close proximity at which Kit and I stood together attracted the curiosity of some of those queuing at the hospital.

* * *

When I was eventually admitted into the precincts of the hospital, I was directed to a room where I was to begin my medical examinations. I was asked to strip naked so that my height, weight and blood pressure could be recorded. It became apparent immediately that the building was not centrally heated. Individual rooms housing white-coated staff each had a coal-fired brazier to provide a measure of warmth.

I peeled off my clothing as required; first my padded leather overcoat, followed by my Harris tweed jacket, my brown corduroy slacks, my beige turtle-necked sweater, and finally my woollen undergarments, all of which ended up in an untidy heap in the arms of Kit, as she waited coyly outside the room.

Rather than dress again before proceeding to the next stage of the examinations, I merely retrieved the overcoat to hide my modesty before going for an examination of my eyes, ears and throat.

Part of those procedures gave me my first shock. The medic in charge took out a wooden spatula from a jar of purplish liquid, which I had assumed to be a solution of potassium permanganate, pressed it upon my tongue and asked me to say "ahh". I almost gagged because I noticed that the instrument had discoloured patches on it, no doubt from having been soaked for too long in that purplish solution. The spatula was the kind that medical staff in Hong Kong would only use once before discarding. The fact that the air smelt overpoweringly of disinfectant did not help.

The next ordeal was no less disconcerting. I was required to provide a sample of blood for testing. The veins in both my arms were unusually thin, so that anyone wanting to extract blood had to be fairly practised at the task. What I had not realised at the time was that disposable syringes and hypodermic needles were too expensive for single usage in China. Therefore they appeared to be generally sterilised for re-use on economic grounds. The blunted needles made for several failed attempts to connect properly with my veins.

The next set of requirements was for me to provide a sample of urine to be analysed, to have my reflexes tested and to have the state of my prostate thoroughly probed. Somewhere during those processes, the medic in charge unceremoniously took hold of my testicles and ordered me to cough. The situation reminded me of an old home truth attributed to President Nixon, to the effect that when a man held one by the balls it usually made sense to obey his orders. So I promptly coughed.

The final stage of the examinations consisted of being guided by Kit to another part of the hospital for X-rays to be taken. There I was in for another shock. The machine used simply took my breath away. It consisted of an antiquated wooden box with two lead-lined gloves sticking out from either side. The contraption gave every appearance of having been handed down from either Wilhelm Röntgen or Marie Curie! I wouldn't have been the least bit surprised if I were to learn later that I had been rendered completely sterile after my exposure to that antiquated piece of equipment.

What I had gone through brought home to me how primitive and backward so many of the basic health and other facilities in China were. One had to admire the sheer audacity of the country's leaders. They were facing monumental problems in every direction and yet they seemed determined to drag the nation forward into a new socialist future — even by the hair if necessary.

* * *

At the conclusion of the various tests, just as Kit and I were about to leave the hospital, a terrifying series of thoughts struck me one after another. What other tricks might local cadres get up to? Could they tamper with the medical findings and allege that I was suffering from some rare and incurable disease? Would that put an end to my chances of ever marrying Kit or at least playing ducks and drakes for months without end?

The possibility was not so far-fetched as all that. After all, both the private medical specialists and the Queen Mary Hospital consultants had failed to identify the cause of my recurring pancreatic attacks. Any allegation made by cadres in China could well take time and stupendous effort to disprove. I realised all at once that I was in thoroughly unfamiliar terrain. Whom could I approach to even lodge a protest or to seek a second medical opinion? Who would even entertain an appeal by an outsider from Hong Kong? All the money in the world would be of no use to me.

But rather than alarm Kit with those dark and outlandish thoughts, I merely asked: "How long will it be before I can get my results?"

"It should take no more than a few days," she replied.

"I can't wait around here for very long, you know. I've got loads of work piling up in Hong Kong."

"There's no need for you to wait for results here. When they're ready I can lodge them with the Home Affairs Department and seek a date for the wedding. That is, if you're still minded to go through with it." There was an obviously teasing note in her voice.

"Do you think I went through everything here today just for the fun of it?" I cried.

"Just checking," she said.

On that more lighthearted note we both broke into a laugh.

* * *

In less than a fortnight I was back in Nantong, armed with a time and date for our wedding. My fears had been totally misplaced; I had been given a clean bill of health, pretty much on all fours with what the Queen Mary Hospital had originally provided.

It appeared that the Home Affairs Department had taken over a former mansion of a gentry family as an adjunct for conducting wedding ceremonies and settling minor domestic disputes. Kit and I duly turned up at a great hall which, judging by the carved and painted crossbeams in its ceiling, must have once served as an ancestral hall for some venerable family. But the cracked and pitted state of the cement floor spoke depressingly of its inadequate upkeep as a public facility.

The hall was divided into two unequal parts by a low wooden fence with a hinged gate at its centre. The greater part of the hall was used as a dedicated public waiting area filled with a number of stout wooden benches which were already fully occupied. Most of those present consisted of prospective pairs hurtling into matrimony, overly-made-up young women and fidgety young men in new but ill-fitting suits. Naturally they were accompanied by entourages of their respective families. One or two of the prospective brides surprisingly had on traditional embroidered bridal gowns but, for the most part, the more proletarian substitutes prevailed.

The overflow from the benches loitered around the entrance to the rear of the hall which opened onto what had once been a privately landscaped garden, with the remnant of an impressive rockery on display. Kit and I joined those idling around the entrance. By design, no Chiu family member turned up for the occasion, to underline their distancing themselves from Kit's decision.

The wall of the smaller section of the hall was dominated by one of those ubiquitous portraits of Chairman Mao. In front of the portrait, a wooden dais rose a few inches above the floor. Upon it was a long zitan bench of uncertain original usage. It was complemented by three seats to form an improvised magisterial adjunct for official purposes. A metal ashtray half-filled with cigarette butts was left in front of each of the three places. A couple of paces away from the dais, two chairs stood at the lower level facing the bench, with their backs against the wooden fence separating the two parts of the hall.

Presently, three officials entered the smaller section through a side door and took their seats behind the zitan bench. A hush descended upon the hall. The official who sat at the centre had thinning grey hair, though he appeared to be younger than myself. His companions were obviously his subordinates for they were in their twenties and had those dull and unimaginative faces of people satisfied with their lot as note-taking functionaries. Each carried a stack of files and notebooks.

After the three had settled themselves at the bench, one of the younger men stood up and called out two names. They were unexpectedly mine and Kit's. We made our way forward through the crowded hall till we reached the low wooden fence separating the two parts of the hall.

As we moved forward, someone called out: "This is the case the whole town has been talking about." A murmur of interest rippled through the assembly.

Upon reaching the fence we were asked to pass through the hinged gate and to take the two seats facing the bench. We were then asked to confirm our names and other details.

The grey-haired member of the trio then addressed us. "My surname is Yim," he began. His voice sounded cultured and well-modulated. "I have been assigned to process your application to be married. There appears to be several unusual features about this application. You have both been found to be medically fit and in good health. So that is not an issue.

"However, though we get many applications for marriages, the number involving one of our citizens marrying an outsider, especially someone from Hong Kong is rare. I have a responsibility for ensuring that marriages are freely contracted and are fully in compliance with the laws and regulations of the People's Republic of China. The young and the vulnerable have sometimes to be protected from their own indiscretions.

"There has, in the present case, been in addition a letter of objection lodged by the parents of the prospective bride, which was subsequently withdrawn. Some local cadres and the central authorities have also become involved in the case. These are all matters which bear looking into."

Listening to Comrade Yim's summary of our application, I became a little troubled by his approach. I had no experience over marriages in China. The available evidence suggested it might be more akin to a trial. Comrade Yim did not strike me as a Kafkaesque ideologue standing with those bent upon frustrating my marriage; I could detect in his tone of voice and in his choice of words some sense of humour and an inclination towards human sympathy. Yet his mouth seemed compressed firmly into a no nonsense mode. Perhaps he had once been a class enemy now attempting to prove his usefulness to the new regime. I warned myself I had to tread carefully.

"Let me begin with you, Mr. Wong," Comrade Yim said. "According to my papers, you first met Miss Chiu on the Great Wall of China. Not the most romantic spot for a meeting in my book. Now it appears you are proposing to marry her. Can you please explain your reasons? Why should a mature and successful businessman from Hong Kong want to marry so young and fervent member of the Nantong Communist Youth League?"

"We fell in love," I said.

"Ah, yes! Love! The perpetual illusion that lies just a little beyond our ability to grasp. Do you see all the young people here in this hall? They and their families are all anxious for them to rush into a state of wedded bliss. And yet, within a few years, half of them would be right back here trying to untangle the messes they've made of their lives. But you have an advantage over them, Mr. Wong. You've already been down that rocky road. Your first marriage had ended in divorce, had it not? Why would you wish to travel down that road again?"

"Hope springs eternal, sir. My first wife and I discovered belatedly that we did not want the same things out of life. I'm hoping to do better this time, having benefited from my past mistakes."

"And have you and Miss Chiu reached accommodation on your common objectives in life?"

"More or less. In theory, at least."

Comrade Yim allowed himself a wry smile. He then fished out a package of cigarettes from one of his pockets, extracted a stick and lit it. After blowing a cloud of smoke into the air, he turned to Kit and said: "Now Miss Chiu, is this marriage you have applied for one made entirely of your own volition, without pressure or inducement from any quarter?"

"Yes, it is entirely of my own free will," Kit said. "I am of legal age."

"Then why did your parents initially object to your marrying Mr. Wong?"

"They did not know Mr. Wong at all. Perhaps they also thought I was too young to be married."

"Did some of your former comrades and instructors at the Communist Youth League also considered you to be too young to marry?"

"I don't know what they thought. My getting married was none of their business."

"Please help me to understand your situation, Miss Chiu. You could have chosen a husband from among millions of young men of your own age in

China. Yet you have chosen a divorced Hong Kong man, one you hardly knew but decades older than yourself, old enough to be your father, one might say. Why?"

"Oh, no, that is not so. Mr. Wong is not old enough to be my father. My father is two years older than him."

"Ah! I stand corrected, Comrade. But there still has to be a reason, since you apparently just bumped into him in some remote corner of the steppes somewhere."

"Because he's got lots of money!" a voice in the public area cried out, to a peel of raucous general laughter.

"Was that the real reason?" Comrade Yim asked, indicating with his head the rough location from where the shouted remark had apparently originated. "Was that also the reason for your parents withdrawing their objection?"

"No, no!" Kit cried. "That subject never came up. My family leads a very simple life. After my parents got to know Mr. Wong, they liked him. They became convinced he would take good care of me. That was why they withdrew their objection, I suppose."

"But what about your own feelings towards him? How did you jump from a chance meeting at the Great Wall to a decision to marry him?"

"It did not happen in such a simple way. I had won a prize from the Communist Youth League to visit Beijing. While there, a friend of mine and I decided to visit the Great Wall. We bumped into a group of about a dozen older compatriots from Hong Kong. They were very friendly. They wanted to know about life in China, while my friend and I wanted to know about life in Hong Kong. We got talking and they invited us to lunch with them at the Ming tombs. Mr. Wong was part of that group. That was how we first got acquainted."

"Mr. Wong must have made a big impression on you. Swept a young girl like you off your feet, wouldn't you say?"

"Not exactly. He both baffled and impressed me. He seemed very sure of himself and what he wanted. For example, within less than two hours of meeting him, he asked me to marry him. He did it quite openly, in front of everybody. It came as a complete shock to me. I had never met anyone like him. Chinese men do not behave that way. They worry about losing face. In addition, he seemed to know a lot about China and aspects of Chinese history which I did not know. It was very interesting just listening to him talk about the various Ming emperors. It became quite natural to enjoy his company."

"It appears that Mr. Wong not only knows a great deal about Chinese history but he also knows some quite influential personages in the capital. Otherwise, a representative of the United Front Work Department would not have made a journey to Nantong to talk to the cadres at the Communist Youth League opposing your marriage."

"I don't know anything about that. All I know was that they stopped bothering me and my parents."

"Well, it's obvious that there are people in high places who look with favour upon your union with Mr. Wong. So unless I can find evidence of illegality or impropriety, there is no call for dealing with your application in any other than a normal way. You have both answered my questions and I have found nothing that bears investigating further. Unless either of you have something else to say, I suggest you come back here tomorrow and I will issue you with your marriage certificates."

A small outburst of clapping met Comrade Yim's announcement.

Kit and I stood up, said: "thank you, Mr. Yim," and gave a small bow in his direction.

* * *

As we left the hall in high spirits, with our arms around each other, I said: "I'm not sure whether we're now technically married. But so far as I am concerned, tonight will be our wedding night and I want you registered at my hotel so that we can spend the evening together."

"I wouldn't advise that," Kit said. "You have to remember that Nantong is still a very small and conservative town. The hotels here wouldn't register any man and woman together in a room for the night unless they have seen proof that they are lawfully married. We can't produce any proof as yet. It's better to avoid an unnecessary row and not provoke a fresh round of salacious rumours."

"Bloody hell! You mean we have to wait till tomorrow before we can enjoy a night together?"

"Not necessarily. There is an alternative. My father has found a nice antique double-bed and had it installed in my room. The only trouble is that you would come in for a lot of scrutiny from the children in the neighbourhood. We're all used to living our lives in public, without too many secrets from one another. It's safer that way."

"I imagine common courtesy demands that I first pay my respects to my new parents-in-law. Let's do that then."

Kit's parents lived in a very modest and sparsely furnished two-bedroom house with a tiny sitting room in front. Its walls were decorated with only a solitary Chinese landscape painting and a Chinese calendar. No portrait of Chairman Mao was to be seen. Kit's room ran off from the modest sitting room. But it had no door. Only a dark blue calico curtain hung over the entrance. The curtain had a length of bamboo attached to its bottom, to weigh it down.

Within two minutes of our arrival, the doorway and the two barred windows on either side of the door were swamped with children of all ages and sizes. But they seemed to follow the rule of some unwritten protocol. They stayed well clear of crossing the threshold, though they showed no inhibition over voicing and exchanging their prejudices and opinions on a whole range of matters.

"Elder Sister Kit is now married and this is supposed to be her wedding night," someone said.

"She's supposed to fight like a wild cat to protect her Pearl," another responded.

"If we hang around long enough we should be able to hear how much of a fight she's going to put up."

"Maybe she's lost it already. Can never trust these Hong Kong types. They'll sweet talk you into all kinds of things."

"Her husband does not look that old at all."

"He must have lied about his age."

"I've told you Hong Kong types can never be trusted."

"She has made her choice; now she must live with it."

While that incoherent chatter flowed back and forth, some in Mandarin and some in the native Nantong dialect, my in-laws and I played out a pantomime of quietly sipping tea and exchanging inconsequential pleasantries. I did, however, summarise for them the essentials of that morning's marriage rituals.

After another hour or so of pantomime, it occurred to me that dozens of children at the windows and doorway and myself had been going through our respective *Passage to India* or *Tale from Bali* moment. They were scrutinising me not because I happened to be a man who had married their neighbour; rather I had become the prototype of a type of "Hong Hong man" loaded down with their preconceptions and prejudices; the type who could not be trusted.

I became very conscious of E. M. Forster's injunction to connect. But how could I? I completely lacked the tool to engage with them. In a very short while they and I would probably never set eyes on each other again for the rest of our lives. What did it matter what they might think about a Hong Kong man throughout the rest of their lives?

And yet, it seemed somehow inexplicably important that human beings should reach out and touch another human being, should the opportunity present itself. I had during the course of my life made connections with people in Paris and Amsterdam, Munich, Venice, Florence, Los Angeles and many other faraway places. And in every case, I and those opposite numbers had known enough about each other's cultures to make the exchanges mutually meaningful and rewarding. My life had always been expanded and enriched by such encounters. It was a pity I could not follow through with that in Nantong. I was anxious to show Kit how she too could enjoy and benefit from that approach to life.

*   *   *

When Kit and I finally retired to our room, she told me something which took me by surprise.

"We have no toilet facilities in the house," she said. "No one in this entire neighbourhood has. This used to be part of a village. We all use a public latrine just a short distance away. But I don't want you to try and head there because the lighting in public areas are poor and I don't want you to have an accident. I've put a chamberpot next to the bed. Please use that if you have to obey a call of nature."

"That's very considerate of you. What you have suggested makes excellent sense to me. If I tried looking for a public latrine in a strange place in the middle of the night, chances are that I will end up falling into it. I think too many of us in Hong Kong never fully appreciate how desperately poor many parts of China remain to the present day."

"We get by somehow."

"That's a marvellous spirit to have," I said. And just to tease her a bit, I added: "And you mustn't forget that all your neighbours are waiting outside to hear you fight like a wild cat tonight!"

"They'd be disappointed. We're going to be as quiet as mice!"

"Yes," I said. "It is only during those moments of telling silences that lovers can begin to sniff out the deepest secrets and vulnerabilities in each other."

With that we cuddled tightly and kissed beneath a large hand-made quilt with many colourful patches.

*　　*　　*

The next day we called upon Comrade Yim as directed and he received us alone in a private office with an elaborate show of courtesy.

"I'm sorry if some of the questions I had asked yesterday had been a little close to the bone," he said. "I meant no offence, just a demonstration I was taking my responsibilities seriously."

"Of course," I replied. "I had been a bureaucrat myself for a spell, so I know how things sometimes have to operate."

"I'm grateful for your understanding. Well, here you are. I have much pleasure in presenting each of you with your own copy of your marriage certificate. And may I take the opportunity to offer both of you my congratulations and my best wishes for a long and happy marriage."

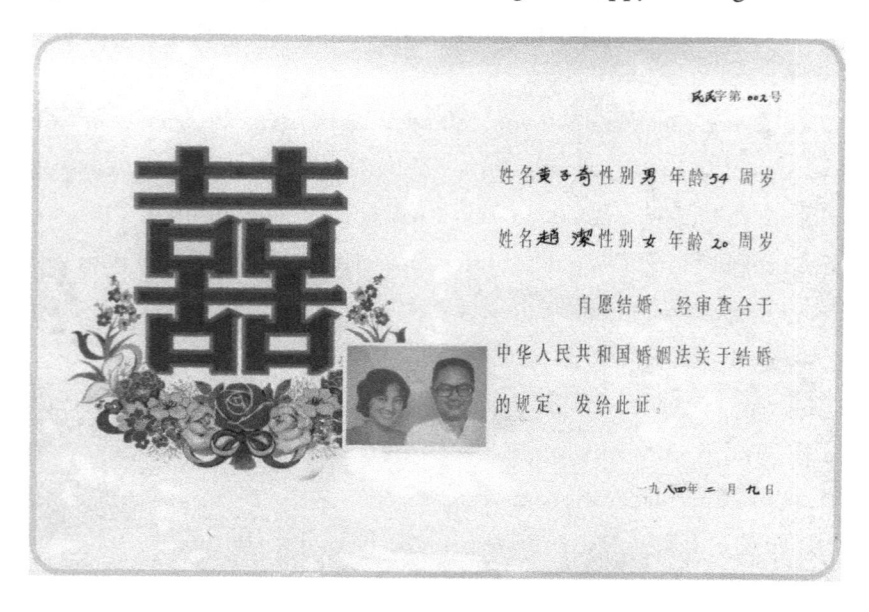

The certificates were identical except for a serial number. They were crimson on one side with bold golden characters stating "Marriage Certificate". The reverse side was white but half the space was taken up by a traditional symbol signifying "double joy" or "double happiness". The rest of the space was used to include a coloured photograph of the couple and their personal details.

After receiving our certificates, I remarked casually: "I suppose the next logical task would be to apply for one of those family reunion visas here to allow my wife to take up residence in Hong Kong."

"That depends on how quickly you wish your wife to join you in Hong Kong," Comrade Yim said.

"I naturally would want her there as soon as possible."

"I hear Hong Kong people are very entrepreneurial. I understand that for a fee certain people known as 'snakeheads' can get a person into Hong Kong very quickly."

"Yes, most things are obtainable in Hong Kong for the right fee. But people getting there without any proper documentation would be considered illegal immigrants, liable for deportation if caught. I'm not willing to turn my wife into an illegal immigrant."

"I fear the normal waiting time for a family reunification visa issued from Jiangsu Province is approximately eight years."

"What! How can that be? The British and the Chinese have a long-standing agreement. The British would allow 150 Chinese per day to take up permanent residence in Hong Kong. That should be more than enough to take care of *bona fide* cases like mine."

"One hundred and fifty per day, seen in isolation, does appear a generous number but is it possible that Mr. Wong has overlooked certain developing realities? There are 23 provinces in China, plus four municipalities and five autonomous regions. Moreover we have 21 ministries and 26 cabinet-level executive departments under the State Council, not to mention various commissions and organisations like the Central Bank, the National Audit

Office and the like. Once you have distributed quotas to each of them, 150 per day do not add up to very many for any of them.

"We must also not forget that the present is also a time when we are supposed to open up to the rest of the world. Everyone wants to set up a representative office in Hong Kong, staffed by its own people so that it can bring in foreign investments and expand economic ties outside of China. Their staff sent to Hong Kong also have a need for family reunification. Official requirements must always take precedence over personal requirements.

"Mr. Wong, you are a man with good connections to both the British and Chinese authorities. May I suggest that it may be more efficient and productive for you to explore some other channels as well, rather than to rely solely on your wife's theoretical entitlement for a family reunification visa as a native of Jiangsu Province."

"I am deeply indebted to you, Mr. Yim, for taking the trouble to draw my attention to the great complexities in the situation. I shall certainly give full weight to your helpful advice. Thank you once again. It has been both a great pleasure and a privilege to make your acquaintance."

"We are both Chinese, Mr. Wong. If we do not do what we can to help one another, who else can we turn to?"

* * *

After receiving our marriage certificates from Comrade Yim, I tried to reassure Kit that I would move heaven and earth if necessary to get her to Hong Kong. Until that had been achieved, I would return to China every month to spend a few days with her.

This could be easily arranged if I took two or three days of leave from work commitments by linking up weekends and Hong Kong public holidays. That would give us a reasonable bank of time together, which we could spend in historical and picturesque Chinese towns studded along the Yangtse valley —

like Hangchow, Soochow, Wushi, Yangchow, Nanking and so forth.

In order to provide flexibility for my business commitments, I urged Kit to give up her job at the textile factory and instead spend her time mastering the rudiments of the English language by using the Linguaphone lessons I had supplied.

And so it was that I began a series of monthly visits to notable Chinese destinations like Soochow, Hangchow and Yangchow to link up with Kit. I would take two or three days of leave each time and fit them in with weekends and public holidays. In that way we managed to enjoy regular reunions of reasonable duration each month.

* * *

Naturally, the moment I got back to Hong Kong, I sought the help of my friends at the Hong Kong Chinese General Chamber of Commerce to get over the latest obstacle I was encountering. They all agreed that the demand for visas for permanent residence in the colony was very high and the number available for family reunification very limited. But, like true friends, they all promised to do whatever they could.

My return to Hong Kong coincided with the Chinese General Chamber hosting an investment and business delegation from China headed by the Chairman of the All China Federation of Commerce and Industry. His name was Mr. K. L. Chang and he was from Nantong. It turned out he was a descendant of the celebrated Chang Jian, the first scholar from Nantong to attain the top spot in the national Imperial Examinations.

When Mr. Chang indicated that he would like to talk to some people knowledgeable about Western corporate culture during his stay in Hong Kong, my friends naturally introduced me to him.

It transpired that one of Mr. Chang's companies had secured a concession to develop a holiday resort on Hainan Island and Mr Chang would like two of his daughters to involve themselves in the project. However, neither of them had any experience in dealing with foreign corporations and he would like to sent them to Hong Kong for a spell to get a flavour of how things were done.

I expressed my willingness to tell them what I could when they arrived of the ethical considerations — or the general lack thereof — when corporations went hellbent after profits.

A meal with Mr. K. L. Chang, Chairman of the All China Federation of Commerce and Industry

* * *

Another Nantong personality who descended on the colony in that critical year of 1983 before my marriage was Mr. Xu Jia-un. He had just finished a six-year stint as Party Secretary of Jiangsu Province to assume the post as the

Director of the Hong Kong branch of the New China News Agency.

Such a posting might appear, on the face of it, to be a demotion for the veteran Communist, for he was a member of the Central Committee of the Party. But in fact the post made Xu China's top representative in the colony at a time when the country was about to embark upon tortuous and deliberately ambiguous negotiations with Britain on the return of Hong Kong and its people to the Motherland.

An extraordinary degree of diplomatic skill was required of such a person because even when a matter was agreed the recording of the agreement needed a great deal of creative ambiguity, so that both parties could claim to have got the better of the other side.

The nakedly neoliberal capitalism rampaging throughout the colony must have been something of a shock to a Communist cadre of Xu's standing. Nonetheless he quickly recognised the power that wealth could wield and he tried reaching out to the traditional class enemies to rally them to the national cause. Such moves drew some criticisms, however, from the more conservative elements back in China.

Xu belonged to the reformist wing of the Communist Party and was a close associate of the then Party General Secretary Zhao Zi-Yang. When Zhao fell from grace because of the Tiananmen débâcle in 1989, Xu also fled into exile in the United States. He was expelled from the Communist Party in 1994.

Like most true Chinese, Xu had that special sense of place and unalterable attachment to his homeland through thick and thin. He longed to return to spend the final days of his life there. But the authorities refused to allow his return. He died in America in 2016, at the age of 100.

* * *

Mr. Chang and Mr. Xu were among the personalities and organisations that my friends at the General Chamber lobbied on my behalf to secure a family reunification visa for Kit. I have never kept a complete list of those they approached. But I do know that it was towards the end of 1984 that someone from the Hong Kong and Macau Office contacted Kit to inform her a family reunification visa was being issued for her.

CHAPTER 14

Awkward Passages

ONCE NEWS CAME towards the end of 1984 that Kit had been approved for a one-way exit visa, steps were immediately taken to bring her to Hong Kong. It was eventually decided that I would meet her in Canton to escort her over.

We booked into the White Swan Hotel on Shameen for a few nights, to familiarise Kit with the sights and sentimental locations of the city where I and many of my ancestors had once lived, before crossing the border into what must be — for Kit — a totally strange and different type of society.

But before our rendezvous in Canton, there was a host of chores and arrangements I had to attend to. Foremost among them was the clearance of an appropriate number of closets and drawers in the Seymour Road apartment for the use of the new permanent sharer of the flat. This included bidding a fond farewell to my extended bachelorhood and disposing of all compromising photographs and other items left-behind suitable for feminine use. Otherwise various kinds of explanations or white lies might have to be employed.

A more difficult task was to give up smoking altogether. Although I had experimented with smoking when I had been a teenager, mainly to make myself appear older and more sophisticated, I did not pick up the habit till I was studying at the Institute of Social Studies in The Hague in 1965. From then onwards, I became a regular cigar smoker.

However, after meeting Kit at the Great Wall, I noticed she always averted her face whenever I blew a cloud of smoke into the air. Since we were going to live together as man and wife, it seemed wise to eliminate a possible point of conflict right from the start.

Next, I had to negotiate an expanded deal with Ah Seam, the chubby and cheerful part-time maid who came three mornings a week to clean my apartment and to do the laundry. The arrival of another occupant was bound to entail more washing and ironing. Perhaps Kit would sometimes even prefer dinner at home, whether by candle light or not, but that would surely involve certain errands to and from the local wet market.

Since I would be at work every day, I had to arrange beforehand for daily tutorial English lessons for Kit, with a former English teacher who had now become the wife of an Administrative Officer. She had agreed, for a fee of several thousands of dollars per month, to pick Kit up at Seymour Road every week day at 9.30 a.m., to take her to her home for lessons appropriate for an adult beginner for two and a half hours, to provide lunch for her, and then to drop her back at Seymour Road.

Of course, there would be other tedious details like getting Kit a set of the front door keys, informing the security office of the building that my wife would henceforth be going into and coming out of the apartment and alerting the Jockey Club — on its very centenary year, by the way —that my wife would henceforth be signing chits for food and drinks and other expenditures on my account.

After Kit's arrival in the city, a whole range of other arrangements and briefings would have to take place. For instance, I would have to show her the locations of the nearest supermarket and wet market, as well as where both a suitable hairdresser and an expert dressmaker could be found. Likewise the most convenient route for walking down to the centre of town from the apartment and the number of the bus to be taken to get to the gymnasium facilities of the Jockey Club at Happy Valley.

Then there would be the more complicated business of introducing Kit to Mr. Yeung at the bank, to start a banking account in her own name, into which I would transfer a specified sum each month for personal and out-of-pocket expenses.

Finally, there would be a series of meals and other functions to introduce my wife to friends and associates. The most important of whom would naturally be Ip Yeuk-Lam and his wife, Suze, since they had long before assumed the role of adoptive parents. Suze, in particular, would become instrumental in showing her where to shop and, in particular, the level of prices pertaining to products generally used by women and within a home.

During that process, a reality brought immediately to attention was that most of my dearest friends were a few years older than myself. Since I was myself 34 years older than Kit, the generational gap yawned mightily between my wife and my closest friends. In addition, most of my friends did not know enough Mandarin to communicate effectively with Kit.

Nonetheless, this was not to say that all parties did not take readily to one another. My friends enjoyed the cheerful company of Kit — to whom they quickly affixed the more phonetically pleasing sobriquet of Kitty — but they all indulged her excessively, as if she were a recently discovered granddaughter they had never met before! Kitty, for her part, lavished upon them the respect and consideration appropriate to family elders. All parties got along quite swimmingly in their respective ways.

My close friends, being very clued-up people, soon began insinuating their children and their respective spouses into our company, because their offspring were obviously much closer in age to Kitty than themselves. It then became my turn to feel slightly out of place.

* * *

Among my closest friends was the widower, Leslie Sung, the erstwhile editor-in-chief of the *Hong Kong Standard* and now a senior partner in the long-standing law firm of Lo & Lo. He had a daughter called Elaine, a graduate — like her father — of the University of Hong Kong.

The four of us soon arrived at an arrangement whereby we would on certain specified Sundays gather for a day's recreational swimming and substantial meals at the Jockey Club country club in the New Territories.

After a while, Elaine would seek out a private corner with me and say: "Uncle David, you and Kitty seem to make such a happy combination. Do you think you could help find someone like Kitty for my father? He's getting a bit lonely in his old age."

"I'm not a matchmaker, Elaine," I fended her off immediately.

It was not because I disagreed with her assessment that her father was in need of some caring feminine company; it was just that I knew Leslie's personality too well. I had been familiar with it for many years, at both work and play. He was a man of high principles, but he was also one who was far too intellectual to suffer fools gladly. I could recall vividly how he had reacted against his poor deceased wife, Lorraine, whenever she had made one of those silly mistakes he had taught her to avoid at the bridge table.

But in the face of the entreaties from Elaine, I said to her finally: "I do think it would indeed be good for your father to find an appropriate mate. But because of your father's temperament, he will have to hunt for one himself. Neither you nor I can pick one for him. If we tried, we could both end up in tears."

* * *

Our pleasant and regular Sunday adventures came to an abrupt end, however, not because anyone did or failed to do something, but because of an unforeseen development in the tragic life of Leslie's younger sister, Greta Sung.

I may, in some future volume of these family memoirs, deal more fully with Greta's life. But for now, in the context of the present narrative, I would offer only a summary of the more salient and relevant points, as follows:

When Chairman Mao and his comrades took power in Peking in October of 1949, Leslie and his wife left Shanghai for Hong Kong, where he subsequently took over the editorship of the *Hong Kong Standard*.

Greta, however, elected to remain in Shanghai, where she had an agreeable job as secretary to the head of a British company doing imports and exports with China. Since Britain had been among the first countries to recognise the new regime, she figured she would be safe working for a British firm. Moreover, her mother had been Swedish.

Upheavals usually occur after revolutions and civil wars. Unexceptionally, one of many subsequently broke out in China. Greta had developed a friendship with a British girl who had been the secretary of the British consul in Shanghai. Greta often had to contact that British girl to put through an enquiry from her employer as to whether a particular product was sanctioned in trade with China or not, particularly after the United Nations embargoed trade with China for its involvement in the Korean War.

In any case, the two girls quickly found common interests in jazz, ballroom dancing and tennis. They took to meeting often out of their offices to pursue their mutual interests. Greta confessed to a weakness for Cadbury's chocolates which the British girl promptly procured for her from the consulate canteen. So the relationship blossomed into a friendship between two like-minded young women.

Then, after the British girl had already finished her tour and had returned to Britain, Greta was accused by the Chinese authorities of being a British spy. She denied the accusation, of course, but the prosecution produced photographs of Greta receiving regular packages from the British girl. Greta's nationality was somewhat uncertain. Although her mother had once claimed Swedish nationality for her, she had also at one stage claimed Chinese nationality. She certainly was not British.

In any case, she had already eaten all the chocolate bars passed to her and could not produce anything to prove she had received only bars of chocolate. Neither the British consulate nor a representative of her company came forward to support her version.

The upshot was that Greta was found guilty of being a spy and was sentenced to a lengthy period of imprisonment and corrective detention. Thereafter she was reduced to just a number within a complicated internal security system and no family member could find out where she was being detained at any given time. All contact was hence eventually lost.

Then, suddenly, several decades later, news came to Leslie that Greta had finished her sentence and was being expelled from China by way of Hong Kong. But where was the poor woman to go? With the passage of time she had become virtually stateless. Lengthy imprisonment had also turned her into a complete physical wreck, in need of all kinds of medical and dental attention.

Time had also shrunk the size of the Sung family to just three siblings — an elder brother, a petroleum engineer, working in the oil fields of Brunei and incapable of overseeing care for Greta. His wife was living in Sweden but she spoke neither Chinese nor English and was of an age where she could largely only look after herself. Then there was Leslie and his daughter, Elaine. There was no other family member anywhere.

Leslie was quite willing and financially able to attend to Greta. The only problem was that Hong Kong had a policy of not taking in refugees because of limited space. Leslie went to see the then Chief Secretary and, because of his long record of public service, Leslie had asked for a visa for temporary stay for Greta, so that she could at least receive much needed medical and dental attention.

But the Chief Secretary had replied that if an exception were to be made, then the whole government policy would fall to the ground. Greta had to leave Hong Kong within the number of days specified for refugees on transit.

Somehow, through some legal loophole, Leslie managed to get Greta into

Macau as a tourist. There she managed to stay at a hotel for an unimaginable number of years for medical and other attention, with Leslie footing all bills.

She stayed for so long that she eventually qualified to become a Macau resident! That was when she could obtain proper legal documentation as a Macau resident and visited Hong Kong. That was when I met Greta for the first time and heard her side of the story.

During those long years, Leslie had gone to Macau religiously every weekend, as a devoted and loving brother would, and that was why our original Sunday swimming trips came to an abrupt end.

* * *

In the meantime, other less tangible and yet more personal considerations in the relationship between myself and Kitty came into play. For example, how could I explain to someone like Kitty why the tempo of life in Hong Kong had to be lived at such a frantic noon-day pace? I have found that insane pace in no other city I had ever visited; certainly not in New York, which seemed almost sedate by comparison.

It was as if everyone in the colony was in a rush for some inexplicable reason. I could not put a finger on it myself. So I tried to evade the issue by ordering two middle-of-the-road daily Chinese newspapers to be delivered to the apartment, in the hope that Kitty would gradually, with their help and her own experiences, form her own impressions of her new home.

But there were plenty of other issues. What about the various subtle snobberies virulent in Hong Kong? How should one explain to a girl brought up in a classless society why residents on Hong Kong island commonly looked down upon the residents of Kowloon, or why they, in turn, tended to look down upon those living in the New Territories?

It had, so far as I could see, nothing to do with wealth or education or genealogy, for that same kind of one-upmanship existed between those who were wealthy, depending on whether their riches came from new or old wealth. Likewise regardless of whether one got one's education at a local or an overseas university.

I found myself floundering repeatedly for the right words to explain the complexities. It dawned on me that playing Pygmalion was not at all easy, neither in the original form nor in the later Shavian version through Professor Higgins. My attempts at any explanation could be so easily misunderstood and lead to inappropriate responses.

To take one concrete example: I told Kitty after her arrival that should she ever take a taxi or have a meal in a restaurant alone, she should always pay at least 10% in excess of any bill presented. It was known as a tip. Otherwise the person receiving the money might take umbrage if a tip was not given.

"Why?" Kit asked. "Do people here not find dignity in performing labour?"

"They probably do," I fudged. "But that practice of a tip happens to be a well-established local custom."

Little did I foresee the hilarious chaos that would ensue when Kitty tried to give a tip to a vegetable seller at the wet market, with whom she should customarily bargain for a deal. And then later, with a cashier at the supermarket! The fact that Kitty did not speak or understand Cantonese and the other parties not speaking Mandarin compounded the problem.

Likewise, I woke up later than usual one morning and found Kitty and Ah Seam trying to conduct a conversation in their respective versions of Chinese.

Ah Seam was asking where Kitty had gone to university and Kitty was explaining that she had not secured a high enough grade in the entrance examinations for university. Therefore she had to be assigned a job in a textile factory by the authorities.

Whilst interrupting the conversation, I did not say anything at the time. But after returning from work that evening, I suggested to Kitty that protecting her own privacy was quite important. She should therefore not tell other people too many details about herself or her family, especially to a part-time maid.

"Why not?" she said. "My adoptive mother, Suze, asked me a similar question along time ago and I gave her the same answer. Is it wrong to tell others the truth?"

"No, of course not," I said. "But one has to be careful. Suze is a respected elder who you could trust with private information."

"You mean Ah Seam is not to be trusted?"

"No, no! Ah Seam is a very decent and trustworthy person. Don't get me wrong."

Kitty's questions had me momentarily stumped. How could a person explain class distinctions to someone brought up in a classless society? How could one point out that some were more equal than others and that it would not do to share too many confidences with just anyone.

What was I trying to do to the innocence and outgoing personality that I had originally found so endearing? Was I in fact trying to destroy those very qualities to adapt her to life in a bourgeois capitalist city? It became apparent that it was not only her transition from a mainland society that was awkward but my adjusting to her socialist values as well.

In the end, I said that Hong Kong was a very tittle-tattle sort of town and filled with gossip. It was collectively like a bunch of nosy parkers around a parish pump.

"You'll have no conception of what I'm trying to convey because you don't know what a nosy parker or a parish pump is," I said. "But a person in Hong Kong cannot be too open and above board like back in Nantong. Every little nugget of information here can be twisted out of all proportion. It would be best if you make a habit of keeping as much as possible of your personal information to yourself and not put everything out in the public domain."

"You mean I shouldn't tell other people about myself?" she said. "Even when they ask?

"No, I mean you should only give such information to those worthy of your trust," I replied, which was a rather sneaky way of giving non-answers to truly difficult questions. Under certain circumstances, it might even be considered a form of intellectual bullying.

* * *

Kitty in 1985, shortly after her arrival in Hong Kong

There had been a long-standing arrangement between the British and the Chinese authorities that a certain number of Chinese people should be allowed to cross the border every day to settle permanently in the colony. At the time that Kitty crossed the border, the agreed figure was 150 per day.

I assumed that each side must have made its own calculations as to the perceived advantages and pitfalls in such an arrangement. From the British perspective, I imagined Chinese cooperation in guarding the other side of the border was immensely helpful, to prevent any sudden mass exodus to escape from a natural or politically-made disaster in the mainland. After all, it had long been a standard Chinese requirement for anyone leaving the country legally to first apply for an exit visa.

Therefore to have someone enforcing Chinese law on the other side would quell British humanitarian voices protesting against the colony turning away refugees. But most important of all, the British side must have figured that some trafficking and illegal immigrants would continue to get through to provide a pool of cheap and able-bodied labour for the city's mercantile activities and burgeoning industrialisation.

But the Chinese, initially at least, must have had a different set of calculations. Since most of Hong Kong's population had originated from Kwangtung Province, there was bound to be a persisting demand for family reunifications. Those left behind were apt to be from the older generations, all becoming less productive as they aged and more prone to illnesses and disabilities. Facilities for the infirm and the medically challenged had been quite rudimentary in Kwangtung. Why not meet that popular demand by granting exit visas so that they could be reunited with their more prosperous families in Hong Kong?

So, during the early years of the scheme, a whole procession of aged, blind and otherwise handicapped exited the mainland to take up permanent residences in the colony. But, as both sides probably expected, illegal immigration and trafficking kept up a steady supply of cheap labour.

It was only after China had decided to modernise and to open up the country to new ideas that a scramble began for other provinces, metropolitan cities and autonomous regions to be allocated a share of the daily quota of visas, in order to set up representational and promotional offices in Hong Kong, to be staffed by their own provincial personnel.

* * *

A peculiar aspect of that daily quota system was that, though a person might be given the right of permanent residence in Hong Kong, that person had to complete a full year of residence before he or she could apply for a colonial travel document to venture outside the colony.

That stipulation prevented me from taking Kitty to visit Singapore to pay her respects to my father and to meet some of my siblings. Neither could I take her to Canada to meet my mother and my remaining siblings, let alone my two children who happened to be still studying there.

It was only the sudden arrival of one of Kitty's relatives in town and my need to offer hospitality that my mind was sent scrambling in several different and unfamiliar directions with fresh perceptions.

The visitor concerned was named He Wei. She was the wife of Gao Shu-Mao, the younger brother of Gao Lin-Mao, who had married Kitty's eldest sister.

First of all, He Wei was a seasoned member of the Chinese diplomatic service and was, naturally, a member of the Chinese Communist Party. She had been assigned for years to diplomatic posts in the Indian sub-continent. Her husband was likewise in the Chinese diplomatic service but they had never been allowed to serve abroad at the same time. Her husband had once been an aide to Zhao Zi-Yang before the latter became the Chinese premier, which implied that he might have been a cadre with a fairly liberal cast of mind. I was to confirm that speculative image when I met him some years later, during a visit to Ottawa, and found that he was in post at the Chinese mission there.

He Wei and her husband had a young daughter, currently being looked after by grandparents. The reason He Wei was in Hong Kong was because she was a member of a study group sent to the city to learn how the city and its government functioned.

That piece of information gave me pause. This was during 1985, a full 12 years before the city was due to return to Chinese sovereignty in 1997! Could the Chinese authorities be so far-sighted as to plan and prepare so far ahead?

And what of the British authorities within the city? Were they also sending groups of local civil servants to the mainland to study how the Chinese bureaucracy functioned, so that a smoother integration could be achieved after 1997?

If no step was contemplated, did that mean an absence of long-term planning or did it imply a continuation of the old failed and divisive policy of keeping the younger generation only educated and money-hungry enough for a hard-scrabbled and materialist existence? If youngsters could really think for themselves, would they not start questioning their rootlessness, their moral confusion and their lack of attachments, on top of their uncertainties about identity? After 20 years in the local bureaucracy, I feared that would be the case, just more political and psychological *ad hoc*ery.

I was very pleasantly surprised, however, when Kitty introduced me to He Wei. She appeared a mature, sophisticated and very self-possessed woman in her early forties. Outgoing and with a well-modulated voice too. Since she offered me my first opportunity to interact socially with a *bona fide* member of the Chinese Communist Party, I was determined to be friendly and courteous for Kitty's sake. But I also wanted to gain whatever knowledge I could out of the unexpected visit.

After we had shaken hands and welcomed her, I said: "I have booked dinner at a restaurant serving European meals; I hope that suits your taste. We can always go somewhere else if you prefer a Chinese meal."

"No, a Western meal would be excellent," He Wei replied.

"I've also booked for four, in case you've a companion."

"That's very thoughtful of you. But I've got no companion; my husband's home in China."

"Oh, I was given to understand that Chinese officials on missions abroad are seldom allowed around unaccompanied by some other official or minder. I must have been misinformed."

"Hong Kong's hardly 'abroad'," He Wei reminded me pointedly. "But, in spite of regulations, I've found a loophole. That particular regulation does not apply where family reunions are concerned. Since Kit's eldest sister is married to my husband's elder brother, that places us within the same family. Now you too. This evening can therefore be considered a family affair. The state has to recognise that long-standing basic social unit, a concept in place since before Confucius."

She and Kitty gave out a joint conspiratorial laugh as they linked arms to negotiate the narrow pavement up Wyndham Street to the restaurant of long vintage known as Jimmy's Kitchen.

Not wishing to be outdone so easily, I observed: "A splendid Chinese attitude regarding families and regulations. But some people seemed to have forgotten to think that way during the Cultural Revolution."

"That had been an aberration, now well gotten over," He Wei said, rather light-heartedly, as we arrived at Jimmy's Kitchen.

* * *

I have now forgotten what the womenfolk had for dinner. As for myself, I always followed the same menu whenever I dinned at Jimmy's Kitchen — half a dozen escargots smothered in garlic to start, to be followed by a medium-cooked black pepper Australian steak. We all accompanied our meals with suitable amounts of house wine.

Under the influence of the wine, we mellowed and chatted freely, though the conversations were in the main between He Wei and myself, especially when the inadequacy of my command of Mandarin forced me to elaborate on some of my points in English.

"Our team's here for ten days," He Wei said. "Can anyone get to understand such a bewildering place like Hong Kong in ten days? I understand you've been here most of your life. What do you make of it? How would you sum it all up for me?"

I shook my head. "An outsider like you might get a better sense of this town in ten days than I possibly can," I said. "You may have a much better perspective to begin with. When I look at this place, I keep seeing too many details and too many problems. Also too many unknowns and missing pieces to the puzzle. I keep thinking of conspiracies and guilty flesh athwart the dark purple of the night. It's like looking into one of those distorting mirrors at fairgrounds. Everything becomes fluid, blurred, protean and multi-layered, full of paradoxes, contradictions and conundrums."

"You sound almost poetical. Are you a poet as well? Most educated people in ancient times used to be."

"Definitely not in my case! We've all become less educated since. With me, I'm just lost for finding the right words to express myself. For example, there's great wealth here. But, as Balzac has quite rightly observed about his native post-Napoleonic Paris, behind every great fortune lies a great crime. But one and a half centuries of British colonialism has failed to produce anyone as penetrating or as perceptive about Hong Kong, in either Chinese or English, as Balzac had been about Paris."

"Why do you think that has been so?"

"I don't know. Many possible reasons. Perhaps nobody could love this mongrel town enough, because its imperfections and anomalies had been so rudely displayed. Or because nobody wanted to study and understand the fundamental circumstances giving rise to those defects. Some respectable writers have passed through — Maugham and his *Painted Veil* and Edmund Blunden's collection of poems in *A Hong Kong House,* after spending a spell as English professor at the University of Hong Kong. But such writers have not really been rooted here, they remained mainly birds of passage, using the place as backdrops to their own stories or perhaps to illustrate something they had been more specifically interested in, like triad society rituals.

"Or perhaps because some of the great crimes here have never been fully uncovered, because balanced investigative journalism has largely died or has been taken over by corporations focused on politics, trivia, readership, hidden agendas and profit. The yellow journalism of William Randolph Hearst, for example, has just about conquered the world. And the libel laws here, like those in Britain, are pretty strict, while the economics for independent journalism simply do not add up at all. I could go on for hours on such subjects, without giving you any clearer picture of what this society is really about."

"Why don't you try your hand at portraying a panoramic picture of the ambiguities of life here, like Balzac did for Paris?" He Wei asked.

"I'm not a writer, I don't have anywhere near that type of talent. I'm at most only a clumsy chaser after dreams."

"Aren't we all, in some sense or other? But you're now also supposed to be a big capitalist. Why not begin by telling me about the business ethos and practices in this town? Our leaders in China want our nation to learn from the outside world."

"I'm not a true capitalist either, in that I am not instinctively conditioned to maximising profits at all cost. I just happen to be a fellow who had signed up to work for a capitalist corporation.

"I could well go on for hours on the neoliberal flaws in the Reagan-Thatcher ideology, on unregulated free markets, privatisations, dog-eat-dog competition, rampant individualism, exploitative inequality, trickery and knavery, the absence of social responsibilities and cohesion, and so on. People, out of isolation, loneliness and empty lives, could easily fall prey to the attraction of religious cults and dead-end ideas. That type of capitalism is being practised at full throttle here. It does indeed contain the seeds of its own destruction, as pointed out by Marx. I might add that total freedom, practised without moral constraints, can be equally self-destructive.

"Our country ought to be very wary of what and of how much of a quasi-capitalist system ought to be allowed into our own country. Our people might still be wedded to a straightforward and old-fashioned way of recording cash in and cash out. When clever outside accountants start introducing a time element to the booking of profits and deciding when an overdue debt should be declared a bad debt, then confusion can reign. Add in off-balance sheet accounting and intra-subsidiary loans and most of the toxic ingredients for fraud would be present.

"Such a free enterprise system may well produce some material benefits for a few. But in the longer term, it is bound to unleash human greed, selfishness, inhumanity and corruption. How can any obviously profit-obsessed system be allowed to run amok in China? The country is still too vulnerable. Can socialism with Chinese characteristics ever produce, for example, those vital components of a civilised society like sages, philosophers and public intellectuals?"

I paused and sighed. I then added: "Since we are, at this very moment, supposed to be in a 'private family gathering' I would rather switch to subjects I seldom get to discuss with a person of authority from the other side. For example, how did you become both a diplomat serving our nation and a member of the Chinese Communist Party?"

He Wei gave another of her light-hearted laughs. "What you've asked me is far too easy," she said. "I've nothing to hide. We're all Chinese, more or less members of one family. If we started drawing lines between this and that, between Communists and non-Communists, where would we end up? Where would you expect Kit to stand?"

"You're right," I said. "We're all Chinese and want what's best for our nation. But tell me a little more about yourself; you have me at a slight disadvantage at the moment."

"Well, I went to school like countless millions of others," He Wei said.

"Like Kit, I joined the Communist Youth League at a young age, at 14, I think. I guess I must have somehow distinguished myself in the League. I was also fortunate enough to get good enough grades in the national university entrance examination.

"At university, most of the kids went in for the sciences or some form of engineering. I took a different path and studied anthropology. I developed an interest in ancient civilisations along river banks, like the Yellow River, the Nile, the Euphrates and the Indus. I got particularly taken by the urban development of the Harappa civilisation. Their urban centres were well laid out and had very impressive plumbing and drainage systems. But I don't think you want me to go on and on about their steatite seals, their terracotta figurines, and so on.

"When I graduated, I applied for a job and also to join the Communist Party. The latter was more difficult than I had imagined. It appeared that millions might apply but few were chosen. Kit's father applied more than once but was repeatedly rejected. To think that when the Party started in 1921, there was only about 50 members; now it has well over 80 million. How many political parties around the world can claim that kind of membership? In the Western world, any political party would jump for joy if membership even reached six figures.

"Being a woman counted against me in becoming a Party member because only about a quarter of the Party were women, although we are supposed to hold up half of heaven, according to Chairman Mao. I had to serve a year's probation before I could be admitted. On the other hand, being a university graduate helped, because more and more graduates are being admitted, compared with the early days when farmers, fishermen and workers predominated."

"How did you feel about having to serve an authoritarian state and being an obedient cog in a vast machine?" I interrupted deliberately.

"Do you believe that over 80 million people could suddenly turn themselves into automatons, without the ability to think for themselves?" He Wei countered. "We must serve the masses, to make their lives better. That has been drilled into us. 'Serving the people' has been written in Chairman Mao's own hand and displayed at the main entrance of Zhongnanhai, the former imperial gardens and now the residential compound for our top leaders.

"When the Party came to power in 1949, the average life span in our country was only 40 years. By the 1970s, the average life span had gone up to over 60 years. I could cite other statistics to show we're making progress."

"I could cite statistics too," I teased. "But that only means that all governments have mastered how to lie with statistics or at least confuse their citizens with the selective kind."

"All right. I accept that some Party members have been greedy, self-serving, corrupt and careless over statistics. Yes, they've made big mistakes too. Some of our leaders have also misread the patriotism and good sense of our people. They've made too many complex regulations on that basis. For example, to maintain control and fearing too much choice, they've figured that most would head straight for bright lights and easy money.

"Well, I and my husband have been sent outside of China for several years, and there's really no place either of us would rather be than amongst the sights, sounds, smells of China and sharing the warmth of our families and the fellowship of our compatriots. We would never contemplate living in exile no matter how luxurious life might be in another country.

"You must also remember that our Party is a broad church; it has to accommodate a wide range of opinions. Meanwhile, there also has to be discipline. After individual opinions have been expressed, we must be humble enough to defer to the collective wisdom of the Party. We have to adhere to policies once agreed. That is what democratic centralism is all about."

"What if an individual member still disagrees, if he still visualises a future for our nation that is different from that envisioned by the Party — economically, environmentally or in some other way?"

"Then he has to submit and live to fight another day."

"That all sounds very well and perhaps even romantic. But how does that reconcile with a person who has heard about the Stalinist show trials in Russia?"

"We all have to retain hope."

"Well, my hope is that we can have another family gathering before the end of your mission."

"I'd like that too. You've given me a lot of food for thought. Kit is in good hands. I'll see whether I can persuade my team leader and my comrades."

Thus the wine-fuelled hours of loosened tongues at Jimmy's Kitchen passed all too quickly. During the process, my respect for the integrity of He Wei grew. She was from a generation of cadres, unlike many of those who had joined the Party immediately about the Liberation, simply because they fitted the right social backgrounds or because they were crypto-bourgeois turncoats out to preserve their old elitist positions. There would be better hope for the country if enough members of He Wei's calibre could reach the higher levels of the Party.

But at the same time, I was assailed by doubts about whether Kitty, at the still untested age of only 21, would develop sufficiently and intellectually to see behind the bright lights and the glitter of her new home town, to detect the plethora of fakery abounding in the background. I was certain that Kitty would be quite lost for a considerable time following the kind of conversation I had been having with He Wei.

*   *   *

One of the first things I noticed after He Wei's visit was that Kitty had been much more relaxed in the company of people she had known — in spite of the conversation being beyond her depth — rather than in the new Hong Kong company I had been introducing her to. It therefore came to me that since she would not be able to travel for lack of travel documents, it might assist in her adjustment process if members of her family could be with her for a time to soften the cultural shock.

Since I possessed more money that I really needed, I could easily invite her various family members to the colony and present each, through Kitty, with a reasonable gift of money to acquire many of the electrical appliances I had around the apartment should they ever take a fancy to the electric kettle, rice cooker, vacuum cleaner, coffee percolator, fruit blender, dehumidifier, microwave oven or whatever for use in their own homes.

Our apartment was, of course, not big enough to accommodate them *en masse*, but they could take turns coming throughout the year, beginning with her parents. After Kitty had given an enthusiastic nod to the idea, the year-long project was set in train.

* * *

Kitty's parents were on the top of the list of invitees and they stayed for nearly a month. They were an absolute delight to be with, for it enabled me to deepen my links with Chiu Bun, who was only two years older than myself.

He and his wife were a simple and undemanding couple. Kitty acted as a tourist or shopping guide for part of the day until I returned from work. Then we would either venture out for a meal or else Kitty together with her parents would prepare something simple at home. Afterwards, there would be ample opportunity for me and my father-in-law to explore the contents of my liquor cabinet.

Otherwise, recurring diversions were provided in explaining the novelties of Cantonese television or in illustrating the types of clothes and music which some officials in China might regard as "yellow culture" or cultural pollution.

Conversation with my mother-in-law was much more difficult because she spoke only the Nantong dialect; thus requiring either Kitty or her father to act as an interpreter. Although our exchanges had been mostly confined to pleasantries, it was obvious from the smiles wreathing her face that she was enjoying her visit. Since she came from farming roots, she became something of a celebrity within her family upon returning home, because she became the only family member who had ventured so far outside her own district.

* * *

Shortly after the old folks had returned to Nantong, to spread the word about their sojourn, it became time to bring the next couple of the Chiu family to the colony — Siu Wah and her husband, Yam Kwan-Lam. They had appeared even more country bumpkin-like than they had been when they had visited Shanghai a couple of years earlier. The variety and cornucopia of goods available in Hong Kong simply bowled them over with amazement. If they had the means, they would have happily taken a couple of container-loads of goods back home with them.

After a day of wandering around the centre of town, Yam Kwan-Lam returned home and declared one evening: "Your town must be very rich. All anyone has to do is to go to some hole in the wall to be supplied with money!"

"They're money-vending machines," I explained. "A person must first deposit money with a bank before he can take money out."

"But there's nobody there to tell whether you're the one who originally put money in."

"When you open an account, the bank will issue you with a debit card and a password. Everything is getting computerised."

"Amazing!" Yam exclaimed.

I felt certain that if I could look into the young man's mind I would see it furiously calculating how he could take a money-dispensing machine home with him!

* * *

During the visits of Chiu Bun and Siu Wah, I picked up some random mentions in casual conversations which intrigued me. Chiu Bun, for instance, let it drop that he and his wife had seen little of their eldest daughter, Shu-Ching, once representatives from the Cultural Services Department selected her at a young age for training as a dancer in an academy in Peking.

Siu-Wah, on the other hand, mentioned that her elder sister had resided for a time at Zhongnanhai and had taken her there twice to meet Chairman Mao.

It did not seem appropriate to quiz guests too closely about family events which they had not voluntarily disclosed. So I had to wait, hoping for supplementary details from Kitty. But my wife proved unhelpful about her elder sister, for she had disappeared from their home long before she had been even born in 1964. However, she did hear proud talk by elders during her infancy of her sister having been selected by Chairman Mao to dance for him.

As for Siu-Wah's encounters with Chairman Mao, she was not at all sure. She herself had gone to Peking as a child with her mother in 1971. Her elder sister was no longer living at Zhongnanhai then. She had become a member of the People's Liberation Army and had married Gao in 1970. She was expecting her first child in 1971 and that was why her mother had gone to help.

The bits of information I had received left me on tenterhooks. They had been like tiny unconnected pieces of a gigantic jigsaw puzzle which told me less than nothing about the big picture, like how the two Chiu girls had interacted with Chairman Mao. That might well constitute part of the hidden history of one of the leading figures of the 20th century I had an interest in. I became increasingly anxious to get Shu-Ching to the colony to learn more.

But the original programme called for a visit by her brother, Chiu Bing-

Hsin, first. That proved harder to arrange than I had imagined, because of a number of inter-personal reasons.

In the first place, it appeared that Bing-Hsin harboured a deep-seated inferiority complex. He somehow was on bad terms with his sisters, probably because, being the only son in the family, he expected being deferred to within the family. And yet, while he was stuck in a dead-end job as a low grade civil servant, his sisters seemed to be distinguishing themselves in their chosen endeavours.

Moreover, he had married a woman from a Nanking family, who regarded marrying a Nantong man as sliding down in social status. Therefore she had been agitating for her husband to be transferred to another civil service job in Nanking and not be beholden to his Nantong family. Hence when Kitty invited her brother and his wife to visit Hong Kong, his wife had adamantly refused the invitation.

Thus it was left to Bing-Hsin to decide what to do. But further complications came into play. A date initially suggested by Bing-Hsin conflicted with the timing of a business trip I had to make; so a postponement was necessary.

Then a secondary matter occurred to me. Kitty's brother was a heavy smoker. Since Kitty did not take kindly to smoking and I had recently to give up smoking cigars to accommodate her, I specified to Bing-Hsin — through Kitty — that any smoking during his visit would have to be conducted from the outside balcony of the sitting room or else in Seymour Road or in the adjoining Robinson Road.

The restriction was considered by Kitty's brother to be an unwarranted infringement upon his personal freedom and in the end led to his staying in the city for only a week. It was by no means a successful visit.

CHAPTER 15

Mistress of Mao

ONCE KITTY HAD SECURED the right to a travel document, priority had to be given to introducing her to the widely scattered and generationally divided members of my family. At the same time, I also had to begin fulfilling — at least in part — my pledge to show her the hitherto unseen world outside of China. This included a quick trip to London to show her the tomb of Marx at Highgate Cemetery.

As for myself, I was also saddled with my travels on behalf of Li & Fung (Trading) which did not include Kitty, especially those to overseas offices. I had a special responsibility for visiting Seoul in South Korea since I had opened an additional office there and its staff was made up entirely of Koreans.

On top of those family and business commitments, I was dead keen to see as many of the hitherto unvisited parts of China as I could. Therefore, when Ip Yeuk-Lam suggested gathering a small group of friends and relatives for a cruise along the Yangtse River, before the projected Three Gorges Dam could change the river basin too much, Kitty and I signed up with alacrity.

The cruise ship stopped at a number of towns and villages *en route*, while a tour guide on board provided a running commentary while the ship passed sites of particular significance in Chinese history or literature. It proved truly enlightening to see the precise settings for historical battles and other happenings which I had previously only read about or imagined.

For the aforementioned reasons, it was only in September of 1986 that

Kitty and I were free enough to consider inviting Kitty's eldest sister, Shu-Ching, and her husband, Gao Lin-Mao, to visit us as guests.

However, before that invitation was actually issued, something out of the ordinary happened. An unexpected announcement was made by the British Council and the University of Hong Kong to initiate a short story competition in the English language to be conducted within the next two months. Such a competition was quite unusual for a mercantile city with an unenviable reputation of being a cultural desert. Inhabitants and visitors alike took the place as one mainly for replenishing one's pocketbook or bank account or acting out one's fantasies rather than for nourishing one's inner life or improving one's intellect.

Once in a while, however, a transiting stage or musical group of some renown, heading home towards Europe after a tour somewhere else, might well put on a couple of tragedies by Euripides or concerts of Bach's cantatas or fugues to break its journey. Such performances in Hong Kong, pricey though they might be, would provide local moneybags with an excuse for putting on their finery and pretending they were not entirely the money-grubbing philistines that they actually happened to be.

Curiously, the organisers of the short story competition made no mention of the nature of the winning prize, except to assure entrants that the winning entry would be published in the local English newspapers.

Their announcement, nonetheless, triggered something buried and long left unresolved in my own psyche. It sent my memory hurtling back to my ignominious attempts decades ago to make a few quick bucks or a decent living by writing short stories.

The first attempt happened in the second half of 1952, after I began a master's degree at Stanford University. Although I had been awarded a fellowship, the stipend was hardly sufficient to make ends meet. Being at the economic margins had been a recurring condition in my life since I was 12, when I was suddenly evacuated from Singapore to Australia as a refugee, together with my paternal grandmother, my siblings and their mother, because of the invasion of Singapore by the Japanese during World War II.

While doing my master's degree, I had to do a variety of odd jobs, like washing dishes, waitering at a cafeteria or mowing lawns, in order to get by. It was perhaps relevant to note that such work at the time had been set at the then minimum wage of 75 cents an hour.

It was under such circumstances that I bumped into a gentleman by the name of Robert North on campus. He was the editor of a quarterly academic magazine called *The Pacific Spectator* with offices in the Hoover Tower. We had known each other casually for some time. I had, during my undergraduate years, established a small reputation on campus for publishing feature articles and topical interviews with certain professors in the *Stanford Daily*, the student newspaper.

After we had exchanged salutations, Mr. North asked if I had ever considered penning short stories. He said his quarterly had started a section devoted to short stories by Asian writers. Because the independence of many Asian countries together with the outbreak of the Korean War, there was a burgeoning interest in Western academic circles for stories reflecting different aspects of Asian culture. His magazine would pay $35 a story, if I felt like working in that genre.

My ears pricked up immediately at the mention of that sum. I would have to wash dishes or push a lawn-mower around for many hours to earn that kind of money. Although I had never written a short story in my life nor had I ever given any thought to writing one, I nevertheless kept the door open by implying I had indeed occasionally tried my hand at it. Now that his magazine had provided an outlet, I would certainly try again.

Upon returning home, I sat down before my typewriter and mulled over the situation. A short story would essentially be no different from writing a news report, I told myself. Before entering Stanford, I had worked for over two years as a reporter for the *South China Morning Post* in Hong Kong. A news report was basically a concise narrative of what happened to whom, when, where and why. The only difference between the two was that one was based on an actual sequence of events while the other would take place in the imagination.

Upon reaching such a conclusion, I started fabricating a story about a merchant who had married a beautiful wife but it dawned on him one day that their lives were not blossoming because he had been regarding his wife as a lovely ornament and possession rather than as a human being. Of course I was without any experience of married life; I could only observe it among friends and relatives. I tried to draw analogies with what little I then knew about fine Chinese ceramics and decided to title the story "The Vase".

After a decent interval of two or three weeks, I went to Mr. North's office and handed him the story. He did a quick read, accepted it, and made arrangements for paying me $35. I was as pleased as Punch, feeling I had pulled off a tidy return and passed some kind of test of creative acceptability.

It was not till the spring of 1954, however, that *The Pacific Spectator* published my story. By then I had completed my MA studies and was back in Hong Kong, where I had secured employment on a month-to-month basis as a night sub-editor at the *Hong Kong Standard*. I was also allowed to write an occasional editorial page article on a subject of my own choosing.

It had taken some time for the magazine to reach me but when I re-read in print what I had written several months ago, I was appalled. The story somehow did not seem at all convincing. The theme appeared contrived and not fully matured, while the main characters and their actions came over as unnatural and wooden.

Perhaps the magazine had arrived at the wrong time, when another trauma had occurred in my life. I had in fact just been summarily fired for writing an article which someone high up in the Hong Kong government had deemed politically objectionable. Indirect pressure was applied upon the *Hong Kong Standard* to dispense with my services.

The coincidental occurrence of those two events reinforced my view that trying to make a living in Hong Kong with a pen was an unrewarding and precarious affair, unless one were resigned to writing jingles for some advertising outfit. I was also beginning to doubt whether I really had any writing talent that was in any way out of the ordinary. An old saw had it that those who could, do; while those who could not, teach. It came back forcefully to me. So thinking, I changed to the more steady and safe profession of teaching and registered for a job to teach English and modern European history at secondary schools.

I might have reconciled myself to that humdrum teaching life if I had not come across an account of an incident concerning Pablo Picasso, the most prolific and influential artist of the 20th century. According to that account, Picasso had an agent in Paris selling his paintings, drawings, sculptures, etc. while he lived in the south of France.

One day, that agent visited Picasso with a painting. He told Picasso he had found a buyer willing to pay a good price for it, if only Picasso would sign to authenticate it.

Picasso however refused to sign, dismissing the painting as a fake.

"But, *Maestro*," the agent cried in amazement. "How can this be a fake? I saw you painting it myself!"

"Yes, I sometimes paint fakes," Picasso replied.

Picasso's remark was both thoroughly honest and revealing. It implied that great artists — be they painters, writers, musicians or whatever — existed to convey whatever they saw as truths — convenient or otherwise — to the wider world. To produce anything less than the truth because of laziness or carelessness or other private reason was to forsake their missions and to indulge in parodies or, indeed, fakes.

That thought gripped my consciousness for a time and then I began re-examining the circumstances under which "The Vase" was written. Had I been too cavalier over my own command of English words, to think that I could get by as a writer without accepting his duty to uncover truths? Or worse still, did I strike a posture for a mere 35 bucks? If so, to what depths could I not sink if I pretended to become a writer?

Pondering those questions, I felt thoroughly ashamed of myself. I decided that if I were to make amends, I would need to seriously engage with life and with art. If I earnestly want to write short stories, then a good starting point would be to study the works of some of the acknowledged masters of the genre — Maupassant, Chekhov, O. Henry, Saki, Kipling, Somerset Maugham and several others.

As I read story after story, the deficiencies in "The Vase" became even more glaring. For that reason, I have avoided including "The Vase" in any of the subsequent collections of short stories published under my name. I also became increasingly humbled and amazed over how many human hopes and frailties, how many individual sorrows and joys, could be so superbly packed into the limited number of words in a short story. That challenge to do likewise grew on me.

After two years as a teacher, I had saved up enough money to repay my Eighth Granduncle part of the loan he had extended me to attend Stanford. However, instead of repaying him, I asked if he could extend the loan for a further year or two. I told him I wanted to go to London to try my hand at writing short stories. The West was reported to be increasingly interested in Asian culture and I intended to set out some of what I saw as truths and to debunk a number of the current myths. He readily agreed with my plan, probably because he pitied me for being already 28 and still bumbling around without a clear direction in life.

With my Eighth Granduncle's further concession, I began working out a strategy for London. Like Dick Whittington of fairy tale fame, I had high hopes but not very clear expectations of London. Realising that my resources would be very limited and success quite uncertain, I took some precautions. I made arrangements with the *China Mail* in Hong Kong and the *Straits Times* in Singapore to accredit me as their London correspondent with the British Foreign and Commonwealth Office.

Such deals would be mutually advantageous, I persuaded them. They could claim they had their own correspondent in London without bearing the full cost for one. I would be there on the spot if they wished to pursue any timely British story. But they would only pay me by the column-inch used for any material I provided. I would in fact be, in the lingo of journalism, only a "stringer".

For my part, I would be on the distribution list for British government press releases and be invited to press functions. In that way I might spot a happening with a Hong Kong or Singapore implication for an article. Thus I would augment my income in Britain.

Once those arrangements had been finalised, I embarked in 1957 on an Italian passenger liner for Genoa. The plan was to go across the continent in a leisurely manner by train to Calais, and then to board a ferry to cross the Channel. The total journey would take well over a month. But once it ended, I could repair to that proverbial London garret favoured by struggling writers to pen whatever obsessed them.

And write I did, assiduously. During the following year I wrote more than ten short stories. Unfortunately, I managed to sell only one! The rest simply made the rounds of all likely publications and collected rejection slips. It seemed that the Western interest in Asian culture that Robert North had spoken about six years earlier at Stanford had still to take root in London. Or else the outlooks of those who sent me their pro forma rejection slips had remained too insular.

After a year, my funds were exhausted and I had no alternative except to seek refuge at my paternal grandfather's home in Singapore. Through the good offices of my brother Francis, I secured a job as night sub-editor at the *Straits Times*. Thus my second attempt to become a writer of short stories also ended in defeat and failure.

* * *

Therefore, when I learnt in 1986 that a short story competition would be taking place in Hong Kong, my memory naturally hurtled back to my impoverished years and my two ill-fated attempts so make money by writing short stories. Since my intervention into the foreign exchange market in Hong Kong in 1982, I was left with more wealth than I would ever need. Thus I had no further need or incentive to write more short stories for gain.

Nevertheless, I felt an irresistible urge to enter that competition. I did not know exactly why. Perhaps it was just the injured pride of a middle-aged man egging me on. Or perhaps I had harboured a subconscious thought that my writing still had some merit. Alternatively, I could just be seeking confirmation that stories which did not make the grade almost 30 years ago had been fairly judged and still did not make the grade today, laying to rest finally any notion of my writing ever rising above mere journalism.

For whatever reason which might be actually spurring me on, I rummaged in the bottom drawer of my desk and found the bundle of stories with rejection slips I had stored away since 1957. From that bundle, I eventually selected a story called "The Card Index" for entry into the competition. It was a story of a henpecked history teacher who suddenly discovered that the prospect of committing murder was not altogether intellectually repugnant to him.

The impulse to enter a story for that competition was to determine ultimately how I would spend the twilight decades of my life. I will detail the various stages in that long and inevitable process in a subsequent chapter of these memoirs.

* * *

Before Kitty could get around to inviting her eldest sister, Shu-Ching, and her husband to visit Hong Kong as our guests, the wheels of Fate had already been set into motion.

A reply duly came back saying that her husband, Gao, was regrettably committed to working on a film for the next several months. However, Shu-Ching herself would be delighted to take up our invitation. Some time from October onwards would be ideal.

On receiving the news, I recalled that Chiu Bun had remarked during his stay how little time he and his wife had spent with their eldest daughter before she had been recruited away from home to undergo dance training in Peking.

I had always much enjoyed the company of Kitty's parents ever since I met them. They struck me as very pleasant and uncomplicated folk who were much closer to my own age. So I suggested that Kitty invite them to come again, since Shu-Ching would be coming alone. The parents readily accepted the chance for a mini gathering of the Chiu family in Hong Kong in October of 1986.

* * *

Of course, when I invited Shu-Ching to come, it was not merely to get to know her as a sister-in-law but also to find out how she got into the Cultural Division of the People's Liberation Army. The references to her having lived for a time in Zhongnanhai, the exclusive residential complex for China's top leaders located in the former imperial Forbidden City, possibly as a companion of Chairman Mao, was also likewise stirring my curiosity.

* * *

Shu-Ching and her parents in Hong Kong in 1986

When Chairman Mao stood up at Tiananmen on October 1, 1949, to proclaim the establishment of the People's Republic of China, he not only secured for himself a place in world history as one of the most successful political leaders in modern China, he also set the direction for the development of his nation for the foreseeable future.

Gradually political leaders from other nations began paying attention to what Mao had to say and how he sought to put his ideas into practice. By the time of his death in 1976, there was a thriving and veritable industry churning out commentaries and books about him and his policies.

I had only a moderate interest in Chairman Mao, except that he had been recognised as by many as one of the greatest modern Chinese leader. I held neither a brief for nor against him. However, when I dipped into the material about him, I was usually left dissatisfied. They tended to be too ideologically coloured, either with too much praise or too many condemnations, but nearly always with inadequate hard evidence. He seemed too off-handedly labelled as this or that.

To compound that problem, Mao himself was a character of many parts, with his fair share of human flaws and talents. If he had been good at one thing, it did not necessarily follow that his words ought to be taken as gospel in some other subject, and vice versa. But his strengths and weaknesses appeared seldom to be objectively analysed and expounded. Perhaps I had approached the subject expecting a recent leader such as Mao to be weighed and assessed in depth, set in a proper historical, environmental and psychological context.

Let me give some examples of what I have been driving at. Mao had frequently been described as a military strategist and was known to have studied Sun Tzu's 13 essays on *The Art of War*, probably in a similar way to how a young Napoleon might have studied them when Jesuit Father J.J.M. Amiot translated them into French and published them in Paris in 1772.

Much has been made of the Red Army's guerrilla tactics in escaping from the various Kuomintang encirclement campaigns and of Mao leading those forces on their epic Long March. That endeavour was no doubt epic, heroic and spectacular. But bearing in mind that the Red Army of that time was largely composed of illiterate farmers, ill trained, badly equipped and vastly outnumbered, what else could that motley group do other than to adhere to the principles of war set out by Sun Tzu more than 2,000 years ago?

That hardly qualifies any leader of the Red Army to claim to be a military strategist, any more than a French general during the Napoleonic wars could, if he had mounted an attack on an enemy in a line formation or a square one. The general would merely be following the standard rules of engagement prevailing at that time.

To be a true strategist, to my way of thinking, one would have to enunciate fresh principles of warfare in the light of new technological realities and circumstances of the era and to have them proven good for the foreseeable future. The character of war had been changing over the centuries because of technological advancements, from the Gatling gun to tanks and airplanes. Obviously, a military strategist who had merely talked about waging war with muskets had to be considered obsolete.

During World War II, the distinction between combatants and civilians had already been erased by all parties through the carpet bombing of cities like Coventry and Dresden. Ultimately, Hiroshima and Nagasaki were wiped out through having atomic bombs dropped on them.

So, on that basis, could Mao be considered a true military strategist for the nuclear age? In November of 1957 he had led the Chinese delegation to a conference of Communist and workers' parties in Moscow where the subject of thermonuclear war came up. He created a sensation when he declared that the Chinese people had not yet completed the country's re-construction and that they desired peace. However, if the imperialists wanted war then it would be fought to the end. Even if half of the world's population perished, there would still be half left.

The statement implied that he was unafraid of nuclear war and the "paper tigers" of America's hydrogen bombs. One writer went so far as to interpret Mao's remarks as indicative of his indifference to human suffering.

Had Mao been using a hyperbole or merely indulging in a bit of bravado, knowing China's limitations in the face of nuclear weapons? Or could he be following the alleged Marie Antoinette's throw-away of "Let them eat cake." upon being informed of the people lacking bread? A person could well interpret the statement as a revelation of Mao's ignorance of the real effects of a nuclear and genocidal conflict.

But whatever unresolved questions Mao might have left in the air about nuclear weapons, he was at least not as twisted as American strategists like Herman Kahn who devoted his calculations to "winnable" nuclear wars. Such a "winnable" nuclear war, it seemed to me, would be a pyrrhic victory for humanity. It would amount to signing up to a suicide pact.

That possibility of nuclear conflict remains today the dominant issue facing the human race. This did not mean we should be leery or hesitant over technological and scientific progress but rather that we should re-emphasise the old Chinese intellectual habit of melding technological and scientific progress with ethical and moral progress.

After all, it would be relevant to remember that Sun Tzu had stated that kings and commanders should adopt a moral stance in war and that an enemy subdued without fighting was the acme of skill in warfare.

Unfortunately, since the ending of World War II, the inept and posturing political leaders of countries possessing nuclear weapons have managed to come up with nothing more than the prodigiously wasteful, unworkable and dead-end strategy of "Mutually Assured Destruction". Instead of coming together to ban the existence of all nuclear weapons for good, they are even now busy updating the development of new generations of such weapons. Such moves are indictments of the unforgivable intellectual and moral bankruptcy of our times.

As nuclear technology spreads, more countries would want nuclear weapons for their own protection against more powerful foes. Sooner or later, some political leader with a suicide-bomber mentality would emerge to suck the world into a devastating nuclear war. Or it might happen by accident or by miscalculation. Our entire world would then end as it had begun — with one mighty and awful bang!

Yet some idiotic politicians are advocating the scrapping of such limited non-proliferation treaties that do exist instead of building on them. It boggles the mind of any sane citizen.

If Mao had been a military strategist of a significant calibre, he would have addressed the fraught issue of nuclear conflict and made some thought-provoking pronouncements on how to rid our world of the threat. But I have yet to come across any sound pronouncement by him.

* * *

Many writers on Mao also mentioned him as a poet and calligrapher. But that tells me almost nothing at all. For thousands of years, educated Chinese who have risen to occupy official positions have frequently indulged themselves in poetry and calligraphy. Some have left their marks on their culture; others have simply disappeared without trace.

For an ordinary Joe like myself, I would have been quite interested in knowing how experts looked upon Mao's poetry and calligraphy. If those who have written about Mao had felt incompetent over offering assessments in those spheres, then they should have said they were leaving it to future experts to give their opinions. It would appear a disservice to both Mao and their readers to mention such subjects and then to leave them hanging in the air with a few superficial comments.

The history of Tao Yuan-Ming, the naturalist poet of the Jin Dynasty, is illustrative of this approach and of the long perspective taken in respect of Chinese letters. Tao had resigned from a position at court to lead a reclusive life in the countryside, to farm and write poetry. His poetry was little known during his lifetime except within his own circles.

His work was not brought to a much wider public for more than 200 years, till the two leading Tang poets, Li Po and Tu Fu, discovered him and praised his work. Many more centuries were to pass before Su Tung-Po, the foremost poet and calligrapher of the Sung Dynasty, also highly praised him. Su declared Tao's work to be the paragon of authenticity and spontaneity.

Thus after the Sung Dynasty, Tao attained lasting fame as the father of reclusive poetry. Today overlooked by his contemporaries, Tao had written poems like the following:

> *The sun sets, no clouds are in the sky,*
> *No murmur of the world's dust.*
> *The mountain air is fresh at the dusk of day.*
> *The flying birds two by two return.*
> *In these things there is a deep meaning;*
> *Yet when we would express it, words suddenly fail us.*

Today, it seems highly appropriate that Tao should be regarded as one of the greatest Chinese poets in history.

Because of the lack of detailed expert commentaries on Mao's poems — so far as I am aware — the common man or woman is left uncertain as to how representative they could be of his or her time. A thousand years from now, would Chinese children still be reciting Mao's poems as they would those by Tang and Sung poets or to copy in calligraphy his distinctive style of brushwork?

* * *

On a more frivolous note, let me turn to writers who have suggested that Mao was a womaniser. The basis for this allegation has historical roots, dating partially back to the 1930s when Mao and his third wife, He Zi-Zhen, a long-time Communist, were holed up together in the North China rebel sanctuary of Yanan.

Along came a left-leaning film actress by the name of Jiang Ching, bringing with her the casually bourgeois and easy moral lifestyle of the acting world. Although Mao was around 45 then and married, while Jiang was about half his age, they soon ended up in a torrid affair. It was not absolutely clear who preyed upon whom as the two worked together. But the Communist elders with a civil war on their hands were greatly scandalised.

Eventually, a compromise was arrived at. Mao was given permission to divorce his wife and marry Jiang. This took place in 1938 on the condition that Jiang would lead no public political role as Mao's wife for the next 20 years. That pledge was largely kept before the two began living separately in 1973. Thus Mao clocked up having had four wives — clearly more than the average man — but gossip about other subsequent sexual partners had not been equally well recorded.

Let me examine separately the possible components in that womanising reputation. Would the mere fact of having had four wives automatically turn a man into a womaniser? I doubt it very much. Nowadays married couples could change spouses almost as easily as they could change breakfast cereals.

During the time of my own paternal grandfather, he had nine wives. I had lived in his home in Singapore for a number of years and I have had close contacts with two of my grandmothers as well as a large number of his offspring by other deceased wives — that is, family relationships with many aunts and one uncle and their respective families. I can testify that neither I nor any of his circle of friends and relatives ever considered him a womaniser.

It was true that, apart from having had four wives, Mao had been rumoured to have had other sexual partners. But documented evidence has not been forthcoming. There should at least have been some sort of analysis of Mao's intellectual or emotional predisposition in this direction by those delving into Mao's life, instead of just repeating odd rumours.

For example, during the middle of the 20th century, there had been some intellectual movement towards free love. A notable instance had been the relation between Jean-Paul Sartre and Simone de Beauvoir. To what extent had Mao been influenced by Jiang — who was also rumoured to have had a stable of her own lovers — or by the idea of free love or the development of the women's liberation movement?

After all, Mao was not an ordinary Joe. He had been heavily guarded at all times since becoming the Chinese head of state. He could not just go to Majorca for a holiday fling or casually link up with some unknown woman he had met on the beach or in a bar.

Moreover, Zhongnanhai was and is very much like the White House in Washington. No one could go in or out without following a lot of security protocols. And where security protocols existed, there had to be records. Did those who merely repeated rumours search for confirming records? Where are the records now and who has them? Why has none surfaced in public so far?

If records could be examined, it might be established where Mao might fit into the womaniser scale compared with, say, Casanova or Don Juan. In the case of Casanova, at least he had left a memoir of his peccadilloes whereas, to my limited knowledge, Mao had left none. It has not therefore been possible to determine, for instance, where Mao would stand in relation to President John F. Kennedy or President Bill Clinton in the womanising league.

If a person were to believe half the stories circulating about Roosevelt and Madam Chiang Kai-Shek or Nehru and Lady Mountbatten, then he would no doubt realise that Mao would not be the last political figure to be distracted occasionally by a bit of skirt.

For future historians who might be interested in the sexual predilections of political leaders, I can at least offer the name of one woman who had sex with Mao and part of her story. Her name is Chiu Shu-Ching. She had been a dancer in the Cultural Division of the People's Liberation Army and she is my sister-in-law.

* * *

When I first met Shu-Ching in 1986, she was already 41. Yet she still looked very sprightly and lithe after having given birth to two children. In the mornings, she would still limber up with dancing exercises in my home, using the back of a dining room chair as a barre for her stretches.

Playing host to Shu-Ching and her parents was like a very pleasant breeze so far as I was personally concerned. I went to work as usual each day, while Kitty took her family members to explore the host of shops and department stores in the city and the wide variety of cuisines available, as well as the standard tourist sights. I would only join them for the evening meals and on weekends. After dinner, we would return home to raid my liquor cabinet and to sit around my sitting room taking in some television show or shooting the breeze.

Sometimes Shu-Ching and I nattered on after a fashion after her parents had gone to bed. She had acquired that refined way of speaking Mandarin common to Peking residents.

It was through those relaxed evening interchanges and some sly and seemingly innocent questions from me that I slowly pieced together, as best I could, a summary of a part of Shu-Ching's early life and her reported relationship with Mao. Perhaps I have even stumbled upon a glimpse of a hitherto unrevealed part of Chairman Mao's character.

* * *

Shu-Ching was born in 1945, the eldest of four children. She was an active and attractive child and displayed an interest in dancing at an early age. This gained the attention of a former dancer living in the neighbourhood and, out of neighbourly kind-heartedness, she taught her a few classical Chinese dances. The child became so fascinated by them that she practised them whenever she could.

In China, it was normal at that time for children to begin schooling at the age of eight. But since Chiu Bun was himself an educated man and since his wife had just given birth to a son that year, he began teaching his daughter some basic characters at the age of six. Among the first ones she was taught were "Long Live Chairman Mao!" — a standard slogan all children were required to chant at school and to learn to write. They also normally bowed before a portrait of Chairman Mao and wished him a long life before each day's lessons began.

Because of Shu-Ching's early acquaintance with written characters, she had stood out in school. She could write more characters than her classmates. But she remained more interested in dancing than in formal subjects.

When she was about ten years' old, the former dancer in the neighbourhood approached Chiu Bun and told him she had judged Shu-Ching to be a girl with a real love, talent and aptitude for dancing. If the child had set her heart on dancing, it might be best to give her a proper foundation at an early age. The problem was that no top notch teacher existed in Nantong; the most famous ones all seemed to have gravitated to Peking.

Chiu Bun replied that though his daughter was very young he had no objection to her following a dancing career. However, he was not in a financial position to send her to study dancing at the capital.

The former dancer said she understood the position. But if Chiu Bun would grant her permission to explore some possibilities, she would see what could be done.

The woman neighbour came back a few weeks later to report that she had been in touch with an old friend who was one of the leading women teachers in classical Chinese dances in Peking. She had a reputation for nurturing dancers with good potential for just a fee sufficient to cover the student's meals. She would be prepared — on the neighbour's recommendation — to take Shu-Ching into her home and studio for a year to really test her potential. The child would, of course, continue her normal schooling at the same time. If she made the grade in dancing, then the arrangement could continue.

As for the *hukou* regulations, which governed the movement of citizens from one place to another in the country, to which was also linked the medical, educational and other social benefits, Shu-Ching could be passed off as a child whom the teacher had undertaken to look after and bring up for a sick relative in Nantong.

And so Chiu Bun agreed to the modest outlay involved with sending his daughter to Peking to train as a classical Chinese dancer.

*   *   *

A year or so after Shu-Ching had arrived in Peking, the lady who had taken her under her wing took up an appointment to teach classical Chinese dancing at the Peking Dance Academy. The academy was the first professional dance school to be set up since the establishment of the Chinese People's Republic in 1949. It was located adjacent to Zizhuyuan Park and had been authorised to issue university degrees, although it was also affiliated to a secondary school for younger students.

Although Shu-Ching was enrolled only in the affiliated secondary school, she was represented as a relative of one of the academy's instructors. She was therefore allowed now and then to use the facilities at the academy. In that way she got to know some of the other instructors, notably Dai Ailian, who was also teaching at the academy at the time.

Thus she heard stories from teachers about famous foreign dancers like Fanny Elssler, Anna Pavlova and Lola Montez and gained insights into what each had contributed to dancing and the different types of music accompanying their dances. Those tales inspired her to master her own dance form, in the hope that she could one day become just as famous.

Soon after she had turned 16, her teacher told her that the academy had been asked to put on a show for senior government officials. It was rumoured that Chairman Mao himself might attend. Everyone went into a frenzy. Because Shu-Ching herself had developed such a fluid and enchanting style in classical dances, it was decided to include her doing a solo number in the show.

The performance duly took place and it proved a great success. Chairman Mao was indeed in the audience. A few days later, word came unexpectedly that Shu-Ching had been asked to go to Zhongnanhai to dance for the Chairman again.

* * *

Shu-Ching was rendered almost speechless with excitement. She did not know what was expected of her nor how she should prepare herself. Ever since she could remember, she had been taught to love Chairman Mao, to obey his every command and to wish him a long life. Now she was being asked to dance for him. She had hitherto only seen him at a great distance, like during National Day rallies, when countless tens of thousands raised their fists and cheered him. He had appeared like a god, worshipped by the entire nation.

Now, suddenly, she found herself singled out to dance for that godlike figure. What did it mean? There had been dozens of other dancers at the concert, not to mention the tens of thousands of admirers of the Chairman at every mass rally. The Chairman could have picked anyone of them to entertain him. Why did he pick her? Did it mean that the years she had put into training in classical dances were paying off? Had her dancing impressed the Chairman? The very thought filled her with pride.

Her mentor had seemed just as proud on learning that her *protégé* had been spotted. But she sounded a warning and gave some advice.

"You've come a long way since you came to me in Peking and I have every faith in your skills. Otherwise, I would not have pushed for your inclusion in the show. Now that the Chairman has spotted you, there is one thing that you must always bear in mind. A command performance is an opportunity. You have to do your very best to please him, because one word from him can make or break forever your dancing career. Never forget that, but at the same time keep calm."

*   *   *

When Shu-Ching and her troupe of accompanying musicians presented themselves at the entrance of Zhongnanhai, their papers were checked before they were escorted to a building known as the Chrysanthemum Library. There their documentations were checked again before being assigned to guarded quarters. They were eventually provided with food and drink and told to make themselves comfortable while awaiting a summons. But everyone was too on edge to relax. The musicians tuned their instruments while Shu-Ching went through some of her moves.

However, they were not summoned that day. When late evening came, they were told they were no longer needed and could go to sleep.

The next day the troupe was taken to a hall with fine curtains and exquisite ornaments and told to ready themselves for a show. A fair while later, the Chairman appeared together with his entourage. They took seats and upon a signal the show began.

When the music struck up, Shu-Ching bowed deeply to the Chairman before beginning her dance. Seeing the Chairman at close quarters for the first time, he appeared to her like a well-nourished elder in his sixties rather than like a god. Her repertoire lasted for close to an hour before she ended it with another deep bow.

The Chairman clapped and so did his entourage.

"You dance excellently," the Chairman said, in his usual Hunanese-accented voice. "Congratulations! But you must not become too enslaved by our past. It is the impetus of the new that pushes every society forward, No doubt you will one day learn the new dances in honour of the Revolution. The future of our nation will depend on young people like you."

Shu-Ching did not know what new dances he might be referring to. She had not been taught any. Perhaps a pair of baggy trousers would be called for instead of the flowing robes of the classical dances; possibly also the red scarf of the Communist Youth League and a clenched fist. Unable to visualise what the new dances might involve, she simply bowed again.

The Chairman must have made some gesture which she had failed to notice, because an aide quickly came forward to offer a glass container holding cigarettes. The Chairman helped himself to one and the aide lit it for him.

After blowing a cloud of smoke into the air, the Chairman said: "I would like to talk to this young lady for a while. The rest are excused."

The musicians were escorted out while another aide brought up a chair for Shu-Ching, placed within talking distance from the Chairman. His entourage duly rose and quietly dispersed.

* * *

The Chairman then asked Shu-Ching to tell him about her family.

"My father is working as a civil servant, a sub-manager in the Nantong office for allocating fuel oil quotas to government institutions and some private enterprises; my mother is from a farming family and is a simple housewife," Shu-Ching began. "My mother can speak only the Nantong dialect and cannot read or write."

The Chairman nodded, almost in approval. "Both in good health, I hope. Do they have other children?"

"Both healthy, thank you, Mr. Chairman. I have a brother of ten and a sister of three."

"Does your family find life in Nantong agreeable?"

"Yes, Mr. Chairman."

"What about fellow citizens in the town? Is life continuing to improve for them?"

"I do not know, Mr. Chairman, because I've been in Peking for more than five years. I've only been back to Nantong twice during that entire period, for just a few days on each occasion during the Lunar New Year holidays."

"Why not go back more often? Did you not miss your family?"

"Oh, yes, I did. But my family does not have enough money to pay for my travelling expenses. It has already been helping me with fees and living expenses."

The Chairman frowned and his mood appeared to darken.

Shu-Ching became afraid she might have given the wrong answer. She did not discover until much later that the shift in the Chairman's mood had nothing to do with her answer. It had been due to an extraneous political matter of which she was entirely ignorant.

The truth was that the Chairman's mood had been vacillating over the last few days because of criticisms made by some Party elders concerning one of his policies. He had initiated the Great Leap Forward movement back in 1958, because he had wanted to accelerate changing China from an agricultural economy to an industrial one. One of the aims and one of the slogans used had been to overtake Britain in steel production within 15 years. Farmers accordingly set up backyard furnaces to produce steel, to meet that target. But that turned out to be detrimental to their farming work. Moreover, the steel thus produced was far below standard. So agricultural production began to fall, setting the stage for the years of the Great Famine which was soon to hit the country.

But even before that tragedy was to occur, the Great Leap Forward had come in for criticism from some of the elders in the Party. Local officials, fearful of missing their production targets, began massaging their figures. Some of the elders saw this and began criticising the policy as flawed.

Indeed, on the days prior to Shu-Ching's arrival at Zhongnanhai, there had been yet another internal meeting and the Chairman had reacted petulantly to all his critics.

When Marshal Peng Teh-Hua voiced criticisms, the Chairman said: "You don't touch me, I don't touch you; you touch me, I touch you. Even though we had once been like brothers, that does not change a thing."

Thus the two old comrades fell out over the way to take the country forward. That confrontation had already soured the Chairman's disposition even before he had sent for Shu-Ching to dance for him. The shadow of that tetchiness had unaccountably resurfaced during his chat with Shu-Ching.

After a few more questions, the Chairman apparently lost interest in further questions. He stood up abruptly to signify that the meeting had ended. Shu-Ching was escorted back to the quarters assigned to her and to the musicians.

* * *

Throughout the following day, Shu-Ching and the musicians waited anxiously to be called to put on another performance. But no summons came. They therefore spent the time fidgeting in their quarters. They were closely guarded and discouraged from wandering around at will.

The call for a further show came the day after that, to take place in the same hall. The Chairman appeared in a lighter mood and the show proceeded as that previous one. After the performance, the Chairman said he wanted to talk to Shu-Ching again and the musicians and the rest of the Chairman's entourage were dismissed.

"What made you want to take up dancing?" the Chairman asked.

"I don't really know," Shu-Ching replied. "It just came to me naturally as a child. I just felt like jumping around and dancing. When a neighbourhood lady saw me, she taught me a few classical dances. She said she had previously been a dancer. I guess it just continued from there."

"And what made you come to Peking?"

"The neighbourhood lady told my father that all the best dance instructors were in Peking and suggested that I be sent here to study. She also had connections with a good teacher here who was prepared to mentor me if I went to Peking."

The Chairman nodded. "I suppose your neighbour has been right. There are a lot of talented people here. My wife is always going on about cultural development in a new China. She has been sending people all over the country scouring for youngsters straight of limb and pleasing of visage to be trained in song, music, drama, dance and so forth, to become the cultural face of a new and modern China. I should put her in touch with you."

"Oh, thank you, Mr. Chairman!"

"You're still a student, are you not?"

"Yes, but I will be finishing secondary school this year."

"What do you intend to do then?"

"Try to get a job as a dancer, I suppose."

"Have you considered joining the People's Liberation Army? It has a Cultural Division, making films and shows for the Army. It could well do with a person who could dance as pleasingly as you."

"I know the People's Liberation Army is prestigious but difficult to get into. I did not know it had openings for dancers."

"I will ask Marshal Lin Piao if there are suitable openings."

"Thank you, Mr. Chairman. That is very kind of you."

*   *   *

After a few more questions, the Chairman stood up and said: "Come with me." Shu-Ching obediently followed, as the Chairman walked slowly out of the hall and in the direction of his personal suite.

The two armed guards outside the suite snapped to attention on the Chairman's approach, saluted and opened the doors.

Once inside, the Chairman said: "I feel a little tired. I think I will take a nap. You must be exhausted too after your performance. Take a nap too."

"Thank you, Mr. Chairman. I can rest on one of the sofas here."

"No, it is more comfortable on a bed. I have a big one. Come with me. We can rest together."

*   *   *

Shu-Ching, in fact, felt quite physically worn out by the tensions, the preparations and the performances over the last few days. So she followed the Chairman into the bedroom. The bed was indeed a large one and the Chairman lowered himself onto half of it.

"You can rest on the other side," he said.

He did appear to Shu-Ching at that moment like a weary, harmless elder, so she obeyed. Within a few minutes she was fast asleep.

She had no recollection of how long she slept. But through the haze of waking, she became aware that the Chairman was caressing her and trying to remove her clothes. She became petrified. She was only sixteen and did not know what to do. She had never been touched by any man before, especially by one so powerful and universally adored as the Chairman. She remembered the words her mentor had given about her dancing career and her instincts told her she should pretend she was still asleep and that whatever was happening was not really happening. She therefore feigned sleep.

But the caresses of the Chairman and how his lips moved over the exposed parts of her body filled her with a tingling sensation she had never experienced before. Her heartbeat and her breathing were quickening uncontrollably and when she finally turned to face the Chairman her whole body seemed unable to do anything except to respond to him. That was how the Chairman turned her from an innocent and frightened girl into a woman.

* * *

When Shu-Ching's narrative reached this point, I shook my head and sighed. "What a pity I did not get to hear of your story 20 years ago, at the height of the Cultural Revolution." I said. "I could have made a handy bundle selling it to one of the Sunday tabloids in the West."

"If I had known you 20 years ago, I would never have told you my story, because you would not have been a part of my family then," Shu-Ching said. "Besides, there is nothing very edifying about any of it for those concerned. I'm now a married woman, with a husband and two grown-up sons. It would be best for the past to remain in the past."

"But Chairman Mao is a historical figure. There is such a thing as historical accuracy."

"Would you really have made much with my story back then? There must be millions of girls around the world being led astray by men or boys every day of the week. What was so special about it happening to a Chinese girl?"

"Ah, you have little idea of the appetite for sanctimony and celebrity scandals in the West. What befalls girls do not matter unless they happen to be Lolitas or Jezebels. But if you can pin it on a famous man then you're in the money. With Mao, I can imagine the headlines even today: 'Exclusive! True Confession! How Chairman Mao Stole My Virginity!'"

"Western newspapers are not as crass as that, are they?"

"You'd be surprised. If you were to write a book about your relationships with Chairman Mao today, I'm sure there will still be a lot of takers in the West."

"That would be a very stupid thing to do, after so long. Did you know, after Chairman Mao died in 1976, the government locked me up for several months?"

"No, I didn't. How come? What did you do wrong?"

"The government thought I was part of some Maoist clique, as it went after the so-called Gang of Four. I can laugh about it now, but at the time I was really scared. I didn't know what was going to happen.

"It was all politics, of course, and the irony was that I knew almost nothing about politics. I didn't know why Lin Piao was designated as the successor to the Chairman at one moment and then, a short while later, was accused of being a plotter for power. I didn't know anything about what Mao's wife, Jiang Ching, and her friends might be up to either. Everyone around the Chairman seemed to want to get something out of that poor old man. But he and I never spoke about politics, only about personal things, dancing and developments within my own family. I thought that was what he wanted me to do, take his mind off politics and his own health problems."

"Politics everywhere is a murky business," I observed. "Presumably the government eventually gave you a clean bill of health?"

"More or less, I guess. I managed to convince my interrogators in the end that I was only interested in dancing and entertaining the Chairman with my skills. They confiscated a couple of poems the Chairman had written for me in his own hand and warned that everything that had transpired between us was now considered important state secrets. I was forbidden to disclose any of our goings-on to anyone, or I might be arrested again. I guess I must be committing some kind of crime now by talking to you."

"Don't worry. I'm now family. I won't report you."

"And you won't be writing anything about what I have recounted? My sister tells me you used to be a journalist."

"If I write anything about you, it would not be published within any timeframe which would possibly cause trouble for either of us."

* * *

Shu-Ching and I sat in momentary silence in my sitting room for a while, each nursing a drink selected from my liquor cabinet and each pursuing a slightly different chain of thought.

Eventually, I broke the silence. "Tell me," I said, "how do you remember the Chairman now, after all these years? What stands out most about him in your recollections?"

"A lot of minor things, I suppose. When we ate together, for example, he always enjoyed those spicy Hunanese dishes. But they were too hot for my taste, so he would laugh and declare that I would never make a good revolutionary if I could not eat chilli. I suppose he was right about me in that respect. He was always kind and understanding towards me too, regardless of what else might be on his mind."

"No one seems to have touched on those more human qualities about him in the articles and books I've come across."

"Perhaps the writers just never knew enough about him. I also did not know what he often thought or did. For example, I did not know why recruiters from the People's Liberation Army sought me out after I finished my secondary school and suggested that I take some entrance examinations. Was that a routine in place for all who had finished secondary schools or did the Chairman arrange it?

"I took the examinations and passed. Or maybe I didn't. But I was enlisted into the army in any case and after a while I got assigned to the Cultural Division and was allowed to participate in some dancing programmes. Was that all arranged as well? I never knew and I never asked.

"While I was with the Cultural Division, I met Gao who was already working there on films. We fell in love after a time and considered getting married. Was that arranged too? I don't think so. But I did not know how to break the news to the Chairman and to get his permission. When I eventually did ask, he was very understanding about it. He said it was time for me to marry and start a family. Gao and I duly got married in 1970.

"After I had my first son in 1971, the Chairman continued to ask me to talk to him every now and then about my family affairs and how my boy was developing. He even asked me to bring my 13-year-old sister, Xiao Wah, to Peking to see him, so that he could determine whether she was growing up to resemble me.

"He was not a well man, you know. He kept smoking too much, in spite of problems with his lungs. He had other health problems too. Towards his final years, there was something infinitely sad about him, which went beyond just ill health and the ups and downs in the fortunes of the country. It struck me he was finally coming to terms with the reality that the human span had its limits, regardless of how many great tasks remained undone in the world."

"Yes, a rather sorrowful conclusion for an ambitious man to reach towards the end of his days," I said. "We are all brief candles. How history will judge our puny efforts is something we can never know, for it can only be made long after we have gone.

"That's the reason I always spend two or three hours wandering around the cemetery at Père Lachaise whenever I visit Paris. Have you ever heard of the place? The remains of many people who had once shaken the world are buried there. It is a humbling thought to realise that no matter how important you might have once been in life, upon death we all just get the same tiny piece of dirt. Gives one a different perspective on life."

"No, I haven't heard of the place," Shu-Ching said. "But Deng Xiao-Ping, the Paramount Ruler of China after the demise of Mao, had judged Mao's decisions to have been 70% good and 30% bad. That has been the official Chinese judgement ever since."

"It would be instructive to know how long that will remain the case," I said.

* * *

Sometimes, when I shave myself in the mornings, I often have to look at myself in the mirror. When I do, I cannot help wondering how many people could look upon their whole lives with brutal honesty, and how many would conclude that his or her life had been 70% good and 30% bad.

All I know is that I am afraid to ever submit myself to such a self-assessment.

CHAPTER 16

Taking Up the Pen

AFTER THE DEPARTURES of my parents-in-law and Shu-Ching for their respective homes, I received a whopping surprise. The organisers of the short story competition informed me, privately and confidentially, that "The Card Index" had won the first prize in their competition. I was invited, like all other participants in the competition, to turn up at an appointed hour on an appointed day at the University of Hong Kong for a formal announcement of the results. I was completely flabbergasted. I had expected perhaps a honourable mention at most.

How could a story written 30 years ago and rejected by a succession of august British literary magazines be considered a winning entry in a contemporary Hong Kong short story competition, I asked myself. A number of possibilities drifted through my mind.

The first was that the inhabitants of the city had lived up to their reputation of being in a cultural desert, with hardly anyone else entering the competition. Furthermore, news had leaked out that the folding stuff, which would normally constitute the prize, was not the kind meant for a wallet but a collection of books published by the Hong Kong University Press. Small wonder I ended up winning by default.

But, on the appointed day, a fair number of people — supposedly participants — turned up with an air of expectation to hear the results. If memory serves, I think the winner of the second prize was an Indian lady.

She received a smaller pile of books published by the Hong Kong University Press than I did.

So both the outcome and the number of people who turned up would appear to contradict my initial suppositions. It also proved a salve for my ego, suggesting that the judges might have discovered an element of appeal in my half-forgotten story. A further consolation came after the piece had been published in the local newspapers. A number of friends took the trouble of telling me they had read and enjoyed my story.

Unless the comments received amounted to no more than the conventional courtesies in social interchanges, then there would still remain a mystery of why so many British magazines had found my story lacking in appeal. Perhaps the standard of English they had expected had been set at a higher level than I had been able to attain. Possibly, over the years, the progressive corruption of the language by the more frequent usage of slang and Americanisms had altered the equation.

However, there was likewise a more alarming possibility. Could the various sub-editors responsible for culling uninvited submissions at the magazines have noticed my Chinese name and promptly returned my submission in my pre-stamped envelope without even reading it? It would not have been an unheard of practice, especially during a time of fading empire and unbridled British upper class snobbery.

It would have been intellectually routine to regard an unknown colonial upstart as being incapable of putting together a couple of sentences of the Queen's English without fracturing an idiom or splitting an infinitive or two!

It occurred to me on a sudden that if such an approach by readers had been taken, then it might explain my dismal acceptance record in Britain during 1957-58. I had written more than ten stories but only managed to sell a solitary one.

On further reflection, I realised I had restricted my efforts to subjects I knew something about — like rickshaw pullers, scaffolding workers, *foki*s in

Chinese provision shops and some rather institutionalised racism in British society. Those might well have been topics with little appeal to the gentlefolks in the shires who might be subscribing to the magazine.

Such attitudes might well have been encountered by many writers from the Third World at that time. I imagined that the Nigerian writer, Ken Saro-Wiwa, might have experienced something similar to have inspired him to pen *Sozaboy: A Novel in Rotten English*.

Ken had been a firm believer in non-violent protests, a man after my own heart in that respect. He campaigned assiduously against the severe environmental damage done to the Ogoni people by the indiscriminate dumping of petroleum waste in the Niger Delta by Royal Dutch Shell and other oil companies. But nonviolence did not protect him from the Nigerian authorities, however. He was soon arrested.

When Ken was arrested, I had demonstrated with others outside the Nigerian High Commission in London for his release. But our efforts were to no avail. The Nigerian government put him on trial on trumped up charges, found him guilty and executed him by hanging in 1995.

It appears that human civilisation has now reverted to a more atavistic age when a price has to be paid by anyone daring to stand by a principle.

* * *

Winning the short story competition gave my dormant creative instincts a decided nudge. But having failed to make a mark some 30 years ago, I deemed it best to let sleeping dogs lie.

Besides, there had been a lot of other things going on which I was endeavouring to handle better. For example, I had signed up for a ten-year stint with Li & Fung and that period had only reached the half-way mark. I had hoped at least to promote a less exploitative atmosphere in commercial dealings, among both staff and customers alike, but that aim had been rather difficult to bring about within the money-mad *à gogo* environment of Hong Kong.

Since my intervention into the foreign currency market a few years earlier, I had been saddled with wealth beyond the dreams of avarice. How to do some small amount of good with that money was still a matter lodged in the back of my mind.

On top of that, the weakening links with my father, my mother, my siblings and cousins, due to physical separations in different parts of the world, also troubled me. Visiting them took up so much more time than I could really afford.

The physical separation from my sons presented an even more acute problem. I could sense we were becoming estranged. They had been in a hurry to rush off to the West, in search of what they had regarded as "freedom", while still unanchored to their own culture and unaware they would turn themselves into free-flowing and autonomous atoms in the outside world, without roots and connections.

Most important of all, I had acquired an innocent and grievously under-educated young wife from a newly-established socialist country. How to mould her into a rational, thinking and sophisticated woman, capable of coping independently with a turbulent and erratic neo-liberal capitalist world, where individual desires often trumped the general public good? It was a heavy responsibility I still had to fully articulate and discharge.

* * *

The extended visit by my in-laws had confirmed my earlier impression that they were a very simple, likeable and undemanding couple. During eras when China still had emperors, a palace maiden catching the fancy of an emperor could usually count on some material benefits for her parents. Shu-Ching might have found favour with Chairman Mao but the only benefits that accrued had been to her dancing career rather than to her parents' wellbeing.

When I had been offered hospitality in the Chiu family home in Nantong on my wedding night, I had discovered to my dismay that their modest house had been bereft of even in-door toilet. I therefore decided that, with my excessive wealth, I should at least ensure that they could spend the autumn of their years in reasonable comfort.

My decision to provide for them was somewhat triggered by a Hong Kong visit by my own mother from Vancouver in March of 1987. She stayed with me for about ten days before moving to Kowloon, where she had promised one of the sons of my Fifth Maternal Aunt she would stay for a few days.

The presence of my mother alerted me to the fact that the wings of time waited for no one. Before any of us knew it, some expression of love or regret we had meant to utter just somehow never found the right moment to escape our lips. Thus the sentiment we had meant to express just remained too late to be expressed at all.

Therefore, shortly after the departure of my mother, I broached with Kitty my intention to provide a new home for her parents. She was absolutely delighted. "Excellent!" she cried. "Give me the money and I'll remit it to them."

"Money is the easiest part in this whole exercise," I said. "To properly realise the project, it should be handled in a way which avoids problems arising in the future."

"What do you mean? What kind of problems?"

"I can easily visualise quite a number. Napoleon had once observed that to foresee was to rule. For a start, it would be far easier to explain to outsiders or anyone with suspicions why you should be buying an apartment in Nantong for your parents, as an act of filial piety, rather than explain why you or I was remitting money to them to buy a property.

"Secondly, given the *hukou* system in effect in China, insinuations are bound to circulate as to how a lowly paid civil servant, responsible for assigning petroleum and other fuel oil quotas in a small city, could afford to purchase a large and new apartment in a well-appointed part of town for his retirement. However, if that apartment were to be purchased by a daughter, newly-married to a Hong Kong businessman, would that not simplify matters to a great extent? Moreover, you would then retain a *bona fide* residential address and a connection with your native town."

"You are implying that I should go back to Nantong to ensure that my parents selected an appropriate home?"

"Yes, and it would not be too early either for you to start making a list of all the features to be included. You have seen more of what is available in the outside world than they, so be sure that their new abode provides them with all the modern conveniences. Don't wait for them to ask for things. They are not demanding folks. They would be accepting of whatever might be made available to them. You will have to anticipate their needs and their wishes."

"How can I know what they might want without asking them?"

I laughed. "My dear wife! You are, like most young people, not paying enough attention to your parents. The young often expect the spotlight to be on themselves all the time. When I visited your home after our marriage, I noticed a few potted plants outside your house. That suggested to me that your father had an interest in flowers and plants. Is that not so?"

"Yes. That has been one of his main hobbies."

"Well, there you are. Make sure that any place purchased has a big enough front or rear garden, so that your father can potter around to his heart's content. He will most likely swoon with delight when that possibility is presented to him.

"During your mother's stay here, she had much interest in the hot and cold running water in our bathrooms and kitchen. So, too, the pull-out larder in our kitchen with its shelves filled with preserved eggs, wind-dried drumsticks of duck, canned goods and Chinese sausages. Be sure that those features, plus other modern conveniences, are incorporated into their new home. If any component is not available in Nantong, you'll have to arrange for it to be imported.

"Also be sure that the place is spacious enough to install an adjoining bathroom for yourself and an extra room for a live-in maid. Your parents will require one sooner or later."

"Looks like I'm going to be loaded with a lot of work."

"That's the least we can do for your parents. Please assure your parents also that you will meet all utility charges indefinitely. Otherwise they might worry over running costs. They could then relax and spend most of your father's pension on food for themselves. My approach should also absolve your siblings from possible quarrels in the future."

"What quarrels? We have no quarrels."

"Your parents are bound to die one day," I said. "If the house were left in your father's name instead of your own, and if he left no will, there may well be a quarrel over how the estate should be disposed of. For example, your brother, being the only son in the family, might claim he ought to get the house outright. How would you and your sisters react to that?"

"I wouldn't care how the house might be disposed of because I would be here with you."

"What if I were to die too? Would you still want to stay in Hong Kong by yourself, without friends and relatives? More so, should we decide to move elsewhere, to be closer to my family and kinfolk."

Kitty threw up her hands in agitation. "Why are you bringing in the subject of death, so soon after our marriage? It is morbid and unsettling!"

"Thinking ahead sometimes requires taking into account the darker prospects as well as the sunny days. Don't forget you have to shoulder your share of responsibility, for agreeing to marry a man only two years younger than your father."

And so it came about that for the next six months and more Kitty had to make repeated shuttle trips between Hong Kong and Nantong in order to identify, purchase, renovate and upgrade a home for her parents. I retained in the background, only exercising an oversight as a consultant and reminding Kitty now and then of some detail she might have overlooked, such as the provision of enough electric sockets in each room.

I was happy to learn that Kitty's parents were fully satisfied with their new home after they had moved in. However, I never saw the final product for myself, because I had no time or opportunity to visit Nantong again throughout my subsequent years

The total outlay for the entire project amounted to only a small fraction of the cost of setting up a similar establishment in Hong Kong.

* * *

During one of Kitty's absences in Nantong, I came across another announcement of an English short story competition being held in Hong Kong, now under the sponsorship of the *South China Morning Post* and Radio Television Hong Kong. Like the competition held a year earlier, publication of the winning entry was also promised. The prize was to be a brace of plane tickets on one of Cathay Pacific's regional routes.

I was in two minds as to whether I should participate again. Since I had won the last competition, I was — in the parlance of boxing — still the reigning champion. It would be cowardly and unsportsmanlike for a champion to hide from a challenge out of sheer cold funk.

On the other hand, I had not written a short story for 30 years. I must be rusty, even if I had not completely lost the knack. For 20 of those years, I had been a bureaucrat, churning out an endless stream of verbose minutes or turgid policy proposals. The trick in both processes was to be noncommittal and to protect one's own backside. The use of lukewarm prose and easily alterable recommendations was the order of the day. Occasionally, one might have to conjure up an apt but obscure Latin phrase to decorate one's outpourings. It would be like laying a wreath upon a grand funeral *cortège* for a dead language.

The possibility of disinterring another unpublished story from long ago did cross my mind. But that struck me as a poorly defendable deception, if not actually cheating. If an entry had to be made, I told myself, then I would have to try my hand at a fresh story.

I thought over the matter with trepidation for a day or two. In writing a new story, I might have to go down in ignominious defeat. But it would be worth a try. So I began work using as background setting one of those perennial daily occurrences in Hong Kong — a cocktail party. It would involve a bitter-sweet ending of a love affair between an ambitious young girl and a married wealthy business tycoon. "The Cocktail Party" was chosen as the title. Amazingly, I managed to finish it in a single day and I duly submitted it with crossed fingers.

* * *

To my surprise "The Cocktail Party" came first in that competition as well. After the story had been published in local newspapers and broadcast on Radio Hong Kong, congratulations from my friends came in and some suggested that I should be writing more stories instead of selling garments, shoes and other mass consumer products. Although I was elated with my showing, I was far from convinced that concentrating on writing again would be a sound idea.

Kitty and I made use of the plane tickets to make another trip to Singapore to visit my father and my siblings.

* * *

Fate, however, appeared to move in mysterious ways. The cocktail party I had written about was such a unique Hong Kong institution that I made every effort to attend as few of them as possible. They could be held for a variety of different purposes, from celebrating a lucrative commercial merger to announcing an unexpected engagement by a son or daughter.

There would appear, on the face of it, a melding of different cultural streams. But whether that would operate in the longer term to the benefit or detriment of anyone remained to be seen.

The attendees would, of course, vary accordingly. Parvenues of various types. But overall, they constituted a happy hunting group for seeking some kind of social, commercial or sexual connection.

There would be, consistently, a few well-dressed professional scroungers who habitually wormed their way into such functions. They would go from one cocktail party to another, day after day, in order to load up on free food and drinks, They could get away with their illegal but fairly innocuous activities because security, back in the days before suicide bombers, was by no means tight.

Apart from them, there was a regular stable of local notables who would figure on most invitation lists — comprising captains of commerce and industry, diplomatic representatives, High Court judges, bankers and so forth. But those personages could not always be counted on to turn up. It all depended upon the amount of *face* expected to be given or exchanged between the parties concerned.

There were, however, a number of more steady presences at cocktail parties. The first group would be the social columnists and their associated photographers. Then there would also be a regular contingent of eager social climbers, always hopeful of having their pictures taken and published hobnobbing with some celebrity or other.

Of such diverse elements was the cult of the cocktail party composed.

* * *

In the weeks following the publication of "The Cocktail Party" I happened to be attending one such party. I cannot remember exactly the purpose or the circumstances, but I imagined it must have been the National Day of one of the countries from which my customers sourced a lot of products.

I had made my number with the host, as required by etiquette, and was searching for a convenient backdoor to make an early escape when I bumped into a lean and hungry-looking European nursing a drink in a corner. He had appeared so forlorn that I felt I had at least to put up a pretence of being sociable.

I helped myself to a drink from a passing waiter and introduced myself.

The man replied that he was from the Netherlands and that his name was Jan Krikke. The mention of Holland gave me an opening and I waxed lyrical on how much I had enjoyed studying in his country, delving into the intricacies in public administration at the Institute of Social Studies in the Hague.

We engaged in various reminiscences and the usual exchange of pleasantries for a while.

Then Mr Krikke asked: "You don't happen to be related to that David Wong who has been winning short story competitions, are you?"

"I'm worse than that, I'm afraid. I am actually that very scribbler," I confessed.

"Congratulations!" he said. "The last story I read was very good and very amusing. Have you written other stories?"

"Yes, a few."

"May I see them?"

"What for?"

"Well, I am actually working for a publisher. Asia 2000. Have you heard of the company? It is being run by an American named Mike Morrow."

"Yes, I've heard a little about Asia 2000 and about Mike Morrow."

"Only the good things, I hope. I was thinking that if your other stories are of the same standard as the one I've read, then Asia 2000 might be keen on putting out a collection of your stories."

We eventually exchanged business cards and I agreed to send along a number of stories for his perusal.

* * *

Hong Kong was a rumour mill and a natural resting place for those who wished to spy on China. The British colonial regime had made no bones about the city being a nest for the dirty business of that cabal of Anglo-Saxon secret service agencies known as the "Five Eyes". The five participating countries, then as now, were the United States, Britain, Canada, Australia and New Zealand. Their aim was to maintain some sort of political and intelligence advantage over the rest of the world, particularly in respect of those they regarded as enemies.

The colonial administration had openly colluded with its partners in crime. It had allowed American agents leeway in interrogating refugees from China within the Immigration Department itself and had set up listening devices at strategic locations to intercept Chinese radio and telegraphic messages.

Of course, I was not without sin myself. When I was appointed by the colonial government to the Post Office in 1980, I did not realise, until too late, that I would be overseeing a system which allowed the surreptitious photographing by Special Branch operatives of private correspondence of citizens whose names appeared on a notorious Q List.

It appeared that the vague excuse of "National Security" covered a multiplicity of sins. And all the while loyal civil servants were expected to repeat the sanctimonious mantra about the "integrity of the Royal Mail."

Thus I could not completely display a clean pair of hands.

I had heard loose talk about Asia 2000 being only a publishing front and about Mike Morrow being in fact a CIA agent. Having known a number of Anglo-Saxon spies in Hong Kong over the years, masquerading as academics, journalists, missionaries, bartenders or whatever, I was not overly concerned about their spying activities against China.

Just like the much-touted China-watchers in Whitehall, they were mostly an incompetent lot and much over-rated. Unless they managed to turn some better educated Chinese into traitors — as the Soviet KGB had tried to recruit me in London during 1957 — they were unlikely to have the cultural accretions to read the more subtle Chinese nuances. It would be idle to think that good spies could be spawned from acquiring a mere university degree. Such people would probably gather only misinformation.

There was probably some justification to the rumours about Mike Morrow being a CIA operative, however, because he was subsequently arrested in Vietnam and accused of being a spy. After some diplomatic kerfuffle over his arrest, he was eventually released and allowed to return to Hong Kong.

When I met him he appeared a pleasant enough type and he was quite knowledgeable about the publishing business. He told me he was thinking of starting a business in China, selling textbooks for those desiring to learn the English language. Whether that would constitute just another cover for other activities or whether he wanted to get me involved, I could not say.

My immediate interest in him and in Asia 2000 was focused only on whether they could usefully provide me with a platform for launching my short stories.

* * *

In due course, I rummaged through the bottom drawer of my desk and put together a *pot-pourri* of stories to send to Mr. Krikke. There was no unifying theme running through them, nor had they been set in the same place. Their backgrounds roamed from Hong Kong to China, from Europe to Southeast Asia.

Mr. Krikke came back with a positive response and asked me to write a couple more to bulk the volume up to sixteen stories.

When I had done that, I took Kitty on a trip to America, together with copies of all the stories. I wanted to show her Stanford and to meet an old friend, Dr. Wilfred Stone. Will was a Professor of English and a prize-winning biographer of E.M. Forster. I wanted to show him my stories and ask him to write an introduction to the book which would be the first one bearing my name.

When I first met Will, he was a teaching assistant at Stanford while I was aiming at my first degree there. In his youth, Will had been a fighter pilot and later on he had been quite active in mobilising opposition to the Vietnam War. We had been in contact ever since. It so happened that when I spent 1957-58 in London, trying to write, Will was also in the United Kingdom, undertaking a teaching assignment for a year.

Will readily agreed to my request and wrote the following excessively flattering introduction:

He wrote: "A craving for something better, sometimes intellectual, sometimes aesthetic, inhabits most of these stories and become virtually their moral imperative. . . . . Always there is a crisis of sensibility that heads to what Sean O'Faolain called a point of illumination or to the verge of one.

"We may claim a sentence from *The Legacy of Liu Pui* as a key. 'He did not want his children to grow up like so many modern Chinese, with the ways of the West half-learned and those of China half-remembered. He wanted them to have the best of both worlds.' David Wong also wants the best of both worlds, but is too honest a writer to fake the evidence and make this ideal come true in 'happily ever after' closures. That ideal is fraught with difficulty and irony, and these stories end — even those with O.-Henry-type endings

— heavy with a sense of unfinished business."

Unfortunately, Will passed away at Stanford in 2014, at the ripe old age of 97. He had been such an active person that many friends thought he would easily make it to 100!

* * *

The book came out in a hard cover edition in early 1990 under the title *Lost River and Other Stories*. My friends had been immensely supportive, buying many more copies of the book than each needed, in order to pass on to friends and relatives. Even my regular *mah-jong* partner, Uncle Lau, who could not read a word of English, bought half a dozen copies to give to his children and friends.

The net result of such generosity was that the book became a best seller and the hardcover edition was quickly sold out. A paperback edition was soon issued by Asia 2000 in response.

* * *

I did not allow the initial robust sales figures to go to my head. I knew they had been manufactured to a large extent by the kindness of friends. But nonetheless it was a nice feeling, especially when local magazines started approaching me to enquire whether I would like to write a story for them.

However, I was quite hesitant over making another stab at a literary career so late in life. But events quite outside my own control were brewing in both my personal and my professional life. Willy-nilly, they forced me onto a path I was disinclined to follow of my own accord.

I will detail those events in a subsequent chapter of these memoirs.

CHAPTER 17

Old Friends Reunited

It had been in the middle of a rather quiet and boring morning in the autumn of 1987, shortly after I had finished checking the over-night exchange of telexes between my staff and overseas customers, that my secretary entered my room to inform me that an elderly Chinese gentleman was in the reception area, asking to see me.

"Who is he?" I asked. "What's his name and what does he want?"

"According to the receptionist, he has been rather evasive and wouldn't say," my secretary replied.

"Very odd! Hope he's not an insurance salesman chancing a cold call. I'm not in the mood for that sort of thing today. Please see if you or the receptionist can get something more sensible out of him."

"Very well."

On her return, my secretary said: "He seems to be responding in riddles. He claims he simply wants to find out how his best man has been doing. Can't make out what he's getting at."

Upon hearing that, I jumped out of my chair and rushed out to the reception area. I had served as a "best man" only once in my life and that experience had been deeply etched in my memory. That had been back in 1948, when I was 19 years old. The occasion had been the wedding between Chan Hon-Kit, a journalistic friend and mentor, and his then fiancée, Frances, a school teacher.

Shortly afterwards, they had left for China seeking — in their own words — "to do some good". That had been a lifetime ago and all attempts subsequently to re-establish contact had drawn blanks. There had been rumours for a time that Hon-Kit had continued his journalistic career with the *Southern Daily* in Canton, but I myself soon went to California after that, to study at Stanford. By the time I returned years later, he had moved on and his tracks had been lost.

It would have been entirely in keeping with Hon-Kit's character, if he were to re-surface, to do so in such a dramatic and unorthodox way.

And surely enough, Hon-Kit was standing with a mischievous smile on his lips in the reception area. He looked little different from how he had appeared decades earlier. The same grave, elevated brow and a head of hair that had remained surprisingly black for a man in his sixties, without the slightest hint of grey. There was also something vaguely familiar about the navy blue worsted suit he had on, before I noticed the creases which had to come from it having been folded up and left languishing for a prolonged period at the bottom of a camphor wood or other chest.

We fell into each other's arms and hugged tightly. A whiff of camphor tickled my nostrils.

"Where have you been hiding all these years, for heaven's sake?" I cried. "None of your friends had a clue. Heard you were with the *Southern Daily* for a while. Then I heard you had moved on, with no forwarding address."

"China's a big country, you know, and I had to go where my work took me," Hon-Kit replied, smiling broadly again.

"Where's Frances? Is she back too?"

"Yes, though obviously not here with me today."

"You've hardly changed, you elusive rascal. More tanned perhaps, but that's all."

"But you clearly have! You're no longer that teenage scarecrow that Frances and I said goodbye to at the border train station decades ago. You've prospered and lost that hungry look. Lavished with all kinds of laurels too, I read, at least according to the rags that pass for newspapers nowadays. You've been described as a business tycoon, a racehorse owner and a winner in short story competitions. You even appear younger than you ought to be. Is that what riches and success do to a man?"

I chuckled. "Appearances are deceptive, just a simple trick learnt from Dorian Gray. I've learned a great deal from you, too, like the need to be an honest journalist, even if you have to do three jobs on the sly in order to make ends meet."

"There's still an enormous need for honest journalists today. Access to reliable information is more vital than ever."

"I couldn't agree more. By the way, do you and Frances have children?"

"Yes, they're all in China, making their own headway in a brave new world. How about you? Presumably you're married and have children too?"

"Three sons in North America, shaping their money-focused careers in a somewhat less brave old world. But we don't keep in touch much. Pity.

"The family used to be the basic unit in Chinese society, not the individual. But modern pressures of life and ease of travel are undermining that. My boys have succumbed to an alien and almost anti-Confucian school of thought in respect of father and son relationships. They feel that since they never had a say in being brought into the world, it is the duty of fathers to give them whatever education and trinkets they want."

"How un-Chinese!"

"Not completely their fault, I guess. Their mother and I broke up a long time ago and the Hong Kong government kept sending me abroad on duty. So they didn't get enough of the family-type of upbringing they should have had. But I've drawn the line after university, however. After that, they're on their own."

"Sad on all scores."

"My marriage had been a mistake from the very start. But wait, I think I've salvaged something at long last. Let me get you into my office first, for a cup of tea; then I'll spill the beans."

Reuniting with Hon-Kit so suddenly seemed to have knocked me off-balance, emotionally and psychologically. An irresistible urge welled up in me, to quickly fill in all the missing years between us.

It dawned on me that I had imagined Hon-Kit burning through all his ups and downs like some "hard and jewel-like flame" whereas my own life had been dogged by missteps and missed opportunities. Perhaps, subconsciously, I was really seeking some form of absolution from my former mentor.

In that state of fuzzy awareness, I ushered Hon-Kit into my office and settled him into the most comfortable of my sofas. In passing through the reception area, I also asked my secretary to arrange for tea.

"Very satisfactory," Hon-Kit said, as he surveyed his surroundings. "You appear very comfortably placed."

"You should know everything here represents just froth and bubbles," I said. "Just the appurtenances of being a capitalist; all quite meaningless. You should know, better than most. After all, you introduced me to Proudhon. 'Property is theft.' Remember? Capitalism is based on the profit motive. And to maximise profits, you have to exploit people at their weakest, people one should not exploit at all. Yet there it is, in the real world. We go to places where labour is cheapest and where the benefits are greatest for our customers, even though I personally dislike making a living that way."

"And how *do* you want to make a living?"

"I'm not sure. That's my problem. Perhaps I'd rather have done some good, like you and Frances."

"I'm not sure we've actually done any."

"Don't say that! I've been envying you all these years, wishing I had gone to China with you, living through all those tumultuous changes in our country. I've a million questions to ask."

Hon-Kit sighed. "I'm not sure I've found very much in the way of answers."

"But you must have! You've lived through everything — the campaigns against the three and five antis, the establishment of the communes, the Great Leap Forward, the Great Famine, the Great Proletarian Cultural Revolution and right now the opening up of the country under socialism with Chinese characteristics."

My mind was now racing far ahead of my speech. No doubt my old friend must have joined the Communist Party for the sake of his ideals. But how had he coped with all the intellectual twists and turns necessitated by the Chinese linkage with their Soviet comrades? He was from an older school than the official who performed the marriage ceremony for Kitty and myself, and older than He Wei, the budding diplomat. How had he adjusted and compromised?

Meanwhile, Hon-Kit was shaking his head and sighing again. "You must know by now what can sometimes happen when a person is young. You think you've uncovered some shining truth and you believe with all your heart in every fibre of it. You couldn't sign up quickly enough to the whole shebang, like a priest committing himself to the vows of some holy order. Then you wake up one morning and start to wonder if God actually existed. That doubt comes as a complete shock and what you had been committed to for years suddenly begins to fall to pieces."

"Are you trying to tell me that you now regret having gone to China when you and Frances did?"

"No, not in the least. Both Frances and I discovered ourselves a little."

"Then why did you deter me from going with you when you did? Otherwise I might also have discovered something about myself."

"You were too young and not yet ready."

"Countless millions of our countrymen were also not yet ready for the changes they had to face. They coped somehow and made their contributions."

"They had no choice. They had to accept their destinies with their families. You had a choice."

"But I kept choosing the wrong path, can't you see? After I had finished university, I met quite a few Chinese graduates heading back to China on the American President Lines ship coming back to Hong Kong. But again I held back, fearful of whether I would be up to the challenges. That had left me feeling I had missed out on something important, something that I still owed to my nation and to myself, solidarity with my fellow countrymen also."

"I'm sure there must have been many opportunities since then for you to contribute to your country, through expanding its export trade or making investments there."

"That's not quite the same. It's like missing that critical moment when a thing had to be done. Missing it taints a person forever and it can't be undone. It's like being born out of original sin or dodging the draft at the outbreak of war. You might try to convince yourself with a thousand excuses, that you've always been a pacifist or a conscientious objector or whatever. But deep inside your heart you know you had been in a blue funk of actual combat, of getting killed or maimed. Time might pass but you can never get to alter that fateful moment."

"That's all in your head, my dear friend. Hasn't it been said that there's nothing really good or bad but thinking makes it so?"

"That is easy for you to say because you and Frances made the right decision. I failed to make the right one."

"Frances and I might have made **one** right decision. That does not mean we made all the subsequent decisions correctly also. By not making a decision when you did, you had been spared the dilemmas of facing all the ones that subsequently followed."

"You're always such a philosopher, employing sophistries to make me feel better. I'm immensely glad, nonetheless, that we've finally linked up again after so many years."

"I'm mighty glad too."

A tea lady brought in cups of tea to interrupt the conversation.

I invited Hon-Kit to partake and we lingered over a few leisurely sips.

Then he continued: "You know, when I employ sophistries it might be just to make myself feel better rather than for your sake. As I've said, so much is inside our heads. Time passes and perspectives change. As our Paramount Ruler has said: 'What does it matter if a cat is black or white so long as it can catch mice?' Changes come and a lot of things get overturned or re-evaluated."

I detected for the first time an undertone of sorrow creeping into his voice and I did not know how to respond. A thought struck me that my old friend might have had to endure spells of the kind of "thought reform through labour" common for Party members straying from the prevailing Party line. Because of the suddenness of that thought, I said the first banal thing that came to mind. "Yes, things here have changed a hell of a lot here, too, since 1949."

"Yes, I know," Hon-Kit said. "We've seen some of them. A cross-harbour tunnel and a very efficient mass transit system. Is your Eighth Granduncle's bungalow on Tsing Yee Island — The Abode of Butterflies — still standing?"

"Sadly, no. Those were simple and happy days back then, were they not? You used to bring your nieces, Irene and Florence, along sometimes. Are they still living in this town or have they migrated?"

"No, they're still here. But you're unlikely to recognise them if you came across them in the street. They were only schoolgirls when they visited The Abode of Butterflies."

"I was only a wide-eyed teenager myself then. I probably wouldn't have recognised my former self if I came across him today. How time has flown!"

"What's standing at the site of the old bungalow now?"

"A couple of blocks of factory buildings, I think. The government has linked up the island with the mainland through reclamations."

Hon-Kit nodded and said nothing further. I was also left with nothing else to say. A silence fell abruptly over the memories of our youth, like the sudden clanging shut of prison gates. Those golden and carefree weekends from long ago could never be revisited by any of us any more.

The marriage in 1949 of Hon-Kit and Frances

"Are you and Frances back here for good?"

"So long as we can survive on our modest Chinese state pensions, I guess."

"Have you never considered staying in China, to be close to your children or grandchildren?"

"Yes, but Hong Kong has always been home for us. When we Chinese reach a certain age, we always long to return to our roots."

"Oh, don't sound so morbid! You're in absolutely fine fettle," I said. "I assume Frances is too. I'm dying to see her again. How about lunching together this weekend? I've got a surprise for both of you. I got married again a short while back, to a Nantong girl who's way too young for me, younger than my two eldest children, in fact!"

"Good heavens! Don't tell me you've turned into a cradle-snatcher!"

"Not exactly. It's a long and complicated story. She's delightfully cheerful and out-going. My friends call her Kitty. I think you'll both take to her. She used to be a leading light in her local Communist Youth League."

"Oh! So it has been one of those unions of both heart and intellect, has it?" That earlier undertone of sorrow lifted from his voice.

"Not quite sure yet. Too soon to say," I said. "Kitty only got her one-way visa at the end of 1984. She's been trying to adjust to the wicked ways of Hong Kong ever since. And not always successfully. It has been an enormous cultural shock for her. Let's have lunch this weekend, so you can meet her. Where are you guys staying? On the island or in Kowloon?"

"Kowloon."

"All right. Do you prefer Saturday or Sunday?"

"Both are suitable for us. But don't you often go horse-racing on Saturdays?"

"You're right. Let's make it Sunday." I named a popular restaurant in Tsim Sha Tsui and said I would book a table for noon on Sunday. "See you both then," I said.

* * *

Seeing Frances again after almost four decades came as a complete shock. Time had been much more cruel to her than it had been to Hon-Kit. She had grown wizened and shrunken. The freshness and beauty that had attended her had vanished; even her voice sounded aged and cracked. I could not help speculating over what physical and psychological trials she must have had to endure since we last said goodbye. Women did not appear to take to ageing as well as men. It seemed so unfair.

Frances in 1948 at the Abode of Butterflies

Introducing Kitty to her merely heightened the devastating passage of time. Although all the generational courtesies between Kitty and my old friends had been observed, the differences in their ages were difficult to ignore. So that initial get-together was by no means an unqualified success.

Nonetheless, a further meal was arranged for three weeks later, whereby other friends who had participated in those outings at the Abode of Butterflies also attended to celebrate the return of Hon-Kit and Frances.

Unfortunately, the number was small, because several of the old crowd had migrated and the rest had gone to their final resting places.

Among the attendees at the subsequent meal was Auyang Ming, that long-confirmed bachelor who had been my roommate for a spell during our youth. He had long ago taken me to a Kowloon whorehouse to lose my virginity.

Auyang Ming also sprang a surprise on most of us. He brought along a newly-acquired wife, who turned out to be a middle-aged lady of a pleasant disposition. I had previously met her briefly at a *mah-jong* party. At that time she had been someone else's wife. Apparently her former husband passed away prematurely and Auyang Ming was conveniently available to fill the breach.

* * *

After that second meal, Kitty and I continued to meet with Hon-Kit and Frances irregularly, on odd weekends. But it soon became painfully clear that not every one had the same motive for attending those get-togethers.

My motives had been more obvious. I had wanted to gain first-hand accounts of the revolutionary convulsions which had taken place in China from friends like Hon-Kit and Frances. I had always been far away from the field of action and I did not trust either the narratives given by the Chinese state media or the Western press. Hence my desire to get more rounded pictures from more reliable sources.

For example, I had read a piece by a Western correspondent about the Great Famine. The man claimed he had witnessed corpses lying by a roadside being chewed by a pack of stray dogs. I had no doubt that the reporter might have seen corpses by a roadside but the description of their being eaten by stray dogs had to be faked, manufactured or sensationalised to dress up the story. During famines, the natural instinct of any Chinese community would be to hunt down every stray dog in the neighbourhood for food, long before any would be left to feed on themselves. I wanted more details of the impact of that disastrous famine in the provinces or localities where Hon-Kit had been.

The long separation between myself and Hon-Kit and Frances certainly made all of us fonder of each other's company. For myself, their presence brought back the frank and uninhibited cut and thrust of ideas and youthful fancies. That spark had already been ignited by the unexpected visit by Hon-Kit to my office.

But the subsequent meetings suggested that both Hon-Kit and Frances harboured a certain reluctance in talking about personal experiences, for they tended to respond to specific questions with only generalities. When I asked them how they thought Deng's policy of opening up the country to the outside world would affect ordinary Chinese life, for instance, they said it was too early to tell.

It occurred to me suddenly that in asking for their personal experiences I was effectively pushing them to justify their lives. How could anyone do that, especially in open company? If I had been asked to do likewise, I would also be stuck.

Kitty, for all intents and purposes, would be "open company" to them. She was from a different generation. Furthermore, she had no interest in either ancient or contemporary Chinese history. Like most young people her age, she regarded occurrences before her birth as matters of little interest or moment. She attended our meetings only because she was my wife and I was keen on them.

With those considerations in mind, I suggested to Hon-Kit that we should perhaps end our weekend family meetings and instead meet bilaterally on an *ad hoc* basis for a cup of tea, whenever convenient. Hon-Kit heartily agreed.

* * *

It soon came out in private conversation that Hon-Kit had taken on a ghost-writing job to augment his pension, penning anodyne or uplifting speeches for a local business tycoon to deliver at his Rotary Club or other similar meetings. Frances, meanwhile, was busy peddling life insurance policies for AIA, on a strictly commission basis.

My heart wrung with sadness on learning of their financial circumstances. What a way to end up in old age and retirement! It was like starting off all over again as had happened in our youth, doing several jobs so that we could make ends meet for that one job that appealed to us.

I felt desperate to do something for them. But how and in what way? To offer them money would seem cruel and heartless, almost cold-bloodedly insulting. It would take no cognisance of the long decades they had both struggled and sacrificed for their ideals; it would be like delivering a cruel rebuke. I simply could not do it. The knowledge of their financial situation, something which I could easily resolve, would have to remain on my conscience as my own form of punishment.

Kitty, of course, could not work out why I should sometimes slip into a melancholy mood after tea with Hon-Kit. She was, unhappily, still too tender in years to read my inner sentiments and my deeper sorrows. She would first have to make mistakes of her own before she could glimpse and be touched by the fountainhead of life's enduring misfortunes.

* * *

Once the one-on-one sessions began between myself and Hon-Kit, the old former warmth of frankness and comradeship returned between us. At an early opportunity, I reverted to the subject of the Great Famine. I asked my old mentor how many people actually perished during those years.

"I don't really know. I wasn't responsible for counting the bodies, you know," Hon-Kit replied. "It all depended on how the statistics had been gathered and disseminated."

"You mean the mainland also know how to lie convincingly with statistics, like the best of economic gurus and confidence tricksters?"

"I'm afraid so. For example, some quarters just took the normal number of births in the period before the famine and subtracted the number of births during the period of the famine to arrive at a number of babies lost through not being born because mothers had been too weakened by lack of food to give birth or to carry their babies for the full pregnancy term. That number would then be added to the reported deaths to make another number. So numbers bandied around are all quite unreliable.

"But another consideration is also important. China's population was about 540 million in 1949, when the Communists took over, and it grew to around 969 million in 1969, well after the Great Famine had ended. Can you imagine what that number would have been and the implications for the country if there had not been those usual Malthusian interventions?"

"It was not till 1979, I think, that the one-child policy was implemented?"

"Precisely," Hon-Kit replied. "So the debate goes on, as to whether a growing population is a good or a bad thing. I don't really know. Is it a good thing to have a shrinking population, like Japan's?"

"I'm glad I'm not responsible for making that kind of decision," I said.

* * *

On the next occasion that Hon-Kit and I met for tea, our conversation settled around the Great Proletarian Cultural Revolution, launched by Chairman

Mao in May of 1966. The revolution lasted for approximately ten years, until Mao died in September of 1976. Afterwards, in the common parlance used inside China, that period was often referred to as "the lost decade".

How could Mao have launched such a destructive movement? I supposed since the Communist came to power in 1949 there had been a steady cult of the personality built around Mao. In the eyes of the Chinese nation and many members of the ruling elite, he had been elevated to the status of a demi-god whose commands had to be obeyed.

But why did Mao initiate such a movement? So far as I could make out, he had written a poem in 1963 which gave an indication of his thinking. He wrote:

So many deeds cry out to be done
And always urgently;
The world rolls on,
Time passes.
Ten thousand years are too long.
Seize the day, seize the hour!
The Four Seas are rising, clouds and waters raging.
The Five Continents are rocking, wind and thunder roaring.
Our force is irresistible!
Away with all pests!

According to my limited knowledge, Mao left no other comprehensive statement of his private thoughts. But further inferences could be drawn from the self-criticism statement that Party elders had forced him to write in 1962, after the failure of his Great Leap Forward policy and from the various public justifications and purposes subsequently given for the mass campaign.

My guess was that Mao thought he had lost power and prestige or — if you prefer — *face*, because of the criticisms voiced by old comrades over the

Great Leap Forward. Mao had revealed some of his difficulties with them in conversations with Jiang Ching, his wife. Being a proud man, he had wanted to recover both. He therefore calculated that by rooting out what he conceived to be the remaining capitalist, traditionalists and bourgeois elements in society, he might retrieve his influence. He also might have genuinely felt that the revolutionary spirit was flagging within the Communist Party itself and that those reactionary elements were making a comeback. So he resurrected a slogan he had coined in his youth that "To rebel is justified."

Chinese officialdom since ancient times had always been afraid of what they had termed "*luan*" or chaos and social disorder. But now it seemed that the chaos and social disorder were being initiated by Chairman Mao himself.

During the early stages, "big character" posters appeared everywhere and revolutionary committees and Red Guard units were formed. Violent clashes duly erupted in virtually every city across the country. Local and provincial government offices and factories were taken over by various revolutionary mobs. Rival groupings all sought opportunities to further their own ambitions and to establish their own power bases. They often fought and killed over who should be in control of each captured entity.

There were some half-baked calls to re-establish a Paris Commune-type of government, like that of 1792 after the storming of the Bastille. Tanks and machine guns stolen from military bases were used by proliferating factions, sometimes numbering thousands, as they fought pitched battles in the streets for control of newspapers, radio stations and other organs of power

Anarchists and Red Guards captured the Foreign Office, published China's secret diplomatic reports and sacked the British Embassy. Foreigners were attacked in the streets. Xenophobia spread like a pox. Poorly educated youngsters often took on the fanaticism and passion of members of religious cults.

Schools and universities were closed, enabling those still wet behind the ears to run amok. They began putting dunce's caps on former teachers and professors and lectured them on revolutionary commitments. Previous leaders of government offices and other organs of authority were openly criticised, humiliated and assaulted. Some were killed and many others were driven to suicide. Numerous cultural and religious relics were severely damaged or destroyed, as were also some military defensive installations.

By October of 1966, Mao himself had to admit in a Central Committee meeting that he had been surprised by the vehemence shown. But he claimed that others were exploiting the disorder to feather their own nests, even waving the red flag only to pursue a reactionary path.

Among the high-level victims of the chaos were Liu Shao-Chi, the President of the People's Republic, Marshal Peng De-Huai, the second-ranking marshal and hero of the revolutionary wars, and Deng Xiao-Ping, the future Paramount Ruler of China. Towards the end, even the much loved and highly-respected Premier, Chou En-Lai, came under attack, possibly because he had always been a moderating voice urging Mao to rein in the more radical activities.

By 1969, even Mao hinted that the Cultural Revolution might have gone too far. A major city and port like Shanghai had already ceased to function by 1967 and factionalism was rife in a number of other cities. Mao increasingly had to rely upon Marshal Lin Biao and the People's Liberation Army to maintain a semblance of control. But he had opened a Pandora's box and there was no shutting the lid again. Developments had acquired a crazy momentum of their own.

One notable side event which happened during that dark period in Chinese history — when the officer corps of the People's Liberation Army was itself also divided in loyalties — was the picking by Mao of Marshal Lin Biao as his successor. Lin had been responsible for putting together that "Little Red Book" of Mao's quotations which soon became so ubiquitously waved and quoted throughout the land. Lin was also responsible for subsequently purging 80,000 rightist-inclined officers from the People's Liberation Army.

But Lin had not been a particularly ambitious or astute politician. He admitted that he had no talent and whatever he knew he had learnt from Mao. He therefore tried not to be designated as Mao's successor but Mao scolded him and told him not to behave like one of the Ming emperors, who had spent more time seeking medicines for longevity than attending to matters of state.

So Lin did the next best thing, by adhering as closely as possible to whatever Mao wished, though he was himself not too supportive of the Cultural Revolution itself. Nonetheless he went along with Mao's ideas and became notorious within the Party for his own "three nos" policy — no responsibility, no suggestions and no crime.

Lin soon sensed, however, that he might be quite vulnerable within the Party after Mao's death, given the devious nature of Party politics. So he began building his own base within the 21-member Politburo. His own wife, Ye Qun, had been a member. As his efforts mustered support, it caused Mao to suspect him of plotting a coup.

Learning of Mao's suspicions and fearing for the consequences, Lin turned even more reclusive than he normally was. In 1972, he and his entire family finally attempted to flee by plane. His son, Lin Li-Guo, was a high ranking officer in the Air Force.

Where Lin had intended to head for was by no means clear. Some said he was seeking asylum in the Soviet Union while others said he was attempting to team up with General Chiang Kai-Shek in Taiwan.

In any case, the plane came down over Mongolia, due either to an accident or to an inadequate supply of fuel. Of course, it was inevitable that a number of conspiracy theories would circulate about the crash. But whatever the theory, the entire Lin family perished with Lin. He was aged 63 and was subsequently condemned by the Communist Party as a traitor.

Mao died in September of 1976 at the age of 82 and the Cultural Revolution petered towards an end. In its aftermath, it proved convenient to blame Lin and Mao's wife, Jiang Ching, for the worst excesses of the Cultural Revolution. The number of people who have been killed or harmed during that decade would always be the subject of partisan debate. But it was significant that the Communist Party itself had to admit rehabilitating three million people who had been "unjustly, falsely or erroneously" dealt with during the Cultural Revolution.

* * *

When Hon-Kit and I discussed the Cultural Revolution over cups of tea, I observed: "Looking from the outside, I'm amazed that such a collective madness can overtake a country like ours. We are supposed to be ruled by a carefully selected Communist Party, a club harder to get into than any of those snooty ones located along Pall Mall. My own father-in-law applied to join twice and was rejected twice."

"The Communist Party is a broad church," Hon-Kit replied. "It contains a great many factions. Although it practises democratic centralism, it is not always easy to predict who would control the majority."

"But can such madness erupt again?"

"Certainly! Why not? Collective madnesses can overtake any party or country. Ours has been particularly vulnerable, because many of its people have been poorly educated. When the country was liberated in 1949, most people were illiterate. Moreover, they had always since ancient times been a naive and superstitious lot. Credulous too. Otherwise they would not have believed that the younger brother of Jesus had led them in the Taiping Rebellion or that performing a few martial arts rituals could make them invulnerable to bullets during the Boxer Rebellion."

I shook my head in despair. "We learn far too slowly," I said.

"Let me tell you a story of the Cultural Revolution which did not gain much traction in the press outside of China," Hon-Kit continued.

"Foreign commentators had been too gleefully writing about the perceived disintegration of a Communist country to remember that such troubles could just as easily erupt in their own countries, if given the right circumstances.

"My story concerns a man in his mid-30s by the name of Chen Li-Ming. He had been something of a revolutionary hero in the town of Hsiang-Tan at one time. But he subsequently lost his mind, and for the last 16 years or so he had been confined within a lunatic asylum in Peking.

"During the Cultural Revolution, a revolutionary group formed by students at Tsinghua University broke into the asylum, in the mistaken belief that one of its members had been detained there. Instead of finding their fellow student, the group found Chen, who excitedly told them he was actually a Red Guard who had been locked up for criticising Liu Shao-Chi. A sort of mob mentality took over and the students began hailing Chen as a revolutionary hero, ignoring all protestations by the asylum staff that Chen had been in fact a long-term inmate.

"Led by Chen, the students went on a rampage throughout Peking and even followed him to other parts of the country to listen to him making speeches. They took Chen's ravings against Liu Shao-Chi as comparable to Lu Hsun's revolutionary work, *The Diary of a Madman*. They even tried to stage shows based on Chen's writing," Hon-Kit lamented.

"What happened to Chen eventually?" I interjected, in disbelief over how far such absurdities could go.

"In 1968, the Central Committee decided that enough was enough. It ordered Chen arrested and put back inside the asylum. For all I know, he might still be there now.

"So you see how credulous even university students could be and why our young must be earnestly educated to think for themselves, to really learn the appropriate lessons from history. Proper education provides a kind of skein which could gather together and constrain all the selfishness, paranoia, greed, ambition, lechery, frustrations, propensity for violence and all those other undesirable emotional or intellectual habits we tend to hide and nurture inside ourselves. The better the education, the more sturdy the integument. Should such demons ever break out from confinement, then farsighted leaders must slay them swiftly and without mercy, lest they spread and infect others."

"I'm beginning to see now what you are driving at," I said. "The Germans were at one time better educated, on average, than the average Chinese. Yet they were still captivated by the ravings of a man with an unbecoming toothbrush moustache and, subsequently — as a nation — did a great deal of damage to the rest of the world. The Italians followed a man, who promised them he could make the trains run on time, with a similar result. History seems to be repeating its lessons with greater and greater frequency.

"Chairman Mao once declared that the mind of a child was like a piece of blank paper. People could write anything they wished on it. I suppose he has proved his point through the Cultural Revolution. Unfortunately, once upon a time, we have all had our own credulous moments. When I was a child, for example, my maternal grandfather told me about a certain Jewish man who was able to walk on water. I believed him and quickly tried to follow suit, at the deep end of a swimming pool. I almost drowned."

Hon-Kit laughed. "You at least latched on to the scientific approach quite early in life. Not everybody did. If this is an occasion for confessions, then I guess I have to make one also.

"When I was young, I read a lot of Tao Yuan-Ming. He was a marvellous poet. When he declared, one and a half thousand years ago, that life was too short to compromise with principles, I believed him and thereby resolved that I, too, would not compromise with my principles. But I soon found I could not adhere to my own resolution."

"That was because you have always been too much of a human being," I replied, with an honest degree of consolation. "The trouble I find with most philosophers and thinkers is that they all seem to visualise human beings as idealised abstractions. It might be fine for Marx to declare: 'From each according to his ability; to each according to his need.'

"But it does not work out that way in practice because those with ability also have their own different needs. Again, we cannot all live like noble savages because man is at bottom a social animal. He needs to live not in isolation but among his own kind and to do that a willingness to compromise is necessary."

"It's always so reassuring for my ego and my self-esteem when I have a chat with you," Hon-Kit said. "You always provide me with such plausible alibis for every failing."

* * *

On the next occasion I had tea with Hon-Kit, he turned the tables on me.

"You once asked me how Deng Xiao-Ping's policy of 'opening up' the country would affect China. You've been familiar with Western ways and have been largely outside of our country all these decades. What do you think? Would it turn our country into as rich and glitzy a place as Hong Kong?"

"Heaven forbid!" I cried. "The wealth and the glitz here, as you must surmise — even from the brief period you and Frances have been back — are only a facade, to disguise the real poverty of the soul and the dire rootlessness among ordinary people. If you remember your Balzac, you will recall him describing post-Napoleonic Paris as a city deprived of love, except for the love of money. That is what Hong Kong is dangerously becoming too.

"But it would be foolish to even pretend to answer your question without first establishing how 'opening up' is defined and the extent to which the government intends to lift the lid. Does it want, for example, a full-throttled Thatcher-Reagan type of free market, with public services privatised, banking deregulated, trade union power cut back and inequality made rampant through a regime where the devil takes the hindmost? Does it want hot money sloshing through our country, like in Hong Kong, looking for predatory pickings and then disappearing with the spoils, or alternatively, legal and accounting firms popping up all over the place selling shell companies in Liechtenstein or the Dutch Antilles for dropping corporate veils over dubious activities?"

"Certainly not!" Hon-Kit replied. "I doubt if the average cadre knows a fraction of what is really happening in Hong Kong or in the wider world. He is likely to be just thinking of incentives to spur productivity and speedy domestic capital formation to invest in national development."

"That is why leaders must tread warily. It is no good announcing grand policies and saying that it was not a crime to get rich, if there are not enough competent cadres on the ground to sensibly and efficiently implement those policies. This is where most countries fall down. It might sound pretty nifty to have modern stock, commodity or foreign exchange markets but unless they are properly regulated they will become just handy tools for insider trading and a range of other malpractices. Even the richest man in Hong Kong has had his wrist slapped for insider trading."

"I see the obstacles and what you mean. But our people have to start learning and making mistakes at some point. Might as well be as soon as possible. Unfortunately, the educational system in China has given too much priority to producing scientists and engineers, to students thinking within certain prescribed parameters, rather than to poets, administrators and generalists, those capable of truly exploring fresh horizons."

"You mean poets like Chairman Mao?"

"No, not exactly like Chairman Mao. But now that you've mentioned the subject, why don't you write an essay setting out the deficiencies and pitfalls likely to arise in opening up our country to the outside world?"

"I'm not an expert in the subject; I don't know the ins and outs of all the complicated tricks. I can barely list the numerous corporations in Japan, Britain and America in oil, banking, tobacco, pharmaceutical, car-making and other major industries which have been lying, cheating and stealing from consumers for years."

"All the more reason for exposing them. It would be a real contribution towards educating our people."

"I'm through with tilting at windmills. Let the youngsters do it."

"That doesn't sound like the young journalist I used to know, the one who said he wanted to be like Zola and take up a pen to defend innocent victims like Alfred Dreyfus."

"I haven't got the talents of Zola."

"You can never know until you have tried, can you?"

"Oh, stop flattering me. I have a much more pressing and personal duty to perform — to prepare my young and innocent wife for life in an increasing cock-eyed world."

And so it came to pass that I ended up once again in poor humour after having tea with Hon-Kit. How was I to anticipate that a silly and boastful remark I had made during my teens would come back to test the validity of my assertion 40 years later!

CHAPTER 18

Gathering Storms

THE FIRST DISMAL AUGURY of things to come happened on the night of December 5, 1986. The Governor of Hong Kong, Sir Edward Youde, died in his sleep at the British Embassy in Peking. He was 62.

The city he governed was deeply shocked by the news. His body was brought back for a state funeral by his wife, Lady Pamela, herself a Sinologist.

Sir Edward had been in China as part of a high-powered delegation, working out with Chinese officials the technical details of reverting Hong Kong to Chinese sovereignty in 1997. This had followed the formal signing of the Sino-British Joint Declaration by Premier Zhao Zi-Yang, on behalf of China, and Prime Minister, Mrs. Margaret Thatcher, on behalf of Britain in December of 1984. It had been a statement that Sir Edward must have had a hand in drafting.

One could not help speculating whether the possibility of his actually dying on the job had ever been considered by Sir Edward himself, before he accepted his appointment as the governor of Hong Kong in May of 1982. Problems with his heart had already been known then, as had the extremely delicate state of Anglo-Chinese relations under a strong-willed Margaret Thatcher. She had just won the Falklands war and was not without some illusions that Britannia could still rule the waves — at least after a fashion. Moreover, her legions of advisors were all badgering her with a chorus of discordant voices.

There were, for example, the legalistic beagles who were focused too much on the meaning of the word "perpetuity" contained in the treaties signed by China ceding Hong Kong Island and the Kowloon Peninsula to Britain. And then there were the myth-makers who truly believed that it was in some way the brilliance of British colonial administrations which had rendered the colony enormously wealthy under a vague *laissez-faire* policy. Surely, to those so inclined, such factors must be worth at least another 50 years of continued British management of the city, albeit theoretically and legally already agreed to be returned to Chinese sovereignty?

There was also the combative instincts of Mrs. Thatcher herself to take into account. When the Chinese side told her in September of 1982 that China would brook no delay over the negotiations and that if it came to a choice between sovereignty and prosperity, China would always choose sovereignty, she had responded by asking her minions whether Hong Kong could be defended.

It was high time that Western leaders like Mrs. Thatcher accepted that the power equations had been shifting radically over the years and that the China of today was quite a different kettle of fish from the China during the Opium Wars. Moreover, the old model for development through colonisation and exploitation of human and natural resources was no longer one which the people of many nations would be willing to tolerate.

Of course, the Chinese side also had its own hang-ups. For several generations, the nation had felt aggrieved over "unequal treaties" with foreign powers and had suffered acute psychological humiliation as a result. The people had therefore preoccupied themselves with their national loss of "face", so much so that no leader could have retained power without promising to rectify an awkward situation left over from history. Their attitude had steadily hardened to become the same as the one which gave rise to the Western knightly motto of "Death before dishonour".

In any case, the opening gambit by the British regarding managing the city for another 50 years got short shrift from the Chinese. However, being a pragmatic people, the Chinese side recognised that the kind of economic and social experimenting that it would be disrupting might well not go down agreeably with many of the five million bourgeois-pampered citizens of Hong Kong.

The Chinese were also conscious that memories of the spill-over of the Cultural Revolution into Hong Kong in 1967 might have raised some local apprehensions. So they agreed to a transitional period of 50 years whereby the corruption-infused capitalist system hitherto practised in the city would remain largely unchanged. Ballroom dancing and horse-racing would continue under Chinese rule, they asserted lightheartedly.

Sir Edward, being a Sinologist and fluent in the languages of both sides and more than alert to their respective concerns, must have been aware of the tricky political and cultural cross-currents he would have to navigate to arrive at a fair and equitable settlement over some old and inglorious episodes in international history. But would either side permit him to steer towards accommodation or merely seek to scupper him? He was likely to have viewed his own inclusion in the British team as both a matter of duty and of conscience.

He had, since his student days at the School of Oriental and African Studies, steeped himself in the language and culture of the Chinese civilisation. He must have quickly become attuned to their many endearing charms, quirks, subtleties and eccentricities.

In fact, he had demonstrated his skills early in life. He had happened to have been on board the frigate HMS *Amethyst* on the Yangtze River when the ship was caught in the cross-fire of the Chinese civil war. His ship had been severely damaged by artillery but he managed to negotiate with a People's Liberation Army commander somehow and freed the vessel. The episode could have left him with an early impression that civilised people could achieve results as readily through talking rather than through violence. For that accomplishment, he was awarded an MBE.

For a foreigner to communicate successfully with the Chinese in their own language could not have been an easy matter, for Chinese was sometimes described as the language of the heart, whereby deep feelings and meanings could be conveyed with simple words or silences. It has remained today a language without grammar, tenses, regular and irregular verbs, masculine or feminine pronouns and so forth.

Sir Edward must have mastered many of its subtleties and nuances prior to joining the Foreign and Commonwealth Office. He had also undertaken several diplomatic assignments in China, the last one being as the British ambassadorship between 1974 to 1978.

When Sir Edward took up office as Hong Kong's governor in 1982, I had already retired from the Hong Kong civil service the previous year. I therefore, much to my personal regret, never had the opportunity to work under him. However, every ex-colleague I could trust and who had worked for him had spoken of him in respectful and glowing terms. He had been variously described as sincere, hard-working, sober and thoughtful, cool and unflappable, well-liked and admired, and always honestly striving to gain practical benefits for the ordinary people of Hong Kong.

Sir Edward was, I think, the only Welshman to attain the governorship of Hong Kong and it was a great pity for its citizens that his term in office should be so abruptly cut short. The number of people who turned up to mourn his demise was ample testimony of the gratitude and affection he had garnered during his brief tenure.

* * *

Earlier in 1986, my friend Wang Kuan-Cheng, erstwhile President of the Hong Kong Chinese General Chamber of Commerce and a member of the Chinese People's Political Consultative Conference, also passed away, at the age of 79. He, together with a few of my other friends at the General Chamber, had been such indefatigable supporters of my pursuit of Kitty that they had pulled all kinds of political strings with powerful personages in China to ensure that I could overcome the various obstacles standing in the way of my marrying a Chinese citizen and a leading member of the Nantong Communist Youth League I had fallen in love with.

Wang joined another bosom friend, Ip Yeuk-Lam, to actually accompany me to Shenzhen to meet Gao Lin-Mao — who happened to have been there making a film— and to persuade him and his wife, Kitty's eldest sister, as members of the Chinese Communist Party, to withdraw their letters of objection against the marriage between myself and Kitty. I would always remember in particular Wang with great affection and gratitude because he had staked his own standing and reputation on my behalf.

It was a pity that circumstances were such that he never got to meet Kitty, the object of his efforts, after her arrival in Hong Kong towards the end of 1984.

In 1985, the year before he passed away, Wang had used his considerable fortune, amassed through the development of his quarry and properties in North Point, to establish an education trust to send Chinese students abroad to study the sciences and technology.

* * *

At the start of 1987, I suffered from another of those severe pancreatic attacks which had been a regular feature of my life since the first attack took place during a *mah-jong* game with civil service colleagues in 1981. I nearly died on that occasion, because my ailment had been initially misdiagnosed as a simple case of food poisoning, before my condition worsened and I was transferred to intensive care.

Since that time, I had undergone a series of ultrasound examinations, endoscopies and other tests, both at government and private hospitals, but no cause had ever been discovered to explain my condition. Hence, periodically, roughly once or twice a year at least, and sometimes more often, I would be hospitalised for a few days after every attack.

The attack in 1987 came in the evening, after Kitty and I had just finished dinner. We were watching television in the sitting room when I suddenly felt the normal early symptom — a gathering of pressure and then pain in the middle of my chest.

I jumped out of my seat to change into street clothes, calling simultaneously to Kitty: "Please pack a suit of pyjamas, a change of underwear and daily essentials like toothpaste and toothbrush. I have to go to hospital."

Kitty was totally unmoved by the sense of urgency in my voice. Although she was aware that I suffered from pancreatic problems, she had never actually seen me suddenness of an attack. The last time I had one she was in Nantong overseeing renovations to the home for her parents.

Therefore she replied without haste: "We have just finished dinner. Why do you want to go to a hospital?"

"Stop asking questions and do what I asked!" I snapped. "In less than five minutes I will collapse with pain and you won't have the strength to carry me downstairs and put me in a taxi."

Events turned out more or less as I had predicted. Kitty just managed to help me into a taxi before I utterly collapsed with pain.

At the Yeung Wo Hospital in Happy Valley, I told the admissions nurse to telephone Dr Joseph Fung, the Li & Fung medical service provider and Fung family elder, who would inform her of the type of medication I ought to be given. It was an altogether steep learning experience for Kitty to realise how quickly I could be reduced to complete helplessness.

* * *

A couple of months after my pancreatic attack, I went out after work with Kwok-Hong and Rosetta for a meal. It was an occasional habit we had fallen into after they realised I was not out to find fault with their work at Li & Fung (Trading), as an excuse for dismissing them. Indeed, they began to see me as a kind of protector, who would assess the performance of their division fairly and objectively rather than blindly following the instructions of H.C.. A feeling of mutual trust and understanding therefore grew steadily between us.

So far as I was concerned, they were a straightforward and reliable couple, not exceptionally brilliant or gifted, but without guile and trying to do their best at work. It would in any case be difficult for me to judge Kwok-Hong's performance since he worked most of the time directly to his uncle regarding all aspects of the fireworks trade. If H.C. really wanted to shunt him out of the company, then he would have to make the case for a dismissal himself and not count on me wielding the knife.

During the course of the meal, Kwok-Hong asked me what I thought of the idea of privatising Li & Fung. He had inherited a block of Li & Fung shares from his father and was under the impression I was privy to the privatising idea. But I was not. It was the first I had ever heard of such a move and I told him so.

Kwok-Hong then explained there had been a meeting of Fung family members and the idea had been discussed. Although the company was a publicly listed company, the overwhelming bulk of the shares were held by members of the family. The shares were therefore seldom traded on the exchange and their price had languished for a number of years, as had its annual dividends. It was suggested that by buying back at a premium those shares held outside the family, the company might be privatised, reorganised and re-launched as a newly listed company.

When I heard what Kwok-Hong had to say, I was not keen to learn any more, for it might make me vulnerable as a possessor of insider information. A slew of troubling thoughts jostled through my mind, almost simultaneously.

I was confident that the initiative for privatising the company had not come from H.C. or any of the Fung family elders. It had to come from someone who had been through the American business school mill. Whoever had talked the elders into the advantages of such a ploy might have other moves up his sleeve.

Shades of Michael Milken, Ivan Boesky and the other Wall Street Masters of the Universe loomed before my mind's eye. They were forever filled with clever ruses and slick tricks. Leveraged buyouts, asset stripping, greenmail, misuse of the company's assets and other forms of financial manipulations had to feature somewhere further down the line if anyone was to pocket anything substantial at the end of the enterprise.

Who knew what else might be in the wind? Some smart American executives were already issuing corporate bonds with a hundred-year maturity, in the certain knowledge that the executives authorising their issue would not be around when they matured. After all, corporations were supposed to have an infinite life! What a wonderful opportunity for financial experimentation and skulduggery! I wanted no association with whatever might be coming.

I was only the head of one of Li & Fung's many subsidiaries, albeit the largest and most profitable one. But I had no access to the accounts of the parent company which were kept in a separate building on the other side of the harbour by the Group Financial Controller.

All I knew was that the trading arm of the company had been growing steadily and profitably since I took over. I had been too busily engaged in my own responsibilities to familiarise myself with activities not of my direct concern. For example, I was aware that the group was trying to establish a series of retail outlets which required considerable outlays but which had not yet become functional. Financing that venture and other projects was somebody else's responsibility, not mine.

In responding to Kwok-Hong's query, I had to admit I had no meaningful answer because I had no idea what might eventually be cooked up by the privatisation project. I suggested that he should really seek an independent legal or accounting consultant's advice, as to how selling his shares to a privatising venture might affect present share holders and who would ultimately benefit most from the change and who would end up owning or controlling the reconstituted company.

Naturally, after dinner, I began contemplating my own ambivalent position in the light of the snippets of information gained from Kwok-Hong. I had signed up to work in a publicly listed corporation under the leadership of a friend of many decades. If that public corporation were somehow to be transformed into a private company at a time when that old friendship was fraying at the edges, over philosophical business differences, then it might well be time for me to move on. The fact that I had not been brought into the privatisation scheme at all — just as I had not been consulted over speculating on the Hong Kong dollar foreign exchange rate — spoke for itself about the growing lack of trust and respect among top executives.

The original agreement had been for me to work for Li & Fung for ten years, with an option on both sides to disengage after five. Well, I had completed six years. So at least that part of the agreement had been met and was operational.

Another minor aspect in my relationship with Li & Fung also niggled me. Before joining the company, I had owned no stocks and shares. Most of the time, as a civil servant, I had been too poor to do so. Indeed, I had to rely on the generosity of the father of my first wife to subsidise me and my family through allowing us to live at his home at Wise Mansion. It was only many years later, after I had risen sufficiently within the ranks of the bureaucracy, that I could afford to make a few investments. But Li & Fung shares had not been sufficiently attractive a choice for me to invest in.

After joining the company, however, I thought it would be a fitting symbolic gesture to my staff if I were to buy at least one small lot of Li &

Fung shares to nail my commitment to the mast.

But based on what Kwok-Hong had told me, I was now in possession of a kind of insider information. Once the word got around in a rumour-mongering city, the only thing clever city-slickers would do would be to buy up available Li & Fung shares at their current depressed market prices and to wait for news of privatisation to collect an easy premium.

It was not a move I was remotely interested in, since I had already gained more wealth than I could possibly use through my venture into the foreign exchange market during the general panic over the Sino-British negotiations.

However, I still possessed my solitary lot of Li & Fung shares and, if I kept it till privatisation was announced, then who knew what fantasies might be circulated about my benefiting handsomely from insider information? To guard against lending the slightest substance to that possibility, I sold my single lot of shares the following day.

* * *

There used to be a strand of economic argument linked to the so-called Chicago school of economics which postulated that — among other things — corporations were entities designed to maximise profits and hence could not be expected to let anything as nebulous as morality interfere with their objective. It had been a line of argument which did not appeal to me at all, regardless of how many Nobel Prizes its advocates might accumulate with their sophistries.

To my way of thinking, corporations were not automated pieces of machinery; they had to be operated by human beings with human strengths and weaknesses, including moral perspectives. They had to acquire different forms of morality from their elders at home or while attending schools, churches, religious ceremonies, youth gatherings, or participating in sports, joining clubs, professional bodies or other social groupings. Even if they had been suckled by a she-wolf, as described in legends about Romulus and Remus, they would have acquired some sense of right and wrong.

Part of the reason why fallacies and outlandish theories have gained currency, I surmised, was because few of the economists formulating them have ever actually dirtied their hands in the nastiness of free market operations. If they had done so, they would have experienced a few aspects of the interpersonal emotions and recurring uncertainties which often came into play.

For example, in former times in China, it used to be quite common for peasants to take their produce and/or some home-cooked food to a nearby village or township to sell, simply by setting up roadside stalls. To bargain with passers-by over the price of a *catty* of cabbages or cucumbers or a home-cooked pork or red bean buns would be a quotidian activity, something which lent a little colour to their otherwise humdrum lives. If a prospective customer happened to be a flighty housewife or a hard-pressed widow, the price might well be adjusted to suit the interpersonal mood of the moment.

But such free and easy ways inevitably came under pressure with the wheels of progress. Local authorities in search of system and order, as well as fresh means of boosting income, soon issued licences for stalls, while local gangsters also got into the act by demanding "protection" money. Combines and companies were not slow to note the demands for certain commodities and brought to bear the economies of scale. Competition developed and with it mass production and the development of complicated supply and distribution chains, each with its many layers of intermediating players and profit-seeking entities.

Transactions gradually became more impersonal and abstract, with more and more of the human and moral elements in commerce being reduced. Intermediaries multiplied, each seeking his own advantage or slice of profits. To look upon one's cup of morning coffee, one would hardly imagine the number of hands those humble coffee beans must have gone through to get into that cup — the growers, the harvesters, traders, processors, roasters, packers, exporters, manufacturers, retailers and others *ad nauseam*.

In the end, anyone who wanted to trade in bales of cotton or sacks of Robusta coffee or any other product could do so by pressing a few buttons or communicating with a stranger at one of the various commodity exchanges. No one needed to know how a product had been produced, or by whom, or exactly where in the world, and under what processes and circumstances. Indeed, the details in the "culture" part in the word "agriculture" would remain known to only a small number of the actual participants in the process.

Everything would be handled behind corporate veils, at a distance, sanitised, impersonal, anything written down would be cloaked in ambiguous legal lingo and without any social, environmental or moral commitments. They would be done by anonymous characters assigned with only numbers and dressed in bespoke suits and displaying clean fingernails. The commodities they traded in would also be classified in numbered lots.

If logs have somehow been illegally cut down and gathered from virgin forests or if fishing quotas have been violated, criminal responsibilities would be defused among umpteen corporations registered in a dozen jurisdictions around the world. Proving any controlling intelligence over the whole shebang before a court of law, and beyond a reasonable degree of doubt, would be well-neigh impossible. Welcome to the globalised world!

Clever economists could make almost any theory— like many conspiracy theories — sound plausible by buttressing it with fancy but misconstrued statistics! They had probably never read Chuang Tzu's warning made thousands of years ago against complicating and confusing our existence so as to render us forgetful of who we really were and become obsessed with what we were really not.

No doubt plenty of city slickers and commercial go-getters would welcome such a complicated arm's length world. So would international bankers issuing sub-prime mortgages or fixing LIBOR rates, insurance companies writing dodgy policies, car manufacturers rigging pollution recorders, tobacco companies faking researches into the risks of smoking, drug makers obscuring side-effects in their medicines, accounting firms cooking their books and so on.

In such an environment each could give unhindered rein to his or her appetite for profits or bonuses. No justification needed to be formulated for whatever might be done in good faith or bad; and all awkward questions from whatever source could be deftly sidestepped.

Adam Smith's *The Wealth of Nations* could be there to provide a hackneyed quote or two to justify most profit-seeking activities. However, Smith's other words, uttered in his earlier and probably more important book, *The Theory of Moral Sentiments,* could be conveniently ignored. Smith had advised on the need to restrain human selfishness and exercise benevolent affection, because basic rules of prudence and justice were needed for any society to survive.

And what about the end-user, the ultimate consumer? What would, for example, a mother wishing to buy a bar of chocolate or an Easter egg for her child think if she were fully conscious that the modest prices for her purchases were rendered possible partly because a million other children in the Ivory Coast and Ghana were working as virtual slaves to harvest cocoa beans every day? Would she still have no qualm over her intended purchases for her child? And what about changing the system, by asking the purchasers of cocoa beans to negotiate a realistic price for each sack of beans with the children who had actually harvested them, instead of leaving them with only whatever remained after everybody else had taken their customary cuts?

It was inevitable in business, as in other spheres of human endeavour, that there should be grey areas and contradictions left without clear-cut answers. How to work them out would always have to depend on an individual's moral make-up and acquired values.

For example, take my own reactions to the marketing of "Black Cat" firecrackers which had been taking place decades before I ever appeared on the scene. Li & Fung had invested massively in touting the brand as the best that money could buy and that its products gave more bang for the buck.

Such brand identification, promoted over decades, was just a form of brain-washing to induce consumers to believe that the product was indeed something which it was not. Some quarters might even call it a form of cheating. The efforts had in any case been so successful that Black Cat products could command a premium of 10% over other brands.

But upon discovering that Black Cat products were being mass produced by a single huge factory in China which also supplied identical products to half a dozen other brands, what should I ethically do? The products were being produced there like cans of beans. The factory had no interest whether customers wished them to be labelled as "Nourishing Beans" or "Tasty Beans" or "White Cat Beans" — so long as they were bought and paid for. Nor would it care about how purchasers handled pricing, advertising the product for its intended market or anything else.

In the circumstances, should I be morally bound to inform customers that the Black Cat products were not superior to other brands, as had been consistently represented for decades, but were in reality no different from other less promoted brands? Or should I reduce the premium charged, contrary to the interests of my own employer? Or should I merely resign from my position?

Such conundrums and moral decisions pervade every commercial relationship — whether openly recognised or not — because all parties had been locked into an exploitative capitalistic system. Each would be seeking an advantage or a greater share of profits from the other. Someone had to give up something and it would nearly always be the weakest party. This would apply equally to corporation as well as to individuals, whether operating as manufacturers or customers, importers or exporters, wholesalers, retailers, shippers, advertisers, sales staff or ultimately as end consumers.

Every now and then some terrible tragedy would occur in some far-off country. A large number of workers would perish in some avoidable fire or in the collapse of some unsafe factory building manufacturing goods with designer labels. There might be some temporary uproar, many crocodile tears and every Tom, Dick and Harry would lament the tragedy and vow it would never be allowed to happen again.

But the sad truth was that it would be bound to happen again and again till everyone involved in that supply chain recognised that, wittingly or unwittingly, he or she had been culpable or complicit to some degree in bringing about that tragedy through some collective whim or wish to have something or to act in a particular way. Only by wholesale change in behaviour or culture could systemic change occur.

* * *

As an illustration of another aspect of the problem, let me recount my personal experience when I first went to America in 1949 to study at Stanford University. I had bought a single pair of Levi denim jeans, which was all I could then afford.

I wore that pair of denim jeans every day for the next four years, winter or summer, like a second skin. I washed it in the student hostel laundromat once in a long while, when it got too dirty from mowing lawns or undertaking other forms of manual labour to earn extra money. I had never been ashamed for wearing that same pair of jeans every day because I knew that in some parts of China people were so poor that all the adults in a family had to share a single pair of good trousers to wear on special occasions.

Now, as the managing director of a multi-national trading corporation, I supervised staff who could source millions of pairs of jeans from half a dozen locations for export to America. Sales depended on what customers wanted regardless of their dubious tastes, the wastefulness of materials or the environmental friendliness or otherwise in the production process. The jeans could be coloured in denim blue or stone-washed, with tapered legs or flared bottoms, with hipster cuts or frayed edges, with simulated threadbareness or patches to suggest wear and tear. It all depended on the vagaries of fashion and styles which would sell better or faster from one season to the next.

Since I joined Li & Fung in 1981 to run the trading arm, the turnover had multiplied manifold, not only in garments but also in other mass consumption products — shoes, toys, handbags, wigs, fireworks, handicraft and Christmas decorations.

If I were to postulate those few selected facts alone, I could no doubt cultivate an impression of my leadership successes. But the truth was much more complicated. The rapid rise in trading volume was a company-wide effort, attributable to multiple individuals — to merchandisers in locating reliable suppliers for the desired goods, to quality control inspectors for detecting early production flaws, to department heads for negotiating mutually acceptable deals between suppliers and purchasers, to shipping clerks for ensuring that good would reach their destinations on time and, above all, to purchasers for knowing their domestic markets and for designing and ordering products which would sell like hotcakes to consumers. Indeed, they were really the ones shaping fashion tastes and manufacturing wants and desires among general consumers.

If all those poor souls within the trading arm, from Kwok-Hong and Rosetta downwards, had not been so desperate about making a steady living and so conscious of their tenuous month-to-month terms, they might have realised with a modicum of reflection that each had a vital role in the entire trading enterprise. Without every single one of them, acting according to some pre-arranged plan, the whole corporate edifice would come tumbling down. If they would act in concert, they could demand better terms or else bring the corporation to a standstill.

It was the job of people like myself, with a nagging weight of conscience, to keep them busy and industrious and leave them without too much time to reflect upon their fraught situations. They were paid at more or less market rates, with scarcely enough fringe benefits. Sometimes when I walked around the offices after working hours, I could see many staff members still hanging around.

At first I was fearful they might be overworked or exchanging views on their existential conditions. Later I discovered that my fears were misplaced. They were hanging around merely because during the hot summer months their offices still provided air conditioning which they could not afford at home! A sorry commentary on their wages and their existential conditions indeed.

Yet there were millions like them in China, hard-working and uncomplaining souls, believing they were living, doing dull and monotonous work until death, to honour their ancestors and to survive and provide for their families. They had been the underdogs since time immemorial. Yet they have nonetheless built the Great Wall with their blood and sinews, the Burma Road with their bare hands against all engineering advice, matched the most advanced military machines in the world in Korea and fought them to a standstill.

I have seen them in their Hong Kong hovels, scraping livings out of rocky hillsides, without water, electricity or other amenities. What could they not have made of themselves and of their nation, if given decent equipment and inspiring leadership!

I had been much relieved to know that my staff members had not been engaging in mutual exchanges of views, for down that road would loom the prospects of unionisation, collective bargaining and the securing of a fairer share of what they had been truly contributing to the enterprise. In short, Marx and socialism and understanding about surplus value would all raise their ugly heads and I would be forced to choose a side.

People like myself existed not because we were inherently bad or mean or exploitative. We had our personal failings and circumstances to contend with. Mine had been a hasty and ill-judged marriage and the bringing of children into the world when I should have found the courage to simply walk away. But I failed to do so, largely because conscience could often make cowards of us all!

So I found myself slipping into an ever-tightening trap. Because I had to earn the means of providing for the physical needs of my family, I could not find sufficient time to provide for their emotional and intellectual needs. When my wife eventually walked out, I could not find a suitable woman to help me discharge my moral and ethical responsibilities towards my children. And in the end, when my children demanded the fashionable thing of their generation, of being sent to North America for their university education, I sold myself into intellectual serfdom — much against my better judgement and instincts — in order to meet their demands. It turned out to be a monstrous price to pay, not only for myself but for my children too.

Mass markets and national culture also came into play in trading. I remembered Kitty telling me that when she was a child and when cloth rationing was enforced in China, she had always been taught at school to be frugal. A little ditty had been sung by children. It urged them that garments should be worn for three years as "new" and three years as "old" before wearing them for another three years as "sewed and repaired" items.

It would appear that in a non-capitalistic society account had to be taken of the national circumstances in addition to the likes or dislikes of individual consumers. It remained, however, a huge question mark to be clarified as to whether the opening of the country to outside influences would gradually alter or water down the emphasis to children about the need for frugality.

* * *

While I was grappling with moral conundrums at the office. I was also encountering some similar problems at home. The main one was the excruciating slow progress being made by Kitty in coming to terms with the

English language. Once she had been granted an exit visa by the Chinese authorities and given the right to take up residence in Hong Kong, I had arranged private lessons for her to learn English from scratch, for five mornings every week.

The tutor I had selected was a former English teacher and the wife of a senior Administrative Officer. I would pay the tutor several thousands of dollars per month to pick up Kitty from Seymour Road, give her lessons and a decent lunch before returning her home. The purpose of the whole exercise was quickly to get her English up to the level for admission to a local university.

Unhappily, that outcome proved rather more difficult than expected. The blame could not be pinned on any single person but on a host of different circumstances which interrupted her studies. For instance, once she had acquired travel documents in 1986, her studies were interrupted because I had to take her to Singapore to meet my father and siblings there. Then I had to take her to Canada to meet my mother and more of my siblings there. On top of that, she had to spend a large part of that year scurrying between Hong Kong and Nantong in order to identify and upgrade a comfortable retirement home for her own parents.

Kitty, unlike myself, had never taken to foreign tongues with any enthusiasm. English was to her just another incomprehensible series of sounds, like the croaking of frogs in the garden or the meowing of cats in the back alley.

When I was a child and introduced to English by Miss Fox at St. Andrew's School, I had taken immediately to the cadences and rhythms of the language. After all, both my father and my grandfather knew the language and our home in Singapore was filled with English books. I accepted my initiation as not just learning another language but as a step towards becoming a grown-up within my family.

I was concerned about Kitty's slow progress with English on another score. Her reluctance to practise with the Linguaphone set I had given her was troubling. It was not that I was expecting right away for the words of Shakespeare or John Donne to drip majestically from her lips. But she should, in the time she had spent, at least have acquired enough command of the language to write intelligibly about cats and dogs and other ordinary things. But she had no such capacity. Her standard was inadequate to get her into a local university, let alone into one overseas.

Moreover, her deficiencies in the linguistic department were not compensated by a sure command of a more traditional Chinese education. She was, after all, a child of the revolution. No *Three Characters Classic* was ever used to cut her teeth on. Nor much of Confucian or Taoist readings or indeed the entire classical range of Chinese literature.

Her Chinese and geography of China might be all right but otherwise her favourite quotations might well be those from Chairman Mao's *Little Red Book*. I had noticed in addition that her choice of recreational reading in Hong Kong had veered towards the Cantonese versions of Mills & Boon romances. No doubt they would be more easily digestible and less taxing than anything by Chuang Tzu.

Or perhaps I had not really fathomed or understood her dreams, the dreams of the mass of the under-informed of her world. Could I have unwittingly and arrogantly just superimposed my own dreams upon her?

My worry following that reflection was that I was fast approaching the age of sixty and that any of those irregular and as yet unidentifiable type of pancreatitis attacks like the first occasion could prove fatal. I was, after all, only of mortal clay.

I had had several subsequent sudden attacks elsewhere, like my collapse at the Taipei airport. If an attack were to occur in a less developed country with primitive medical facilities and if I were unable to communicate adequately in a local language, then I did not fancy my chances.

In that eventuality, I would be failing once again to fulfil a promise I had made to Kitty, of getting her into a university and preparing her for the vicissitudes of life on her own two feet. That troubling prospect haunted me.

* * *

So, one day, I alluded gently to the slow progress she seemed to be making with English and I urged her to apply greater efforts if she really wanted to get to university.

"What do you expect?" Kitty retorted. "All your friends and everyone else around talk to me in Cantonese and I have to concentrate to understand what they are saying. Even strangers only talk to me in Cantonese. Nobody wants to talk in English.'"

"I'm really sorry," I said, regretfully. "You're absolutely right. An English environment would suit much better for you to master English."

"Do you know how boring it can be for me to keep listening to a machine all the time? Even you don't want to speak to me in English. Your first instinct when speaking to me is to find out how to put a common Cantonese phrase or idea into authentic Mandarin. It's all very well for you to want to improve your Mandarin. But what about me?"

"I *am* really sorry. I thought Hong Kong would make your transition to life outside China easier. I overlooked there are disadvantages here as well."

"I'm sorry too. This place makes me feel so useless. I couldn't even explain to the nurse at the hospital what your problem was."

"Never mind. Severe pancreatitis is not a Cantonese term that crops up very much in polite conversation. Let's forget about that and go to London. We can find a place we both like and move there."

"Is London as strange and as unnatural a place as Hong Kong?"

"What do you mean?"

"Well, when you have your regular twice-weekly *mah-jong* games with your friends, I usually meet up with my *kai-ma* or adoptive mother, so that she could show me how to shop for basic necessities at the most suitable places. She always told me not to reveal my liking for any particular item, like for a dress or a pair of shoes or an item of jewellery. She said I should always show coolness or indifference, not my real feelings no matter what, because as we pretend to leave the shop, the proprietor might well come up and offer a bigger discount in order to nail down a sale."

I laughed. "Your *kai-ma*, Suze, might well be right for Hong Kong. Everyone is trying to make the best deal for himself or herself here. She's an experienced and veteran shopper. But it won't be like that in London. Prices are fixed there and on display, with no bargaining. It's different from here, unless you go to a district like Notting Hill."

"Notting Hill? You want us to live there?"

"Oh, no. I just intend to show you what different districts in London can be like."

"So the British also bargain there?"

"Yes, sometimes."

"Do you also bargain during work here, to get the best deal?"

"I'm different. I'm not out to maximise profits for myself. I'm a kind of middleman. I try to accentuate the positive for all sides, so that my company can earn a commission if a deal is made."

"But you had told me previously you would be considered in China as 'a skimmer in the middle'. Is that kind of non-productive activity not found objectionable here?"

"No, not in Hong Kong. We operate a capitalist system here and I'm not exactly non-productive. I offer a service, putting together buyers and sellers, to benefit everyone."

Kitty looked puzzled for a moment. "You mean you're like a marriage match-maker?" she said.

"More like a pimp," I almost answered with tongue-in-cheek. But in the end I answered with a simple "Yes."

"So when are we moving to London?"

"Well, we have to find a suitable home first. London's a pretty big place, you know, and finding the right kind of home is bound to take a bit of time, perhaps even several visits might be necessary to find the right one. Then I'll have to give my employers a reasonable period of notice before leaving. But leave all that planning and other arrangements to me."

* * *

I saw no reason to lumber Kitty with a lot of unnecessary facts and opinions. London was largely unknown to her, whereas I was familiar with the city from many previous visits and prolonged stays. Indeed, I knew where the snooty residential districts were located and also where the relatively safe and agreeable neighbourhoods were, though those two conditions did not necessarily coincide. I was, of course, more concerned with comfort, safety and convenience than with the snob appeal of an appropriate address. I also knew roughly how well or poorly the public transport system served the various targeted locations.

Furthermore, two important conditions — which most migrants would normally have uppermost on their minds — did not enter into my calculations at all, to wit, the economic implications of migrating and the likelihood or otherwise of the recipient country accepting one's residency there. I had more than enough financial resources to purchase whatever property Kitty and I might decide upon and, given my resources and the number of foreigner spivs with money already granted residential status in London, I did not anticipate any difficulty.

There was a common Chinese saying to the effect that, given enough money, a man could even persuade the devil to do his bidding. Or as the 17th century English poet, Aphra Behn, had put it: "Money speaks sense in a language all nations understand." Given the new Babylonic age spawned by neoliberal economics, I had no reason to doubt the validity of such observations. In my experience, money remained the best passport anyone could possess.

Whatever home we might eventually decide upon, I had a number of *sine qua non*s. First of all, the location of the home had to provide quick and easy Underground access to Soho, the location of a wide collection of Chinese restaurants. Decent Chinese meals were a necessity I could not be deprived of for very long, especially since I found Kitty's cooking not entirely reliable.

Secondly, because of my random pancreatic attacks, there had to be a good teaching hospital within a reasonable walking distance from the home. I could not rely on Kitty's English being sufficient to explain on the telephone why she would need an ambulance.

Thirdly, the proposed dwelling should also have easy access to the twin railway stations of Euston and St. Pancras for visits to the soon to be completed new British Library facilities there. I had been using the old library for years, when its famous round reading room was still part of the British Museum at Bloomsbury. I recalled the delightful hours I had spent there, acquainting myself with the finer points of Mongolian cuisine during the time of Kublai Khan and the history of Chinese erotic art during the Ming Dynasty.

No doubt I would have many occasions to make use of the library again because since the winning of the two short story prizes in Hong Kong and the publication of *Lost River and Other Stories*, I had felt a growing urge to write short stories again.

Maybe I was finally approaching an age when Anaïs Nin had spoken of people seeking to write because they wanted to live life twice — once in the moment and the other in retrospect.

As to the kind of home I wanted, I also had very definite ideas. I needed more space than the original bachelor's apartment I had bought at Seymour Road. The room there I had used as my study did not have enough room for my books, let alone provide suitable accommodation for visiting guests.

At the same time I had had enough of living in an anonymous multi-storeyed development with hardly any interaction among neighbours, even when sharing the same lift with them. I therefore preferred a more cosy converted town house with at least about 2,000 square feet of space, made up of three good-sized bedrooms and two bathrooms. Friendly but quiet neighbours would be a definite plus.

Realising that people tended to be less active and more sedentary with age, I took some precautions. I decided to aim for a second floor apartment in a building without a lift. That would force me to exercise by running up and down the stairs several times each day, to collect the morning newspaper, to pick up the morning and afternoon mail, to buy groceries at the neighbourhood supermarkets and stores, to put out the rubbish in the evening, and so on.

All those foregoing considerations, however, would be far too exhausting to explain to an unsophisticated girl from China. So I decided to keep them to myself.

After a couple of days of sifting and considering my prejudices and preferences, I narrowed a suitable home in London down to about ten locations. It was after I had made a list of my own requirements that I asked Kitty what her requirements might be.

She replied at once that we should have much more space than the 1,200 square feet we had at Seymour Road. Furthermore, she requested that her future English school and a good gymnasium be situated within walking distance from any new home.

After adding her requirements to the list, I began contacting estate agents in the specified areas to arrange for viewing potential properties. We managed to start our first home-hunting visit to London in September.

That first visit was not a success, however, for none of the properties on offer in the districts we visited had met our requirements. But the visit did highlight another issue — the remaining length of the lease on various properties. So far as I was concerned, any suitable property with another 30 years to run on its lease was all right by me because, if I were still alive by then, I would not wish to renew the lease as I would probably need institutional care. But it was far from the case with Kitty. She wanted a lease which would not expire till the end of her natural lifespan.

That therefore became an additional requirement. But because of the approach of winter, our next trip to London did not take place till the spring of the following year.

CHAPTER 19

Breaking Up

TRADING HAS BEEN AN ACTIVITY almost as old as humanity itself. Remnants from the Stone Age have convinced some anthropologists that trading had taken place at that time, particularly in obsidian used for sharpening tools.

Most people in modern times, during the innocence and credulity of their childhood, had probably been inducted unknowingly into the spirit of trading. How else should one describe school children learning to exchange marbles, stamps, wooden tops, comic books, cigarette package covers and a whole range of whatnots with fellow or older students for items which the latter somehow mysteriously possessed, such as a whistle, a piece of magnetic rock, a fountain pen or some supposedly magical talisman?

Many could no doubt recall those hurried bargainings taking place in playgrounds as they calculated mentally whether an item they fancied was really worth what they were being asked to give up in exchange. Sometimes part of the lunch money and the bus fare home would also come into the equation.

But loudmouths and smooth-talking senior students were probably only displaying their potential for turning themselves into future politicians or hustlers. In any case, occasionally, by the time the school day was over, a bargain struck before the start of classes or during a brief recess, unless already executed, might turn out to be no longer binding. Second thoughts and cooler calculations would have had a chance to come into play.

Such early experiences would nonetheless be fitting preparations for adulthood, when every person might — at one time or another — be called upon to trade his conscience for some opportunistic grab at power or riches, or else to surrender his pulsating heart to another for that much more elusive will-o'-the-wisp called love.

To the outside world, the British colonial enclave might be promoted as "the Pearl of the Orient" and as the freest of free markets, but for *hoi polloi* there, countless tens of thousands still had to live in over-crowded squatter settlements or precarious hillside shanty towns, without running water, electricity or toilet facilities and dangerously exposed to the vagaries of weather.

For them, it was indeed a spiteful and unforgiving place. They had to learn under those pitiful circumstances the most fundamental forms of trading — the exchange their unremitting toil for the slender right to survive.

Their city had always been a divided place, split along at least a dozen and sometimes overlapping lines — by race and religion, by rulers and ruled, by shades of political or economic attachments into predators and prey, patriots and Quislings, visionaries and the undereducated, enterprising chancers and dull-witted lumpen proletariat, and, of course, into the obviously rich and the plainly poor.

It could not be gainsaid that a selected few from the lower classes could also grow enormously richer through dogged determination, pure sweat and sailing extremely close to the wind. But for the vast majority of the poor, they remained largely without power or influence and served only to provide the fast-paced and energetic backdrop to the entire city.

A bygone Western thinker had once described their lot as solitary, nasty and brutish. But there was paradoxically a silver lining to certain things. When a fire ripped through a squatter settlement in Shek Kip Mei in December of 1953 and immediately rendered over 50,000 people homeless, the normally laid-back government was forced to initiate a public housing programme.

A year later, a housing estate was completed at the original fire site. The victims were allocated space in new multi-storeyed H-shaped blocks on the basis of 24 square feet per adult in a family, with a child calculated at an appropriate fraction. That 24 square feet came to about half the amount of space allocated to prisoners in single cells in British gaols at the time. But at least those resettled had running water, communal bathrooms and toilets and no longer had to engage in the dangerous business of stealing electricity from overhead power lines.

So for the workhorses of society, subsidised housing represented a small step forward in their quotidian existence. They remained, however, too hard pressed to afford decent school books and uniforms for their children or enough elbow room to bring them up properly.

Indeed, one young woman had complained publicly that her cramped home deprived her even of the right to have a bit of undisturbed sex! Hong Kong was unquestionably a very crowded place, possibly the most densely populated city on earth. No secluded spot could be found, like in London's Hyde Park or New York's Central Park, where the young could go to find a degree of privacy. How could they develop into rounded and thinking human beings if they were for long periods confined, like hamsters, inside would-be cages?

But the young, like their parents, had Chinese stock, with plenty of endurance, patience and determination to survive through endless hardships. Their ancestors had already demonstrated those qualities over thousands of years instead of just for a measly two hundred years or three.

Moreover, they had also developed the habit and the willingness to make inordinate sacrifices for the good of the following generation, hoping to be repaid during their old age, through the handed-down and long-practised Confucian tradition of filial piety.

Their bosses — the poor knew only too well — were out to squeeze the most they could out of them. British officialdom was of little help. Its schools taught students about the wisdom of a distant and foreign King

Solomon, but remained largely silent on the sages of other cultures, making virtually no mention of that long line of equally exemplary Chinese officials, euphemistically referred to as *fu-mo guan*s.

Such officials, selected mainly through a series of stiff examinations in the classics, were supposed to dedicate their time and efforts to easing and solving the problems of inhabitants under their charge, as if they were their own children.

British officials, by contrast, seemed aloof, indifferent, and even at times bemused. They often looked upon the behaviour and antics of Chinese subjects like those of an incomprehensible alien tribe with whom they would rather have as little truck as possible, except as servants. Or perhaps as mistresses as well, if the females had attractive physical attributes.

Fellow creatures from the lower strata, be they street pedlars or casual jobbers, were often no more accommodating or reliable. The flame of class solidarity did not actually burn within their breasts. Their shared poverty had conditioned them to obedience and a proneness to stabbing others in the back if some minor advantage could be gained.

Yet, in spite of their cynicism and resignation to their own fate, a vague resentment kept eating away at them. Perhaps the rich were really different from themselves after all. According to the gossip circulated by their household retainers, the rich wallowed in drugs, drink, sexual deviations, hallucinations, neuroses, psychoses, kleptomanias and other types of mental maladies.

As for themselves, no matter how many extra hours of toil they might put in each day, the wealth gap separating them from even the moderately well-off seemed only to stretch progressively wider, rather than shrinking with time. Something had to be amiss.

In addition, the well-heeled, in spite of many questionable deeds, seemed able to easily throw over themselves a cloak of pious respectability, even when consorting with shady characters or sealing under-handed deals.

How could they get away with so much that was undreamt of among ordinary folk? Rumours of different sets of fake accounting figures, tax havens, shelf companies in the Caribbean and Latin American countries and numbered accounts in Switzerland had been doing the rounds for ages.

In addition, it had long been whispered in certain circles that somewhere within the precincts of their city, secreted among the great canyons created by characterless modern edifices of glass and steel, and tucked between streets befouled by the exhausts of too many Rolls Royces and Mercedes, was a staggering kind of subterranean life out-doing the wickednesses and debaucheries which had prevailed in Shanghai during the roaring 1920s.

But to qualify for admission, one had to be first initiated, filthy rich and introduced by one or more of the individuals holding sway and influence within those twilight zones.

Once admitted, a person belonged to a community more exclusive than the most exclusive London club. Anything could be made available for the correct amount of money. An ancient injury or insult to be avenged for the sake of family or clan honour? No problem. A specified piece of Chinese antiquity, possibly once looted or stolen from an imperial palace? Easy, for an appropriate price. Otherwise, how could so many pieces of those rare and exquisite Chinese antiques have found their way into Western museums to be displayed?

Through similar payments, the wildest of their personal whims, predilections or idiosyncrasies could be indulged in within plush settings, with supporting casts of any age or sex specified. A drug-fuelled psychedelic fantasy or a sexual performance outdoing anything described in *The Before Midnight Scholar* or depicted in the erotic paintings of Ming Dynasty? Also no problem. But, horror of horrors! What if their own precious little ones got ensnared into that netherworld of debauchery and defilement? Truly unthinkable!

The poor and ordinary had been brushed by dreams and longings too, as they teetered upon the cusp of sleep. But riches beyond the dreams of avarice would not be among those floating into their minds. Rather more mundane and run-of-the-mill aspirations, like owning some luxury item seen in a department store window or a fancy car that had caught the eye at an automobile showroom. But must those wayward thoughts always remain so far out of reach, simply for being so ordinary and mundane?

Perhaps the only consolation for their unfulfilled desires was the realisation they did not have to be involved in anything illegal, improper or chancy like the rich. They would accordingly be spared dealing with unsavoury underworld characters and being exposed to blackmail, cheating or being taken for a ride.

* * *

For youngsters who might be bitten early by the trading bug, to the extent that they might be tempted upon reaching adulthood to try their hand at becoming traders, they should be aware that beyond a few localised small scale activities, trading was a much more difficult and complicated calling than they had imagined.

At the national and international levels, they would be confronted by an ever-expanding jungle of regulations concerning quotas, tariffs, health, safety, country of origin, product standards and descriptions, advertising and other aspects of trade, plus those suddenly announced and unforeseen governmental bans, interventions, restrictions and sanctions.

During the years between the two world wars, exports as a ratio of global GDP collapsed from around 16% to a mere 6% because many countries wanted to protect their own products and their own domestic markets.

Therefore, when World War II ended, there rose a general desire to revive trade, in the hope that such an activity would in general benefit everyone. Thus 23 countries got together in October of 1947 to sign a General Agreement on Tariffs and Trade, thereafter to be called GATT for short. That arrangement become operational in January of the following year.

The initial aim was to evolve, through a series of GATT decisions, a reasonable and understandable set of international rules governing quotas, tariffs, subsidies, disputes, market disruptions, dumping, mislabelling, country of origin certifications and other trade related matters.

It soon became apparent, however, that as trade increased and supply chains stretched across continents, the problems faced by GATT became interlinked with political and economics tensions within and between various nations and regions. The language previously used by classical writers to describe trade and economic relationships became far too simplistic and inadequate for a rapidly changing and complex reality.

What was, when a person reflected upon it, a free market, an autarky or a comparative advantage? When David Ricardo was theorising about those terms and such issues as the depreciation of banknotes 200 years ago, he had drawn upon the production of wine and cloth in Portugal and Britain for illustrative purposes.

But in the modern interconnected world, a vast variety of wines and cloth are being produced all over the globe. Wines have distinctive flavours, bouquets, maturities, alcoholic content and various venerable house brands.

How to factor in all those differences in calculating opportunity costs? Moreover, consumers might simply favour the qualities of a particular wine from one place over those from another place. One could not produce a sparkling wine in Australia and simply call it champagne nor a hard cheese from America as a Cheddar, if it were not really produced in Somerset. Even the whisky produced in Ireland tried to distinguish itself for the drink produced in Scotland by adding an "e" to its name.

Similar considerations apply to fabrics. Cloth had different "feels" and characteristics which might or might not appeal to different customers. The European Union seemed nowadays to be particularly punctilious about product descriptions and countries of origin.

Cheapness in production could hardly be regarded as the sole or dominant criterion. To pose an absurd question: Would the nations of the world give up producing nuclear bombs and instead buy them from North Korea — just because that country could make them cheaper?

Thus international trade began impacting upon a range of other important issues, like national security, balance of payments, the exchange rate for currencies, inflation rates, capital in-flows and out-flows, national GDP growth fluctuations, poverty-alleviation programmes in less developed countries, and so on and so forth.

In the long stretch of history, trade frequently produced unpredictable effects which could lead to wars and, indeed, to the rise and fall of kingdoms and empires. Numerous examples abound. For instance, after China had perfected the manufacturing of silk 400 years before Christ, silk became a highly valued commodity in parts of Europe. But transporting the product by land across the old Silk Road was a difficult and arduous affair.

The Byzantine Emperor Justinian was anxious to learn how to produce silk within his own realm. He therefore got together with a couple of Nestorian monks — who had been Christian missionaries in China during one of the most open and tolerant periods during the Tang Dynasty — and got them to smuggle out in the year 552 some silkworm larvae in hollowed out bamboo walking sticks. Justinian thus established a silk-making industry in southern Greece, which is still operating at the present time.

Much later, in the 19th century to be precise, it was the British public who developed an abiding fondness for Chinese tea and Chinese porcelain. Those imports had to be paid for, however, in silver, which in turn created an adverse balance of payments problem for the British Exchequer.

The British East India Company eventually came up with the morally questionable idea of rectifying the imbalance by exporting opium from India to China. That inevitably led to gunboat diplomacy and the successive Opium Wars, with enduring consequences not only for a weak and divided

Chinese nation but for much of the world.

In more recent times, most countries made a fetish of paying lip service to free trade but the stronger among them have consistently utilised their strength and bargaining positions to extract advantages for themselves or for important sectors of their own economies. Historical instances had been as common as mud. They had come, for instance, in the form of British corn laws, imperial preferences, quotas, tariffs, state subsidies, national monopolies and a host of other political quirks and other impediments to trade.

Less developed countries, frequently facing obstacles to their own development and difficulties in gaining market access to wealthier countries for their own goods, naturally gravitated towards GATT, to seek greater fairness and protection under a more rules-based regime.

Hong Kong, because of its rapid transition from being a mere entrepôt hub for the transiting of goods to becoming a manufacturing centre of significance in its own right, especially for textiles and other consumer goods, soon became one of the contracting parties in GATT.

The territory often played a pioneering role in decisions made by the organisation. For example, Hong Kong was instrumental in establishing the practice among exporters of enforcing quotas and other restrictions instead of leaving their execution to the vagaries of importing authorities.

Much of the credit for the city's development into a major trading, economic, financial and aviation centre rested upon the efforts of a shy and extremely modest but physically and intellectually intimidating Scottish economist by the name of John Cowperthwaite.

John had arrived in Hong Kong as an elite Administrative Officer in the British Colonial Civil Service at the end of World War II. His early assignments in the colony had, by accident or design, been in the economic sphere. He ended his career as the Financial Secretary of Hong Kong, holding that office for ten years from 1961 to 1971.

I had the rare privilege of working directly under him as Assistant

Economic Secretary for Hong Kong, undertaking foreign missions with him, and learning a great deal about good economic governance from him.

He turned out to be an economic thinker and administrator of the first order, widely recognised as such in academic circles. Instead of simply trying to apply economic precepts he had studied at Cambridge to his work, he decided to go out among the population to observe for himself what they were like and how they actually got things done in real life.

He noted the work ethics of the Chinese, their mean hard-scrubbed existences, their propensity to save what little they had, their concern for the education and wellbeing of their children and their powerful glue of family attachments. Perhaps he had even foreseen a glimpse of what the Chinese could be capable of as a nation once it had been given stability and better opportunities.

Based on his observations and on his own common sense, he decided that little intervention would be needed in the local economy. He judged that the Chinese could make it pick up steam by itself. He thus opposed any fostering of a dependency culture by the government among the poorer sections of the community, even though that dependency was being increasingly pushed by politicians in Europe and among the more privileged local expatriates.

His outlook, coupled with his natural shyness, caused him to remain fairly unpopular and misunderstood among some of his colleagues. He did cultivate, however, a fair number of good Chinese friends.

The proof of Cowperthwaite's economic pudding was actually in the eating. When he retired as Financial Secretary in 1971, with a richly deserved knighthood, he left the city with no national debt, no balance of payment problems, no foreign exchange control whatsoever, no deficit spending, no unemployment, bulging reserves, and the entire economy motoring along at a reasonable clip. What else could anyone ask from an overseer of an economy?

Long before his retirement, he gained admiration from some of the more perceptive members of the community. They saw that there was no cant about him. Although he was a British citizen, he really believed in his country's declaration before the United Nations that those who ruled over non-self-governing territories had first the duty to attend to the best interests of the people they ruled over.

To that end, he consistently battled Whitehall over a wide range of issues on behalf of Hong Kong — an unfair division of aviation traffic rights between British and Hong Kong airlines, the levelling of excessive defence costs on the colony, the requirement for Hong Kong to maintain its reserves in sterling but provided inadequate compensation to Hong Kong for losses suffered when Britain suddenly devalued sterling without notice, and the persistent imposition of various quotas and restrictions against Hong Kong products entering the British market.

Within GATT, Cowperthwaite also exerted a considerable influence, nudging that organisation towards decisions less restrictive to international trade.

By the time GATT turned itself into the World Trade Organisation in 1995, the organisation had 125 contracting parties and its rules covered approximately 90% of world trade. Gradually, the membership in WTO rose to 193 contracting parties and world exports, as a ratio to global GDP, climbed to 25%, before the world financial crisis of 2008 set in.

The world today remains divided in a fierce struggle between nations committed to multilateralism and globalisation and those seeking a more nationalist unilateralism and protectionism. Some countries were now attempting to pervert politically some of the basic WTO tools for orderly trade, like country of origin labels and dispute resolution mechanisms.

The future direction for international trade therefore remains highly uncertain, depending on the quality and wisdom of the politicians many countries might be choosing to lead them.

*   *   *

Since entering the private sector as part of an international trading corporation, I had absolutely no say over how anyone might impose quotas, tariffs, bans or sanctions against goods originating from another country. Such acts, usually spurred on by the slow culmination of perceived or real political and economic grievances, were usually abrupt and hotly contested by those on the receiving end.

Whenever a territory imposed a fresh impediment to trade, all that a trader or agent in the private sector could do would be to act like a by-stander witnessing an unfortunate traffic accident. He could inform his customers of what had transpired and how they might circumvent the unforeseen obstacle by seeking similar goods from alternative sources.

It was only after I had joined Li & Fung that I discovered that the actual network of branch offices which the corporation had touted in advertising had been in fact a rather mixed bag.

Apart from the corporate headquarters in Hong Kong, the only branch of significant size was located in Taipei, whereas the branch in San Francisco, for example, was only a one-man operation, charged with answering queries and identifying potential American customers for the various heads of product divisions to call upon to stimulate business.

I had initially been introduced at the Taipei office by H.C. Fung himself. Most of staff were engaged in trading, under the leadership of the relevant heads of product divisions back in Hong Kong. In some instances, like in garments and shoes, both territories produced goods needed by customers. Other customers, like those for fireworks and handicraft, bought products originating from Taiwan as well as from elsewhere.

It quickly became apparent, however, that the designated head of the Taipei office was not an ordinary country manger in a normal trading structure, for he had responsibilities far beyond trading. He had also been assigned duties by other subsidiaries within the Li & Fung group, like the subsidiary responsible for sniffing out investments opportunities in Taiwan and developing properties purchased there.

Another important function of the Taiwan manager was to strengthen and deepen relationships between senior members of the Fung family and Kuomintang elders in Taiwan. Those relationships had been established long before those elders had been ousted from China by the Communists in 1949. They still mattered in a place where the Kuomintang still had considerable political and economic influence.

It soon became clear to me that I was not really equipped to discharge some of the duties mentioned above. Moreover, I already had my hands full with trading and had no desire for a turf war from the outset. I was therefore more than content for my role in Taiwan to remain opaque and indistinct.

The kind of relationship that H.C. sought to maintain with Kuomintang elders was commonly known among Chinese as guanxi

Many foreigners unfamiliar with Chinese society and culture tended to look upon *guanxi* as more or less synonymous with corruption and nepotism. However, they would be largely mistaken. That term merely referred to social "connections" of various kinds, seeking to place an individual within the wider context of his family and his community. Those relationships were sometimes ambiguous, spreading across boundaries delineating spheres which were personal, official or commercial. But they were of special relevance in a society which tended to be hierarchical in nature.

Such relationships were usually built on Confucian ethics and virtues, like commitment, loyalty, reciprocity, trust, empathy, blood ties and friendship. Once established, those relationships remained largely personal to the people cultivating them and often tended to boil down to a never-ending exchange of favours.

It might begin with something as innocuous as touching an old school chum for a quick loan or asking a cousin, who happened to be a dentist, to give priority in treating one's toothache. A favour thus granted would strengthen any pre-existing bond between the giver and the recipient. It would be generally considered a grave offence if a person who had received a favour failed to reciprocate when called upon to do so.

Were a personal connection to be used and traded for financial gain, then a grey area would emerge. If not properly handled, it could quickly descend into malpractices and favouritism.

Foreigners new to China, struggling with Chinese bureaucracy to register themselves for business, residency, holiday, educational advancement or some other purpose, and faced also with a language problem, would be most apt to encounter an instance of the operation of *guanxi* when seeking help from a local intermediary.

Whether such an intermediary would use his own *guanxi* to get the job done would likely be the first intimation to a foreigner of the operation of *guanxi* The kind of impression formed would depend on whether any fee was charged or whether the intermediary was just doing a favour.

And overarching all *guanxi* connections would be, of course, that ubiquitous Chinese concept of "face". That, too, would not be an altogether easy feature in Chinese life for many foreigners to grasp.

* * *

For illustrative purposes, I recount here an actual instance when I had to exploit H.C. Fung's *guanxi* with Kuomintang elders in Taiwan in order to get myself out of a pickle.

It happened in the following way: a significant European importer of Chinese handicraft called upon me in Hong Kong to explore the terms under which Li & Fung (Trading) would be willing to act as his Far Eastern agent for porcelain vases, flower pots, garden stools, beaded curtains, rattan baskets and similar items. Most of them were available from factories in China, Hong Kong and Taiwan which our corporation had dealt with before.

I explained our normal terms to him and showed him some of the local factories. He seemed satisfied with what he had heard and seen. He then asked me if I could go to Taiwan with him the following day and show him our operations there. I replied in the affirmative, thinking it would be nice to sign on a new customer with only a further two-day trip.

But when I asked my secretary to make my travel arrangements, I discovered that the normal multi-entry and exit visa I usually used for travel to Taiwan had expired. But I did not consider that a serious impediment, for I knew that for business purposes an entry visa could be easily obtained at the Taipei airport. So I went with the prospective customer and did what was required of me.

However, two days later, when I wanted to return to Hong Kong after sealing an agreement with the customer, I was told by staff at Taiwan that I would not be allowed to leave without an exit visa.

The explanation was simple. Since I had arrived in the island on the basis of an emergency entry visa, the rules required that I apply for an exit visa. That would provide for a proper bureaucratic and security record I had visited the island. Otherwise, my visit would not be recorded.

To process an exit visa usually took a minimum of two or three days. If I had applied for an exit visa the moment I arrived, it might have been about ready by now. As it was, I would have to wait for another two or three days before I could leave.

The news was very disappointing. I had a lot of work waiting in Hong Kong, including the signing of some contracts with other important customers. I had been ignorant of the regulations previously, because I had hitherto just had stamps chopped on my multi-entry and exit visa.

I was desperate not to waste extra days on the island, so I asked the head of the Taiwan office whether the process could be shortened. He said an emergency exit visa could be granted, but it required the personal approval of a minister. He said H.C. was intimate with one of the ministers and he would enquire whether he could grant an audience to one of the top executives of the Li & Fung group.

And so it came about that I called upon the said minister and, after exchanging some pleasantries about this and that and about Fung family members, he granted me an emergency exit visa.

No doubt, should that helpful minister ever transit through Hong Kong on a foreign trip, H.C. would feel obliged to offer him some slap-up hospitality for the favour he had bestowed upon me on my employer's behalf.

* * *

When I joined Li & Fung, the corporation was already acting as an agent for a large chain of British high street retailers of bags of all descriptions — fashion bags, evening bags, shopping bags, totes, purses, wallets and the like. The customer had sourced its requirements from Hong Kong, Taiwan and South Korea and had only one real competitor in Britain, another slightly bigger chain selling similar products. The competitor also sourced its goods largely from the Far East but it was being served by another Hong Kong trading company.

The customer brought out a fresh line of items every year, fashioned by its own designers, for manufacturing in factories in the three locations. When items were to be made in Korea, the division head would send staff members from either the Hong Kong or the Taiwan office to oversee production schedules, quality control, shipment dates and so on. An expensive undertaking on a fixed commission.

Operations at the customer end was co-ordinated by a chief buyer who visited the Far East twice a year. In between, his team of specialised buyers for individual categories of products would visit as necessary, to explain their requirements in detail to my merchandising and inspection staff and to the factories involved in their production.

That chief buyer was a pasty-faced man of about my own age. He was a voluble man fond of his drink and came over as a type of whisky priest so aptly described in the novels of Graham Greene.

I struck up a cordial relationship with the chief buyer and gained some technical understanding of the bag business. For example, I learnt some simple ways of testing for colour fastness and how to apply a drop test to determine the sturdiness of straps attached to shoulder bags. In order to get a more direct feel of industrial developments in Korea, I decided to join the chief buyer on a couple of his trips to that country.

While in that country, I became acquainted with a Korean manufacturer of leather fashion bags by the surname of Chung, from whose factory the chief buyer had been getting some of his supplies.

Chung was an urbane and engaging man, with a fluent command of English. We went out for a couple of meals together and got into some quite serious and stimulating conversations. It turned out that Chung was as eager to learn about Hong Kong as I was to learn about Korea.

According to Chung, a number of his Korean friends had been wondering if there was scope for Korean products, like cosmetics and instant noodles, to sell well in the colony.

I replied that everything depended on whether products were being properly promoted. The Hong Kong consumer market was expanding rapidly with growing wealth. Many long established British staples in food and drink, however, were missing out because they were satisfied with annual growth rates of five or six per cent, not realising that with proper promotion in Hong Kong, some American and European brands were achieving growth rates in double digits.

From those early contacts, Chung and I both found that we clicked. I formed the impression that Chung was a sound, reliable and honourable person with whom I could do serious business. Thus the idea of establishing a Li & Fung branch office in Seoul, with his help in recruiting Korean staff with English proficiency, gradually took shape in my head.

*   *   *

As time went by, more existing as well as new customers wanted to source products out of Korea. That provided me with more opportunities to visit Seoul and deepen personal relations with Chung.

I did a rough calculation on commission income coming from the Korean trade and judged it economically worthwhile to experiment with a small branch office in Seoul in conjunction with a partner who not only knew the language but could tap into Korean exporters eyeing Hong Kong as a market. There would then be no need, from my point of view, of spending money to send merchandisers or inspectors from Taiwan or Hong Kong to oversee shipments out of Korea. On the flip side, enquiries on Korean products suitable for Hong Kong could be answered either by my own staff or referred to the Trade Development Council.

So I eventually put the proposal for an experiment to Chung. I suggested that Li & Fung (Trading) and whatever corporate vehicle he might care to use could form a joint trading venture for a couple of years. It might become more permanent if it turned profitable or be folded after a couple of years if it did not. During the experiment we would share half the income each and half any losses. The new entity would be called a branch office for Li & Fung (Trading) for known brand identification purposes but he would be responsible for overseeing the recruitment of staff and its local management.

Chung thought the proposal a good idea and in due time an all Korean staff was recruited and the new entity brought into being.

*   *   *

Trading had always been an easy way of making a living in Hong Kong. Anyone with no formal education could still become a street hawker and earn his keep by selling newspapers, comics, risqué magazines, cigarettes, chewing gum or other popular items on a commission basis.

At a slightly higher level, there would always be openings for tally clerks, shipping assistants, product merchandisers and quality controllers. Those positions required no special entry qualification other than basic education and some undertaking for on-the-job training. For the unskilled and those without capital, they represented an initial rung in a long ladder towards some imagined prosperity at some future date.

Trading firms had never been either charitable or moral institutions. The Ten Commandments did not apply. Their focus had always been on making profits, through whatever form of human exploitation deemed necessary.

They offered meagre wages consistent with recruiting and retaining suitable staff, and the barest number of holidays and fringe benefits demanded by the law. Extended working hours were the norm throughout that calling, while employers relentlessly separated the wheat from the chaff among employees by maintaining a month-to-month system of employment to facilitate hirings and firings. Long-term contracts were exceptions rather than the rule.

Of course, employees knew how to play that tough and devious game too. Job-hopping was rampant. For the sake of a modest rise in pay, a low-level employee would jump from one firm to another. Quick money rather than loyalty was the deciding factor. Sometimes, for the talented, the mere threat of leaving might be enough to elicit a pay rise or a promotion. Employees worked on the relatively sound principle that if they did not toot their own trumpets then they were likely never to get them tooted at all.

The dream of junior staff was that, once they had mastered the rudiments of the job and developed enough *guanxi* among the factories producing their line of products, they might get lucky one day. If they gained the confidence and rapport of a big foreign buyer, they might well be able to start a small business of their own by poaching that buyer from their own trading house.

After all, for an individual, it was better to be the head of a chicken than the tail of a bull. He needed no plush office or embossed letterheads to start. All he needed was a telephone to communicate with the foreign buyers.

Foreigners were just as obsessed with profits as anybody else. If a person could demonstrate he could do the job on just 3% commission rather than the 6% charged by his employer, why should a foreign buyer not jump at the chance? At 3%, the man's income would still be far in excess of his existing wages while the buyer might gain kudos from his employer.

In the trading world, those at the managerial level had to constantly read and to deduce correctly from the tea leaves of personal ambitions, because the poaching of staff and customers was a recurring phenomenon in the business. If they were read wrongly — as happened in respect of H.C. Fung's suspicions over the ambitions of his nephew, Kwok-Hong — then the results could be very unsettling for all concerned.

* * *

I paid particular attention to the development of the Seoul office because it had been my baby and I wanted it to thrive. However, growth there did not live up to expectations. There had been a few new European customers sourcing out of Korea but they had been generally small firms; the biggest one had remained the specialised British chain of high street stores selling bags.

In my estimation, that customer had more or less reached the limits of it growth potential. The new lines of fashion bags it had been putting out each season were becoming less innovative and exciting and its profit announcements and forecasts had sounded more muted. I calculated that the time was ripe for me to make a play for its main competitor, who was at that time using another Hong Kong trading house as agent.

Therefore, when I next visited the United Kingdom, I made a point of paying a courtesy call on the top management of the rival chain. I made my usual pitch.

Li & Fung was an old established company providing efficient, reliable and competitive services. We had a network of offices in the Far East staffed with very experienced merchandisers and quality control inspectors who were always on the look-out for new products which might appeal to Western markets.

For example, we were placing orders on behalf of European customers with some Korean factories producing very high-quality leather fashion bags and with some Chinese factories making excellent embroidered evening clutch bags. I should be delighted to send them samples to judge quality for themselves, if desired. Our commission rates were naturally quite competitive.

My listeners heard me out with courtesy and attention. They expressed reservations, however, since Li & Fung was already representing their main competitor in Britain. They were afraid of a potential conflict of interests, with trade secrets and upcoming designs and fashion ranges passing too easily to the staff of competitors.

I tried to put their minds at ease on that score. I said that Li & Fung had long been accustomed to serving competitors. Where the volume of trade was significant, we designated entirely different teams to serve different customers, without any overlapping or leakage of sensitive information. We acted like large accounting firms which served as both accountants and auditors for major corporations. We usually built a sort of "Chinese wall" between customers. For example, we bought garments on behalf of Gap in California but we also bought them on behalf of Gap's competitors. Likewise, in respect of toys, we acted on behalf of ToysRUs and also its competitors. No conflict of interests ever arose.

The meeting ended on what diplomats might describe as "a constructive" note. I might not have got my foot inside the door, but I think I at least had left it slightly ajar with the insertion of a couple of toes.

* * *

Meanwhile, from the visits of the various buyers of speciality bags from the British chain, I learnt that their company was undergoing a restructuring of its management. There was likely to be the creation of a new post of buying director and it was rumoured that its chief buyer, who went by the Christian name of Nick, might be in the running.

Nick, that pasty-faced individual, was about my own age. He had both a limited education and an averagely endowed imagination. But he had worked hard on his way up, mastering a set of skills concerning bags and their multifarious uses. He was a reasonable enough man to do business with, because of his competence, but he was not the kind of person who could naturally attract me, either spiritually or intellectually, into a genuine friendship. In other words, if I were to get stuck in a car in a muddy rut on a country road in the middle of the night, I would certainly not ring him up, expecting him to come to help me push it back onto the road.

A short while later, Nick turned up in Hong Kong on his normal twice-a-year visit to the various places in the Far East where his buyers had viewed products and suggested factories where they might place orders. He confirmed that a restructuring exercise was going on in his company but uncertain as to whether he would be promoted or not.

I conventionally wished him luck, although I doubted whether he could radically change the fortunes of his company because he had fallen behind in attuning himself to the changing tastes and preferences of his younger women customers. The demographics as well as the purchasing power were changing in Britain and businesses and their leaders had to adjust.

* * *

After Nick had returned home, I received a message from Chung. He said he had heard rumours that the young Korean he had recruited a couple years back to head our joint venture might be resigning to go into business for himself. If the rumours were true, then the young man might be taking with him the British bag chain customer. He was not so much worried for himself, because he still expected the chain to order fashion bags from his factory, but it might mean that the 6% commission flowing from those orders would no longer go into the Li & Fung branch office.

I told Chung to relax, sit tight and watch developments. In the dog-eat-dog world of trading, no youngster could be faulted for trying to advance his own lot. However, I suspected that the whole saga might have originated from an attempt by Nick to show his own bosses he could somehow cut company costs, to enhance his own advancement upwards.

What Nick had overlooked, however, was that his company had an agency agreement with Li & Fung for all Far Eastern purchases. While the British company might manage to do without Li & Fung in Korea, it could not do so as easily in respect of Hong Kong, Taiwan and elsewhere. I would not be minded to allow a breaking of the agreement in respect of Seoul without the whole agency arrangement coming into question.

Besides, a breach at the present time might actually hide a silver lining. It might enable me to bring in an even bigger British bags customer than the one we had been dealing with. I did not think Nick's company had a strong enough poker hand to enter that sort of game with me.

* * *

A few months later, Nick came to Hong Kong again on the second of his yearly trips. He told me that the restructuring exercise was still on-going in his company. But business conditions in Britain were deteriorating and profit margins were shrinking. In view of the increasing volume of goods being purchased through Li & Fung in recent years, would there be scope for negotiating a lower commission rate, Nick asked.

I replied that it would be reasonable for a commission rate to be re-adjusted if the volume and the profitability went up significantly together. However, that had not been the case from Li & Fung's point of view.

The Seoul office had been opened largely to facilitate his company's purchases, instead of having to send staff from Hong Kong or Taiwan to oversee deals. It was true that the business there had increased but overall it had not developed as well as it might. If one factored in my pay and perks as managing director — because of the amount of time I had to spend establishing and overseeing the office — the whole project would in fact be a loss maker up to now rather than a profit centre. Hence the timing was not at all ripe for considering any adjustment to our commission rate.

I had that conversation with Nick on a Saturday morning, as he was due to fly off to another destination on Sunday. I thought I had put that issue to bed for the time being. But I was wrong. Nick was apparently not satisfied with my response and had decided to go over my head with Victor Fung.

* * *

When I went to my office on Monday morning, the head of the Handbags Division came to see me with a clutch of contracts with factories for signing. He told me that he had received a telephone call from Victor Fung on Sunday instructing him to henceforth reduce to 5.5% the commission rate to be levied on purchases by the British high street bags customer.

I was astonished! How could Victor Fung overrule my decision without so much as discussing the issue with me first? As the chairman of Li & Fung (Trading) he no doubt had the right to overrule me. But to do so without even hearing what I had to say or what my plans had been was corporate autocracy at its worst.

What kind of macho management theories were American business schools spewing nowadays? In my eyes, his decision amounted to one discourtesy and disrespect too many. I realised at once that I could no longer plan for the corporation nor to work meaningfully for it any more.

Besides, with the enormous amount of money I had already made betting against the judgement of Victor on the Hong Kong dollar exchange rate during the Sino-British negotiations, I was no longer in need of any income from either Li & Fung or anybody else.

"It seems Victor has taken over the supervision of your division," I said wistfully, to the division head. "You had best go to him henceforth for all future instructions, including when there are contracts to be signed."

* * *

I spent the rest of the morning pondering how I might disengage amicably from Li & Fung, without leaving too much rancour behind. The problem was that the agreement made with H.C. Fung, under which I would leave the civil service to join his company, was essentially an oral gentlemen's agreement because we had been old friends and horse-owning partners.

Its essence could be summarised in a couple of sentences. To wit, I would work for ten years in the company, and during that period my terms of employment and perks would in no case fall below those enjoyed by the head of a major government department. After a minimum of five years, however, each party could terminate the agreement by giving the other party a year's notice.

At that point, I had completed more than seven years with the company and I had reached the maximum accumulation point of six months for earned leave. I imagined I had been the only employee within Li & Fung who had the generous senior civil service leave rate of 48 days per annum, as well as the ability to accumulate leave for six months. The rest of the staff in the company, except for members of the Fung family, had only two weeks' holiday a year, which they had to take or have it forfeited.

Therefore, with my leave entitlements, I could practically walk out right away, with accumulated or current leave balances covering much of my notice period. I could not see why the company would want to keep me hanging around when my decisions were being willy-nilly overturned without reason.

However, there was one part of our agreement which had been subsequently turned into writing following a discussion with Victor Fung. I pointed out to him that it would cost the company a bomb to provide me with one of those 3,500 square feet luxury apartments enjoyed by heads of government departments. I had been actually living in one of those apartments at Palm Court on Robinson Road at the time.

"I was now a bachelor," I said, "and living without my children while they studied abroad; so I did not need so much space. I would much rather live in a more modest apartment, if I could somehow own it after ten years. That would be a much more economical solution for the company too."

After that conversation, Victor got Coopers & Lybrand to set up a Panamanian company based on bearer bonds. Li & Fung would make an interest-free sum of money as a loan to the Panamanian company for me to purchase an apartment of my choice, with 10% of the loan being written off after every year of service. In theory, at the end of ten years the Panamanian company would be free of debt and whoever held the bearer bonds would be the owner of the company and all its assets. It was a neat accounting trick, sidestepping tax and other considerations.

Because the Panamanian company technically owned my apartment at Seymour Road, I went to consult my old journalistic friend, Leslie Sung, over any possible legal tangle. Leslie, after studies in Britain, had joined as a partner in the venerable firm of solicitors known as Lo & Lo.

I told Leslie that I did not want to stir up bad feelings between the company and myself by suddenly banging in my year's notice. I thought I should at least resolve the ownership of the Seymour Road apartment more obliquely first. After some discussion, we decided the best approach might be to send a cheque in covering the final two years of write-offs for the Panamanian company as a signal I was not entirely happy with remaining in the company, leaving any minor adjustments to be settled later.

We thought that might at least lead to a civilised conversation between the parties on how the final terms of disengagement might be worked out. Thus Leslie sent a fairly brief lawyer's letter with a cheque.

With that in the works, I took three weeks' leave and headed to England with Kitty, to continue our search for a suitable home. I did not attempt to explain to Kitty what was actually going on within the office. I thought that, given her ignorance of corporate affairs, she would have to boggle her mind to understand the key elements involved.

* * *

But before leaving for England, I sent a message to Chung. I told him what had transpired and that I would soon be leaving Li & Fung for good. I said I did not know who would be taking my place but it seems our experiment at a joint venture should come to an end. I apologised for failing to make money for either of the partners in the experiment and wished him every luck for the future.

* * *

That trip to England excited me no end. At the age of 59, the prospect of being freed from the trammels of office routines and producing corporate profits filled me with anticipation and exhilaration. The ability to go to a faraway place to reflect upon the changing nature of my native city — both the good and the bad aspects — and to write short stories about them fired my imagination.

There used to be a popular television programme called "Beneath the Lion Rock". The name came from an outcropping called the Lion Rock in one of the ridges of hills in the New Territories. The episodes told of the grim determination and wry fatalism of ordinary people as they struggled for survival in an inhospitable environment.

At the same time, I remember some of the novel by Balzac I had read when I was young. Balzac had written about post-Napoleonic Paris and he had observed that its citizens were losing the ability of love — all except for the love of money. I could sense that something similar was happening in Hong Kong as the territory rushed pell-mell towards reunification with China.

But I was too much in the midst of change to think about it objectively and dispassionately. I needed distance to gain a degree of perspective. So heading for England was just what I needed.

CHAPTER 20

Odds and Half-Ends

THE FURTHER TRIP that Kitty and I made to London proved unproductive. Although we had visited many properties in various districts north of the Thames, we were unable to find any which came close to our multifarious needs.

"What about Paris?" Kitty suddenly asked one day. "I've heard so much about that romantic city and you've also at times spoken fondly of it yourself."

"Yes, spring time in Paris, chestnuts in blossom, cafe tables along the streets, strolls along the banks of the Seine, the smell of freshly-baked bread and all those images. But if you want to live there, you'd need to learn the language. Do you want to learn French as well?" I replied.

"Well, maybe later. For now, one language at a time. But I'd love to wrap myself in those dreams at some stage."

"And you will."

Kitty's reference to the choice of Paris alerted me to the need to secure residential status somewhere for Kitty and myself. I had been in and out of Britain so frequently in the past, for work, for studies and a variety of missions, that subconsciously I might have taken Britain as almost a natural second home. But to live there permanently for both of us necessitated meeting a set of bureaucratic requirements.

One of the oddities I had noticed previously was that London was such a cosmopolitan playground, with almost every nationality and culture in the world represented. Probably also every kind of law-breaker and misfit as well. It must be either a manifestation of a remarkable tolerant and welcoming streak in the British character or else of a certain universally attractive nature in those green and pleasant isles for so many different types of people to be drawn there.

Yet there was a flip side to things. The British government never seemed too willing to allow many of its former colonial subjects to sink their roots there — unless they came loaded with cash or some rare and unusual talent. So many of the vital staff in its celebrated National Health Service, for example, seemed to have been recruited from abroad.

Well, at least I could satisfy the cash side of things under British immigration rules. So I duly applied for Kitty and myself to be granted permanent British residential status as a couple with independent means.

I was eventually asked to produce not only my bank and brokerage house statements testifying to the sufficiency of my funds and where they were being kept. I was in addition asked to provide a legally certified document indicating that Kitty and I were in fact married, presumably to guard against the human trafficking of young women. It seemed almost as if the Whitehall machinery paid more attention to an immigrant's moral lapses than to his morality.

Having in due course submitted the documents requested, I sat back and waited patiently for the bureaucratic mill to slowly turn. Not having found a home there yet and not having been properly disengaged from my employment, I was in no terrible hurry to move.

* * *

Meanwhile, Leslie Sung's letter and cheque elicited no response from anyone at the appropriate level within Li & Fung. Part of the reason might be that neither H.C. nor Victor knew exactly how to respond.

On the other hand, it might also be due to other developments within the corporation. One of those developments was that the office space occupied by Li & Fung (Trading) at Cameron Road had proved inadequate for some time to meet its expanding activities. The property arm of the corporation, under the leadership of William Fung, had been charged with finding alternative accommodation. Could a suite for a Managing Director and his immediate supporting staff be soon surplus to need? That could have been one of the vexing questions the company faced.

Nobody sought my views about where or how the expansion might best be effected. Since I was, in my own mind at least, on the way out, I did not volunteer an opinion. I had been given to understand that alternative accommodation in a new building at the China Hong Kong City on Canton Road was under consideration.

Likewise, no one saw fit to bring me into the company's privation plans which were first mentioned by Kwok-Hong and Rosetta. I had thought it unwise to stick my nose into those hush-hush family or corporate manoeuvres being made by others with their banks and financial backers. In such matters, an ability to deny inside knowledge was truly important. It was a case of ignorance being bliss.

* * *

While I was pondering what additional move I ought to make to further my disengagement from the company, I was suddenly struck down by another attack of severe pancreatitis.

It so happened that Dr. Joseph Fung, who traditionally provided company medical services for staff of the entire Li & Fung group, was away in America on a prolonged holiday.

I therefore got myself admitted to the Yeung Wo Hospital at once and asked Kitty to urgently contact Ip Yeuk-Lam's youngest son, Shing-Kwan, to get him to use his *guanxi* for a top internal medicine specialist to attend to me there.

Shing-Kwan was a gynaecologist but he had been part of the medical establishment for some years and so knew who were the best specialists in each field. He arranged for me to be seen by a Dr. Lam who had specialised in internal medicine.

Dr. Lam initially gave me the same type of medication as Dr. Joseph Fung had and that quickly eased my pain. But he expressed surprise that I should be suffering from severe pancreatitis for so many years without anyone being able to find a cause or cure for the ailment. He suggested that I should be given another set of ultrasound and endoscopy tests.

I replied that I had already undertaken a large number of those, both under Dr. Fung and under a number of government consultants at Queen Mary Hospital. But none of them seemed able to pinpoint the cause for my attacks.

Dr. Lam said although he had practised internal medicine for a number of years, he could not say he was well up on the latest techniques and developments in the field. However, there was a Professor Leung who had just joined the Chinese University Medical Faculty. He had come with a big reputation from America and Europe. If Professor Leung could be persuaded to accept me as a patient, would I be prepared to place myself in his care, Dr. Lam asked.

I said I would gladly place myself under the care of the Devil himself if he could deliver me from my sudden and recurring attacks.

And so it was arranged that I would be transferred by ambulance from the Yeung Wo Hospital to the Prince of Wales Hospital in the New Territories, where Professor Leung taught and practised.

Professor Leung turned out to be a stern and straight-talking individual. He appeared fairly young in my eyes, being only in his forties, but he seemed very self-assured. He ordered me to take a further set of ultrasound and endoscopy tests.

When the results became available, he shared them with me and pointed out what they showed. But he began by asking if I had been prone to developing stones in my internal organs.

"Yes," I replied. "About 20 years ago I had some gall stones and they had to be removed."

"Well, I don't want to know who gave you your previous tests concerning your pancreas and I don't want to know why they could not see what I am seeing now," the professor said. "You have developed another stone in your pancreas and it is floating around inside. Sometimes it gets itself stuck in your pancreatic duct and when that happens, you get an attack. If you agree, I can operate and get rid of the stone for you. But before I do so, I want to know whether you're a heavy drinker."

"I used to drink a fair bit," I admitted. "But in recent years, I've gone off drink and now limit myself to just a glass of wine or two at dinner, on special occasions."

"If you want me to operate on you, you'll have to give up even that occasional glass or two of wine."

"That's all right with me," I said.

"No, I'm serious," Professor Leung said. "If you touch a drop of alcohol after the operation, so much as a beer or a glass of wine, don't come back to me if you get into further trouble with your pancreas. I won't treat you any more. Is that clear?"

I nodded in acceptance of his condition.

So I had my operation, following which I gave up alcohol altogether. I did not have any further problem with my pancreas thereafter, until about 20 years later, when I developed pancreatic cancer and was treated at the Royal Free Hospital in London.

By then, I had naturally migrated and had to undergo a risky and major operation known as a whipple to cope with that dangerous new ailment.

An interesting aside to the Hong Kong episode was that, since I had been a former civil servant and was then a pensioner, which entitled me to free Hong Kong medical care at government hospitals, I was not charged anything for my stay at the Prince of Wales Hospital nor for the services of Professor Leung.

* * *

After my discharge from the Prince of Wales Hospital, which was considered as sick leave, I was given another week's sick leave to recuperate at home.

When I returned to the office, the atmosphere seemed to be crackling with static electricity. Everybody knew that I had been hospitalised and rumours had circulated that I had refused to take further responsibilities for policies in the bags division. So most of the more senior staff sensed that some major change was in the air. They were filled with curiosity and expectation. A few dropped by my office to ask after my health but there was not a peep out of either H.C. or Victor Fung.

A check with Leslie revealed there had been no response to his letter with the cheque for the Panamanian company loan. I was anxious to bring matters to some quick and civilised resolution but I had to take into account the interests of innocent third parties apart from my own immediate interests. For example, I had to consider the future of my secretary, Mrs. Gina Cheung.

I had engaged Gina as my secretary at the beginning of June of 1982. I could not have selected a more efficient and loyal one. She was a petite and cheerful woman married to an inspector of police who rose later to become a superintendent. She also willingly handled some of my personal correspondence with friends, relatives and ex-lovers and was quick-witted enough to keep her own dossier of important dates on them, like their birthdays and anniversaries, so that she could remind me of their approach if I were absentminded.

Gina was pregnant with her second child at the time and was due for paid maternity leave in the early part of 1989. If I were to leave Li & Fung too early, I would not put it past the company to discharge her as someone no longer needed and hence deprive her of paid maternity leave. So I had to calibrate my actual departure to protect her entitlement.

Although it has now been more than 30 years since we both left Li & Fung, I still receive a greeting card from Gina on festive occasions, although she is by now a grandmother, with her hands full of grandchildren.

For the foregoing reason, Leslie advised me to sit tight till a response came from Li & Fung.

* * *

So I decided to take another two weeks of the 48 days of annual leave I was due and headed for London again with Kitty to continue our search for a suitable home but it again proved a complete damp squib. Upon my return to Hong Kong, there still remained no response from Li & Fung.

But my mind was soon driven towards a much wider and more troubling focus. A flurry of stories had been appearing in both Western and local media about social and economic problems in dozens of cities in China. There had apparently been protests and demonstrations by students and strikes by workers over price inflation, shortages of essential goods, corrupt practices and so on. Amidst those manifestations of discontent, there had also been shouted slogans and demands for "democracy" and "freedom" without anyone spelling out what those words actually meant.

A few of the stories were objective and constructive but most carried an anti-Communist or anti-China undertone. Some of the narratives even reported contradictory demands by demonstrators.

But with the British due to return the colony to Chinese sovereignty looming ever closer, more residents became receptive to those tales of woe and grew alarmed over their own wellbeing after 1997. Those stories encouraged some to contemplate emigrating, while a fair number actually did move later to Canada, Australia and elsewhere.

I had anticipated a number of transitional problems when such a large and impoverished country like China decided to allow market forces to play a bigger role to aid the country's progress. To move from a system where the prices of essentials had been kept stable by the state since the early 1950s into a partially market-influenced pricing system would be challenging enough in itself. But with so many stuck at the margins, filled with unarticulated hopes and unrealised dreams, a transition could be very disruptive and a painful adjustment.

While the transition was proceeding, someone would still have to work in the fields to produce the food and others would have to mine for coal to fight against the cold. Under a dual pricing system, people with the right connections could purchase goods at state specified prices and later resell them at market prices to gain quick profits, leading to corruption and growing inequality in wealth.

It was all very well for the Paramount Ruler to say that getting rich was no crime, without spelling out that some means of enrichment had to constitute real crimes.

It was obvious that the transition would encounter many hiccups. To attempt to do it on the fly, with cadres inexperienced with capitalism's twists and turns, would be challenging enough. Although higher education had been increased, the emphasis had been placed on turning out scientists, engineers and technologists rather than able administrators. Furthermore, out of sheer ignorance or a mistaken understanding of a free market, cadres might well begin to introduce some of the more objectionable features and practices of capitalism into the new system.

There was in addition no shortage of spivs, crooks and profiteers within the country itself to exploit whatever could be exploited for gain. Inefficiencies in distribution must initially create shortages which would in turn spark inflation. In Peking, for example, the consumer price index soared by 30%, making ordinary wage earners no longer able to afford staples. Simple survival stared many unfortunates in the face.

As I took in those media reports, I became worried that fresh turbulence might overtake China once again, especially if stirred by malicious rumours, profiteers and outside forces with evil geopolitical intentions.

Hong Kong under British rule had been a notorious gathering place for provocateurs, local turncoats, rabid anti-Communists and Western spies and counter-revolutionaries. The colony's lack of foreign exchange control made it easy for dubious money to be sent into and out of the city for a range of ideological, criminal and other purposes. Banks were already up to their necks in money-laundering, tax avoidance and other dicey activities.

To add to that toxic mix, a small collection of Chinese pseudo-intellectuals who had "soaked themselves in salt water" but had returned to the country with qualifications in some specialised field, had utilised their status in those fields to offer nostrums for curing the ails of the country in completely unrelated fields.

Some of the more swell-headed gave speeches blaming the country's poverty on its political system and circulated their ideas about freedom and democracy among naive students still wet behind the ears.

History had in fact produced very few public intellectuals or sages whose musings and insights were worth reflecting upon or memorising. The reason was that very few had real competence over multiple spheres of human knowledge. A man might be an astrophysicist or a pioneering neurosurgeon, but why should anyone listen to him when he was sounding off on *mah-jong* techniques or on how to manage a nation's budget?

But it seemed that the entire world had somehow been so dumbed-down as to expect simplified solutions to very complicated problems. No doubt, blindly following the snappy opinions of movie stars, sporting icons and popular personalities was far easier than thinking for oneself. The gullible would have to swallow such proffered pearls of wisdom at their own peril.

To top everything off, the leadership of the country was not in the least united in providing solutions. Some modernisers, like the Premier Zhao Zi-Yang and Communist Party General Secretary Hu Yao-Bang, wanted to speed up changes while many conservatives wanted to slow down the role of market forces. That split in the leadership naturally percolated down to those implementing changes on the ground.

In the face of spreading student and worker demonstrations and repeated breakdowns in law and order, Hu had to resign in January of 1987. He had been accused of being too soft on students and agitators by some hardliners.

Deng Xiao-Ping, the Paramount Ruler and initiator of change himself, began warning against the worship of Western lifestyles and multiparty systems, as such notions undermined not only traditional values but also the leadership of the Communist Party. That showed that Deng himself had reservations about the degree or speed of change. Yet he had allowed Zhao Zi-Yang to assume the position of General Secretary of the Chinese Communist Party during the 13th National Congress in 1987.

In those confusing and unsettling circumstances, I could not help soliciting the views of my friends in the Chinese General Chamber. Unfortunately, they either blamed the Western media for exaggerating problems in China or else they supported the prevailing official line of the government, which was that it was doing its best to adjust to the transition.

* * *

It was inevitable that the situation in the mainland should become central to conversations between myself and Chan Hon-Kit when we met regularly for tea.

"What do you make of those media reports of protests and strikes in different parts of China?" I asked. "Are they being exaggerated? What have your children been telling you? What have the mainland media been saying?"

Hon-Kit shook his head and sighed. "Where can anyone go for reliable news nowadays? China is a vast country with many towns. What might be happening in one place might not get much coverage elsewhere. Besides, the media are now either controlled by government or by media moguls with their own axes to grind.

"When we started out in journalism 40 years ago, our editors used to tell us to go after facts and still more facts, allowing readers to make up their own minds about whatever might be going on. We were told to leave expressions of opinions to the editorial pages. Now we are fed false news and manufactured opinions. Independent news outlets have been steadily dying or are being taken over. I don't know what universities teach in mass communication courses these days. They are probably just churning out an endless stream of new and unprincipled paid hacks."

Now it was my turn to sigh. "Yes, my friend," I said, "it seems that both technology and a changing world are leaving both of us behind. Uncovering the truth and revealing it to the world are now no longer core to our former profession. Anyone with such notions can now be left to weep in his beer — if he is still allowed to have beers! But I am still curious to know what's actually happening in China."

"That's hard to say. It's a very big country. Both the Chinese government and vested foreign governments publicise only what they want to put out with their own spin. Both may use some of the same words to describe events but those words mean different things. So far as can be determined from the bits and pieces culled from the grapevine, things are not going so well with the transition to a more market-led economy. People are encountering many unforeseen problems impacting their lives."

"Perhaps it's time we found a modern Kung-Sun Lung to start another rectification of names, so that everybody has a common understanding of the meaning of the words they use," I said.

Hon-Kit chuckled. "Not a bad idea at all. People may then realise that

'Freedom of the Press' does not include the freedom to spread falsehoods and lies in China.

"When the Communist Party came to power in 1949, you will recall, most of the people were illiterate farmers with no disposable incomes. We had nothing to sell them except faith in our leadership and a hope that the hardships and sacrifices being called for would one day lead to better lives for their children and for the nation.

"Our people are still too inadequately educated today. They are riddled with many superstitions. They still put faith in physiognomy, palm-reading and *fung shui*, for instance. Government has a duty to protect them from crooks, fraudsters and fomenters of political dissent.

"However, exercising control entails problems over messaging and how to address and influence those on the receiving end. Government cannot sell a narrative or a promise without delivering at some stage, just as it cannot condemn capitalist excesses in one breath and try to promote free market reforms in the next.

"We are facing that same old dilemma anew today, in the teeth of many wild and competing narratives and greater ease in communications. In such circumstances, we cannot be completely open with the truth, can we? Can we truthfully admit, for example, differences of opinion within our own leadership? That would undermine both the faith in our leadership and the unity of our country. Then everything gained by the revolution might start unravelling.

"Answer me this, my friend: If you were charged with caring for a child incapable of chewing enough intellectual food for his own needs and growth, would you consider it wrongful for some pre-chewing to be done for him before feeding him?"

That question completely turned the tables on me. I was caught off-guard for a solution. "I can understand the differences of opinion within the party," I mumbled. "I imagine memories of the Cultural Revolution must keep appearing before all their minds' eyes like Banquo's ghost. But in the end we have to trust the good sense of our people somehow. Do you know what the trouble really is with people like us, Hon-Kit? We think too much and we have too many qualms and scruples. We always try too hard to consider things from different points of view. We would never make good leaders. We're not decisive enough."

"You're right! That's why I've never aspired to lead anyone or anything. I know my limitations. But we have both been brought up that way, trying to figure out, for instance, why we had to learn a foreign language just to submit to being ruled by rather mediocre foreigners.

"Was it because our British rulers wanted to produce subjects like us, subordinates of a different race but with English tastes, attitudes and morals? Psychologists say that childhood experiences would affect many of us. Maybe that was what the British were after with their educational system. Have we both been moulded, each in a slightly different way, since our boyhoods and school days? Are we only now at this late stage trying to come to terms with our own country, now that we have been left outside in a ceded place and without a jot of influence there?"

"Let's not start down that road, Hon-Kit. At our age, we probably still have too much fire in our bellies to accept that Lord Macaulay took both of us for a ride. Let's stick with the present subject and try to visualise how things might span out in our country."

Hon-Kit smiled and nodded. "All right, if you feel that time is not yet opportune for serious introspection or self-examination. We can afford to allow my questions to marinate for a while longer.

"In that case, do you remember that ancient story from the time of the School of Names? One of its leading lights was a lawyer by the name of Teng Hsi, as history goes. When the Wei River flooded, a rich man got drowned. His body was picked up by a boatman. When the family of the rich man sought his body for a proper burial, the boatman demanded a huge reward.

The family went to Teng Hsi for advice and he told the family to merely wait, because nobody else would want the body except themselves. Later, when the boatman became anxious about disposing of the body, he also went to Teng Hsi for advice. He was also told to merely wait because he was the only one from whom the family could get the body.

"There has been no historical record or legend handed down about the eventual outcome of that interesting case. That is our present predicament. We too can only wait and watch."

* * *

After my inconclusive discussion with Hon-Kit, I got a message from Leslie that a solicitor's letter had come back from Li & Fung, returning the cheque for clearing the debt of the Panamanian company.

I huddled with Leslie immediately to work out what this might mean. Obviously, the cheque had not led to any approach for ironing out the situation. The letter returning the cheque was terse and gave nothing away.

We appeared stuck in limbo. I could not imagine that the company would want me to continue when my decisions were being overturned without explanation. I felt that some explanation was at least due to me, though I did not want to approach H.C. or Victor lest either would construe me as a supplicant.

In the meantime, something else happened. When H.C. was urging me to leave the civil service to join his company, he said that his company adjusted staff salaries every year in line with movements in the Consumer Price Index and that, as a top executive, I would, in additional, be entitled to an annual bonus based on the profitability of the company.

I had responded to H.C. by saying that an annual adjustment in line with the Consumer Price Index would be good enough for me, although movements in the Consumer Price Index were a very crude and inaccurate indication of inflationary pressures. As to bonuses, I would gladly forego them, so long as my salary and perks did not fall below that of a head of a government department. Moreover, as my work would be largely administrative in nature, it would make for difficulties in aligning bonuses with profitability.

And so it came about that my salary was adjusted every year along with the salaries of other staff. But following the contretemps with the British bag customer, mine had remained unadjusted. That had to be deliberate. What lay behind that omission? Was it a nudge for me to go? But if Li & Fung wanted me to leave, it could openly serve me a year's notice. Why had it not done so?

I asked Leslie what he thought and what Li & Fung might be up to.

"It is hard to say," Leslie replied. "From the return of the cheque and the failure to adjust your salary, the company might be minded to contest some of the terms of your employment."

"After seven years on the job?" I exclaimed.

"The great difficulty is that your agreement was largely an oral one between friends. H.C. could argue, for example, that he was unaware after the conversion to annual leave of 48 days, a head of department could still accumulate leave for up to six months. No one in Li & Fung had such an arrangement. Leave not taken within a particular year would normally be forfeited."

"He wouldn't stoop so low, I think. I had been given permission to accumulate leave for up to six months because I had been roped into the Bermuda II and other civil aviation negotiations. I had specifically mentioned that benefit as part of my package to H.C."

Leslie nodded. "I see," he said. "If you were to give notice, you might have an argument over your accumulated leave and the housing benefit that would go with it."

"How else could I get Li & Fung to begin a dialogue and resolve the matter in a civilised manner?"

"If the company wanted a dialogue it would have started one when we sent in the cheque. Instead it sent the cheque back with a curt solicitor's letter. So the company has obviously taken some legal advice."

"Okay, so why shouldn't we go down the legal route as well? Should I sue H.C. and Li & Fung(Trading) for breach of contract? I am owed a number of other perks, you know, like annual holiday passages for my wife, now that I actually have one. I haven't claimed for any of her trips overseas to visit my mother in Canada or to London to search for a suitable home."

"Litigation is a mug's game, David. The main winners would be the lawyers involved. I would urge you to think it over very carefully. But if you're minded to move that way, I'll have to ask one of my partners to take over your case, to give you the most objective legal advice available. I fear my judgements might be clouded by our friendship."

"Thanks, Les. I think I'll think things over while taking the rest of this year's leave in London. I'll let you know on my return."

* * *

Kitty and I were in luck on the latest of our London visits. We found what we wanted in Belsize Park, within walking distance to the Royal Free Teaching Hospital and conveniently linked to underground transport. In addition, there was a smart private gym located right across the street to cater to Kitty's needs.

The flat was on the second floor of a converted Victorian town house on a 999-year lease. The apartment was slightly over 2,000 square feet and had three large bedrooms and two bathrooms. The asking price was fairly reasonable and the seller and I shook hands on a deal, barring the settlement of a few outstanding legal technicalities.

The place needed refurbishing, however. But I could visualise clearly what I could do with it, where I could install a new electrical fireplace in the sitting room, hang my chandeliers here and there, modernise the kitchen to my satisfaction, re-tile the two bathrooms and so on.

I returned to Hong Kong in such high spirits that I wanted to end all the sophistries and uncertainties concerning my employment as a trader and get stuck into re-designing my new home, so that I could settle in and revive my old passion for writing, while Kitty concentrated on mastering the English language.

Coincidentally, I received word at around the same time from the British immigration authorities that Kitty and I would be granted residential status in Britain as people of independent means, provided that I remitted a sum of not less than half a million pounds into the country. Considering that I intended to purchase the property at Belsize Park and to initiate some other pet projects, I duly remitted much more than the sum specified.

Those two developments increased my desire to pull up roots in Hong Kong and start a new life in London as soon as possible.

In order to bring my relationship with Li & Fung to some kind of conclusion, I asked Leslie to pass my case to one of his partners so that a suit could be initiated against H.C. Fung and Li & Fung (Trading) for the breaches of my oral contract with them.

* * *

Once the lawsuit had been formally lodged and picked up and embroidered upon by a couple of local scandal sheets, the city lived up to its reputation for being one of the most gossip-mongering place in the Far East. Speculations abounded as to what could be behind the break-up of an old and successful horse-owning partnership and a subsequent working friendship.

The first person to contact me on learning of such a conflict between old friends was a businessman and fellow horse-racing fancier by the name of Peter Leung. He had known both H.C. and I for many years and he was aged somewhere between H.C. and myself.

"David, I've known you and H.C. for many years," Peter declared. "You two have long been known as close friends; you've even owned race horses together for decades. If some disagreement has risen between you two, surely you don't need to take H.C. to court, do you? That might be a foreigner's way of doing things but it certainly is not a Chinese way."

"You're right, Peter," I replied. "My suit is not a Chinese way of doing things at all. Perhaps we made a mistake from the very start, by assuming that words uttered between friends were as good as a bond. As a result, there's hardly anything in writing regarding the terms of our engagement. So when problems arose, how can we continue in a Chinese fashion when one party refuses to talk?"

"Is that so? Perhaps what you both need is only a good mediator. Tell me what is at issue between you and I'll talk to H.C."

"There is no need to trouble you with specific issues. They are all relatively minor. Once we can start talking, they can all be fairly easily revolved."

"All right. Leave it with me. I'll talk to H.C."

* * *

A week later, Peter Leung came back to see me, looking crestfallen.

"I've spoken to H.C.," Peter reported. "He says he has handed over the day-to-day running of all company affairs to his two sons and he does not wish to interfere with their decisions in your case. I'm sorry I've not been more successful as a middleman."

"I'm sorry too. But thanks for your efforts," I said. "Did you really believe H.C.? He is still very much the head of the family, you know."

"He seemed to be rather upset with you."

"Yes, I can imagine he well might be. I had refused to stand by him concerning some Fung family dispute which had absolutely nothing to do with my work. You might remember that H.C. never saw eye to eye with his elder brother, Mo-Ying, when he headed the company. Now that Mo-Ying had passed away, H.C. is still trying to take his former dissatisfactions out on his nephew, Mo-Ying's son. It's a shame really.

"The nephew is not exactly a live wire but he spends most of his time working directly under H.C. on selling fireworks. H.C. sets all the policies and pricing. But somehow H.C. has got into his head that his nephew is planning to start trading on his own and possibly take some of the existing customers with him. That is why H.C. wants to get rid of him and he wants me to wield the knife.

"I don't think the nephew is planning anything untoward. He's by no means the adventurous type. Apart from fireworks, he does a reasonable job as the head of his division. I cannot find anything seriously wrong with his or his division's performance to warrant dismissal. If H.C. wants to turf him out, he would have to make the case himself, on the basis of the nephew's work on fireworks. I just cannot manufacture a case against a person I consider to be innocent."

"A sad business altogether," Peter observed. "Family feuds are so troublesome. I guess a man must follow his conscience and do what he thinks is right."

"I agree. But if H.C. finds it difficult to engage with me directly, because of our past associations, the proper conduct would be to send his son to approach me as a senior to iron things out. That would have been in line with proprieties, not the other way around."

* * *

Another friend who contacted me over my lawsuit with Li & Fung was Eric Ho, a former Eurasian colleague in the civil service. Eric had retired in 1987 as the Secretary for Trade and Industry to take on the challenging job of Chairman of the Hong Kong Public Services Commission during the difficult transition period.

"How can Li & Fung breach the terms of a contract with you?" Eric asked. "I know you. You're not a person to go for legal redress unless it were a last resort."

"It more or less is," I replied. "Our contract was largely an oral one, made between old friends, with hardly anything written down."

"Still, that's scandalous, considering what you've done for the two Fung boys. It was on your say-so that I arranged to introduce them into public life, getting one appointed to a social welfare committee and the other to the Cotton Advisory Board. How can the company turn around and be so mean to you in return?"

"Well, I've got a lot to thank the company for as well, Eric. It enabled me to leave the civil service and make a lot of money on the foreign exchange market during the turbulence of the Sino-British negotiations. It would have been quite improper for me to do that sort of thing if I had remained a member of the public service. I now already have more money than I can possibly ever use. So it is a question of fighting for a principle, rather than money."

"It's sad when the ways of our forebears are not followed nowadays. Perhaps the younger generation has been too much influenced by foreign education. If you ever want me to talk to the Fung boys, you know where to find me. I've had interfaces with both of them in the past,"

"Thanks awfully, Eric. No need to trouble you. Unfortunate for all concerned. If the Fungs don't want an amicable settlement, then we'll just have to see how this plays out in court."

* * *

It was possible that the intervention by Peter Leung had triggered a response from Li & Fung (Trading), for I received a formal letter giving me a year's notice for terminating my employment.

So some movement at last! It was also a tacit acknowledgement that a year's notice on either side had constituted a part of our original agreement. However, the letter did not attempt to tidy up any of the details. It did not indicate, for example, whether I was expected to continue working for that year or whether I could take my accumulated leave of six months within that period.

Still, no one at the right level in the company seemed interested in initiating a face-to-face conversation, to indicate what was expected of me during the period of notice, or how the breaches I had claimed in my law suit could be fairly and sensibly resolved.

In the absence of conversation, my turning up each day in the office soon descended into a farce. I would sign contracts for established customers on established terms, except for those concerning the bags division. I made the kinds of authorisations I normally made; but I held no meetings with new customers or pursued discussions with old ones who wanted fresh arrangements. I diverted all matters requiring changes to Victor.

Needless to say, with my equivocal and unsettled standing within the company, I made no more overseas trips to visit possible foreign clients or to drop into branch offices. A sense of unease manifested itself among staff who still had to interface with me. I felt quite sorry for their discomfiture.

*   *   *

I was soon diverted again from my own situation by further events in China. On April 15 in 1989, Hu Yao-Bang, the disgraced former General Secretary of the Chinese Communist Party, suddenly died. He had been one of the leading reformers after the country decided to introduce market-led pricing into the economy at the beginning of the 1980s.

In an outpouring of emotion, students and others began attributing his death to the way hardliners within the party had forced him to resign. They therefore gathered at the Monument of People's Heroes and sang patriotic songs to mourn his death. Most of the assembled crowds dispersed quietly but a small group had to be forcefully removed by the police.

A state funeral had been set for Hu on April 22 at the Great Hall of the People. Tiananmen Square was accordingly closed for that purpose. But about 100,000 students nevertheless ignored the closure and marched there, demanding to see the Premier Li Peng. The demand was naturally not met.

The passing of Hu seemed to have turned into a national focal point for all sorts of grievances, dislocations, complaints and suffering endured by ordinary people since the introduction of market forces into the economy. Price inflation had been a universal phenomenon. But there were a thousand other ways in which ordinary citizens could have been adversely affected.

Take, for illustration, what Kitty had experienced when she went back for a short visit to her parents in Nantong. Her mother suddenly became unwell one evening. Kitty took her to a hospital. But the staff there asked for a deposit of 30,000 RMB before they would attend to her mother. This was a marked departure from the health care system Kitty had known as a girl when medical services, although more rudimentary, were free.

"It's the middle of the night," Kitty protested. "All the banks are now closed. How can I get my hands on 30,000 RMB? And why so expensive? Why can't my mother be attended to first? She's in pain. I will pay the deposit tomorrow, as soon as I can get the money."

But the medical staff would not relent. Those were the new rules, they explained. The sum asked was only a deposit. If the cost came to less, a refund would be made. Kitty therefore had to ask her father to scurry among their relatives and friends in order to raise the deposit.

It was obvious that any major policy shift decided upon in Peking still depended on sensible implementation at the local level, with regulations that suited local circumstances. To simply ask for an unspecified amount as deposit without thinking through the implications could merely shift the burden towards the more vulnerable in society.

For example, how could a reasonable deposit be decided upon without first examining the seriousness of the malady in the patient? Those deciding on the level of deposits would naturally want to play safe by asking for a higher amount to reduce their own liability.

On the other hand, any examination of a prospective patient might discover a life-threatening situation. Could any medical professional seriously turn away such a patient with a clear conscience, if that patient could not come up with an appropriate deposit?

In the case of Kitty's mother, it might appear at first sight that the medical staff had been heartless and bureaucratic and had acted against medical ethics. But on further examination, it became apparent that some other patients had been disappearing after treatment without settling their bills. The new rules had been fashioned by local authorities to ensure that costs could be recovered from the salaries of the staff who had treated defaulting patients without first collecting deposits from them!

Hence the transition to a market-focused pricing system led to enough unintended dissatisfactions and unhappiness to go around. Perhaps a better explanation to the population at large of what was really expected for "Socialism with Chinese characteristics" should have been done before any implementation was attempted. And such minor flaws in carrying out policies all came to a head across many towns and cities upon the unexpected death of Hu, crystallising all the passions, mistaken perceptions and the unwarranted hopes of students and the general public.

* * *

Meanwhile, various student groups in different parts of the country were echoing calls for an end to corruption, greater government accountability, the introduction of democracy and a multi-party system, freedom of the press and other Western practices and slogans. They seemed to have swallowed naively and unthinkingly the standard narratives of foreign propaganda, that such changes could somehow cure all their country's woes. They therefore boycotted classes and held marches and demonstrations to further their vague but so-called "patriotic" demands. They nonetheless gained considerable support from disgruntled factory workers and from the inflation-ravaged general public.

On April 22, the day scheduled for the state funeral of Hu, rioting broke out in the cities of Changsha and Xian. Many cars and shops were burnt and looting occurred. Law and order were breaking down in several locations in the face of sustained agitation. It was unfortunate that most of the young, idealistic or trouble-makers, had not been old enough to remember the madness and the excesses of the Cultural Revolution.

The following day student groups in the capital formed a union and elected leaders to lead them to press for reforms and to protest against the failure of the government to respond to their demands. Thousands of students marched through the capital to head for Tiananmen Square and were joined en route by many more thousands of workers and ordinary citizens.

On April 25, the Paramount Ruler, Deng Xiao-Ping, endorsed the need for martial law. But the Premier Li Peng also warned the students through an editorial in the *People's Daily* the following day, that the demonstrations were considered as an anti-Party and an anti-government revolt.

The students reacted angrily to the accusation and on April 27 began marching in their tens of thousands through the streets again. Joined by non-students along the way, they broke through police lines to reach Tiananmen Square. Protests and strikes also began occurring in other cities and some students from elsewhere began converging upon the capital.

Nonetheless, by April 30, the General Secretary of the Communist Party,

Zhao Zi-Yang, still argued for making concessions and talking to the students to end the protests and the classroom boycotts.

Subsequently, leaks of the discussions in the Standing Committee of the Politburo revealed sharp differences of opinion among its members. Hardliners wanted a condemnation of student violence and a decisive end to demonstrations. But Zhao thought that, while taking all necessary measures to combat rioting and violence, students could still be persuaded to return to their classrooms out of a sense of patriotism.

By then, I was developing an uncomfortable foreboding that things might slip out of control. In addition, rumours began swirling around Hong Kong that anti-Communist Chinese and Taiwanese elements and Western intelligence agencies were getting ready to intervene and stir up further unrest in China. Both local as well as foreign money was being couriered to dissident groups within China. Furthermore, American troops were touted as being ready to intervene if the unrest exceeded a certain critical pitch.

Meanwhile, the names of some leaders of the protesters began appearing in media stories, together with their statements and demands. Some of their demands were half-baked and it was by no means clear how representative those leaders were or how far their writ extended among the tens of thousands camped at Tiananmen Square.

I therefore asked Hon-Kit to meet me as soon as possible, to get a better handle on what might be brewing.

* * *

By the time Hon-Kit and I met the following week, the situation had deteriorated further. Some 300,000 protesters had already occupied parts of Tiananmen for a week. Emotions were running high and the encampments on the square were turning into a chaotic and unhygienic collection of humanity. There had been squabbles and fights among some demonstrators too, for control of the public address system used to broadcast to the crowds. It seemed that whoever had control of the system at a particular moment in fact became a sort of *de facto* leader.

"Had you previously heard of any of the so-called protest leaders?" I asked Hon-Kit.

My friend shook his head. "There appears to be a vast mixture of groups out there, some patriotic, some opportunistic, some just curiosity seekers gawking like spectators at a gruesome accident. I suppose those speaking out now must be the ones with the loudest voices or the thickest skins or the keenest to enjoy his or her time in the limelight. Some might have received foreign money or been promised an imagined cushy exile in the West for acting out a specified role. I doubt if any has really thought through the real problems in their own country or the consequences that they or their families might face as a result of their actions and statements. Numskulls the lot of them! Shouting empty slogans out of emotion or momentary pride."

"A lot of bravado and highfaluting declarations have indeed been tossed around," I said, "and they are being gleefully reported on by many Western media. Those kids are going to find themselves hard put to live up to their words, uttered either before some adolescent damsel or during a moment of mob madness. When the chips are down, they'll find that forfeiting one's life for an abstraction will not come as lightly as a feather, but fall more crushingly than Mount Tai."

"What can anyone expect when you have immature youngsters stewing for days and weeks together, feeding on each other's self-delusions, passions and mob psychology?"

"But I'm puzzled why Zhao cannot foresee what such toxic closeness might produce. Why is he continuing to press for dialogue in opposition to his colleagues on the Politburo Standing Committee? Has he plans for using the students, just as Chairman Mao had done in launching the Cultural Revolution?"

"Not that I know of," Hon-Kit replied. "I've only been a very small potato at the local level all these years. Never got anywhere close to Zhao or anyone near the top. But his offering dialogue has been a big mistake. It has given those kids encouragement and a false sense of their own importance. Can anyone now really speak for that rabble in Tiananmen?"

I sighed. "I suppose the destinies of men, as well as of nations, all depend on making a right decision at some critical point, don't they?"

"Yes, indeed. I seem to recall that ages ago, an outnumbered young Napoleon defending another revolution, resorted to 'a whiff of grapeshot.' to gain the day."

"That phrase was actually coined by Thomas Carlyle, some time after the event. Please forgive and ignore my pedantry. But with so many at Tiananmen, 'a whiff of grapeshot' would mean significant spilling of blood!"

"I'm no hardliner, my friend. But I'm both a realist and a Chinese. The moment for nipping trouble in the bud has unfortunately passed long ago. Acting now might still mean less bloodshed than later. No responsible government can ever allow unruly mobs to take over a nation."

"Mob rule certainly provides no answer. But how to avoid a tragedy?"

"A good question. I don't have an answer either. We in Hong Kong can only be bystanders. The game is being played by others and we do not know when and what silly move is going to be made by someone. The future rests in the laps of the gods; we are helpless."

Hon-Kit paused for a moment and then added: "Odd, isn't it? No matter how much the world changes, human nature remains the same. Aristotle had it spot on thousands of years ago. Did he not say that the young would always overdo things? They love too much and hate too much and the same with everything, because they have not yet been sufficiently humbled by experience to know the limitations in life."

"Ah, yes!" I replied. "How long ago has it been when you and I were acting just like those kids in Tiananmen today? We also kicked against the pricks.

We felt then that something was not right about our lives but we could not work out the wider contradictions within our society. We were miserably paid and we supported the idea of forming a union for journalists but our employers soon put a stop to that. So we just lashed out, without being able to articulate what was actually wrong and what we really wanted!"

Hon-Kit laughed. "Yes, those were the days! But have we grown any wiser from our missteps and mistakes? How much have we really learnt? There are still so many problems to which we have no answers, though we still give way to moments of sentimentality and hope."

"You pose too many unanswerable questions, my friend," I said. "We must meet again fairly quickly to catch up on developments in the mainland. How about a week from now?"

* * *

After that meeting with Hon-Kit, I was informed by Lo & Lo that it had received a letter from Li & Fung, offering a lump sum to settle my claim for breaches of my contract. The sum was not broken down but it added up to roughly 85 or 86% of the amount claimed. The difference by itself was not really of much moment.

Leslie's partner advised me to accept the offer. He explained that rejection might be costly, because legal convention provided that if I failed subsequently to convince a court that I could better the sum being offered, then I might be denied costs and be made liable for the costs of the other side. Those sums could be considerable because barristers would be involved.

I was in two minds as to how to respond. One the one hand, if Li & Fung had made the offer right at the beginning, I would undoubtedly have accepted it to avoid a row and for old times' sake. But on the other, I still felt irritated by the company's refusal to engage in meaningful talks for so long.

There was also another important point of principle to consider.

Corporations had always enjoyed a distinct advantage over their employees whenever a dispute arose. A corporation could always use shareholder resources to scare an employee into accepting a less than favourable settlement for fear of incurring unaffordable legal fees.

Since I possessed a surfeit of wealth, why shouldn't I take on one of those bullying corporations to demonstrate that justice did not automatically go to those with the biggest purses? Also, what was the use of money if a person did not use it to fight for principles?

There were two other related factors to be worked into the equation. First, I had been very astringent in calculating my claims. I was therefore quite confident of being able to prove that the sum outstanding was more than the amount being offered in settlement.

Secondly, I could surmise from the sum offered that Li & Fung had made provision for paying my salary during the entire period of notice. It was not clear, however, whether the company expected me to take my accumulated leave during the notice period, rather than making me work until the end before paying me a lump sum in lieu of leave.

Therefore I asked Leslie's partner to seek clarification on this point before considering the offer. When Li & Fung eventually replied that it had no objection to my taking accumulated leave during the notice period, I realised that, given the lapse of time since the letter of notice, I could end my presence at the company in a matter of weeks if I took the last six months of the notice as leave. Liberation was apparently much closer than I had previously imagined. I therefore wasted no time in instructing Lo & Lo to reject Li & Fung's offer of settlement, to indicate that I would take my accumulated leave during the last six months of the notice period, and to brief a Queen's Counsel and a junior for the ensuing proceedings.

I felt as light as a bird as I turned my concentration to finalising the purchase of the property at Belsize Park and planning the various renovations I intended to make there prior to moving in.

* * *

"I'm afraid the die has been cast," Hon-Kit exclaimed dejectedly, the moment he saw me on May 14th. "A bunch of knuckleheads on Tiananmen decided yesterday to start a hunger strike to pressure the government into making concessions. Do those clowns even know who our leaders are? They are men who have been forged in the crucibles of death, against the Kuomintang during the arduous Long March and against the mechanised might of the United Nations in the bleak hills of Korea. They've seen thousands of their comrades give their lives for a cause. Do those silly kids really think our leaders will bat an eyelid if some of them decide to skip a few meals? It's a recipe for total disaster."

"I hear Gorbachev, the Soviet leader, is scheduled to begin a state visit to China tomorrow too," I said. "It's supposed to be the first state visit between our two countries in 30 years."

Hon-Kit gritted his teeth in exasperation. "Yes, there was supposed to be a grand welcoming ceremony for him at Tiananmen, but the venue had to be changed. It will be a great loss of face. No consideration of national dignity or honour, or any inkling of political protocol among those kids."

I nodded apprehensively. "Their demands also seem to be becoming more absurd and incoherent. It all looks like an unhappily ending on the horizon."

We then chatted in a desultory fashion for a while, exchanging news of students in other cities copying the hunger strikers in Peking and rumours of anti-Communist groups and foreign agents making their way into China to fund protesters. We both grew more despondent as we talked.

"Chaos is apparently gaining momentum and spinning out of control," I said. "National television is apparently planning to broadcast a possible meeting between the Premier Li Peng and student representatives on or about May 18."

"Yes, part of Zhao's softer approach, no doubt," Hon-Kit said. "Could make things worse."

"I'm still curious about Zhao's motives. He was picked by the Paramount Ruler, wasn't he?"

"Yes, he had a pretty good record for dealing with economic problems. He had also been a part of a five-member committee set up in 1986 to look into political reforms. He was elected as General Secretary during the 13th National Congress the following year."

"Was there any gossip about him or his inclinations among cadres?"

"There was some talk of him finding too much corruption within the system but not knowing how to deal with it. Too many powerful cadres involved. It was said that he then started to talk about Western parliamentary democracy being less prone to corruption. Perhaps that was what led him astray."

I chuckled with irony. "If Zhao really believed that self-serving Western theory, then it proves that a little knowledge is indeed a dangerous thing. He would not have thought that way about parliamentary systems if he had known about the little brown envelopes being passed around Westminster to secure peerages and honours and to have a loophole or two incorporated into pending legislation; or about the myriad ways British banks launder money, work tax avoidance schemes, collude over LIBOR rates, foreign exchange, mortgage rates and heaven knows what else; or how J.P. Morgan could stifle competition in America and acquire more wealth in that country than the total value of property in some 22 of the constituent states west of the Mississippi."

I then rattled off a whole string of known abuses and corrupt practices in various Western countries with elected legislatures — price gouging and wrongful marketing of drugs by pharmaceutical companies, misinformation on health hazards from smoking by cigarette makers, manipulation of pollution gauges on vehicles by major motor manufacturers, using tainted meat to produce food, insider and naked short trading options in stocks and shares, fixing sporting events with desired outcomes beforehand, using advertising on a massive scale by public relations and lobbying firms to turn casual wants into compelling needs for paying clients, and so on and so forth.

"It seems that whatever the political system, human greed will always be there," I concluded. "Corruption will just take on new and different and less obvious forms under a different political system."

"You seem to have acquainted yourself with a multiplicity of shady ways of enrichment in the outside world," Hon-Kit observed. "I'm not sure it'll be a good thing for Chinese cadres to learn so many such tricks."

"They'll learn them soon enough, I'm sure, once they're fully exposed to free market practices and their lax regulations," I said. "In actual fact, right now in Hong Kong, I think we have the scariest political and economical arrangement in the world — a snooty, white-dominated colonial autocracy out of touch with its citizens and of dubious competence sitting on top of a neoliberal free-market laissez-faire economic system that is rotting away from its own excesses and contradictions. Yet Western politicians of limited intelligence keep singing the praises of such an arrangement. I just hope Chinese leaders will have enough sense not to use us as a model."

"We must analyse this situation more when we next have tea," Hon-Kit said.

* * *

During our meeting, I also took the opportunity to update Hon-Kit on the state of my dispute with Li & Fung and to inform him of the intention of Kitty and myself to move and settle soon in London.

Kitty had found the Cantonese environment in Hong Kong too overwhelming, I explained, and it had been a real interference to her getting to grips with the English language. A British setting should suit her better.

"As for myself, I'm keen on another shot at writing fiction," I said. "But what can I really write about except Hong Kong and its inhabitants? I've worked here for most of my life and my family's been here for five generations. Yet this place remains so unique, puzzling and poorly understood by me and by outsiders.

"You have contact with a part of it and you think it represents the whole. But it doesn't. This is in fact a mongrel city, superficially Chinese, but lacquered by foreign influences in terms of food, clothing, social habits and class culture. But it is also protean and dynamic, riddled with paradoxes and cross-currents. It is raucous, greedy and divided, given to swashbuckling lifestyles and testing the limits of the law. And yet, somewhere beneath the money-madness, the brassy deceits and outward cynicisms, there exists in many of its inhabitants a streak of compassion and goodness. I just need to distance myself from the place and gain some perspective in order to disentangle the various strands and to make more sense of them. I'm hoping London will be far away enough for me to do that."

"You've given yourself a whale of a task, my friend. Good luck!" Hon-Kit said. "I was born and brought up here too. But after having been away for four decades, I almost find myself a stranger visiting another town."

* * *

Li Peng's televised meeting with students turned out to be a complete disaster for the government. The Premier appeared stiff and ill at ease, without even a trace of charisma. He was, to any practised public relations eye, quite the wrong type of person to stick before a camera for such an exercise.

He had been an engineer by training and was not the least adroit at winning over hearts and minds. Instead of projecting an image of a caring official, sympathetic to the trials and tribulations necessitated in adjusting to a more open economy, he came over to many as doctrinaire, aloof and hidebound.

A measure of his failure to convince was that about a million of the residents took to the streets of the capital to demonstrate their solidarity with those on hunger strike.

On the other hand, the body language of most of the student representatives was distinctly cock-a-hoop, if not wantonly confrontational. They seemed pleased at last to have secured a national platform for their voices. But apart from repeating their mangled litany of slogans, they offered no constructive remedy to the transitional problems faced by the common people. They had, at the very least, failed to display the good manners expected to be taught to the young.

Moreover, it was doubtful whether the students really represented anybody except themselves and their small circles of classmates. Though they and their statements had been promoted and lionised by some foreign media, their writ hardly extended very far among the hordes in Tiananmen Square.

Two or three of those leaders merely sat quietly during the televised show, possibly stuck dumb by the sudden glare of national limelight in which they found themselves.

Zhao, the General Secretary of the Chinese Communist Party, must have deduced from the televised fiasco that his conciliatory approach had been a total flop. The moods of both the protesters and of his own colleagues in the Politburo Standing Committee appeared to be slipping beyond his control.

It was subsequently leaked that Zhao and other members of the Standing Committee had met following the broadcast at the home of the Paramount Ruler, Deng Xiao-Ping. Deng had felt that the demonstrators were being used by elements advocating bourgeois liberalism. He therefore concurred with declaring martial law and using the People's Liberation Army to restore order.

Zhao had responded by saying that he did not want to be the General Secretary who mobilised troops to implement martial law. In making that statement, he surrendered his own power and political career.

In a desperate attempt to reduce the risks and bloodshed that were bound to ensue, he went among the demonstrators in Tiananmen at 4.50 a.m. on the following morning, to plead with hunger strikers to end their strike and for the demonstrators to disperse. He was accompanied by a few aides.

"Students," Zhao announced, tearfully, "we have come too late. We are sorry. You talk about us, criticise us, it is still necessary. The reason I have come is not to ask you to forgive us. All I want to say is that students are getting very weak. It is the seventh day since you went on hunger strike. You cannot continue like this.

"You are still young, there are still many days yet to come, you must live healthily, and see the day China accomplishes the Four Modernisations. You are not like us, we are already old. It does not matter to us any more."

Soon afterwards, Zhao was stripped of his official positions and placed under house arrest. His supporters within the Communist Party were progressively purged. Zhao himself remained under house arrest in Peking until his death some 16 years later, in January of 2005. During his confinement, however, he manage to record a secret journal, which was smuggled out bit by bit by his friends and published after his death as *Prisoner of the State*.

* * *

When Hon-Kit and I spoke on the telephone on May 19th, our hearts were heavy with dread and apprehension. We had both watched Li Peng's meeting on television and had heard of Zhao's visit to Tiananmen and his short speech.

"Can a tragedy still be averted?" I asked. "It will take a while to assemble enough troops in the capital to deal with those massive crowds at Tiananmen. So there's still time for emotions to subside and for people with common sense to disperse."

"Unfortunately, I fear that will not happen," Hon-Kit replied. "People have been hyped up for too long and the psychological and group bonding that has taken place will be difficult to change. Besides, the youngsters have now got the bit between their teeth and think they have the popular will on their side. They're too naive to realise that anti-Communist and foreign forces are merely using them as foolish tools against their own country."

"It's crazy for so many people to remain crowded together at Tiananmen. They've already made their views known. A few calls have been voiced by *agent provocateurs* to overthrow the government. By remaining there, do the crowds really expect to bring the government down? With such numbers, any panic could start a stampede and cost lives. That has happened before at football games and religious festivals. So why can't the more sensible leaders begin urging the crowds to disperse?"

"Those who consider themselves leaders are bickering among themselves. Some hotheads even yearn for bloodshed to legitimise themselves and force the government into a climb-down. I imagine there might be a few unhinged kids among them who think the only way out of their humdrum lives might be to seek glory in martyrdom. Complete idiots the lot of them!

"But the lives of troops might be at risk as well. Troops have long been taught their duty was to serve and assist the people. Hence their frequent use during natural disasters. But now they are being used to disperse and chase them away. That might place them under considerable emotional and psychological stress. They might hesitate when given orders, thus endangering themselves in front of angry protesters."

"What an unholy mess! Are the student leaders so trapped in their own self-delusions and inflammatory utterances to use their brains? Have they thought about the consequences for themselves and for others?"

"If rumours are true, some might be thinking of running for it. If they had been one of the instigators of unrest or had colluded with outside elements, they could well have no other choice. British and American spies, I hear, have been working on an operation codenamed 'Yellowbird' to get people to America. Taiwan-sponsored elements would no doubt be aiming to reach that island."

"Does not say very much for those who claim to be leaders when they think only of saving their own skins. No doubt some could even dine out indefinitely on the mere fact of having been present at Tiananmen. But so have countless thousands of others. They would, however, have to stay behind to face the music. Or readjust themselves to the less heady business of just leading ordinary productive lives at home."

* * *

The portents had been plentiful in the prelude to disaster in and around Peking during the first few days of June in 1989 but few paid much attention to them. It was as if everybody was mesmerised by some great street theatre being enacted in which they all expected, at some stage, to have a role as bit players or as part of some gigantic chorus. No doubt some had been so conditioned to playing an assigned role that they could only follow developments through a sort of collective haze or through the prisms of their individual fantasies, prejudices and false hopes.

When troops from some 30 Chinese military divisions, totalling more than 300,000 soldiers, began arriving and camping around the suburbs of the capital, had the citizens been too absorbed by their own predilections and concerns to notice? When newspapers emphasised the imposition of martial law and called upon everyone at Tiananmen to leave, did those messages fail to reach their targets? Had the repeated broadcasts warning citizens to stay off the streets and remain at home also produced no effect?

For whatever reason, tens of thousands remained lolling about the streets or at Tiananmen, as if they could not bear missing any twist or turn in the unfolding drama around them. Perhaps they had been too consumed by curiosity or by their own everyday grievances. Perhaps they simply could not help themselves, like people drawn to gruesome accidents. It all seemed quite amazing in retrospect!

It has now been over 30 years since those few bloody days in June of 1989 in Peking, collectively known as the Tiananmen Incident. Yet the world is left with no balanced and coherent overall account, with appropriate timelines, of why so many hundreds of thousands of people got caught up in the sporadic events which took place over many neighbourhoods within the capital city. A significant number of people, both soldiers and civilians, got killed or injured. The precise number remains uncertain because different sets of figures have been tossed around.

Among the first people to be injured were troops in a convoy of vehicles entering the city along Changan Avenue from the suburbs. The convoy was ambushed long before it reached Tiananmen, by angry residents who attacked and set fire to the vehicles. According to a Chinese government statement, a total of 65 trucks and 47 armoured personnel carriers were destroyed. It is difficult to imagine how many people must have been seriously hurt in the fracas that followed.

Reports currently available about the Tiananmen Incident are numerous, but most are fragmented accounts by individuals and visiting journalists. They are too often shrouded in propaganda, half-truths and outright fabrications with political bias to be taken at face value. Perhaps another generation or two will have to pass before all governments and their agencies which had any role in that shattering affair would declassify their secret files and diplomatic cables to allow historians and scholars to piece together into an understandable mosaic all the evidence and timelines of the Tiananmen Incident.

* * *

Kitty and I left Hong Kong to begin our new life in London at the start of 1990. As to my lawsuit against H.C. Fung and Li & Fung (Trading), it was left in limbo because the High Court still had to assign hearing dates.

The timing of our departure, on the heels of the Tiananmen Incident, gave rise to unfounded rumours that I, like many others seeking to emigrate, had no confidence in the future of the colony once it had been returned to Chinese sovereignty. My decision to do so had long been made for other reasons. Indeed, for more than ten years thereafter, I looked forward to visiting Hong Kong regularly at least twice each year, usually during April and November, to reunite with my old *mah jong* friends and my relatives. I only ended those visits after most of those dearest to me had gone the way of all flesh.

* * *

Although this volume concludes my memoirs for the period up till 1990, I remain keen to continue writing about the next stage of my life. However, whether a further volume will ever be written depends on my health, my memory and whatever Fate might choose to decide.

About the author

David T. K. Wong was born in Hong Kong and received his early education in China, Singapore and Australia. He has degrees in political science and journalism from Stanford University in America and a post-graduate diploma in public administration from the Institute of Social Studies at The Hague. Later, he also became a Fellow in Economics at Queen Elizabeth House at Oxford.

He worked as a journalist in Hong Kong, London and Singapore for a number of years before joining the Administrative Service of the Hong Kong Government. After retirement from public service, he became the Managing Director of an international trading firm for eight years before migrating to London to embark upon a writing career.

To date he has published four collections of short stories, two novels and four volumes of memoirs. His short stories, some of which have earned him a number of awards, have appeared in various magazines in the United States, Great Britain, Hong Kong and other Asian countries.

Many of his stories have been broadcast by BBC Radio 4 in Britain, RTHK in Hong Kong and other stations in Ireland, Holland, Belgium and elsewhere. A number of his short stories have appeared in anthologies.

He is the founder of the annual David T. K. Wong Fellowship in Creative Writing at the University of East Anglia in the UK. The Fellowship awards £26,000 to a successful candidate to write a serious work of fiction set in the Far East.

All of Wong's fiction is available for free download at his website, www.davidtkwong.com.

EXPLORE ASIA WITH BLACKSMITH BOOKS

From retailers around the world or from *www.blacksmithbooks.com*

Lightning Source UK Ltd.
Milton Keynes UK
UKHW010716260521
384398UK00001B/30